RICHIE!

The Fast Life and Times of NASCAR's Greatest Modified Driver

The Richie Evans Story

by Bones Bourcier

COASTAL 181
PUBLISHER

COVER PHOTO CREDITS

Front:
Sonny Richards photo

Back:
Background image: Marc Rohrbacher photo/courtesy of *Speedway Scene*
Coupe image: Lynn Evans collection
Daytona image: Dorsey Patrick photo/Lynn Evans collection

ISBN: 0-9709854-6-0

For additional information contact:

Coastal 181
29 Water Street
Newburyport, MA 01950
(877) 907-8181, (978) 462-2436
info@coastal181.com
www.coastal181.com

Copyright 2004 by Lew Boyd. All rights reserved.
No part of this book may be reproduced in any form, or by any means, without permission in writing from the publisher.

The author and publisher shall not be held liable for any incidental or consequential damages that might result from the content of this book.

First printing December 2004
Second printing March 2005
Third printing July 2008
Fourth printing December 2009
Fifth printing January 2011
Sixth printing December 2011
Seventh printing March 2012

Printed in the United States of America

For Pete Zanardi and Mike Adaskaveg,
whose writing and photography introduced me to
the world within these pages;

for Val LeSieur,
under whose guidance I stepped into it;

and, of course,

for Richie,
who was always more of an open book than he realized.

Contents

Acknowledgements and Applause — vii
Foreword — ix
Prologue — xiii

PART ONE
Farm Boy — 1

Westernville — 2
Drag Days — 7
Family Man I — 8
Round and Round — 10

PART TWO
Winning — 15

Coupe Days — 16
DPW Orange — 23
Gas Station Life — 25
Broke, Broke, Broke — 28
Winning — 35
Work Hard, Play Hard I — 40
Outlaw — 43
Redemption — 52
Family Man II — 60

PART THREE
Champion — 65

Big Dreams — 66
Gene's Machine I — 67
Daytona Rookie — 71
A Title Won — 73
A Title Lost — 84

Work Hard, Play Hard II	90
Cookie	95
The Capital of Modified Racing	102
Billy	103
Change of Focus	105
Shop Talk	113
R-E-S-P-E-C-T	120
Family Man III	123
1978	131
Shifting Sands	140

PART FOUR
Richie! — 143

"Where Modifieds Belong"	144
Fun in the Sunshine State	148
That Orange Camaro	152
On the Road Again	160
Top Gun	168
The Natural	174
Gene's Machine II	181
Keeping it Simple	185
"Bo-Diddley"	191
On a Roll	203
Most Popular	215
Work Hard, Play Hard III	223
Side Jobs	232
"I Like What I Do"	242

PART FIVE
"You Gotta Be 40 To Drive One of These Things" — 251

Rebound	252
The Competitive Fire	257
Headliner	261
Lucky Man	265
From Outlaw to Company Man	268
Smelling the Roses	276

1984: Some Excitement with Jimmy	285
"Milk and Cookie Racers"	294

PART SIX
Just Passin' Through … **297**

Nine-Time Champion	298
"We're All Just Passin' Through …"	303
Martinsville: Home Away From Home	307
The Day the Music Died	311
And Where Were You?	319
Goodbye, Champion	322
Mystery	327
Missing Man	330
Scattered	335
Legacy	342
"Like He's Still Here"	346

Epilogue	349
Feature Victories	352
Track Championships	354
Index	355

Acknowledgements and Applause

UNLESS OTHERWISE CREDITED, all the quotes contained herein were obtained in exclusive interviews conducted by the author. Most were done especially for this book, although some are leftovers from on-the-record conversations across the last 20 years. We thank all those who shared their thoughts and memories with us. In cases where we borrowed quotes which first appeared elsewhere, we credit the authors rather than the publications; this was done because many of the journalists whose work we researched wrote simultaneously for newspapers and magazines, meaning that several quotes appeared in more than one forum.

We extend special gratitude to John Bisci, Phil Smith, Mark Southcott, Mel Thomas, Dan Pardi, Ken Meisenhelder and Doug Zupan, archivists who keep racing's past alive through their collections of statistics, photos and films. They do this for the best reason of all: their love of the sport.

We also tip our hats to Ray Evernham, who—despite the obvious demands on his time these days—enthusiastically agreed to write the foreword because of his high regard for Richie Evans. Ray is a man who has not forgotten his roots, and won't.

The author wishes to thank the following for their help, for their hospitality, and for services above and beyond the call of normal friendship: Richie's entire family, as well as his various mechanics, crewmen and companions; Dick Berggren and his staff at *Speedway Illustrated*; Val LeSieur and his staff at *Speedway Scene*; Mike Adaskaveg and John Grady; Andy Fusco; Mike McLaughlin and Ralph Solhem; and the New England Auto Racing Hall of Fame.

Additional appreciation to Lew Boyd and Jim Rigney for their editorial and logistical assistance; Sandra Rigney for her interior design (and for putting up with Jim); Cary Boyd for her proofreading (and for putting up with Lew); Heather McIntosh for her proofreading (and for putting up with the author); Joyce Wells for her wonderful cover design; MaryRose Moskell for helping keep the Coastal 181 office relatively sane; and all the rest who indulged us while this book took shape.

Foreword

by Ray Evernham

I CAN'T REALLY REMEMBER the first time I actually saw Richie Evans. It had to be way back in the days of the old All Star League, maybe at Flemington Speedway. I already knew who he was, because I was a huge modified fan and I'd heard and read about him. But once I noticed him, he reminded me of Big John Milner, the hot-rod character from the "American Graffiti" movie with his T-shirt sleeves rolled up and that pompadour-looking hair-do. He was just the kind of guy you had to watch.

Once I actually got to race with him, I think what I respected the most about Richie was the way he treated people. In my eyes, as a kid trying to race modifieds, he was a big, big star, and yet he would always talk to me. It didn't matter who you were, Richie would always give you more than just the time of day. Over the years, he had a reputation for partying as hard as he worked, and he *earned* that reputation. But the racing came first. He always cared about that, first and foremost.

I remember joking around with him one day at Pocono, when we were there for the Race of Champions. Richie had probably the best two cars in the whole place sitting in his garage stall, and there I was with a car that was kind of a junker in comparison. Well, I was playing around, telling him I'd trade him my girlfriend Mary—who is now my wife—for a ride in his back-up car. He kidded me about that for years, and he kidded Mary, too. He was always really nice to the both of us.

Richie was the racer's racer. He could build his own cars, and he really understood them. He was certainly way ahead of his time on a lot of things, especially tires. He'd mount dozens of tires for those big races, and then he'd settle on exactly what he wanted.

Another thing I loved about him was that he proved that you don't always have to conform to what everybody else is doing. When chrome wheels and chrome bumpers and chrome nerf bars were the hottest things in modified racing, Richie bolted on his orange wheels and his flat-black bars and bumpers. Certainly, if he'd wanted to be flashy he could have done that with the sponsors and the product deals he had, but that wasn't him. He knew that the most important things were horsepower, a good-handling car, and hard work.

Because he's still so well-known, a lot of people who know I raced modifieds will ask me if I raced with Richie Evans. The correct answer is: Not quite. There were a lot of nights when we were on the same track, but he was always way ahead of me. In fact, probably the proudest day of my driving career came one November at Wall Stadium, when he and I shared the front row for a heat race at the Turkey Derby. We both used the number 61 and we both had the same initials, so I told my friends, "Look, I've got the same initials, I've got the same car number, and I'm on the same row. This might be the closest I ever get to running with Richie Evans."

Richie had opportunities to move up beyond the modifieds, but he wanted to stay in that division. He loved what he was doing, and he loved the people he worked with and raced with. And, you know, I really respect that. The only shame of it is, I'm certain that he would have been a *great* Cup driver. I can remember him running his Camaro at Daytona back in the superspeedway modified days, and he ran a lot of laps at over 200 miles per hour when that was still pretty unheard of. He had that kind of racing figured out, that's for sure. And, honestly, to this day a lot of the things I do with our Nextel Cup teams are based on the fundamentals I learned from watching Richie Evans.

I can't stress this enough: The things that impressed me about Richie, the things that have stayed with me over the years, were not all technical and mechanical. That stuff is obvious, because you *had* to look up to a driver who won like he did. But purely from a *guy's* perspective, there are just some individuals in life who stand out as being cool. To me, Richie Evans, Dale Earnhardt, John Wayne and Elvis all had that characteristic, whatever it is. It's hard to define, but those kinds of guys just have the ability to make people look up to them. They're *stars*. They're like the cowboy with the white hat in the movies who looks after the kid; they're the gunslinger who always gets the job done. I don't know how in the world you acquire that level of cool, but Richie certainly had it.

Unfortunately, this can be a tough sport. When you choose to make racing your career, you inevitably end up going through some tragic times. Twice now—with Richie and then with Dale Earnhardt—I've experienced days when I realized that The Man was gone, that the one race driver we all thought was indestructible *wasn't*. I remember very vividly the day Richie died. I said right then that modified racing was never going to be the same, and I don't believe it has been. It was the same when we lost Earnhardt; it was the same kind of dark day, and he was the same kind of indestructible man, and you just couldn't believe he was gone.

I'd like to think that somewhere, right now, Richie Evans and Dale Earnhardt and a lot of their friends are having a hell of a race. And, I'll tell you, Dale would have his hands full with Richie. I'm sure they'd have a beer together later on, and they'd laugh, but first they'd put on one amazing race.

Richie Evans was quite a guy, and he left a big impression on a lot of us short-track racers. I'm just saddened to think that a lot of the younger people on the modified scene—racers and mechanics and fans alike—never got the chance to know him. The good thing is that now, through this book, they'll get that opportunity.

RAY EVERNHAM
Evernham Motorsports
October 2004

Evans and Evernham, 1979.
(Ray Evernham collection)

 Prologue

ON A COOL BUT BEAUTIFUL autumn day, the last remnants of an early snow hiding in whatever shadows the bright sun could not find, Wilbur Jones walked into the pit area of the Utica-Rome Speedway like he was walking into a church: tentatively, quietly, respectfully. And that was proper behavior, because to some folks the place remains sacred ground. Something very big—the stock car racing career of a fellow named Richie Evans—started right here in 1962, and it impacted the lives of thousands of people, Wilbur Jones included.

"How long since you've been here?" I asked him.

Jones said, "Whew. Probably back in the late '70s."

Utica-Rome, just south of the New York Thruway in Vernon, is a half-mile dirt track these days, but it used to be an asphalt bullring a bit over a quarter-mile around. On any given Sunday in the late 1960s and early '70s, to stroll this same pit area was to walk among modified royalty; depending on the season, you might find Maynard Troyer, Pete Hamilton, Bill Wimble, Jerry Cook, Lou Lazzaro, Kenny Shoemaker, Don MacTavish, Rene Charland, Fred DeSarro …

Wilbur Jones motioned toward a section of chain-link fencing. "Right about there, that's where we always used to park." He meant Evans and whatever spirited collection of friends made up his crew on that particular race night. Jones looked at the site for a long moment, and then he grinned.

"Bugsy Stevens used to park next to us," he said.

The tour continued, its guide dressed in a heavy denim jacket and wearing a ball cap to keep the chill at bay. "The welder, he used to park over there," Jones said. "And right here, this is where Eddie Flemke used to pit."

Now Wilbur laughed. "You know the story about Eddie driving Richie's coupe in the 400, don't you?"

Do I ever. Growing up, it was one of my modified racing catechisms. The year was 1970, the race was Utica-Rome's famous New Yorker 400, and Steady Eddie Flemke was in the Evans coupe because Richie had been tossed out of NASCAR for racing at unsanctioned tracks. Flemke was welcome, but Evans, an outlaw, wasn't allowed into the pits. So he and his guys set up camp in the parking lot just outside the pit gate, and that's where they tuned the orange #61. Flemke, enjoying the whole thing immensely, waved his pit pass at the gate guard every time he drove in to practice and race. Then he turned a neat little story into regional folklore by winning the 400 in a romp.

Wilbur Jones walked over to a spot beneath a telephone pole. "This is where we pitted Eddie that night," he said. "They've moved the fence, because the pits didn't used to be this big. Where we're standing, this was actually part of the parking lot. Yup, we pitted Eddie right here."

Sacred ground.

We walked a bit more, checking out the rest of the facility. Some of it looked new, Jones said, "and bigger." And yet so much of it was nostalgic, familiar. We stood for a few minutes on the lowest row of a small set of pit bleachers, and Jones, waving a hand in the air, traced the layout of the old paved track. In the infield, just inside turn one of the dirt oval, a backhoe was moving some earth. I don't think my friend Wilbur even noticed it. I'm pretty sure he was seeing 1968, or 1973, and some Sunday night when his man Evans duked it out with Cook or Ray Hendrick or Geoff Bodine.

"There's a lot of good memories here," Wilbur Jones said.

This book is the story of a life. That makes it a bit different, in my mind, than calling it a life story; to do a by-the-numbers "life story" of a guy like Richie Evans, you'd have to get all bogged down in statistics and exact dates, and that didn't interest me. Oh, don't worry, a lot of the major numbers are in these pages, because there is no way to get around the fact that Richie won and won and won. Thompson Speedway announcer Russ Dowd once described Evans as "the defending champion of almost everything you can think of."

So, yes, you are going to read about the nine NASCAR national modified titles, the Daytona wins, the Race of Champions victories, the repeat scores in the Oswego Bud 200, the Spring Sizzler at Stafford, the Thompson 300. But, again, this is the story of a life, the fast life of Richie Evans, so we will visit those grand moments mostly as milestones along a colorful highway. Because this was a man who did more than just win; this was a man who also lost a bunch, who raced on his own terms, who worked hard and played hard, who knew struggle, who laughed, who loved, who lived. His friend and rival Maynard Troyer has said, "Richie was a package deal," meaning that it wasn't accurate to look at just one side of Evans. "If you took away one part or another," Maynard declared, "you wouldn't have had that same package." In this book, then, we are going to look at all these parts, hopefully giving each the proper attention it deserves in the "package deal" that was this man's life.

So don't be surprised to see more space given to Richie's suspension from NASCAR than to, say, his 1982 modified championship. One played a bigger role in defining his life, that's all. And you may read less about what happened during some races than about what happened *after* them, because only a portion of the Evans legend was forged between the green and checkered flags. We are going to get a little bit playful before you come to the final page, that's for sure.

I've often thought that if it wasn't for Richie Evans, I might not be sitting at this desk, having made a life out of writing about race cars and the folks who drive, own, build and maintain them. A bit over 30 years ago, I was a 13-year-old Connecticut kid with deep interests in both racing and writing, but it hadn't ever occurred to me that you could connect the two.

Richie Evans and Bones Bourcier, Thompson Speedway, 1977. (Mike Adaskaveg photo)

Why would it? What little coverage the daily newspapers gave to automobile racing consisted mostly of summary reports: "Stevens passed Ron Bouchard on lap 24, and led his fellow Massachusetts driver by two car lengths at the finish." Even the magazines lacked any real zest; an "in-depth profile" of a champion driver might waste 3000 words telling you little more than how long the man had raced, what he'd won and where he'd won it, and what his future goals were. You could spend an entire evening reading the thing, and still come away feeling like the guy was a complete stranger.

Then I picked up the April 1974 issue of *Stock Car Racing* magazine and opened to a feature on Richie Evans, the 1973 NASCAR modified champion. It was written by Pete Zanardi, a name I knew from his work at the old *Hartford Times*; he was the only newspaper guy in my area who, given the space, would actually tell you a little something about the heroes who raced at the local tracks: Flemke, Bugsy, Gene Bergin, folks like that. Zanardi's magazine piece opened in a Rome tavern called Coalyard Charlies, with Evans "smiling, engrossed in playing an elaborate electric TV-like paddleball machine ... It became a giggle when he stopped the streaking 'ball' and sent it back at his opponent with all sorts of bleeping bounces. By the end of the game—it takes eleven points to win and Evans usually does—people had gathered around him."

(Reading those words today, I can still hear that goofy Evans giggle. Zanardi described it as "an infectious laugh that gives the listener the impression that he shares it only with his close friends.")

You could smell the cigarette smoke and the beer in the sentences. You could see the smiling faces. It was the first hint I'd ever had that writing about racing might be a great way to hang out with some really interesting people, to look over their shoulders as they led their lives.

The idea that you could actually get paid to pass their stories along almost seemed like stealing.

Well, I've been getting away with that sort of thievery for better than 25 years now, and I suppose it all started with that Richie Evans story. In time I wrote plenty of Richie Evans stories myself, and although in hindsight I was only a kid—just 16 when I first started pestering him, 25 when he died in 1985—I felt like I came to know him pretty well. I saw him plenty at race tracks, in party settings, on the road, and in Rome, the place he called home.

In this business, you try to stay as neutral as you can when you've got a notepad or a word processor in front of you. But sometimes, off duty, you find people you just happen to like. It wasn't until fairly recently that I finally figured out what attracted me to Evans. It's complicated, and yet it's really very simple; it's all about the balance between work and play. Racing, obviously, involves a great deal of labor. Writing, done properly, is an awful lot of work, too, more work than most people would think. And yet anyone lucky enough to earn a living at either job is doing something he loves. The key, I think, is that balance. I watched some racers and writers have too much fun and thus never tap the potential they had; likewise, I saw some racers and writers work so hard that, despite whatever success they found, they seemed to find very little joy in the whole thing. Then I watched Richie Evans get that balance just right, and I told myself that this was the way to do it. He worked as hard as anybody I've ever known, but he was also a man who knew how to enjoy himself.

Way back in the spring of 1984, Richie and I had a couple of conversations about collaborating on a book. He was interested in the process: what kind of format I had in mind, how we'd work, things like that. But then spring became summer; he had races to run. Maybe later, he said. Twenty years later, here we are.

This is, without question, the hardest single project I've ever taken on. I've co-written the autobiographies of Tony Stewart, Bill Simpson and Bugsy Stevens, all of them intriguing subjects, but that is a different sort of work. On an autobiography, the job is to help a fellow tell his own story; you pry from him as much as you can, you shape his words a bit, you get his stamp of approval, and you go to the printer. It's his life, explained his way. But when you're writing *about* someone rather than *with* someone — especially when that someone is not around to confirm things—there is a much greater pressure to get things right, to dig through the documented history and sort through the hundreds of undocumented stories. Dig and sort, dig and sort, dig and sort. Honestly, I don't know that there's ever been another book on a race driver, living or dead, as thoroughly researched as this one.

I wanted to get it right. I wanted to produce something Richie Evans would have appreciated, not so much for its content as for the effort that went into it. How do you write about a full-bore guy like him without doing it full-bore? So I spent Lord knows how many days and nights retracing his steps, and I went through a million hours of interviews, and I dug into stacks of old magazines and newspaper clippings, and I ate a few lunches at Coalyard Charlies, and I drank a little bit of beer with some friendly old faces.

And now I'm going to step out of the way and let his story unfold. It is best told by Richie's family and friends, and his teammates and rivals, the people who knew him best. People like Wilbur Jones, standing on the bottom plank of that tiny pit grandstand at Utica-Rome and looking out at all those wonderful yesterdays.

"This place was it," he said softly. "This was *it*.

"This is where it all started."

BONES BOURCIER
Indianapolis, Indiana
October 2004

Mike Adaskaveg photo

I thank you, Lord, that I am placed so well,
That you have made my freedom so complete;
That I'm no slave to whistle, clock, or bell,
Nor weak-eyed prisoner of wall and street.
    BADGER CLARK, Poet Laureate of South Dakota
    (from "Cowboy's Prayer," 1906)

I'm content. A lot of my friends carry lunch pails and work in factories, and I'm pleased that I don't have to do that. I like what I do. What else do you need in life to be happy?
    RICHIE EVANS, NASCAR National Modified Champion
    (to Bones Bourcier, 1983)

PART ONE
Farm Boy

Sandy Jones collection

Westernville

EVEN BEFORE HE ARRIVED FOR REAL, Richie Evans was making a commotion. His mom, a tiny spitfire named Satie, was due any day, but there was always work to do on a New York dairy farm, and so Satie Evans, nine months pregnant or not, was pitching in. Her husband, Ernest, was off attending to one of the hundred or so tasks a farmer has to deal with every day—feeding the livestock, cleaning the barns, fixing machinery—and Satie, despite the summer heat, was out in the field.

Inside her, there was some movement: a shift, maybe, or a kick? Whatever it was, the baby was up to something, which was nothing new.

Sandy Jones, Richie's kid sister by two and a half years, heard the story forever. "The day before Rich was born," she says, "he was bouncing around while his mother was raking hay."

These prenatal interruptions ended on July 23, 1941, when Richard Ernest Evans was born at the old Rome Hospital. The commotion, however, lasted for about the next 44 years.

The new parents brought their first child home to Westernville. Rome to the southwest and Utica to the southeast are the closest cities of any real size. Even today, when you roll up State Route 46 and detour off into Westernville, there is the very real sense of being on the edge of something old, something between colony and wilderness. From there to Canada, some 100 miles straight north, you aren't going to run into anything resembling a large town unless you happen to slip off the path into Watertown. This is a scenic land of deer and dairy farms, great fishing in the summer and great snowmobiling in the winter, at the foothills of the grand, green Adirondack Mountains just to the northeast.

The sign out in front of the town library reads:

Western
Oneida County
March 10, 1797
Formed from the Town of Steuben

Something old, something between colony and wilderness. This is quiet, beautiful country, with Westernville at the quiet, beautiful heart of it.

The Evans homestead was on South Hill Road. Everything in these parts seems to be a hill of some sort; Gifford Hill, Buck Hill, Star Hill, Canterbury Hill and more. Ernest Evans had something like 200 acres, upon which roamed several dozen cows, a couple of workhorses, the family dog, and these two children, Richie and Sandy. The clan lived in

Mom and Pop: Satie Hall Evans, Ernest Richard Evans, 1938.
(Sandy Jones collection)

three different houses in their time there, and yet never had a telephone. Mom Satie was "the hub of the wheel," according to Sandy Jones. Satie Evans kept one and all nourished with "good old-fashioned foods like meat and potatoes, homemade pickles, and fresh vegetables from the garden: corn, tomatoes, cucumbers, onions, radishes, string beans, loose lettuce, peppers, pumpkins." For dessert, there was homemade ice cream; for breakfast, French toast made with homemade bread, topped with maple syrup Satie had boiled down from sap drawn from the trees ringing the fields. Daughter Sandy marvels, "She could work in the barn *and* have food on the table."

Growing up in a place like that could be fun, sure. Sandy remembers simple pleasures like "watching the deer with their fawns come out of the woods to eat and play in the new meadows" and camping in the woods along a stream, where they'd "watch the minnows swim and catch crayfish."

But it could be plenty of work, too. On a dairy farm 50 years ago, any able-bodied kid amounted to a hand. The two Evans children picked stones out of the new-plowed fields, mended fences, chopped and hauled wood, you name it. Mornings, Richie rode with his dad as they hauled milk from their own barn and neighboring farms to a plant in the nearby village of Holland Patent, the son standing on the floorboards and hanging onto the dash so tightly that, according to Sandy, his fingers "wore the paint off." One day the boy overslept, so Dad rode the route alone; that turned out to be a stroke of amazing luck, because that same morning ol' Ernest Evans dropped a wheel off the road and rolled the truck.

The Evans farm in Westernville, 1959.
(Sandy Jones collection)

(left) Brother, sister and faithful dog Blackie.
(Sandy Jones collection)

(right) Richie Evans with sister Sandy and the family milk wagon.
(Sandy Jones collection)

The oversleeping came as no great surprise to anyone who knew either Richie Evans the farm boy or Richie Evans the racer. His second wife, Lynn, to whom he was married from 1976 until his death in '85, says, "Rich wasn't ever an early riser in the time we were together. I think that was something he detested from back in the farm days, the idea of *having* to get up." The dairy cows required milking twice a day, mornings and afternoons, and the sunrise shift was murder on young Richie, who on a number of occasions was found asleep on the job, seated on the stool, his head laid up against the side of one lazing cow or another.

After the morning milking came school. In the earliest years, that meant a mile-long walk to a one-room schoolhouse filled with farm kids. You want wilderness? You want colonial? In the cold Oneida County winters a pot-bellied stove served as the school's furnace, and come Monday any and all traces of Friday's warmth were long gone. To thaw her shivering students, the teacher heated bricks atop the stove, and then placed a single hot brick beneath each desk. In the late 1940s, that was a Westernville radiator.

Evans eventually moved on to Holland Patent Central School and then Holland Patent High, where his sister says he became something of a fave with the softer side of the student body. "I had girls who'd invite me to eat with them in the cafeteria," she giggles, "because they wanted to get to know Rich."

This much is certain: By the time he was in high school, Richie Evans was one of those kids who seemed destined to become *somebody*. Already, he possessed so many of the qualities that would serve him well in the years to come …

He had an entrepreneurial spirit. As a boy, he talked his parents into letting him raise and sell rabbits, a profitable little venture that ended only when he underestimated the romantic tendencies of his bunnies; his father put an end to the business because, Lynn remembers Richie explaining, "there were freakin' rabbits everywhere." From there, he moved to Christmas trees, planting something like a thousand seedlings he'd gotten through the 4-H Club. That worked out better. Many of those trees decorated the living rooms of various family and friends every December for years to come, and today—half a century later—hundreds still still stand on a hillside near the old Evans farm.

He had a scheming independence. When his mother slid him some money to buy a senior class ring, teenaged Richie—no doubt figuring he'd earn it back in time for the actual ring purchase—used the money instead for a trip to Daytona with some friends. His parents learned of the trip, sister Sandy recalls, only after he'd already left town. "My father, he could yell," she says. "Well, my mom and I had to listen to all that yelling—Richie *this*, and Richie *that*—and by the time Rich came back he was all done hollering."

And he had, early on, a strong work ethic. "We worked very hard on the farm," Evans once reminisced to writer Pete Zanardi. "A time clock was something we didn't have. You worked until the job was done. You had to."

Evans once theorized to a friend that by the age of 18, almost everybody is essentially the person he or she is going to be. By that point, he figured, the ingredients that form each individual—the personality, the likes and dislikes, the drive—were too well blended together to be changed much. "By then, you're done," is how he put it, as if describing a cake being baked. And in his case, that seems to have been true. He was miles and years away from becoming a Saturday-night hero, much less a NASCAR national champion, but he was, yes, essentially the person he ended up being.

The challenge of mechanical problems thrilled him. "You have to be a mechanic on a farm," he told Zanardi. "My father had equipment that was supposed to last for 10 years, [but] he had for 30." And if whatever mechanical contraption he was working on had wheels and an engine, so much the better.

Lynn Evans remembers Satie telling a story about her boy, who was "somewhere around six years old" at the time: "She was up at the old farmhouse, looking out the window. I guess Rich had grabbed up his sister Sandy and put her in a car with him, and they were driving around the field until Satie went running down there and stopped them. It just goes to show you, he was already intrigued by motorized things."

The intrigue did not fade. Sandy tells of another day when the two of them, just teenagers, took turns driving the family's Studebaker around the farm. Ernest Evans didn't object to the joyride itself, but he wasn't happy about the deep tire tracks in the meadow, which indicated that this had been more than an average spin around the property. "I took the blame," Sandy smiles, "because I was only learning. But, of course, Rich was the one with the heavy foot."

"I think he got a lot of his driving ability out there in Westernville," Lynn says, "because there are some roads out there where, if you're driv-

Check out the dude! Sister Sandy says, "I had girls who'd invite me to eat with them in the cafeteria because they wanted to get to know Rich." *(Sandy Jones collection)*

ing along a little fast, you'd best know what you're doing."

And Richie Evans knew what he was doing. Well, most of the time. There are tales of him attempting to round one particular sweeping turn up on Gifford Hill, losing traction, and knocking down a huge portion of some farmer's cornfield before managing to make his getaway.

It was, all the old stories would seem to indicate, a fairly happy-go-lucky childhood and adolescence. This was a good kid, a good older brother—Sandy says, "Rich was more than protective," adding, "he would check out my boyfriends, and he would always tell me his opinions"—and by all accounts a good son, occasional motorized horseplay aside. Plenty of folks in exactly those circumstances have inherited family farms, worked them through their own lifetimes, and then handed them down to *their* own sons and daughters.

And yet something inside Richie Evans—that scheming independence?—kept pulling him away from the cows and the land and the hay and the machinery up on South Hill Road. It wasn't any fear of hard work; that never scared him. The best guess anybody seems able to offer is that he simply found the early-to-bed, early-to-rise lifestyle too restrictive.

"Rich didn't talk much about those days," says Wilbur Jones, who knew Evans from the time they were both in high school. "But I do know that he didn't care for that farm life."

The deepest Evans ever got into the subject, at least publicly, was in this line to writer Zanardi: "I might have become a farmer, but at 16 it became more than I could handle." Across his career, it was sometimes Richie's style in interviews to say more with the words that *didn't* come out than with the words that did.

At any rate, there came a point when the farm boy had to get away from the farm, or maybe stay there for good.

Actually, for years it had been clear to Sandy Jones—Sandy Evans back then—that the old homestead was never going to be able to hold her brother. She grins and talks of their toddling days, and of how he was always trying to wander up and over the hill toward his grandfather's house. Their mother, too busy with the chores and the housework to keep chasing down her active son, resorted to tying him up by rope in the backyard. No doubt pleased with her own ingenuity, Satie Evans left young Richie there in the yard, playing with the family dog, while she went into the kitchen to fix dinner.

"After a while," Sandy chuckles, "Mom looks out the window, and there's the dog and Rich, walking together up the road to Grandpa's. He had gotten the dog to chew through the rope!"

Drag Days

AT 16, RICHIE EVANS TOOK HIS FIRST JOB outside the farm, working for a Westernville neighbor of sorts by the name of Joe Jones. Just three years older than Evans, Jones had grown up on nearby Buck Hill; he had known this kid Richie "from the time I was 15, 16 years old. He was a good kid who got along with everybody."

And so when the Jones boy took over ownership of a local filling station—and he *was* still only a boy, just about to reach 20—he hired the kid to pump gas, help keep the place clean, and do a little light mechanical work.

Jones found out pretty quickly that young Richie Evans could handle a lot more than light mechanical work.

"When you come right down to it, if Richie had had any kind of education at all, he could have been a mechanical engineer," says Jones. "He was really, really good. Oh, hell, he could fix cars, engines right from the ground up. It was born right in him."

And so, in hindsight, was the need to compete, to race. *To win*. Evans, like so many kids, enjoyed souping up his cars, and in short order he was squaring off in street races. "I did a little bit of it, too, sure," admits Joe Jones. "But I mostly liked working on the cars; I wasn't really much of a driver. Richie, he liked to drive."

It was certainly dangerous, not to mention highly illegal, and therefore not the least bit smart, no getting around that. But these were the boom years of the hot rod craze, and every teenaged boy bright enough to extract more horsepower from his Chevrolet or Mercury couldn't wait to put his know-how to the test by matching it against the next guy's Ford or Plymouth. It was a way to prove you knew what you were doing under the hood, and that appealed to the mechanic in Evans. Toss in that desire to compete, and you had yourself one bad-ass street racer, a guy who took the game very seriously.

This time card from January, 1960 shows Evans taking home $48.11 for his 48-hour work week at Joe Jones's Westernville Flying A Service. *(courtesy of Joe Jones)*

Just one of Richie's red-hot drag cars from the early 1960s. (Lynn Evans collection)

Billy Nacewicz, who later traveled with Evans thousands of miles up and down the highway and crewed him to, what, a few hundred modified wins, asked for and heard plenty of old-days hot rod stories.

"Richie did all the stuff you hear about from those days," says Nacewicz. "He raced guys on the streets, running for $50 or maybe running for 'pink slips,' which is what they used to call the registration. Richie was well-known for that stuff. They'd go out to [Route] 365, which of course wasn't as busy as it is now. That road had a nice long, straight stretch, and they'd pair off.

"He'd work all night on his car after working in the gas station, changing motors and doing whatever he had to do, just to get ready to go out and run against somebody out on the four-laner."

Later, Evans got into organized drag racing, though he initially kept operating with the stealth of a midnight street racer. His sister Sandy recalls their father asking Richie about some bars he had added to his car's rear suspension. "Of course, Rich didn't tell him it was to stabilize the car for drag racing," she says.

He competed when and where he could, running in various amateur "door-slammer" classes at area strips like the one which still sits inside the Fonda Speedway. Local lore has it that one of Evans's early matches there was against a speedy Schenectady lass named Shirley Muldowney, who, nicknamed "Cha Cha," went on to become an NHRA legend.

"I was an avid drag racer," Evans told Connecticut radio show host Arnold Dean in a 1979 interview. "I spent all my time and money on drag cars."

Nacewicz says, "Richie wasn't a star in drag racing, by any means, but he was a winner. In fact, he was a *big* winner. He won more than his share of drag races."

Family Man I

ANY GUY WHO EVER HAD A TEENAGE JOB pumping gas will tell you that when the sun is shining and the birds are singing and you've got the first real money of your life in your pocket, there isn't a better gig imaginable. The world is yours, and none of it seems like work. Remember that "service with a smile" cliché? It came from guys in high school, or just out of it, grinning through a windshield-cleaning and a quick check under the hood.

So here was Richie Evans, 18 years old and putting in a day's work for Joe Jones at the Flying A service station in Westernville in 1961. Just then, a local girl named Barbara Peters, two and a half years his junior, happened to be strolling past with a girlfriend. Barbara was a student at Holland Patent, from where he had graduated, and she remembered seeing him in the hallways, but they never so much as said hello in his school days.

"He was a farm boy and I was a cheerleader," Barbara says. High school social divides being what they were, this apparently precluded conversation.

But anyway, there he stood, and here she came, and he did what any red-blooded American boy did back then when a pretty girl walked by.

"He whistled at me," she says.

And she and her girlfriend did what all red-blooded American girls did in response to so bold an action.

"We stopped and talked to him."

Forty-odd years later, Joe Jones says he has never heard that story. "But," he adds with a laugh, "I don't doubt it."

Richie Evans, already a fast mover, asked the girl out on the spot. "We went to the drive-in that night in his 1958 Thunderbird," Barbara says.

His nickname around town, she recalls, was "Oil Can," just because he was always working on cars. Many of their dates, she says, revolved around stuff that went fast.

"He always had nice cars," Barbara remembers, "and we used to drag a lot, up and down the boulevard in Utica. People would actually say, 'Hey, Evans is in town,' and they'd come out to race him."

And how did Oil Can Evans do in those impromptu street face-offs?

"He never got beat," Barbara says. "Never got beat."

Richard Ernest Evans and Barbara Peters were married in 1964. Down the road, they had four daughters—Jodi (born in 1965), Janelle (1966), Jill (1969) and Jacki (1970)—and hundreds of great nights and a thousand ups and downs. All Barbara Evans knew in those early days was that she had signed on for something that seemed like it might get interesting.

"You could just see it in him," she smiles. "I knew he was going to be something."

(left) Richard Evans and Barbara Peters tie the knot in 1964. *(Sandy Jones collection)*

(right) Do you suppose Pfeiffer's Restaurant was ever the same? A ticket from Richie Evans's 1964 stag party. *(courtesy Jodi Meola)*

Round and Round

"THE BIGGEST MISTAKE I made," Richie Evans once told writer Dick Berggren, "was starting oval-track racing at 22." He forever regretted not having started younger, and mentioned that in a dozen different interviews. He often talked of having "wasted too much time" drag racing, because it didn't seem to be leading anywhere. It was fun, yes, but it was nothing *but* fun. "If I had applied that drag time to oval racing," he said to Berggren, "I would have done much better."

Well, it's hard to imagine how much "better" his oval-tracking career could have gone, but, yes, Evans did get something of a late start. He was 21 when he spliced together his first stock car, 22 by the time he got it really rolling.

It might not have happened at all, had it not been for the advice of a colorful local dude named Chuck Mahoney. A Rome native, Mahoney had done a bunch of stock car racing in the sport's wild early years, driving and winning at tracks all over New York and actually making it to the big leagues. Between 1949 and '56, he competed in 16 races in NASCAR's Strictly Stock and Grand National divisions, which evolved into what is now the Nextel Cup series. His most memorable season was 1950, when Mahoney ran 11 Grand National races, finishing six of them in the top 10, including a second-place finish at the old dirt Charlotte Speedway, a third close to home at the long-gone Vernon Speedway—where he qualified on the pole—and a fifth at Darlington.

In his post-driving days, Chuck Mahoney did a bit of local racing, dabbled in track promotion, and was known in the area, one old-timer recalls with a smile, as "a character's character." And at some point, probably in 1962—no one thought to record the date, because no one imagined what it all might lead to—Mahoney took aside a Rome youngster named Richie Evans and passed on a bit of wisdom.

"You've got to stop racing for trophies," Mahoney said. "Those trophies ain't going to buy you nothing.'"

And if Evans wanted to race for something that *could* buy him things, there was a place he could do that, although the dollars initially would come in small amounts. Just south of Rome, in Vernon, the Utica-Rome Speedway was fast becoming a Mecca for local fans and for stock car racers from around the Northeast. Built by a fellow named Joe Lesik on some farmland along Route 5, the new track, a paved quarter-mile, opened in September of 1961. Lesik ran three races that year—won, in order, by Billy Rafter, Rene Charland and Ed Ortiz—before shutting down for the winter. Charland, a fun-loving practical joker from Massachusetts, was named track champion that year, and he repeated in 1962.

Utica-Rome ran two classes: NASCAR sportsman coupes—essentially modifieds with small-block engines and carburetors—and an entry-level division called hobby stocks. What Richie Evans ought to do, Chuck Mahoney told him, was cut up his drag car, get a set of rules for Utica-Rome's hobby class, and try stock car racing.

So that's what Evans did. He and Joe Jones and a fellow named Clarence "Speed" Williamson, an area racer of some note, welded and bolted together a hobby stock car. Construction took place in a bay at Jones's gas station in Westernville's center, "where the Nice N Easy store sits now," Jones says.

Richie Evans and Joe Jones were partners on that first car, a hacked-up 1954 Ford. The number on the side was PT 109, after the Navy torpedo boat piloted by Lieutenant John F. Kennedy in World War II. By 1960, Kennedy was America's dashing young president, and among his admirers was this would-be stock car racer in rural New York. Barbara Evans says, "Richie really liked John Kennedy, and he had seen a movie about the PT 109."

The Utica-Rome debut of Evans and ol' PT 109 came one summer Sunday evening in 1962. In the bleachers that night sat a Rome resident about Richie's age, a lad named Ted Puchyr, whose interest in stock car racing dated back to the days when his father ran a late model car at the old Vernon track. A couple years down the road, he and Evans would become friends; some 20 years later, Puchyr would be a familiar face in Northeastern racing circles as the fellow who oversaw the sponsorship activities of the ADAP and Auto Palace parts chains. But in 1962, he was just a skinny kid shaking his head at this funny-looking hobby car, the PT 109.

History in the making: the first Richie Evans stock car. *(John Bisci collection)*

The best guess on this shot is that it was taken after a Utica-Rome heat race. And doesn't Richie look racy? *(John Grady photo)*

Round and Round 11

"That car seemed like it stood about eight feet high," Puchyr recalls, "and it had these big springs on the front, so the nose was up in the air like a drag car. It was comical."

The thing didn't drive much better than it looked. Standing atop the flagstand was John Tallini, already an established NASCAR official who in time would work hundreds of Evans's races. "I can still remember the first time Richie raced," Tallini says. "He came out with that hobby car, and he couldn't have made it run in one direction if his life depended on it."

Only a handful of Sundays passed before a crash tore that unwieldy Ford to pieces. Also destroyed in the wreck was the Evans-Jones partnership. "The first time I totaled the car," Richie told writer Pete Zanardi, "Joe turned the whole operation over to me."

"True story," Joe Jones grins. "When Richie smashed that thing all to hell, that was the end for me. I said, 'I've got a family to deal with. I can't be dealing with this car, too.'"

Before long, Evans himself almost threw in the towel when his next hobby car didn't show any immediate improvement. His late friend Fred Ulrich recalled the struggling young driver having a conversation with Cliff Kotary, patriarch of one of the area's great racing families and a man for whom "Richie always had a real fondness," according to Lynn Evans. Ulrich said, "Richie told him, 'Cliff, I'm having all kinds of trouble. I just cannot keep the car on the race track.' But Cliff talked to him, and of course he stuck with it."

Without any of them realizing it, the cast of players in the great saga that was Richie Evans's life and times had begun to assemble. It swelled and changed faces over the years, as the wins piled up and his notoriety grew, but it started for real with those hobby cars on Sunday nights at the Utica-Rome Speedway. Joe Jones helped build the first one. Dick Abbott, a pal of Richie's, knew how to weld and was thus invaluable. Max Baker, another chum, pitched in from the start. Cliff Kotary was generous with his counsel.

Wilbur Jones had gotten to know Evans in their high-school years, although Richie went to Holland Patent and Jones attended Rome Free Academy. They met just bumming around—"I ran into him a few times here and there," Wilbur says—and got to be friendly for the best reason in the world: "Girls! Rich was going with this one girl, and I was going with another girl, and somehow we ended up double-dating." Now Richie had a stock car, and Wilbur wanted to help.

Fred Ulrich was on the scene more and more, too. He was a local builder who had lived "just a couple roads over" from the Evans farm in Westernville, and they had been acquainted from "when Rich was probably 15 years old." Ulrich was friendly with Dick Abbott, which deepened his association with Evans. "I knew Dick," said Ulrich, "so I started going to Utica-Rome and hanging around the pits."

On the other side of the grandstand fence, the same sort of thing

Getting the hang of things: Evans and his blue Nova. *(John Grady photo)*

was happening. Young Ted Puchyr stopped laughing at the newcomer, and started pulling for him. And a Westernville couple, Bill and Millie Hatch, had inadvertently become Evans fans, too. Two decades later, Millie would work alongside Richie as his fan club president, but the initial attraction was accidental. "My brother and his girlfriend wanted to go to the races one night," Millie shrugs, "so we all went over to Utica-Rome, and that's when we first saw Rich race. Everybody there seemed to be rooting for him, so we did, too."

As 1962 became 1963, and then '63 melted into '64, Richie Evans plugged away. And a curious thing happened: that hobby car—by then a blue Nova whose number had been streamlined down to a simple 109—began to get smoother, faster.

"I think the biggest thing that went against Rich early on was that he didn't know how to make the car go around in circles," says Wilbur Jones. "He knew how to turn the steering wheel—he knew that naturally—but he knew nothing about the mechanical end of it. But he picked it up, picked it up, picked it up. And if he did something wrong, he learned from it."

Evans himself said as much in 1979, remarking to radio man Arnold Dean, "It took me quite a while to keep going, because I never knew which way to turn the bolts. When we started, we knew absolutely nothing. And that's probably what makes you remember stuff so well [once you learn it]; you did it wrong so many times that when you finally did it the right way, you were *forced* to remember it."

He finished 19th in the Utica-Rome hobby division standings in 1964. The class champion was Frank Mathalia; interestingly, second in points was Sonney Seamon, who would play an important role in Richie's future. Other notables in the '64 hobby rankings: Dave Kotary fifth, Dick Clark eighth, Dick Fowler 10th.

Certainly, 19th in the standings in the second division was nothing to get overly excited about. But there was something starting to show in Evans, a determination which would in time become one of his hallmarks.

"You know, just from his attitude alone, I thought Richie would make it," Wilbur Jones says. "Because, see, he absolutely hated to lose. Once he got the hang of things, he was just determined to get better."

Already, he had come so far from the farm.

PART TWO
Winning

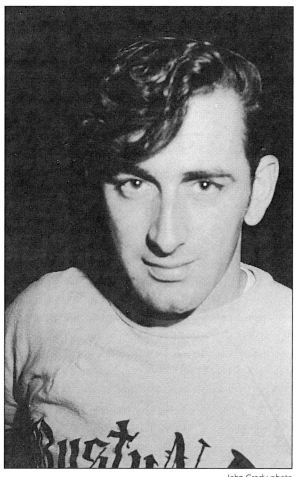

John Grady photo

Coupe Days

RICHIE EVANS WAS MOVING FAST—particularly off the track—in those early days. In addition to having gotten married, he had moved to Rome and run through a series of jobs, putting in stints as a mechanic and gasoline-slinger at the 'L' Truck Stop in Yorkville, Tommy Frank's Mobil station on Rome's Black River Boulevard, even Griffis Air Force Base. Now, as he fought to get this stock car stuff figured out, he was operating his own Shell service station on West Dominick Street in Rome and racing temporarily out of a tiny garage not far away on Spring Street.

And one evening in the winter of 1964-65, Evans was moving fast down Erie Boulevard, Rome's main drag, when he spotted a familiar face in the next car. It belonged to Dick Waterman, part of the Utica-Rome Speedway's new ownership group.

Waterman's involvement with Evans's home track was an interesting story in itself. The owner of an upholstery shop in Camden, he was something of a race fan, having been to several supermodified shows up at the Oswego Speedway, but he never as much as sat in the grandstands at Utica-Rome in its first three years of operation. Then Waterman and his friend Bernie Ingersall, an area moving company owner, took their wives on a February trip to Daytona Beach for the big NASCAR Speedweeks, and—with a spot of help from the weather man—Dick Waterman's life changed forever.

"Once we got down there," Waterman remembers, "Bernie and this other fellow started talking with Joe Lesik about buying Utica-Rome Speedway. I wasn't involved at all [in the negotiations], but because it happened to rain almost all week long at Daytona that year, they held all their business meetings in my car at the track. So I basically sat in on the meetings, because it was raining outside and I had no place else to go.

"Anyway, we got back home, and the other guy backed out of the deal. So Bernie said to me, 'Do you think you'd want to take half of this speedway?' I said, 'I don't know if I can handle half, but I'll get together with a couple of my friends and see what we can do.'" To shorten up a long story, Waterman and Ingersall and a couple of partners bought the track, and over the next few years Waterman took sole control.

"So the first time I ever watched a race at Utica-Rome Speedway," he laughs, "I owned the place."

Now Dick Waterman was driving along Erie Boulevard on a winter's night. "I heard somebody frantically blowing his horn," he says. "I look over, and it's Richie, waving for me to follow him. I followed him over to Spring Street, where he showed me his very first modified, a coupe."

The previous autumn, Evans had dropped a 326 Chevy engine into that little Nova, slapped on a set of wide tires, and run with the modi-

(left) Coupe construction, back before modifieds were production-line race cars.
(Lynn Evans collection)

(right) An early Evans mod, still carrying the number 109, gets ready to roll.
(Lynn Evans collection)

fied-sportsman cars in the final race of the '64 Utica-Rome season. With the coupe, he was going to challenge the modified guys for real, on equal terms. Well, at least as equal as his budget would allow.

Waterman says, "He was really proud of that coupe, you could see that."

Evans found the jump from hobby cars to modifieds almost as challenging as the transition from drag racing to ovals. The modifieds did everything better—accelerate, slow down, corner—and at a bullring like Utica-Rome they seemed to lap at warp speed. On top of that, the depth of talent was so much greater. On any given Sunday night in 1965, the modified field might include four-time NASCAR sportsman champion Rene Charland, New England star Ed Flemke, a hot Western New York kid named Jerry Cook, New England invaders like Billy Harmon, Elton Hill and Don Moon, Rome's own Dave and Tom Kotary, and a couple of hobby graduates named Sonney Seamon and Frank Mathalia who had climbed the ladder right along with Evans.

But Richie showed some flashes of brilliance that summer, particularly in a 30-lapper on July 11 when he finished second between a pair of Kotarys, winner Tom and third-place Dave. And on the final night of that season, September 19, Richie Evans won the first modified feature of his career, edging Seamon and Bernie Miller.

The job got tougher in 1966, as Utica-Rome's stature in the Northeastern racing world grew. In addition to the tough holdovers from previous years, Bill Wimble, who rose from the obscurity of the tiny dirt ovals near his home in Northern New York's St. Lawrence River Valley to become NASCAR's 1960 and '61 national sportsman champion, added the Vernon track to his weekly menu. Kenny Shoemaker, a burly, tough-talking dirt-track hero who was also an above-average pavement chauffeur, became a Utica-Rome regular, too. Also crossing over from the dirt were Utica's Lou Lazzaro, who in time would come to dominate at Dick Waterman's track, and Johnstown's Andy Romano, for years one of the region's popular travelers. From New England came lightning-fast Gene Bergin, chasing checkered flags, and Ernie Gahan and Don MacTavish, chasing the points that would bring them, respectively, the 1966 NASCAR national modified and sportsman championships. And often parked next to Eddie Flemke was a blond-haired Massachusetts kid and Flemke disciple named Pete Hamilton, learning to chase points himself; in '67 he would succeed his pal MacTavish as NASCAR sportsman champ.

"We had the best there was, every Sunday," Waterman proclaims. "It was like a who's-who of modified racing. Let me tell you, when they dropped that green flag at Utica-Rome, you had to be on the ball."

Starter John Tallini, the man charged with dropping that green flag, says, "We used to start 24 cars in the main event. Well, you could look down the list, and 20 of 'em were guys who had won a feature race somewhere. Some of 'em might have won two or three times that week. It probably didn't sink in with me back then, but that place was full of champions."

In the grandstands, Richie's wife Barbara and his sister and a growing contingent of Evans fans sat and cheered—"That was what you did on Sunday nights, you went to Utica-Rome," Sandy says—and watched him slug it out with the big dogs. Though he went winless in '66, Evans was in fact running better than ever, staying in step with the biggest names in the sport.

On May 15, he chased Flemke and Wimble to the checkers, like a student studying the masters. And in the 30-lapper on June 16, Richie figured prominently in what, in retrospect, has to be one of modified racing's all-time greatest top-five rundowns for a regular weekly show: Shoemaker, Evans, Hamilton, Flemke, Wimble.

By 1967 and '68 he was hitting the road on a more or less regular basis, heading east toward the Albany-Saratoga Speedway in Malta—another Joe Lesik creation, best described by three-time NASCAR modified champ Bugs Stevens as a "roomier" version of Utica-Rome—or north toward Airborne Park in Plattsburgh or west toward Fulton. Malta and Plattsburgh were NASCAR facilities, while Fulton Speedway was an "outlaw" track, affiliated with no sanctioning group.

And it was in the process of all this skipping around that the fellow whom the modified faithful came to recognize across the next 18 seasons as Richie Evans—a winner as popular among the racers and other assorted hangers-on in the pits as he was with fans—began to emerge. Within a couple of years, according to those who were there, it seemed like Evans *knew* everybody; if he hadn't raced beside you, maybe he'd spoken to you about tires or carburetors, or autographed your souvenir program.

"He was the same guy back then that everybody knew later on," says Wilbur Jones, who made most of those early road trips with his buddy. "He was always just full of life."

Robin Pemberton, born in 1958, was just a kid race fan from Malta dividing his time between the Albany-Saratoga bleachers, the L&R

"Evans, man, he was cool," says 1960s coupe fan (and present-day NASCAR vice president for competition) Robin Pemberton. *(John Grady photo)*

Speed Shop operated by the Len Bosley family, and his own mom and dad's eatery, Dunster's Restaurant. Dunster's was a hangout for racers who were hungry, and L&R was a haven for racers who needed parts or just a place to work. Pemberton went on to become a winning Winston Cup crew chief, served some time as Ford's NASCAR field manager, and in 2004 took a job as NASCAR's vice president for competition. But he still beams like that Malta boy when you get him talking about the '60s modified scene.

"Because of the restaurant, I got to know all those guys," Pemberton says. "I knew Rene Charland when I was a kid. I knew Don MacTavish. Heck, it'd be nothing at all for me and my brother to be outside working on our bicycles while Eddie Flemke and Pete Hamilton were adjusting the valves on their race cars right alongside us.

"I remember seeing Richie, and actually meeting him, in those coupe days. I was still a kid, so I can't say we developed a relationship or anything like that. But when you're a kid, you've always got a few racers you think are just cool. With me, Pete Hamilton was one. Eddie Flemke was another. And Evans, man, he was cool, too."

Dave Lape and Merv Treichler, standout drivers from different ends of the Empire State, also thought Evans was pretty cool.

Lape, a Canajoharie native who cut his teeth on the Fonda Speedway dirt, was trying to find his footing on pavement when he first encountered Evans. "I remember Richie being a guy who would help just about anybody," Lape says. "And, believe me, he helped me quite a few times. We used to take our dirt car to Utica-Rome and Albany-Saratoga to run against the pavement guys, and we were basically a bunch of kids who didn't know anything. And Richie – who was pretty much our age, or just a little older, but had already won a lot of races on asphalt – was always somebody we could go to. If you asked him something, he was very honest, and he would try to help you."

If that help made Lape a tougher man to beat—as on July 28, 1968, when he hounded Evans all the way to the checkers at Utica-Rome—well, that was fine.

Treichler, out of Sanborn, north of Buffalo, didn't need much help. Raised on the open-competition tracks of Western New York, Merv had the mechanical side of things well in hand by the time he started seeing Evans regularly at Fulton. But that, it turned out, was their common bond, the launching pad for a 20-year friendship. "We talked about race cars a lot," Treichler says. "Back then, everybody was basically a driver/mechanic, and Richie understood the nuts and bolts of it."

It was also at Fulton that Evans caught the eye of Donald "Dutch" Hoag, from the tiny town of Bath on New York's Southern Tier. Hoag has gone into the history books as a modified god, having scored *five* victories in the National Open—precursor to the Race of Champions—on the treacherous Pennsylvania mile known as the Langhorne Speedway. More incredibly, Hoag won that grand old 100-miler three times (1956, '60 and '63) while Langhorne was still dirt, and twice (1967 and '68) after it was paved.

"Right from the start, I thought Richie was really talented," Hoag recalls. "I mean, he was a good, competitive runner right from the first day I saw him."

In the mid-'60s, Hoag was driving for a pair of brothers named Ray and Donnie Turner, who owned a Rochester-area construction company and housed their potent modified in an old chicken coop in the suburb of Scottsville. The Turners, friendly types, had an open-door policy at the shop, which attracted a number of race-crazy youths from a nearby town. Hoag, once he'd asked the boys where they were from, dubbed them "the Spencerport kids." A few of those kids went on to make serious impressions on the sport in the years to come, including Gary Reichert, Mike Loescher and an ex-motorcycle racer named Lee Osborne, who dated Hoag's daughter Donna from 1964-66.

"Anybody who was young and raced out of that area, the Turners started all of us," Osborne says. "In 1965, I told Ray I wanted to race. He said, '*Everybody* wants to race.' I told him, 'No, I really want to do this.' He pointed to a car they had out back, an old coupe Bobby Hudson had run for them, and he said, 'That thing needs a new front clip and a new rear clip, but we'll show you how to do it.' They let me use part of their shop, and I put on a new front end and a new rear end. We flat-towed it all the way from Rochester to Shangri-La on opening night in 1965—Dutch's car was on the truck, and my car was behind it—and we blew a tank off the truck's radiator on the big hill heading out of Ithaca. But, you know, I think we ran third or fourth in the feature that night."

Lee Osborne went on to win 55 modified features in the next four seasons, including "something like 29 or 30 in 1967." His beat was generally the Spencer Speedway in Williamson, the Shangri-La track west of Binghamton in Owego, and Fulton. Evans raced mostly at Utica-Rome

A young Richie Evans leads one of the sport's giants, the great Dutch Hoag. *(John Bisci collection)*

and Albany-Saratoga, mixing in stops at Plattsburgh and Fulton. Toss in "all the specials at places like Oswego," Osborne says, and "we might have raced together a dozen times a year. We ran a lot of big shows, 100-lappers and stuff like that." For Osborne, the memories remain vivid.

The racing: "Richie's stuff wasn't very fancy. In fact, I remember the gas tank flying out of his car one night at Fulton. Came out the right side of his car in turn three, and it was laying on the race track. His cars were a bit on the crude side, but they worked. And he was already a hell of a driver."

And the camaraderie: Evans's gang, in addition to the usual Rome bunch, was joined for a short spell by energetic mechanic Billy Taylor, who in years to come would wrench many winning cars for Richie's rivals, including Maynard Troyer and Geoff Bodine. "We were friends," Osborne says. "We got along real good, me and Richie and Billy Taylor and those guys. We were a pretty good bunch of characters."

Ozzie was four years younger than Evans, but they had hit their modified strides at about the same time. Therefore, Osborne grins, "It was us against the old guys, you know? Dutch was winning, Don Diffendorf was running good [in Western New York]. We were 20 years younger than those guys. And on the NASCAR circuit you had Bugsy Stevens and Eddie Flemke, and those guys were a good bit older than us, too."

It was a peer thing, the same sort of alliance Evans would forge with another fellow destined for modified greatness, Rochester's Maynard Troyer. The two men began clashing on a regular basis at Fulton, and before long they were clashing everywhere, with one or the other often winning. Had they been different sorts of men, it might have gotten nasty and stayed nasty. Instead, Troyer and Evans managed to be rivals *and* friends.

"We started running modifieds at roughly the same time," Maynard says, "so we kinda grew together."

They were all part of a booming scene, a thriving New York asphalt modified community. Osborne says, "You ask anybody from out this way who grew up in the 1960s, and they'll tell you the same thing. Back then, you just assumed that everybody went to the stock car races on the weekends. I thought that was simply what you did; I didn't know there were people who *didn't* go to the races. You could go to any track, and you'd see the same faces in the same seats, week in and week out. You wanted to go, you *had* to go, because you felt like you were a part of it. It was a soap opera: *What's going to happen next?*"

It was the perfect environment for drivers to become heroes. That's how Lee Osborne views it in hindsight. But in 1967 and '68, he didn't allow himself to think that deeply. "You did what you did, and you went home," he says. "Yeah, we kinda knew who the other hot guys were, but it didn't really matter. We were all grubs. We were all gas station guys. And if you raced, there were always going to be people who looked down on you like you were the lowest form of life. We had greasy fingernails, and we drove these old, ratty trucks, and we towed these pieces of junk down the road. But you know what? We didn't care."

Dave Lape says, "I don't think any of us knew what was ahead. We were just racing, and I'm sure we didn't realize what might happen for us. The main thing back then was just getting to the track that night, getting to the next race."

And maybe waiting for the next break. That seemed like it might have arrived for Richie Evans early in 1968, when one of modified racing's most coveted rides opened up. Big, bad Kenny Shoemaker had driven the A-to-Z Automotive coupe for more than four years and piled up an impressive portfolio of victories, particularly on dirt but also at blacktop joints like Utica-Rome and Malta. When car owners Cliff Wright and Donnie Zautner fired Shoemaker in a tiff over a crash, they tapped this promising Rome driver Evans as his replacement.

His own cars were good, and getting better, but Evans took the seat. As long as the ride was fast, why not let some other guy's wallet pay the freight?

Alas, the association ended after Richie had only run the #24 a handful of times at Albany-Saratoga, Plattsburgh and Utica-Rome. Its owners had a chance to hire Don MacTavish, and they quite sensibly jumped on it, handing Evans his walking papers. In his autobiography, "They Called Me the 'Shoe'," Shoemaker suggested that the A-to-Z guys canned Richie "because they didn't think he'd ever make a driver." More likely is that Cliff Wright and Donnie Zautner simply saw a chance to replace one proven champion, Shoemaker, with another proven champion, MacTavish, and it took getting rid of Evans—fast, yes, but still something of an apprentice—to make room for the new hire.

Shoemaker, who died in 2001, called the breakup "a shame," and wrote that Evans and the #24 had the potential to be "a combination that could have continued for many years."

But Richie never held a grudge. For one thing, the record book proves that he ended up doing quite well, thank you, without the A-to-Z Automotive coupe. Besides, the whole episode gave him a chuckle for the rest of his days. Anytime he stumbled upon a photo of himself in the Wright/Zautner #24, he'd share it with anybody in the room and reminisce about "the only time I ever got fired."

 # DPW Orange

THE MOST FAMOUS COLOR/NUMBER combination in the history of NASCAR modified racing had nothing to do with anybody playing favorites, and picking out something that looked or felt right.

No, Richie Evans ended up driving an orange #61 mostly because he was backed into a corner.

First, the paint story, which has become fireside lore in modified circles. The stock car in which Evans had first begun to turn heads, that little hobby-class Nova, had been a dark blue. But when it came time to lay a coat of paint over one of his first modified coupes, blue was out of the question.

"For one thing," says Wilbur Jones, "Rich didn't have any money to buy paint."

But he knew where he might be able to find some at a pretty fair bargain. Like most municipalities, the City of Rome happened to keep a stash of orange paint at the Department of Public Works garage; it was used mostly for touching up the city's battle-scarred snowplows, and, hey, it was just sitting there ...

Besides, Jones says, "Richie had always liked the black and orange colors at Rome Free Academy."

What happened next is a little bit fuzzy. In the romanticized version, Evans either picked a lock or vaulted a fence and helped himself to a couple of gallons. Others hint at an inside job, suggesting that an Evans crony who worked at the department might have spirited the stuff out for his pal.

Wilbur Jones knows the truth, but he isn't about to give it up. Smiling, Jones says only, "Richie didn't do it. Now, one of the people *around* him might have done it, but it wasn't Richie."

At any rate, the #61 coupe had a new look: "It's DPW Orange!" Evans exclaimed. Later, once he could afford to purchase paint legitimately from body shops, the color changed in subtle ways. According to Bill "Bondo" Clark, who took a part-time job sweeping floors for Evans as a teenager in 1973 and ended up painting his cars for years, "technically it's a yellow, but it leans a little toward the orange side. The paint code is number 1021. You go down to the paint store and ask for 1021, and you'll get that same orange."

As the years rolled on, Evans used to give different answers to different people about what color his cars were. He might say "Omaha Orange," or he might say "Swamp Holley Orange," and both were legitimate automotive shades similar to his. But Clark swears that it was always "just plain 1021," and that any variations in the colors occured in the mixing stages and not in the Evans shop.

"We used to buy it by the gallon," he says, "and we used it just the way it came."

But Richie Evans always got a kick out of that "DPW Orange" designation.

"The price of that paint was just right," he'd say with a wink.

The number story also has a bit of a mystery to it. Nobody seems to remember just why Evans switched from his Kennedy-inspired #109 to the number 6; the best guess is that several tracks were cracking down on three-digit numbers, in some cases because they were a nightmare for manual scoring and in other cases because the new electronic scoreboards could not accommodate them, but it's still unclear just why he chose #6.

What *is* clear is that, from the beginning, the number was a bit of a headache for him, simply because other guys were using it. At the NASCAR tracks, the #6 was the property of a genuine New York State legend, Dick Nephew, who had been the national sportsman co-champion (with Bill Wimble) in 1961. And whenever Evans snuck away to the north or west to run at some of the area's non-NASCAR speedways, a rising Rochester driver named Maynard Troyer always seemed to be there with *his* sharp-looking #6. If a promoter happened to frown on two cars having the same number, neither Nephew nor Troyer was likely to volunteer for re-lettering duty.

"Richie was the new kid on the block, so he always had to change his number," says former Oswego Speedway track manager Dick

Who knew that swapping numbers would lead to "61" becoming one of asphalt modified racing's hallmarks? *(John Bisci collection)*

O'Brien. "And I'm sure that adding that '1' was the easiest thing to do; put a little tape down, or a little bit of paint."

In 1969, tired of the constant swapping, Evans made things permanent: he would run as #61, and that was that.

"It became something that was really traditional," O'Brien says. "And today, the two are synonymous. That number *is* him. When you think about Richie Evans, you think about that orange 61."

 ## Gas Station Life

THE AD IN THE OLD Utica-Rome Speedway souvenir program reads:

> *Rich Evans' Shell Service*
> *Major and Minor Repairs – Gas – Oil*
> *General Repairs – Goodyear Tires*
> *401 W. Dominick – FF6-9630 Rome, N.Y.*

Evans was just 19 when he took over the place, helped along by a loan from his parents. Strangely enough, Ernest and Satie Evans had little interest in their son's racing; as near as anyone can tell, Richie's father never once saw him race. Sister Sandy says, "He wasn't dead set against it, or anything like that. He did visit the garage, I remember that. Why he didn't go to the track, I don't know, because he always liked the idea of working on tractors and cars and things. I suppose he was just always too busy." Only after Ernest's passing in 1978 did Satie begin attending races, smiling broadly whenever her son made it to victory lane.

Way back when, they were more interested in seeing him succeed during the week than on the weekends. Barbara Evans remembers them happily helping their boy, whom everyone saw as "a real go-getter, a real hard worker," says Barbara.

That hard work, and the skills behind it, quickly earned Evans a fine reputation around Rome. Fred Ulrich said, "Even early on, Richie was known as one of the best men around when it came to carburetors and transmissions. He could take them apart and put 'em together like it was nothing."

By every account, Evans enjoyed the gas station life. He wrestled some with the financial realities of being self-employed—as we shall come to see—but he was comfortable with the life itself, the work and the interaction with the folks who brought their cars in for fill-ups and snow tires and oil changes.

"I had to work with people," he once reminisced to Pete Zanardi. "You know that stuff about the customer being right? I always believed it."

Ah, the good ol' days: a modified coupe parked outside a service station. (John Bisci collection)

The proprietor of Rich Evans' Shell Service had a creative, plotting mind. The Christmas trees he'd planted as a kid on the ridge up in Westernville? "By the time we were in our early 20s, they were getting to be full-sized," Wilbur Jones remembers. "So every year, we'd go up there and cut down 200 or 300 trees, then haul 'em all down to the gas station and sell 'em outside. He kept right on planting new ones every time we did that. I think he looked at it like this was going to be a life-time deal, a way to always make some extra money. In fact, he did that right up until he got really successful, winning championships and all that. After that, he just didn't have the time to race full-time and do the trees, too."

Across the 1960s, the gas station became a meeting place, a mandatory daily or nightly stop for the loose confederation of friends and casual acquaintances who would, in time, morph into something resembling a pit crew. They were, really, the first real racing help Richie Evans ever had, and they found themselves turning up at 401 West Dominick Street on a regular basis.

Young Ted Puchyr, who had become something of an Evans fan in that Utica-Rome bleacher seat, happened to be tooling down West Dominick Street when he noticed something really cool in the end service bay of the Shell Station on the corner of Madison.

"That orange coupe sat there, and it was *visible*," Ted Puchyr says. "And I just walked in."

He walked in and he stayed. There were others, of course, friends who lingered into the long nights in the bay which housed the coupe. Fred Ulrich was around all the time, as was Max Baker, one of Richie's oldest friends. And Wilbur Jones, who had double-dated with Evans in their school days; the two lost touch for a while, but reconnected, Jones figured, "in about 1963, at the Shell station."

Jones, who in those days was employed with Baker at Revere Copper Products, says, "The gas station was a regular stop every day, before work

Crewman Ted Puchyr (foreground, left) at the ready prior to a Utica-Rome feature. *(courtesy of* Speedway Scene*)*

and after work. I worked at Revere, me and Max, and we both worked [second shift]. So I'd get to the gas station at about nine o'clock in the morning, and Max and I wouldn't leave until about three. We'd work at Revere until about 11:30 at night, and then we'd head back to Richie's until about one o'clock in the morning. It was a way of life for us. We *wanted* to be there. We couldn't wait to get there."

And still others. Joe LaMonica, Ron LaMandia. A young guy named Danny Morgan. Anthony Evans, whom everybody called Weasel, and Dominick Marcello, whom everybody called Donny.

"I met Richie in, I guess, 1968 or '69," Marcello says. "I was working as a machinist, and I had a 1949 Pontiac Catalina. Nice car. But one day I was driving and I heard something strange underneath, and I said, 'What the hell is that?' So I drove it into Richie's garage, and they were sitting around playing [a card game called] joker poker. I said, 'I got something rattling on this car. Would you check it out?' Richie said, 'Yeah, bring it in and we'll put it on the hoist.'

"So I pulled it into the bay, and I remember his coupe sitting there in the other stall. We got my car up onto the hoist, and he found a loose bracket on the exhaust system. But, see, the brackets I had on there were not stock; they were really nice pieces I had made myself at the machine shop. Well, that got Richie's attention. He said, 'I've got a question. I need to get some shackle-bolt brackets made for my race car ...'

"We started looking at his coupe, and then he drew me a picture of what he wanted. He said, 'Can you make me a couple of these?' I said, 'No problem.' I couple of days later I brought him the brackets—nice pieces, with ball bearings and the whole nine yards—and he said, 'Oh, they're perfect. Can you make me a couple more?' We were friends from that day on."

There was always *something* happening at 401 West Dominick. Ted Puchyr remembers the night when Evans pulled some customer's nice automobile into a bay to be worked on the next day, and then got back to fiddling with the coupe. "Richie was revving the motor up on the race car, and the flywheel disintegrated," Puchyr says. "It came flying right through everything [on the race car] and hit the customer's car. It tore up that car just like a machine gun hit it." All work on the modified stopped, Puchyr recalls, while Evans figured out how to patch up the poor guy's ride.

It was a vibrant, dynamic place, full of young men brought together, Jones figures, by "our common interest in racing. It wasn't *work* to us. I mean, don't get me wrong, we worked really hard on those race cars. But we loved it."

What the Shell station was *not,* Jones says, was "a place to just hang out. Rich didn't really like it if guys just showed up and stood around doing nothing. See, the problem was, we always had some beer there, but it was there in case we wanted to have a cold one after the work was done. You didn't just pound down one beer after another all night. But a lot of guys knew he kept beer in the refrigerator, and they'd just hang around and help themselves to the beer. Rich would get a little ticked off about that."

In time, the hang-around guys got weeded out, and the good help became part of that Shell station, part of Richie Evans's everyday life.

"Richie was at that gas station all the time," Wilbur Jones says. "*All* the time. He pumped the gas, he worked on the cars. If he was busy and I was there, I might go out and pump some gas just to help him out. We all did stuff like that."

 ## Broke, Broke, Broke

DESPITE HIS GROWING REPUTATION for solid mechanical work, and despite the fact that an ever-widening circle of friends were hanging out at his service station and therefore buying his gasoline, the last half of the 1960s found Richie Evans in near-constant financial upheaval. He seemed to have a terminal case of that most pernicious of all racing illnesses: poverty.

It was no big secret.

"When he had the Shell station, he was notorious for it," remembers Ted Puchyr. "Like, he had to pay cash when the tanker came. There was no credit. The reason for that was because there had been times when the tanker would come and Richie would write them a check, but there was no money [in the account]. So he'd bounce the check, and Shell Oil would go out of their minds, and after a while he started to be a C.O.D. customer. They would call and say, 'Now, don't forget, when the truck gets there, we need, like, $2200,' or whatever it was for a load of fuel back then.

"But the thing is, everybody liked Richie. There were times when the tanker would be ordered for Monday, but he'd have a bad weekend at the track and the money wouldn't be there. So Richie would go to Joe Carillo, who was a snowmobile dealer up the street. Joe would peel out the $2200—no questions asked, nothing signed—and Richie would pay the tanker guy. And during the week, as he got some business, he would pay Joe back."

There were two very solid reasons for this ongoing fiscal crisis on Dominick Street.

The lesser of the two—but an important one nonetheless—is that according to friends, Evans had a tough time being a hardass in a business where hardass behavior is almost required. Somebody he knew from the race track, or maybe from the local pub, would roll in with a mechanical problem that needed fixing today but couldn't be paid for until Friday. Come Friday, Evans would be off to the races, and by the time he reconnected with the customer, they'd be a little bit short again and ask if he might be able to carry them until the *next* payday. His collections skills were essentially non-existent. Half the time, his friends say, he was too sympathetic to pound on customers for the money he was owed, and the other half of the time he was too busy to chase them.

But the biggest thing stabbing Evans in the hip pocket, no question about it, was that orange coupe in the last service bay. His then-wife Barbara says, "I think the gas station itself did very well, but I'm sure it was hard for him to race on that money, too."

He was spending every nickel he had on the modified. Hell, he was spending nickels he *didn't* have. In 1979, Evans reflected on those hungry times in a radio interview with Arnold Dean: "I invested just about everything I could get ahold of," he told Dean, "right from sales tax money …"

Even as he laughed—and Richie had a warm, goofy, staccato laugh—you could tell that he hadn't forgotten the feeling. *Nobody* ever forgets what it's like to be broke, broke, broke, week upon week.

"It was," Evans told Dean, "a matter of robbing from Peter to pay Paul to keep the car going."

He used to joke that he turned plenty of bill collectors into race fans in those days; they'd go to Utica-Rome on Sunday nights and root for him to do well, so they'd have a chance to get paid. "It got to be a ritual to see who could get to my garage first on Monday morning," he later reminisced to Dick Berggren, "to get a piece of what I'd won over the weekend."

He told Berggren, "Somebody was always trying to put a lock on my door."

"Richie didn't have any money," says his old employer Joe Jones. "If he smashed the car, he'd bring it to my shop and put it on the frame rack and try to straighten it around. Anything to keep going."

The solution, obviously, would have been to quit racing. That apparently never occurred to Evans, not even in the hardest times.

And there were lots of hard times. As the money got tighter, just getting to and from the speedways became a crapshoot.

"I'm coming back from Malta one night, towing the race car," Ted Puchyr recalls. "We had a '59 Oldsmobile and a rickety old trailer. I'm coming down a hill on the Thruway, and the motor blows. I mean, everything just comes right down through the oil pan. The Oldsmobile fills up with smoke, and I can't see, so I just ease it over to the side and I finally get stopped. I'm sitting there, and a state trooper comes by.

"Now, the car isn't registered. The trailer isn't registered. I'm in deep trouble, right? Well, luckily, the trooper never asks for my license, never asks for anything. He just says, 'We've got to get this thing off the Thruway. I'll call a wrecker.' So he calls for the wrecker, and away he goes. A few minutes later, here come Richie and Barbara driving down the road in Richie's '62 Ford, his red convertible. He sees me, and he stops. He says, 'What happened?' I tell him, 'I blew the motor up.' He says, 'Well, what's going on now?' I say, 'The trooper called a wrecker.'

"Richie says, real serious, 'We ain't got no money to pay for a tow truck. Take the rear binder off the car. Take off the chains. We've gotta figure something out.' So we're crawling around underneath this thing, wrapping these chains around bumpers and axles and spring hangers. We're going to tow this whole thing with his Ford. I ask him, 'What are we gonna do when we get to the Thruway exit? They're not going to let us go through the tollbooth like *this*.' He says, 'We'll take care of that when we get there.'

"We get rolling, and he's towing me so close that I can't even see his brake lights, at, like, 50 miles an hour down the Thruway. When he slows down, I'm hitting the back of his car, because he's stopping his Ford, me in the Oldsmobile, and the trailer, and we didn't have electric brakes on the trailers back in those days. We get off at the Fultonville exit, and he cons the lady [in the tollbooth] into letting us pull through and park it off to the side. We went home, and the next day at 8:00 in the morning we headed back there with two pickups to haul everything home."

It is the kind of thing that never seems to happen when you've got cash in your pocket and money in the bank. Misery can't resist pestering you when you're tapped out.

Puchyr again: "One night, Richie wanted to race at Plattsburgh. The crew that night was going to be him and me, that's it; everybody else was either working or doing something else. He says, 'You take the race car up to Plattsburgh. I'll go home and get cleaned up and change, and I'll drive your car up there.' I had a 1966 Pontiac GTO, the first one in the city of Rome, and that thing would run like a bear.

"Anyway, I take off from the gas station. To get to Plattsburgh, we'd go north out of Rome on Route 12 and then run cross-lots, through the woods. Well, the truck stops running. Just *stops*. I pull over and look under the hood, and I see that the fan belt has come off. What happened was, the crank broke in half, and when that happens, the pulleys stop turning and the belts come off.

"I get ahold of a guy I know, and I get the thing towed back to Rome, to the gas station. I never did see Richie, and he never did see me. Now, this is the '60s, and nobody's got cell phones. I'm trying to call the speedway, trying to call the speedway, and finally I get through. I tell the guy there, 'As soon as Richie Evans gets there, have him call the station.' So finally, he calls. I say, 'We've got a problem. I blew the tow truck up, and I'm back in Rome.'"

Puchyr says he can still hear the anguish in his friend's voice. "He just said, 'Aw, *man.*'"

Just another weekend in the struggling years. Some race nights were tight: "We'd all chip in to buy a clutch or a tire if that's what it took," Puchyr smiles. And other race nights were *really* tight. Wilbur Jones says, "There were a lot of times when we had to pool our money just to pay the toll on the Thruway. I'm serious about that. We'd be riding down the highway with the race car, and I'd say, 'Rich, you got any money?' He'd say, 'I got a little. You?' That's just the way it was."

But remember what Puchyr said earlier: *Everybody liked Richie.* And those who could help, did help. If it wasn't Joe Carillo, the snowmobile dealer, bailing him out on a gasoline delivery, maybe it was old Fred Ulrich coming up with the cash to keep the race team going.

"I don't know if Richie would've stayed a racer," Jones says, "if it hadn't been for Fred."

Puchyr echoes, "When Richie didn't have anything, Freddy was there. Nobody knows what Freddy put in that car. He bought tires, he bought motors. Freddy did everything he could within the means that he had."

It was something Ulrich shrugged off for years. "Well, Rich didn't have any money," he said in 2003. "He couldn't buy the same stuff the other guys had in the modifieds, and that was tough for him. So I'd buy him a few tires—you could get a tire for 50 bucks—and he'd use my truck sometimes to haul the car to the races. What the hell, I was doing pretty good, building houses.

"I could see that Rich had the potential to be a good race driver. I remember thinking, 'If this guy can hang in there, he can really be one of the top dogs.' And, you know, I guess that's why I wanted to help him."

There were a couple other folks who thought picking up a tire bill for Evans might be a good gamble. Utica-Rome promoter Dick Waterman says, "There came this one point when Richie was absolutely out of money. Well, my partner Bernie Ingersall and I heard about this, and we very quietly bought him a set of tires. It's something that maybe we shouldn't have done, as track promoters. But, see, he was from right here in Rome, and he was getting to be very popular. So, to be totally honest, we were as concerned about ourselves as we were for Richie, because it was a way of keeping a very good local driver racing at our track."

Writer Andy Fusco, an upstate New York fixture, concurs: "Don't forget, half of Waterman's crowd came from Rome!"

Somehow, Evans kept afloat, but barely.

"One day," says Donny Marcello, "I had to leave my car at his place, and he said, 'Take mine.' Well, I jumped in that thing and took off, but I didn't get halfway down the block before I ran out of gas. That's how it was with Richie back then. Things were tight."

Writer Tom Neff recalled leaning into the cockpit of an Evans coupe at Albany-Saratoga and seeing the phrase "Think $" lettered on the dash. It wasn't just some cute slogan put there to rev up the driver. It was Richie's way of reminding himself that a foolish move tonight might mean having to skip a race tomorrow night. But even when he did "think $", it was no guarantee that things weren't going to go haywire.

Words to live and race by! *(Lynn Evans collection)*

Evans told Dick Berggren about the time in the 1960s when he found himself leading a big-dollar event with just 10 laps to go. "I started counting the money, figuring what I was going to do with it all," Richie said. "I don't do that anymore, because just about the time I got it all counted, the motor let go on me. A race isn't over 'til it's over. That one sure wasn't. I really needed that race. I didn't have anything. I had no property, no money in my pocket, nothing. All I had was people wanting money I didn't have."

Today, with Evans at or near the top of everybody's list of all-time great American short-track racers, it's tempting to gloss over his hard times as if they were just some little slump. In fact, they lasted years. He might have been winning races, and he might have looked to smart bystanders like a star in the making—in '68 he grabbed his first Fulton victory and finished second to Jerry Cook in the Albany-Saratoga track standings—but Richie Evans spent an awful lot of time in the ditch.

"Back in 1967 and 1968 it was pretty close, a race-to-race situation for me," he told writer Pete Zanardi. By '68, he added, he was "running junk, just trying to keep things together."

And not always succeeding. Ask anybody who was around Evans back then. Ask Ted Puchyr. In 1968, he and Richie set out for Martinsville, Virginia, hauling the coupe behind a pickup truck they had borrowed from Fred Ulrich. Even back then, Martinsville was one of Eastern short-track racing's holy grails. Only the best won there, but not only the best made an effort. Every backyard racer longed to make the spring and fall trips south to the half-mile oval with the hairpin corners. Evans decided to go after a conversation with Bernie Miller, for years one of the strongest competitors at Utica-Rome and other New York speedways.

"Bernie used to have some beautiful coupes," Puchyr remembers.

Evans accepts an All Star League helmet. He was winning big in the late 1960s, even as his financial well ran dry. (J&H photo/courtesy of Speedway Scene)

"He knew how to do it; he was a craftsman. Anyway, he really had the Martinsville bug. He would make the trek down there every year. He was always saying, 'Richie, you have got to go to Martinsville.'"

Puchyr was the lone crewman on that trip for the simplest of reasons: "I had weekends off! I was working in construction then."

So off they went. When they pulled into Martinsville Speedway and parked their borrowed tow rig, the weary travelers could not believe their eyes. "In the pit next to us were the Wood Brothers and Donnie Allison with their number 21 coupe," Puchyr recalls. "It was a beautiful burgundy, and it looked like a show car. Inside, everything was naugahyde, rolled and pleated leather. We said, 'You don't *race* that thing, do you?' And, of course, there was also Ray Hendrick in Jack Tant's Flying 11, another beautiful car."

They thought they had gone to modified heaven. Instead, it turned out to be just another weekend in modified hell for Richie Evans.

Puchyr says, "Everybody in New York back then ran these dovetail coupes, like Dutch Hoag did, because Dutch was The Man and he set the style. Whatever Dutch Hoag did, everybody did. Well, at Martinsville, you had all the Southern NASCAR officials in charge. They looked at our car, and they said, 'What is *that*?' We said, 'It's a modified.' They said, 'Ain't like no modified we ever saw before.' See, down there they were all running the full trunk and [partial] fenders. They said, 'We can't let you run. Your fuel cell is exposed, and we don't allow that.' They told us we needed to go someplace and fabricate a tail, or we couldn't run."

They headed out of the track and into nearby Ridgeway, home of a well-known racing hangout called Clarence's Steakhouse; its owner, Clarence Pickerall, fielded fast modifieds for years with drivers like Paul Radford and Satch Worley.

"Down by Clarence's," says Puchyr, "there was a Sunoco station that had four bays. We pulled in there and said, 'Hey, man, we've got to work on our car.' The guy actually shut down three bays—*he gave us three bays!*—and got us some sheet metal. That's the way it was back then: Guys would give you their whole garage just because you had a race car, and they didn't care where you were from. We got to work and fabricated a tail so the tank wasn't exposed, and we put these little Mickey Mouse fenders on it, too. We showed up back at the track and we were legal, but I'm sure it still looked like we really didn't belong there."

Their troubles were not over yet, because those Southern officials weren't done cracking down on this Yankee newcomer with the orange modified. But others noticed Evans's tenacity, and came to his aid. Years later, Richie recalled to writer Rich Benyo that his coupe was made up of "about half Virginia parts" by the time he passed inspection that weekend at Martinsville.

It got worse, of course, because everything seemed to get worse in those days.

"We had gone down there with a fresh stroker big-block Richie bought from a guy in Utica," Puchyr says. "He had scraped together the money to buy that thing, because you *had* to have a stroker to keep up with those guys. Well, it lasted maybe 10 or 12 laps in the race before it just hand-grenaded."

Evans robbed Peter, paid Paul, and somehow kept on going, with hard luck shadowing him every step of the way.

"We were at Fulton, and we blew a hole in the radiator early in the night," Puchyr remembers. "It's spitting water out. Richie tells me, 'Go to the hot dog stand and get all the relish you can.' I say, 'Relish?' He says, 'Yeah, *relish*. Every time I come in, pop the cap and pack it full of relish and water.' I guess it was some old mechanic's trick he'd learned. See, one piece of pickle in the relish would find the hole and plug it temporarily, and when that one blew out, the next piece of pickle would find the hole.

"In those days, they used to have these jars of relish sitting there at the food stand, and I was grabbing all I could. The concession guy was going crazy: 'What are you doing? You're putting me out of business!' I told him, 'I need this for our race car.' We made three or four pit stops [in the feature], but Richie finished the race. It was just wild.

"Of course, that radiator was half-full of pickle relish when we got done. We just threw it out."

There were nine NASCAR championships and hundreds of wins and barrels of laughter in his future. All Evans knew that night at Fulton was that somehow, he and his guys were going to have to come up with a new radiator.

"You know what it was like?" Ted Puchyr says. "It felt like us against the world."

Winning

"One night near the end of my career," says the great Bill Wimble, "I was racing at Albany-Saratoga. It was a long race, a 100-lapper maybe. Early on, in my mirror, I could see Richie coming. Well, he must have tried to pass me for 90 of those 100 laps. We weren't fighting for the lead, but we did battle really hard for probably third position. He never got by, but what impressed me was that he never, ever gave up. I've seen very few drivers as bull-dogged about what they're trying to do as Richie was in that race. And there's one other thing: We never did touch. It was a good, hard, clean, fair race. I remember thinking to myself for the first time that night, 'This guy has got something that most drivers don't have.' I could feel that."

Wimble pauses. "See, once you've run that close with a guy for that long a time, you can recognize those who are really good and those who maybe aren't as good. I had run with Richie quite a few times by then, of course, and I had watched him race in the lower-division cars before he ever got into modifieds, so I knew that he was good. But I never really recognized just *how* good he was until that night at Albany-Saratoga."

Evans's friend and crewman Wilbur Jones recalls a similar epiphany: "I can't say I ever *noticed* Richie getting better. It was a little bit like watching grass grow; all of a sudden you've got a lawn."

By the closing years of the 1960s, there was no doubting that Evans had become a terrific driver, one capable of beating the best from time to time. "I remember him winning some of the 100-lappers and some midweek special races [at Albany-Saratoga]," says Robin Pemberton. "You could tell he was good."

The problem was, Evans *only* seemed able to win from time to time. There were still too many nights when his car didn't handle, too many nights when the feature ended with his orange coupe in the pits, oil or water or both leaking out as it sat crackling from the battle.

His was the curse of every talented young racer not born into money: Richie Evans had grown far better than his equipment. He didn't have the technical side of racing—the chassis, the tires—mapped out the way the big winners did, and he didn't have time to learn that stuff because he was always attending to burnt pistons, busted cranks, thrown rods and broken rockers. From the scraps, he would piece together his next engine, and, predictably, the next engine would meet the same smoky end.

Billy Nacewicz, still a few years away from working with Evans but already a familiar face, says, "I remember Richie praying that he could just get one good, reliable engine. It didn't necessarily have to be the most powerful engine, as long as it would last."

In time, Evans pulled together enough dough to buy a powerplant from John Clement, a Rochester-area builder who had assembled some winning mills for Merv Treichler and others. "I went and picked it up for him," Fred Ulrich said. "It was a big-block, like everybody ran back then, and it was a hell of a motor."

There's no telling what would have become of Evans or his racing operation had that engine blown up, too. Maybe he'd have hit the skids and given up. Instead, Ulrich remembered, "all Rich ever did to that motor for the whole summer was change the oil and tune it up a little bit." He started finishing races, which meant hauling in more money at the payoff window. Evans, still struggling to pay down his bills and to keep the gas station afloat, squirreled away a few bucks at a time until he could get another good engine, this one from Rochester's B&M Speed Shop. (A side note: the "M" in B&M Speed was Milt Johnson, father to a couple of kids named Alan and Danny who grew up to become dirt modified legends.) With some reliability under the hood at long last—"For 40 races, I did nothing but adjust the valves," Evans once said—he had more time to pay attention to the rest of his program.

"That's when he was able to start worrying more about working on the car itself," Fred Ulrich said. "That really helped him."

Something else helped, too. Just as there had always seemed to be another person ready to help Evans out of his latest financial jam, there were always folks willing to give him a hand straightening out his race cars.

Two stand out in Evans lore: Sonney Seamon and Ed Flemke.

Clayton "Sonney" Seamon had been part of the local racing scene since the birth of the Utica-Rome Speedway; he had, in fact, done some welding work on the track's original retaining wall. Dubbed "the Mayor of Vernon Center," the popular Seamon came up with Evans through the hobby stock ranks, and his 1968 Utica-Rome modified championship testified to Seamon's ability behind the wheel. But from the start, his relationship with Evans was more than just driver-to-driver; to watch them chat, perhaps standing with their feet up on a tire, was to come to the conclusion that Sonney—the older of the two by several years—was something of a big-brother figure to Richie.

"Sonney and Richie were really close," says Ted Puchyr. "They were buds. They raced together, and they worked a lot together."

Puchyr remembers Seamon and Evans combing Oneida County's dairy barns and swamps for abandoned coupes—1937 Chevrolets and '36 Fords—they could haul off and chop into their next modifieds. When it came to car construction, Seamon, who built and sold a small handful of cars each year, was certainly a man worth listening to. Says Billy Nacewicz, "Sonney was an excellent fabricator, one of the best in that time period. He worked with Dick Abbott—who welded up a lot of our cars later on—and Sonney built a really nice modified."

Fred Ulrich recalled Evans telling Seamon that he ought to exploit

Sonney Seamon was a champion driver, a terrific fabricator, and one of the key mentors for Richie Evans. (courtesy of Speedway Scene)

what was then a wide-open field, and mass-produce his handiwork. "Rich tried to talk Sonney into doing what Maynard Troyer did later on," Ulrich said. "You know, build cars for sale, and try to get a lot of customers. Rich would say, 'Sonney, somebody's eventually gonna do this, and it would be perfect for you.' But Sonney's attitude toward racing was a little different than Rich's. He was more *relaxed* about things. He had his little garage, and he was happy, I think, doing what he was doing."

Richie Evans has gone down in modified history as one of the division's most successful builder/drivers, but in 1969, still in the learning phase of his career, he chose to do with his cars what he'd done with his engines: He left them to the experts. In the Rome area back then, that meant Sonney Seamon, and for the next several seasons the Evans coupes—and the earliest Evans Pintos—rode on Seamon-built frames.

And when Evans wasn't bending Seamon's ear about car-building tricks, he could be found picking Flemke's brain about chassis setups. Not only was Steady Eddie a wizard when it came to suspensions and such—he had pioneered the "Flemke front end" which took pavement coupes out of the buggy-spring age—but he had also been *everywhere*. In the early '60s, Flemke was the unofficial leader of a band of racing gypsies tagged the Eastern Bandits; its other regular members were Rene Charland, Melvin "Red" Foote and Denny Zimmerman. The Bandits, based in New England, made weekly runs into Maryland and Virginia with occasional dips into North Carolina. There was a method to this seeming madness: The Southern modifieds of the day, while incredibly high-powered, were heavy and ill-handling, and thus Flemke, a weight fanatic even in that junkyard era, looked at the Dixieland tracks the way Willie Sutton looked at banks on payroll day. The flyweight coupes of the Bandits might as well have been getaway cars, because they hauled off the cash on a regular basis.

By the time he got off the road and settled into the relatively tame routine of racing three and four nights a week in New England and New York—becoming the dominant Utica-Rome driver of the mid-'60s—Flemke seemed to have setups for tracks of every configuration. Better than that, he was more than willing to share what he knew with any young driver who came calling. And as the two men began to see more and more of each other at places like Albany-Saratoga and Utica-Rome, Ed Flemke was sharing that knowledge with Richie Evans.

"Richie and Eddie Flemke got very tight," Dick Waterman recalls.

Ed Flemke Jr., now a successful NASCAR modified driver and car builder in his own right, says he has no idea "what the attraction was" between his father and this young racer from Rome. But it went back, he says, a lot further than most folks realize.

"I know it was even before Richie was in the modifieds," Flemke Jr. remembers. "Whenever we were at Utica-Rome, we'd have to stay after the modified feature was over because my dad wanted to watch Richie

Says longtime Evans cohort Wilbur Jones, "Richie looked up to a lot of guys, and Eddie Flemke was number one." Here's Richie and Eddie at Albany-Saratoga in 1973. *(Mike Adaskaveg photo)*

run the hobby cars. Now, that was very unusual. We had a four-hour ride home, and my father always had a rule: 'Five minutes after the checkered flag, you'd better be at the car or you're walking home.' But he would stay at Utica-Rome to watch Richie.

"I do know that what my dad admired in *anybody* was their tenacity and their focus. He liked people who would see the goal and let nothing stop them from getting where they wanted to go. Maybe that was it, but I'm just speculating. I know he thought very highly of Richie."

Highly enough, apparently, to spend as much time helping Evans as Evans needed.

"Eddie helped Richie a lot with the chassis," says Wilbur Jones. "Remember that Flemke front end? Richie's car had that setup on it, and in the beginning he didn't have it figured out. Now, the thing about Richie was, he really wanted to *know* how something worked. Once Eddie explained that front end, Richie had it dialed in."

All that time around guys like Sonney Seamon and Eddie Flemke transformed the way Evans viewed the coupe in his gas station.

"He got to the point where he was always thinking," says Donny Marcello. "He knew I was a machinist, so every time we got together he was coming up with different projects for me. If he had to put a pulley on the front of the engine, he'd want me to turn it down to a smaller size. 'The lighter, the better,' he'd say."

And, to be clear, not all the knowledge Evans picked up was in the pits or in garages. Modified racing was full of grandmasters in the second half of the 1960s, and the smartest young drivers were the guys who paid attention on the track.

Lee Osborne says, "That Eddie Flemke, boy, he had some tricks. Utica-Rome was such a tight track, and the car had to slip a little bit to turn. Well, Eddie would run down into the corner and lay his left-front tire against the other guy's right rear, and it would make the other guy push up just a bit. Then Flemke would back off, turn his car, and drive right under the guy. He'd do that to car after car, week after week, and he was so smooth about it that the other guys wouldn't even know it happened. It was amazing."

And Osborne's own mentor, Dutch Hoag, took plenty of young drivers to school, among them Richie Evans. Wilbur Jones says, "I remember this one particular race at Spencer Speedway. Richie's leading, and Dutch Hoag is right on his tail. Well, Dutch keeps pushing him harder and harder, and Richie's going faster and faster. Finally, Richie pushes up and Dutch drives under him. Dutch wins the race. Later on, Dutch came over and asked Richie, 'Well, did you learn anything out there?' Richie said, 'Yup. Next time, you're going to have to go *around* me.' And he really did learn from that."

Hoag got a kick out of that, just as he did from another lesson on another night, also at Spencer, also featuring Evans in the pupil's role. "I went around him coming out of four on the last lap," Dutch says. "Some people in the pits asked him afterwards, 'What went wrong?' And Richie said, 'Nothing. That ol' man is gonna get you sooner or later. You just don't know when or where.' I liked hearing that."

But as his engines got more reliable and his cars got faster and his experience deepened, Richie Evans began to give as good as he got. "He got to the point where he was good everywhere," says Wilbur Jones. "Utica-Rome, Fulton, Albany-Saratoga … just everywhere."

And against just about everybody. In 1967, Long Island promotional geniuses Larry Mendelsohn and Lou Figari had come up with a traveling modified road show called the All Star Racing League. Its concept was simple: a summer-long series of Wednesday-night 100-lappers featuring "teams" of drivers representing prominent Northeastern tracks, asphalt and dirt alike. Non-league drivers were also invited to participate, and in no time flat the All Star races were magnets for the best short-trackers the region could offer: pavement wizards like Flemke, Fred DeSarro, Charlie Jarzombek, Fred Harbach and Bill Greco, dirt specialists like Budd Olsen, Fuzzy Van Horn, Frankie Schneider, Will Cagle and Al Tasnady, and guys who could handle either surface, such as Lou Lazzaro, Buzzie Reutimann, Ron Narducci, Rene Charland and Jerry Cook.

On consecutive weeks in the summer of 1969, Richie Evans won All Star features at Lancaster and Albany-Saratoga. Not bad, huh? Well, check this out: he lapped the entire field in both of those 100-lap shows.

Years later, racing historian Tom Neff noted, "If one were asked to point to one happening that elevated Richie's status from a capable Empire State contender to a blossoming national star, his 1969 All Star upset at Albany-Saratoga would be an astute choice."

Dick Waterman, seeing his Utica-Rome star catch on in places far and wide, recalls thinking that Evans "was getting to the level of a Bugsy

Evans lapped the entire field in winning this 1969 Lancaster All Star event. *(John Bisci collection)*

Stevens." That was high praise, incredible praise, given the times. In 1969, Bugs Stevens was in the process of winning his third straight NASCAR national modified championship.

Work Hard, Play Hard I

TED PUCHYR HAS THIS THEORY about why his friend Evans went from being a hot young local racer to being a region-wide star and then to being the most popular driver in the long history of asphalt modified racing.

"People," according to Puchyr, "love to party."

And Evans was happy to oblige them.

"Let's put it this way," says Dave Lape, looking back on all the late nights at Albany-Saratoga and Utica-Rome. "If you wanted to have a good time, you knew where to go. Just go see Richie, and hang out with him and his guys."

They stood on the gas when they won, and they stood on the gas when they lost. "It didn't really make too much difference, as I remember it," Wilbur Jones says.

Of course, maybe the party went a little *longer* after a victory, because in those wonderful days when just about every purse was paid after the race, in cash, a victory gave Evans and the boys a bit more ammunition. Puchyr says, "We'd win a race, and Richie would throw the money down on the bar and say, 'When it's gone, shut us off.'"

Almost from the beginning, it became a routine: You got done racing, you loaded up your stuff, and then you made the most of what remained of the night. Sometimes that meant cracking open a beer cooler in the pit area, and sometimes it meant communing with fans in the speedway parking lot, and sometimes it meant heading off to whatever local tavern catered to—or, in some cases, simply tolerated—large groups of loud, laughing racers.

"We didn't leave any track without partying," Puchyr says.

Barbara Evans adds, "We always had to stop somewhere to have something to eat, something to drink."

The names of the places still spin off the tongues of the old Evans crowd. The Hutch, down the road from Albany-Saratoga. The Nutshell —"*Everybody* went there," Barbara Evans says—over in Vernon, near Utica-Rome. Closer to home, Coalyard Charlies just off East Erie Boulevard on Depeyster Street in Rome, or the Rusty Nail right there on West Dominick Street. The Rusty Nail, in fact, became something of an unofficial clubhouse when its proprietor, Charlie Houseman, threw some money into the Evans racing operation and the little orange coupe became, in race reports and pre-race introductions, the Rusty Nail Special.

"They had a flagpole outside the Rusty Nail," Barbara Evans remembers. "Whenever Richie won, they'd put up a checkered flag."

That sort of thing was standard operating procedure for short-track drivers and mechanics across the nation. What Richie Evans did was, um, raise the bar a bit, at least in his neck of the woods. Before him, the standard bearer for outrageous modified behavior may have been Bugs Stevens, who across his long career was the toast of race-town saloons up and down the East Coast.

"If there was a party going on," Bugsy cheerfully admits, "I wanted to be in on it."

Sometimes, Stevens remembers, the hijinks got a little out of hand. There were occasions when the locals took a dim view of the more raucous behavior and there was, shall we say, some intervention by law

Evans, looking rather Fonzie-like in a Rusty Nail Café T-shirt. *(John Grady photo)*

enforcement. "Everybody we ran around with got carted off in handcuffs at least once," he says.

But even The Bugman whistles softly and shakes his head when he thinks about his old pal from Rome. They had first gotten to know each other at tracks like Albany-Saratoga and Utica-Rome, and grew better acquainted across dozens of post-race bashes.

"Richie used to say it was a good thing we came down the road 10 years apart," Stevens says. "And he was right, because we were too much alike: both crazy. But Richie was crazier than I was, believe me."

Dick Thompson, who served as the Martinsville Speedway public relations director for better than 20 years, saw early on a side of Richie Evans which looked awfully familiar to him. As a sportswriter, he had covered the intersecting careers of 1960s NASCAR heroes Curtis Turner and Joe Weatherly, pioneers remembered as much for their antics away from the speedway as for winning two straight Grand National championships (as Weatherly did in 1962-63) or conquering two of the toughest ovals man ever created (as Turner did by winning Grand National events at Darlington and Langhorne). Weatherly, flush with prize money, bought an airplane and flew it from race to race without knowing the first thing about navigation; for guidance he relied on the railroad tracks and highways below, and of course on a good strong drink. And Turner, who landed *his* plane on a city street to visit a liquor store when his passengers ran dry, and who once drove a rental car into a swimming pool, was known to console friends who were sorry about missing a particularly wild party with this: "Don't worry, we're going to start another one in about five minutes."

Turner and Weatherly were the poster boys for antisocial, often irresponsible—OK, just plain stupid—behavior among stock car racers. There is no way to pretend that they lived exemplary lives. But if you can't look back on the things they did and laugh, if you're the type to frown and cluck your tongue over such shenanigans, you probably wouldn't have had much fun around Evans, either.

"Richie Evans was born too late," Dick Thompson wrote. "He should have raced with Weatherly and Turner."

Billy Nacewicz says, "You know that phrase, 'You work hard, you play hard'? Well, that might not have been invented by Rich, but it was sure invented *for* him."

Nacewicz and Thompson are both right. Richie Evans also did a lot of antisocial, often irresponsible—OK, just plain stupid—things. And he happened to have a ball doing them.

"One night, a bunch of us are at the Rusty Nail, and we hear this noise," Donny Marcello remembers. "We look outside, and here's Richie, parking his stock car right on the sidewalk. He had driven it from the gas station, right down West Dominick Street, and over to the Rusty Nail. I said, 'Richie, are you nuts?' He said, 'Don't worry about a thing. Nobody's going to bother us.'"

Another Rusty Nail night: "It's closing time," begins Marcello, "and you know how that goes. Richie says, 'Let's go get some breakfast.' There's a bunch of us. He jumps into his Fairlane, and we all head down to a place called the Hollywood Restaurant. There were four cars in line, and we're playing around, racing. We're all heading down Dominick Street, right through town."

The rule on such occasions, everybody recalls, was: Last driver to the restaurant buys breakfast for everybody. Some nights, the run between the Rusty Nail and the Hollywood looked like Daytona on the white-flag lap.

"Wilbur Jones had his Firebird, and he was in front," Marcello says. "Then came Richie in his Fairlane, me in my Pontiac, and then Max Baker. Well, Wilbur won't let Richie get by. So as we're coming up on a stoplight—right in front of Goldberg's, the big department store—Richie turns right and swings up onto the sidewalk. He's driving down this sidewalk, trying to pass Wilbur.

"Now we look up, and there's a cop standing there. The cop holds up his hands, and Richie stops. The cop knew Richie, because *all* the cops knew Richie. He walks over—we're all stopped at the red light, so we're listening—and he yells, 'Richie, it's two o'clock in the morning. What the hell are you doing driving on the sidewalk in front of Goldberg's?'

"Well, Richie looks up at him, and he says, 'Window shopping!'"

Of *course* all the cops knew Richie. He was a fun guy, a good guy, one of those late-night gearheads who might get into light trouble every now and again and require a halfhearted talking-to at the stationhouse. Whenever something like that happened, one friend says, "they took him in the front door, and right out the back door."

This time, the cop did the same thing any cop would do if he ran into a familiar face goofing around like that, driving down the sidewalk in front of a department store in the middle of the night.

He told Richie Evans to hit the road, and to slow down a little.

Do you suppose that *ever* worked?

Outlaw

LOOKING BACK AT IT TODAY, the degree to which NASCAR controlled its drivers in the 1950s and '60s—or, more correctly, *tried* to control them —seems absolutely incredible. A modern-day short-track fan might have a hard time believing that signing a NASCAR competitor's license back then was, in a very real way, like signing a bond of indentured servitude. For years, NASCAR members were completely forbidden from racing in events at non-NASCAR tracks. Later, this insane restriction was relaxed just a bit, and NASCAR drivers were allowed to run *wherever* they pleased, but certainly not *whenever* they pleased. If they happened to compete at an outlaw track within, say, 50 or 100 miles of a NASCAR facility operating that same night, they might be fined, docked some arbitrary number of points, or perhaps suspended altogether.

Iron-fisted as its practices seemed, NASCAR had its staunch defenders. Utica-Rome promoter Dick Waterman says, "From the standpoint of any race driver, I think NASCAR was the greatest thing they had going for them. Bill Wimble and I used to argue about this; he told me one time that he wasn't sure how important NASCAR really was. I said, 'Well, where would you have gotten if you just ran little dirt tracks in upstate New York? Who would have ever heard of Bill Wimble?' NASCAR is what made auto racing successful, and from the standpoint of a promoter—even though they did things that I wasn't always 100 percent in favor of—the things they did were for the good of the sport. If you raced at a NASCAR-sanctioned track, you knew you were insured, and you knew you were going to get paid. That wasn't always the way it was everywhere."

Heavy was the hammer swung by the NASCAR bosses in Daytona Beach. And yet, racers being racers, many of them flirted with that hammer on a pretty regular basis. The sheer number of cars and tracks in those days, coupled with the fact that thin media coverage meant local news often *stayed* local, made things easy for teams tempted by the fat purses that popped up from time to time at non-NASCAR facilities.

"There probably wasn't a modified driver out there who didn't sneak off once in a while to run a non-NASCAR track," Waterman says. "They had all kinds of tricks; they'd paint their cars, change their numbers."

And, of course, they'd use phony names. In the Northeast, this gag was elevated to humorous art form in the early 1960s, when the biggest stars from the NASCAR-sanctioned Fonda Speedway would concoct various aliases in order to run at the old Victoria Speedway and later at the monthly open-competition shows at Lebanon Valley.

In their cult classic "FONDA! An Illustrated and Documented History of the Legendary Fonda Speedway," co-authors Andy Fusco and Lew Boyd revealed some of the better ones: "Jokester Jeep Herbert was the king of pun-motivated monikers, using Pete Moss, Flex Hose, and Bob Alou. The latter was a brilliant send-up of Ricky Ricardo's Cuban theme song on the No. 1-rated TV show of its day, 'I Love Lucy' ... Some drivers enhanced the ruse with a phony hometown as well. Bill Wimble was supposedly Bud Smith of Glens Falls ..."

The generation which followed Herbert and Wimble got wrapped up in the same surreal scenario, trading in their identities for purse money. For the right cash, Lee Osborne, one of the hottest New York drivers of the day, was happy to masquerade as an unknown newcomer called

Andy Davidson. And in the mid-1960s at Fulton, there was a modified driver by the name of Milton Carpenter who looked suspiciously like that Evans kid who was beginning to make waves down at Utica-Rome. But how could that be? Fulton, an outlaw track, ran Sunday afternoons; Utica-Rome, a NASCAR facility, ran Sunday nights. It *couldn't* be the same guy, could it?

It was a silly, wink-and-a-nod game, and some of the very best drivers played it.

Ted Puchyr says, "A lot of guys—Dick Fowler, Sonney Seamon, Richie—would sneak up to run Fulton. We'd cover our cars with this water-based paint on Sunday mornings, and everybody would run different numbers and funny names. Richie raced under the name 'Milton Carpenter' because Milton was one of his mechanics at the gas station. We'd use a primer red and the number 109, going back to Richie's original number. Richie was just there for the extra money. I mean, he ran good at Fulton, but guys like Maynard Troyer and Dutch Hoag just dominated those outlaw tracks. We were more like a filler car.

"We'd run the race at Fulton, then we'd all stop at a car wash in Cicero and hose off the water-based paint, and underneath it would be the NASCAR numbers and paint. Then we'd haul ass to Utica-Rome."

Again, it was a winking thing. Any man—or, indeed, any sanctioning body—would have had to be blind not to see it was going on. Here would be guys like Fowler, Seamon, Evans and more, all arriving late at Utica-Rome each week, with their cars, according to Puchyr, "still dripping-wet when we pulled into the pits." And, really, what was the harm? Had these teams raced at Fulton and then skipped Utica-Rome, maybe NASCAR and its officials would have had a beef, legitimate or not. But whatever they were doing on Sunday afternoons, they were certainly supporting their neighborhood NASCAR track on Sunday evenings. And so, nine times out of 10, nobody in a position of power caused a stink, no matter what the rules or regulations said.

Ah, but that 10th time …

"One Sunday after Fulton," says Puchyr, "we stopped, washed the car, and headed for Utica-Rome. Ralph Ouderkirk, the NASCAR chief steward, was waiting for us. Keep in mind, he had already let Sonney Seamon and Dick Fowler into the pits in front of us. But when we got to the gate he said, 'You guys can't sign in. We know you've been running non-NASCAR races.'

"Now, this was a Sunday night, but Richie somehow gets ahold of somebody with NASCAR—I have no idea who he called—and he pleads his case. He's standing at a pay phone at Utica-Rome Speedway, and he keeps putting money in there. Well, apparently whoever he talked to [at NASCAR] called the track and said to Ouderkirk, 'Let him race.' So we get the word, and we pull up to the pit gate. Ralph says, 'Where are you guys going?' Richie says, 'You were just on the phone. They just *told* you I could race.' Ralph said, 'That's right. *You* can race. Your *car* can't race.'"

It was a petty bit of pit-gate justice, to be sure, and Evans was furious. His first impulse was to head home, but that would have been a mistake. If he left Utica-Rome, all lasting records would indicate that he had missed a NASCAR event after running an outlaw race that very day, and who knows what sort of penalty they'd have in store for him then?

It was getting late, and there wasn't time for a second round of phone calls and negotiations. Luckily, to the rescue came car owner Frank Trinkhaus, a Fonda Speedway fixture who regularly hauled his Saturday-night dirt modified, number 62, to the Sunday-night pavement races at Utica-Rome.

"Frank heard what was going on," Puchyr recalls, "and he said, 'Richie, go ahead and sign in. I'll pull my driver out, and you can run my car.' So Richie drove that big dirt modified that night." Car #62 raced, while car #61 sat in the parking lot.

By the tail end of the 1960s, the whole NASCAR-versus-the-world situation seemed to have settled down. Oh, the organization still had its draconian rules about members and their outlaw activities, but there wasn't quite the old urgency about these things. Most of asphalt modified racing's top drivers, and indeed most of its premier speedways, were NASCAR-affiliated. Sure, there were a number of tracks across New York, New England and New Jersey running unsanctioned events, but NASCAR had the names. If one of those names wandered off and showed up at an open show someplace, the folks in power tended to look the other way.

Why cause a fuss? Come the next big NASCAR show, all the key drivers and cars were going to be there. Unless somebody really wanted to put the screws to a guy, why raise an eyebrow over him running a small-time outlaw race?

With all that in mind, the rift that developed between Richie Evans and NASCAR in 1969—and lasted until late in the summer of '71—smelled like the worst sort of witch hunt.

That 1969 season began well enough, with Evans beating a terrific Albany-Saratoga field in a 100-lapper run in honor of Don MacTavish, killed just that February in a late model sportsman crash at Daytona. Once the weekly season started, Utica-Rome and Fulton continued their fight for Sunday cars and Sunday fans. As usual, Utica-Rome was a top priority with Evans, and in its opener he finished second between winner Jerry Cook and Lou Lazzaro. Then, for three straight weeks, rain and late-spring snow wiped out racing at the Vernon track; seven times that year, weather derailed all attempts to go racing at Dick Waterman's track in Vernon. One such wet Sunday derailed Richie Evans's career.

"Utica-Rome rained out," says Wilbur Jones. "And it rained out early enough in the afternoon that we had time to get up to Fulton, which *hadn't* rained out. So we all beat feet to get up there. I mean, there were a bunch of us: Lou Lazzaro, Jerry Cook, Sonney Seamon, Dick Fowler, everybody. Richie won that Fulton race, and the next morning he got a

(left) Evans receives a late-1960s Utica-Rome banquet trophy from NASCAR founder Bill France Sr., who clearly had no idea yet what a handful this driver from Rome could be! *(Lynn Evans collection)*

(right) Victory lane at the 1969 Don MacTavish 100 at Albany-Saratoga, one of Richie's last big NASCAR wins before Daytona Beach dropped the hammer on him. *(John Grady photo)*

call from NASCAR telling him he'd been suspended.

"Richie said, '*Suspended? What for?*' They told him it was for running a non-NASCAR race. Hell, Utica-Rome had been rained out! Not only that, but what about those other guys? Cookie didn't get suspended. Louie didn't get suspended. But they didn't want to hear it. Richie was out."

Maybe the earlier incident, the one where Evans hopped into a borrowed dirt ride while his own coupe sat idle, had left a bad taste in some local official's mouth. Or maybe this was somebody in Daytona Beach deciding that it was time to once again crack down on those wandering modified boys, and Evans just happened to be the fall guy.

In hindsight, they sure chose the wrong wandering modified boy to pick on.

What NASCAR always banked on, in the association's most dictatorial days, was that its drivers would take their penalties quietly; fines would be paid, points would be forfeited, suspensions would be served, and then the offender would be welcomed back into the fold like a lamb that had strayed. For 20 years, that had basically been standard practice. But there was nothing at all standard, they were soon to learn, about Richie Evans.

In the gas station on West Dominick Street in Rome, Evans picked up a paint brush. On the sloping tail of his orange coupe, in a size you couldn't miss, one word appeared in stark black letters: OUTLAW. And when he beat a Lancaster All Star field which included a bevy of NASCAR heavyweights, Evans couldn't resist peacocking a bit. "I beat them in the Don MacTavish 100, then [NASCAR] threw me out," he told *National Speed Sport News*. "So I just had to beat them again tonight, and I did."

This was war.

Let somebody at NASCAR fine him; Evans had already decided they weren't going to see a dollar out of his checking account. Let them take his points, too; he was through with NASCAR, he told anybody who would listen. He would go racing instead at tracks like Spencer, Lancaster, Fulton, Oswego, and anyplace else where he felt welcome.

It was a gutsy move, and not just because he was thumbing his nose at America's most powerful sanctioning body. It would also pit him on a regular basis against the same group of tough racers who had beaten him weekly in his "Milton Carpenter" phase, including Maynard Troyer and Dutch Hoag.

Puchyr says, "Maynard's equipment at that time was unbelievable. He had his big cab-over hauler and his Falcon-bodied car, and he was the trendsetter. And Dutch, he had those lightweight cars; you'd look at his roll cages and think, 'Oh, my God!' But at these outlaw tracks they didn't have any weight rules, so the lighter you could make it, the faster you could go."

Lee Osborne, who parlayed his meteoric rise on that Western New York circuit into a terrific sprint car career—after the 1968 season he moved to Pennsylvania and then to Indiana, where he eventually starred for years with the World of Outlaws tour—knew what his pal Evans was up against.

"Our cars were light before anybody else's were," Ozzie says. "The modified I built at Turner's, for example, had a conduit roll cage, thin-wall tubing. These were 2200-pound cars when a lot of modifieds were still up around 3000.

"The guys from Eastern New York and New England, most of 'em, their focus was on horsepower. They ran big-blocks and fuel injectors, and we ran carburetors. They had us out-powered, but chassis-wise we could usually handle 'em. Their cars had a ton of nose weight, and with those big motors they'd just squirt from corner to corner. We ran 336 cubic inches—that's a 327, .060 over—with a lot of RPMs in light cars, and we really worked on our chassis. I think we were a little bit ahead on things like stagger and weight [distribution]."

Dutch Hoag says, "In all the years I drove—for the Turners or anybody else—I never had a 427. Hell, I won on the mile at Langhorne [in 1967] with a small-block. Did it with handling."

Against those kinds of cars in the past, Evans had struggled. Recall Puchyr's earlier description of their Fulton efforts in the mid-'60s: "We were more like a filler car." Now, basing himself on their home tracks, Evans was going to have to either learn to swim with the sharks, or get eaten.

At first he treaded water, trying new setups and no doubt cutting corners here and there to get his cars into the same weight class as, say, Hoag's or Troyer's. He won a few in '69—including his first career score at Spencer and four Lancaster wins—and was soon a regular threat. Osborne believes it was in this period that "Richie really got into things like stagger, cross-weight, spring rates, and all the stuff that matters." By the dawn of the 1970 season, it was clear that Evans had caught up. That

(left) Another Fulton score. In his Outlaw years, both Richie and his cars improved dramatically. *(Lynn Evans collection)*

(right) At the dawn of the 1970s, Evans was loose, unstructured, and fast. *(Lynn Evans collection)*

year he won at all of his regular stops, but really stood out at Fulton, where he won eight races and the track championship.

On one Friday night, Evans won the modified feature at Fulton—beating, incidentally, a visiting Lee Osborne—and then stuck around to drive a sedan-bodied car for Jack Griffiths in the limited sportsman main. Despite a serious overheating problem, he won that feature, too. Western New York scribe John Bisci wrote, "The car overheated in victory lane and let loose a geyser of water vapor as Evans posed with the checkered flag." In the checkered flag photos, Richie is grinning as if he'd never enjoyed racing more.

And maybe he never had. Clearly, this loosely-structured outlaw life agreed with him, to the point where Evans decided to double his fun. He prepped his backup coupe to full NASCAR specs, and called upon his old friend and mentor Eddie Flemke to run it when Flemke's schedule allowed. That meant most Friday nights at Malta—"For two years, Richie would go to Spencer with one car, and I'd take the other one to Albany-Saratoga for Eddie," said Fred Ulrich—and the odd Sunday at Utica-Rome.

It worked like a charm.

"I'll never forget, this one Friday night [in 1970] there were two big races," Ulrich recalled. "Rich had a special show out at Spencer, and we had the Don MacTavish Memorial race at Albany-Saratoga. Well, at Albany-Saratoga there was a pay phone in the pits, and Rich told me to go and stand by that phone as soon as the race was over. So I did, and I wasn't there for 10 minutes when the phone rang.

"I pick it up, and Rich says, 'What happened?' I tell him, 'Well, Eddie won down here.' Rich says, 'Good. I won up here.'"

Writer Andy Fusco theorizes that Evans supporting those NASCAR events as an owner might have been a peace offering, an olive branch extended from Rome toward Daytona Beach. "Fielding that team car for Flemke was a pretty diplomatic stroke from a guy not known for his diplomacy," Fusco says.

Others insist that it had nothing to do with politics, and everything to do with pragmatism. Look at it from Richie's viewpoint: had he run both his cars at, say, Spencer, his best-case scenario on any race night would have been a one-two finish. On the other hand, sending Flemke one way and then going the other way himself could literally be a win-win situation.

Ed Flemke Jr., who often tagged along with his dad on those trips to New York, falls into the pragmatic camp. "I think Richie and my father both saw an opportunity to win a lot of races and make a lot of money," he says. "And they *were* making money. So the motivation behind it all was, 'It's better for both of us this way.' They had an agenda."

There may have been one other small bonus. Like Evans, Flemke had an anti-authoritarian streak. His son suggests that Steady Eddie might have delighted in the notion that "having that orange 61 still there in the pits at Malta and Utica-Rome [despite Richie's suspension] was pissing off NASCAR. I'm sure that part of it didn't bother him any."

This much was becoming clear: Evans might not have been winning his fight with NASCAR—in racing, as in life, you never truly beat City Hall—but among modified followers the whole affair was beginning to take on a David vs. Goliath flavor. And David had plenty of support in the grandstands.

In locking Evans out of its bedrock tracks, NASCAR was essentially telling upstate New York fans that if they wanted to see the most popular young racer in their area, they should head instead to one of the area's many open-competition ovals. For some, that was an attractive option. Fulton, for instance, was less than 60 highway miles from Utica-Rome, and Fulton had Richie Evans in the pits every Sunday. "It hurt us at Utica-Rome," says Dick Waterman. "There's no getting around that."

Yes, the suspension hurt Evans, too, because it kept him from two of his bread-and-butter tracks, Albany-Saratoga and Utica-Rome. But on the bright side, every so often he was able to exact a measure of revenge at both those NASCAR ovals, and whenever that happened it only made his underdog's battle seem more heroic.

On August 15, 1970, he went to Albany-Saratoga for a 100-lap open-competition event, and took the win after a race-long battle with Bugsy Stevens. The two men were friends, but it pleased Evans immensely to beat Stevens, at the time NASCAR's hottest modified name.

Just two weeks later was a Labor Day weekend straight out of the dream factory. On Saturday night, Evans blitzed a modified field at Lancaster. And on Sunday came a victory that Richie always called one of his favorites, even though he wasn't at the wheel.

Between 1964 and '69, the New Yorker 400, right there close to home at Utica-Rome, had established itself as one of the region's most prestigious NASCAR events. Its first six editions were run using a twin-200 format, and in those years an amazing cast of modified characters posed with the checkers after winning one of those 200-lappers: Flemke,

Running wild: Richie Evans in his Outlaw phase, winning and gaining popularity. *(John Grady photo)*

Steady Eddie Flemke aboard the backup Evans coupe. Among Flemke's victories in this car was the storied 1970 New Yorker 400. (John Grady photo)

Wimble, Fred Harbach, Don MacTavish, Robbie Kotary, Lou Lazzaro.

In 1970, Dick Waterman opted to stage the New Yorker as a straight 400-lapper. Evans entered a car, listing Flemke as its driver. Not surprisingly, given the level to which things had deteriorated between Evans and NASCAR, that led to a standoff at the sign-in shack.

"They wouldn't let Richie in, even though he wasn't driving the car," Wilbur Jones says. "They had no problem with Eddie, but Richie was another story. So Richie said, 'Fine, we'll just pit the car out here in the parking lot.'

"Well, every time Eddie drove into the pits for practice, he'd wave his pass to the officials. I think he was getting a kick out of the whole thing. And, you know, Richie got a kick out of it, too. He named me the official chief steward of our little pit area. Back then, women weren't allowed in the pits at a lot of tracks, so Richie said, 'Wilbur, can we have women in *our* pits?' I said, 'Why, certainly we can.' I didn't allow any beer, though. I'm not saying there wasn't any beer out there, just that I didn't allow it."

Donny Marcello recalls, "I'd watch the warm-ups from the grandstands, and then run back out to the parking lot. That was something else. I mean, here's Eddie, driving back and forth through the pit gate. Ain't that some shit?"

That's some shit, all right.

And it got better. Steady Eddie Flemke and the orange Evans coupe dominated the New Yorker 400, winning in a cakewalk over Robbie Kotary, Dick Fowler, Gene Mangino and Maynard Troyer. His car owner wasn't able to join him in posing for the victory lane photos, but that only made this evening more fun.

"Boy," grins Marcello, "did we ever party that night!"

And can't you just picture the outlaw grin on Richie's face as *that* bash rolled on?

Redemption

HERE WAS THE PROBLEM NASCAR faced in its ongoing banishment of this fellow whom folks were beginning to call the Rapid Roman: Richie Evans had become a genuine modified star, on the track and off it. No, NASCAR wasn't lacking for names; it had the charismatic Bugsy Stevens, it had Jerry Cook on the rise, it had Flemke prowling around, it had Ray Hendrick and Paul Radford holding down the Southern front, it had Gene Bergin and Leo Cleary in New England, it had Fred Harbach and Charlie Jarzombek on Long Island, it had a great 1970 national champion in Fred DeSarro. But there was a hum building around Evans, a buzz. It shows through even in the old clippings, in stories of races where, win or lose, he was big news.

In October of 1970, Evans went to Langhorne for his second stab at the Race of Champions. (On his first trip, in '69, he had qualified fifth and finished seventh behind the powerhouse cluster of Hendrick, Roger Treichler, Cook, Chuck Boos, Merv Treichler and Guy Chartrand.) There was no getting around the fact that, despite its non-NASCAR status, the ROC was the single most prestigious race on the modified calendar. It annually attracted well over 100 cars, many of them guaranteed starters thanks to a series of qualifying events staged throughout the summer at as many as 30 Eastern tracks. With all those winners heading for Langhorne every autumn, the Race of Champions might have had the most appropriate title in the sport.

"I'll tell you how big a deal Langhorne was," says Lee Osborne, who took a hiatus from dirt-tracking to steer a Dutch Hoag car in the '70 Race of Champions. "Back then, nobody ever really *prepared* for races. Sure, you'd go through the valves, and check the tires, and tighten up the bolts, but that was about it. But when it came time to start thinking about Langhorne, guys took their whole cars apart and really got 'em ready.

"To us modified guys, it was like going to Daytona. You had to travel pretty far to get there, and you'd show up in the middle of the night just to get in line with what seemed like 200 other cars. All your heroes were there, plus a ton of guys you'd never even heard of."

Richie Evans damn near beat 'em all, heroes and unknown alike, in 1970.

Ray Hendrick, driving the famous Flying 11 coupe owned by Jack Tant and Clayton Mitchell—which Bugs Stevens has called "the best modified of its time"—was running away with the 200-lapper when his car uncharacteristically broke on lap 159. That appeared to give the lead to Evans, whose strategy had been perfect; his pit stop sequencing had placed him ahead of some of the day's other contenders, among them Maynard Troyer, a youngster named Geoff Bodine in a radical home-

Geoff Bodine and Richie Evans in 1970 at Langhorne, the biggest modified bash of all. *(Lynn Evans collection)*

built Valiant, and Guy Chartrand in Ed Cloce's famed and feared Hemi-Cuda.

Evans was in a pretty sweet position: leading a big-dollar race, riding in a car that—thanks to the chassis lessons he'd learned and the reliable engines he could now afford—might have been the sweetest piece he'd ever sat down in. And then things got weird.

Dick Berggren later wrote, "When a yellow flag followed a few laps [after Hendrick's departure], the pace car picked up Evans. After [it led] Evans around for several laps, the announcer shocked the crowd by relating that the chief scorer had decided that Evans wasn't really leading at all … and that Roger Treichler was in front."

And yet, in a startling bit of incompetent officiating, the Evans car was left up front on the restart, nearly a full mile behind leader Treichler, who was "buried in the pack," Berggren wrote. From there, things got even more blurry. While Evans played catch-up, Roger Treichler led until the final lap, when his cousin Merv nipped him at the checkered flag. It was the closest modified finish in Langhorne history. Evans and his orange coupe were scored third.

Richie, as baffled as anyone about how he went from being the apparent leader to being just another guy on the lead lap, filed an immediate protest. It was summarily denied. Yet, as Berggren wrote, "There probably will be no way to convince some fans that in fact Evans did not win the event."

He was a headliner at Langhorne, and yet he was not a NASCAR guy. He was winning with the All Star League, and yet he was not a NASCAR guy. In 1971 he topped the Genesee Championship Trail, a high-profile New York chase which awarded points to the A-division drivers at every track regardless of affiliation … and he yet was not a NASCAR guy.

In the summer of '71, an item in the Syracuse-based *Gater Racing News* suggested that Evans was "considered by many to be the finest modified driver in New York State." And yet he was not a NASCAR guy.

Steve Hmiel, then just diving into a mechanical career that would carry him through modifieds and all the way to Nextel Cup victory

Lancaster's All Star 100, 1971. Action like this (involving Gordy Treichler in the 47 and Ray Hendrick's Flying 11) helped make Evans "the baddest cat in the alley," says Nextel Cup team boss Steve Hmiel. (John Bisci collection)

Randy "Buster" Maurer was Richie's right-hand man in the early '70s. (Maurer collection)

lanes, says, "The thing I always found interesting about Richie was how much he turned his career around. I was a Malta guy, a Utica-Rome guy, a Plattsburgh guy. When Richie ran at those places in the '60s, he was just a gas station owner from Rome who had a modified and ran OK. He was fast and he won a little, but not too much. Then he went away, and he ran all those places out in Western New York—Spencer, Lancaster, places like that—and all of a sudden, he was the baddest cat in the alley."

And yet he was not a NASCAR guy.

Evans was simply running up and down the road, winning races and grabbing ink, creating that hum, that wonderful outlaw buzz.

In 1971, he was doing much of that in the company of a new mechanic. Randy "Buster" Maurer had been casually acquainted with Evans for a few years, thanks to Maurer's role as a crewman for Frank Trinkhaus and his driver, Don Wayman. Then a terrible crash at the New York State Fairgrounds mile in September of 1970—the Trinkhaus 62, Lee Millington in the cockpit, vaulted the third-turn wall and killed two spectators—drove the veteran car owner out of the sport. "Frank pretty much cut the car up and dissolved the operation," Maurer says.

Evans, who knew Maurer's father, mentioned a few times that if the kid wanted to hook up with another race team, he could use the help. He had sold the Shell garage and opened up a Sunoco outlet just a few blocks down on West Dominick Street; between the gas station and the modified, there was plenty of work to be done. Early in the '71 season, Buster took him up on it. "I finally stopped by Richie's, and we went to the races," Maurer remembers. "The first few times, I actually went with Wilbur and we took a car to Malta for Ed Flemke. Then one weekend I ended up going out to Spencer Speedway with Richie."

Buster Maurer sighs and smiles. "And one thing led to another."

He was working in an auto parts store, and mulling over an employment offer Evans had casually slipped into a conversation—"Richie asked me one time, 'Why don't you come work for me at the gas station?'"—when he found himself at odds with his boss over something or other. "I went up to Richie's on my lunch hour," Maurer recalls, "and I said, 'Have you still got a job available?' He said, 'Sure. You can start this afternoon.' I went back to the auto parts store, and I said, 'I'm done.' Then I went to work for Richie. I worked at the gas station days, and worked on the race car nights."

As the only full-time help, Maurer was listed as the team's crew chief. "But," he points out, "we didn't have titles then. I was Rich's only employee, but he had an awful lot of guys who helped him: Max Baker, Wilbur, Freddy, Danny Morgan, Anthony Evans ... the list of guys goes on and on. Mechanically it was Rich and I, but those guys were always around."

Right away, they became more than simply boss and employee. "Rich taught me a lot," Maurer says. "I think I learned my competitiveness from him. And he became like my big brother. In fact, when we'd go to a track where not everybody knew us, we had people thinking we *were* brothers. Will Cagle was one of the people who thought that."

Maurer's life became a non-stop blur of highways and pit passes and wrenches and post-race beers. "In '71, we spent an awful lot of time on the road," he says. "We were doing all the Friday, Saturday and Sunday night races, plus the All Star League races and other special shows during the week. Then, there were all the Genesee races at the New York State tracks. That was difficult, because during the week it was just Richie and I. We'd drive to the track and do our thing, and then we'd party a little bit, of course, and then we had to go to the next track. It didn't leave much time to go home and fix the cars.

"The good thing was, Richie was the kind of guy who was always digging right there beside you. There was nothing he asked you to do that he wouldn't do himself."

Onward they rolled, to places they knew well – Evans won six times at Lancaster that year, four more at Fulton – and places they'd never been: Devil's Bowl Speedway and Catamount Stadium in Vermont, late model joints which occasionally hosted modified specials; Wall Stadium on the Jersey shore, where Evans copped an All Star League feature in August of 1971; the strange tri-oval in Lee, New Hampshire, where, Maurer recalls, "the track ran down a hill, around a corner, up a hill. It was *weird*. I'll never forget Rich laughing about it. He told Bugsy Stevens, 'This place is a riot!'"

In the summer of 1971 they showed up at another quirky track which Evans didn't find quite so amusing. Though he was to see fantastic success there in the years to come, the Trenton Fairgrounds Speedway and its 1.5-mile layout came as quite a shock to Richie when he rolled in for the annual Trenton 200.

"The first time he ever went to Trenton, we still had a coupe, and it sat pretty tall," Maurer says. "I remember we drove all night from Shangri-La or somewhere to get there. To get to the infield pits at

Trenton, you used to cross the track off the fourth turn, and as you pulled across you could look down that long front straightaway. Man, it looked like it went forever. Richie, myself, Fred Ulrich, and I don't know who else was in the truck. Well, Richie looked down that straightaway, and you could see he was thinking, like, I don't know if I want to do this or not. You could read that in his face.

"That was the first hesitation I'd ever seen out of Rich. But we got into the pits, and he said, 'I'll take it out and see what happens.' He practiced pretty good, and when he came back in and he said, 'We'll give it a go.' He later made the comment that in that coupe, he'd be driving down the straightaway and it would change lanes all by itself, because it was so aerodynamically bad. But once he got going, he was fine."

If ever a race signaled the changing of the modified guard that was starting to take shape, that 1971 Trenton 200 might have been it. Ray Hendrick and Bugs Stevens led early but ran into trouble, Hendrick cutting a tire and nailing the wall with the Tant/Mitchell #11 Camaro and Stevens blowing an engine in Sonny Koszela's Woodchopper Special. With those old pros out of the running, the last 150 laps were dominated by young studs. The top three finishers were Geoff Bodine (whose Valiant was an aerodynamic marvel compared to the coupes), Ron Bouchard (in the Dick Armstrong #1, an ex-Tant/Mitchell machine) and Richie Evans.

Bodine had already become something of a sensation in New York, shining at NASCAR and outlaw tracks alike. The son of Chemung Speedrome owner Eli Bodine, he kicked off his modified career in 1969 with a used coupe he had patched up and improved, showing the grasp for chassis science which would come to be his calling card. In 1970 Bodine won 12 features; in '71 he took 18 more.

Bouchard, too, was clearly one of the division's rising stars. In winning four straight track titles at the Seekonk Speedway in his native Massachusetts, he had caught the eye of Armstrong, who made lots of money manufacturing costume jewelry and spent lots of it assembling a first-class modified team. Aboard the Armstrong coupe, Bouchard had dazzled everybody in a summer show on the three-quarter-miler at Pocono, blasting from 40th to fifth in just a few dozen laps before a hard crash left him with three broken ribs.

"That was an exciting time," says Bouchard. "I was just getting used to racing with the New England guys—Bugsy, Freddy [DeSarro], Eddie [Flemke]—and then along came Richie. And he was really a good race car driver."

Too good, really, to keep operating outside NASCAR, and both parties knew it. The story of how Evans finally patched things up with the gang from Daytona Beach has been muddied in the telling across all the years, and too many of the people on both sides who knew the real truth are no longer around to tell it. The bumper-sticker version is that

Seeing double: a pair of 61 coupes, one for Evans and the other for Eddie Flemke, turned up at several tracks after NASCAR allowed Richie back into the fold. (John Grady photo)

Richie Evans, citing New York's "right to work" laws, either threatened or initiated legal action against NASCAR, and so in the summer of 1971 his suspension was rescinded. It's safe to say that NASCAR—whose sharpest minds have always recognized the power of a good drawing card—probably wanted him back anyway.

And it's worth noting that never again was a NASCAR modified driver penalized for racing where he wasn't "supposed" to.

The best part about all this for Evans was that it happened just in time for Utica-Rome's New Yorker 400, the race his car had won the previous year in another man's hands. When he showed up for the big home-track show in '71, he was a better driver than he'd ever been, and his latest coupe was a match for any car in the place. He made it clear immediately that he meant business.

"I don't think I've ever been as psyched up as I was that night," he told writer Pete Zanardi. "I wanted that one badly. I remember going all out in warm-ups. I was there to win, and I wanted them to know it."

If anyone missed that point, he reinforced it soon enough. He took the lead in the 1971 New Yorker 400 and sped off and hid, running every lap as if it was a time-trial and knifing through lapped traffic. It was a stunning display of aggressiveness, of authority. And it was something else, too: It was Evans throwing the finger to NASCAR, to every official who'd had a hand in his suspension, and to anyone who had seen him as just some "outlaw" racer.

Wilbur Jones has a vivid memory of the evening. "Eddie Flemke had dropped out. Richie kept running faster and faster, and Eddie was trying to slow him down. He ran out to the edge of the track, signaling Richie with his hands: *Slow down! Slow down!* Richie just kept on trucking. He didn't pay any attention.

"Well, finally Eddie bent over and he picked up a pretty good-sized rock. He held that in his hand and showed it to Richie, as if to say, If you don't slow down, I'm gonna throw this damn rock at you. That got the message across. Richie slowed down, and we won."

Fred DeSarro, Jerry Cook, Billy Hensley and Lou Lazzaro—NASCAR heroes all—finished second through fifth that night. None of them was in the same area code as the orange #61 after the 400 laps.

This was sweet redemption.

Richie Evans was on top of the world.

How confident was he feeling in those days? Well, as the 1972 season approached, he made a move that led him directly into the kind of career, and the kind of life, he would enjoy for the rest of his days. He sold off his service station, and moved his race team and indeed his everyday existence around the corner and down the block to 608 Calvert Street, and a building he bought from a fellow named Tony Pettinelli.

"It used to be New Systems Laundry," says Pettinelli's son, Tony Jr., who later spent several years as an Evans crewman. "They'd had a fire at the laundry, and my dad bought the place. We lived right across the street. Dad rented it out for a short time, and then Richie moved in."

He moved in with his race cars and his tools and the very same phone number, (315) 336-9630, he'd had at both his gas stations. He moved in, and he never moved out.

While Evans got the new shop up and running smoothly, his crew chief was also gearing up for the '72 campaign. "Back then," says Buster Maurer, "you spent your off-season building cars, going to the junkyard and digging through the snow, getting parts you needed. I spent about half that winter over at Sonney Seamon's shop, building the new car, the first Pinto." (Those were, after all, the early, exciting days of what came to be called the Pinto Revolution. It started on Labor Day of 1971 in Connecticut when Gene Bergin, wheeling a red number 2X Pinto for owner Bob Judkins, dominated the Stafford 200. It swept through the division so quickly that on the starting grid for the 1974 Race of Champions, by then running at Trenton, *Speedway Scene* writer Joanne Davies counted up 25 Pintos, 12 Vegas, 11 Gremlins, three Mustangs and three late-model bodies, but not a single coupe or sedan.)

The new #61 Pinto—built by Seamon, tweaked by Evans, Maurer and the Calvert Street crowd—was a rocket. True to what became Richie's later form, he didn't roll it out immediately, preferring instead to test-hop the new car while relying on the trusty coupe come race time. But once he had the Pinto running to his liking, he couldn't resist loosing its reins.

Writer and historian John Bisci recalls the new car showing up at Lancaster on July 1, 1972. "Richie was only going to run it during warm-ups," Bisci says. "But it went so well that he decided to qualify it and race it."

And how, Mr. Bisci, did Evans fare in the Lancaster feature?

"He lapped almost the entire field."

Eleven days later, that Pinto carried Evans to his first Oswego victo-

On July 12, 1972, the first-ever Evans Pinto carried Richie to his maiden victory at Oswego. *(Lynn Evans collection)*

ry, a 50-lapper. That same summer, it brought him his first scores at Shangri-La and the Freeport Stadium on Long Island. He was winning sanctioned and unsanctioned races alike; he told Pete Zanardi that it was "so great running NASCAR and opens, too."

In 1972, Evans did quite a few things. He raised his All Star League win total. (By the time the series folded in '74 after founder Larry Mendelsohn's death, Richie was its all-time king with 10 victories.) He also won another Genesee championship. He won eight features at Lancaster, one a Race of Champions qualifier. In his own backyard he won his first Utica-Rome track title on the strength of three victories; he beat Lazzaro, Cook, DeSarro and Ollie Silva to record the last of those, which was his second straight New Yorker 400 triumph.

In August of that year, the Evans #61 was one of 98 modifieds in the pits at Pocono for the Flight 216 race, named after a curiously-labeled oil additive. The event was shortened slightly by a late-afternoon downpour and tainted by a mid-race scoring dispute, but it was a stellar day for Richie, who beat out Maynard Troyer, Ray Hendrick, Ron Bouchard and Flyin' Bryan Osgood. Buster Maurer recalls, "We pushed the car back to the garage area, and the water was so deep it was pouring into the floorboards. They had declared us the winner, and when we got into the garage area we partied a while because you didn't get paid right away. Wilbur and I and Fred and Rich, whoever was there, we stood in the garage area and we drank beer and raised hell.

"After a while it was time to go to the pay window, and Rich says to me, 'Buster, go down and pick up the money.' It was a pretty good distance away, so Wilbur says, 'Come on, I'll give you a ride.' We drive to the pay shack, and we're standing in line. We get up to the pay window, and I give the guy the car number. I sign the form, and the guy says, 'How you want the money?' I says, real loud, 'Cash!' Because, knowing Rich, he wouldn't want no *check*.

"Now, I think we got $2800 or $3800. Whatever it was, we'd never

Buster Maurer says the modified division was "put on notice" by the Evans gang in 1971-72. Was it ever! *(Bill Balser photo/courtesy of Speedway Scene)*

won that much money before. We'd won maybe a thousand bucks a few times, and that was a big deal for us back then. So the guy counted out the money, mostly all wadded-up $20 bills, and we brought it back to Rich. We walked into the garage and gave it to him, and, *poof*, he threw it all up in the air! Money all over the place!"

It was a thrilling, spontaneous moment in a thrilling, spontaneous period.

Buster Maurer says, "I can remember pulling into Catamount—we'd driven overnight from *somewhere*—and having people look at our truck like, 'Oh shit, he's here.' That was a real cool feeling. We were feeling like any place we went, on any given night, Richie could win.

"I think we put the modified division on notice: *This guy's coming*."

 ## Family Man II

BY THE TIME MARRIAGE and fatherhood came along, Evans was already a confirmed rowdy, and domestic life did not do much to slow down his anything-for-fun attitude. His wife Barbara says, "Richie was a great bowler. Back then, he was in a league. Well, one night he and his bowling buddies had gone drinking, and they all came back to our apartment. But first they put all their bowling balls in the clothes dryers in the apartment building, and turned them on. *At midnight!* I'm sure they woke up everybody there."

Doing the dad thing: Richie and Barbara Evans with daughters Jodi and Janelle; Richie with Jodi at an amusement park in Old Forge, NY. *(Jodi Meola collection)*

He tried hard to do the dad thing, struggling at times early on. Barbara grins at all the talk about Evans being so mechanically inclined, thinking back to some Christmas Eves when he seemed anything *but* gifted with tools. "The children would get doll carriages and other toys, and he could not put them together," she says. "He could not put together a sled, a high chair. He couldn't put up the Christmas tree! He couldn't fix a lot of things in the house. But I look at it like, he was born to race. He could work with his hands, as long as it was on those cars."

And she tried hard to do the wife thing, looking after the children—one, then two, then three, then four—and attending as many of his races as she could sensibly fit in.

"I'd go to Utica-Rome, and I loved that," she says. "I took the girls there quite a bit. That was before Richie was as big a name as he was later, but he was already winning an awful lot at Utica-Rome. Most of the time I'd go alone, because I didn't like the idea of the kids being exposed to all that noise when they were little. But I'd go with Rita Seamon, Sonney's wife, and sometimes we'd take the kids.

"And I remember going to Fulton. In fact, I'll never forget this one trip to Fulton; he had a Corvette, and I was driving while he slept. Well, he woke up, and I guess he thought I was going a little slow. He said, 'Christ, this car was made for *racing*. Will you move it?'"

But he was getting to the point where his ambitions as a traveling racer and the demands placed on any young family man were getting ready to intersect. There's no getting around the thought that when they did, his own fast lifestyle was bound to figure into things, too. When all those different sides of the early-'70s Richie Evans finally met up at a crossroads, there began a long, grinding wreck.

"Rich was gone a lot, and I couldn't always go with him because the kids were so little," Barbara says. "I think that's more or less what ruined our marriage, just the fact that he was gone all the time."

And there were the normal jealousies. These days, she laughs about

Good news, bad news. Photos like this mean victory, but they can also mean trouble on the home front! *(John Bisci collection)*

it; 30 years ago, such emotions could start a World War. "I used to see his pictures with the trophy girls," Barbara says. "There was 'Miss This' and 'Miss That.' One night when he still had the gas station, I opened up the racing paper, and there was a picture of him kissing this girl. I got so mad that I backed into the gas pump and knocked it over."

She sighs. "The life that we were living just got me so *angry*. He'd go race, and then he'd go party, and that was so hard for me because I had to be home with the kids."

They were both too temperamental to do anything but fight, both too stubborn to talk things out, both too ... well, maybe too immature to be married. Evans turned 30 in 1971, but there were moments when he had trouble acting 18. And it takes absolutely no prodding for Barbara to admit that she did not always play the role of the peacemaker in the relationship.

The two of them had their share of public spats, maybe none louder than a verbal donnybrook one Sunday in the Utica-Rome pit area, right there in front of friends and foes and strangers.

"Richie and I were arguing," Barbara says, smiling. "Eddie Flemke came up to us and said, 'Look, you two, can you please just *try* to get along?' I'll never forget that; Eddie was so nice about it."

The crazy thing was, in the midst of all this unrest, with his whole life upside down, Richie Evans was driving better and winning more than he ever had.

Wilbur Jones says, "I don't know how he did that. But I think it's because he was always able to get in that car, put his helmet and his belts on, and tune out the whole world. That race car was probably his sanctuary. In there, he didn't have to think about anything except, 'How am I gonna get to that finish line first?'

"That's all I can think of, is that the race car was Rich's own little world. Like, 'In here, nobody can touch me.' You know what I mean?"

In their life as husband and wife, that single-mindedness used to drive Barbara Evans crazy. Later, she came to understand that to him, the garage and the race car and the growing travel were not a job, but a *pursuit*. Racing was both his career and his oxygen, and she sees that to some driven men like Richie Evans, the choice between those things and an unsettled marriage is really no choice at all. This was not like trying to fix a union between a husband who habitually went out with the boys after their 9-to-5 shift at the mill, and a wife who wanted him home each evening for dinner. Counseling and compromises weren't going to solve anything here.

"Racing was his life," she says. "It was *in* him."

They were divorced in 1972.

Donny Marcello, who for a while worked part-time in the kitchen at Coalyard Charlies, set up his friend in an apartment above the bar, and Evans, free from the constraints he had come to see in matrimony, dove headlong into the single life. Lettered across the back panel of that first Pinto modified was a slogan which pretty much summed up his feelings on domestic bliss. This was in the heyday of the popular, nationally-syndicated "Love Is …" comic strip, in which a sweet young boy and girl, holding hands and smiling innocently, provided a different daily ending to that sentence.

On the tail of the Evans #61, it read, "Love is a bedful of sweat."

Love is a bedful of sweat! *(Lynn Evans collection)*

Though he drove her mad on a frequent basis back then, today Barbara Evans—she has never dropped his surname—says, "I think back a lot. I think about Richie. He was quite amazing. He had a finesse about him, a charm. You wanted to hate him sometimes, but you couldn't. And even after we were divorced, I relied on him a lot. He took good care of me and the kids."

Time really does heal all wounds. Thirty-odd years after they split up, the first Mrs. Evans grins as she looks for a way to sum up Mr. Evans.

"Richie," she says, shaking her head, "just wasn't the marrying kind."

PART THREE
Champion

Lynn Evans collection

Big Dreams

THERE IS THIS TENDENCY TODAY for people to remember Evans's career as not truly taking off until Gene DeWitt's support arrived in 1973. Well, DeWitt's financial backing enabled Evans to do a lot of great things, true enough—and Richie was always the first to proclaim that—but this is also true: in the four seasons spanning 1969-72, Evans won something on the order of 70 modified features all over the Empire State (including the 1971 and '72 New Yorker 400s), captured two track championships at Fulton and another at Utica-Rome, and was almost always up to the task of running with the biggest names in the Northeast when they invaded his turf for major NASCAR modified events or All Star League shows.

Clearly, he was already a man who was going places, spurred on by a rare combination: He was talented, he was likable, and he had a burning, restless will.

Lynn Evans, who is as much a student of her late husband's career as any fan ever was, says, "I like reading stories about people who are self-driven, because it's amazing to me the way some people want something so badly, and *love* something so badly, that they'll pursue it with everything they have. It's in their blood, and that's that. And when I read about anybody like that, I'll think: That was Rich. He was just so driven to succeed."

By late 1972, his race team had become essentially self-sufficient. It didn't make him a lot of money, but it wasn't nearly the drain on his personal and professional finances that it had been in the coupe days. Driving race cars was his entire life, and life was getting better, a little bit at a time.

"Richie was one of the first guys I knew who was really a full-time racer," says Dutch Hoag. "Well, him and Jerry Cook, because Cook never did anything but race."

Ah, Jerry Cook. If Evans ever wondered in those days just how realistic it was to be a full-time NASCAR modified racer, he needed only to look across Rome, to the home and shop out of which Cook had built a nationally-recognized short-track name. A native of Lockport, New York, out Buffalo way, Cook had gotten into racing young, building his first coupe in 1958 at age 13. He hired hotshot drivers like Cam Gagliardi and Kenny Meahl until he was old enough to take the wheel himself. By 18 he was driving, and soon winning, at places like Utica-Rome, Albany-Saratoga and Fonda. But Cook's career truly hit top gear in 1968, when he moved to Rome, married a local girl named Sue Ray, and immediately hit the racing road, chasing points.

Few seemed as comfortable with the highway-and-speedway life as

All Star League chief steward Big Bob O'Rourke interviews Richie after a 1972 All Star League victory. (Mike Adaskaveg photo)

Jerry Cook. He was, no question, a modified traveler in the great road-dog tradition of Don MacTavish and Pete Hamilton, the two Boston-area kids who roamed the East Coast en route to winning the NASCAR sportsman titles in 1966 and '67, respectively, and of Bugsy Stevens and car owner Len Boehler, who teamed to win those three consecutive NASCAR modified championships from 1967-69.

Cook's solid backing from Rochester-area trucking company owner Pete Hollebrand, his willingness to haul anywhere and everywhere, and his amazing ability to grind out frequent high finishes had led him to NASCAR national modified crowns in 1971 and '72. It isn't hard to imagine the impact that had on the psyche of an eager, increasingly driven Richie Evans: *If Cook can win a championship racing out of Rome, well, why can't I?*

Years later, when he was interviewed for a promotional video produced by Winston to showcase its NASCAR short-track involvement, Evans was asked what made him so good at chasing points. Richie responded, "We had a good teacher when we got started. We had to figure out how to beat Jerry Cook."

By the winter of 1972-73, Evans had no doubt been studying Cook long enough to pick up a few title-hunting tips. He also had himself a couple of great Sonney Seamon-built Pintos and a small collection of B&M big-block engines, enough firepower to give him a fighting chance against Cook or anybody else. He had a solid, familiar crew chief in Buster Maurer, and help from the likes of Wilbur Jones, Anthony Evans, Kenny Tomasi, Donny Marcello, Jim Small, and a half-dozen other Calvert Street loyalists. He had all of the ancillary equipment—from spare toolboxes to, *finally*, reliable trucks and trailers—to carry him through a long, hard points race.

He had everything a championship wanna-be could ask for, except the money to make it all happen.

Gene's Machine I

GENE DEWITT HAD BEEN A RACE FAN as long as anybody who was anybody could remember. By his own admission, he had owned his first stock car, a jalopy-class rig, at 14 years of age, and had sponsored a number of cars later on. Dutch Hoag remembers meeting him "in the early '60s" at an indoor three-quarter midget race at Rochester's War Memorial, where DeWitt was an enthusiastic spectator. Already, Hoag remembers, DeWitt was running "a hell of a business."

The business was B.R. DeWitt, Inc., a construction juggernaut founded in 1923 by Gene's dad, Byron R. DeWitt. The company is gone now, but in the 1960s and '70s it was enormous; among other projects, B.R. DeWitt, Inc. played a part in the building of the St. Lawrence Seaway Project, which linked the Great Lakes manufacturing belt to the Atlantic shipping lanes and the world.

But work was work, and pleasure was pleasure, and as soon as the construction executive met Dutch Hoag—easily the biggest racing name in Western New York in those days—DeWitt saw an opportunity to get even more pleasure out of his favorite pastime. In "oh, '63 or '64, somewhere in there," Hoag says, DeWitt confided that he had some big ideas.

"Gene wanted to go to Daytona," Hoag says. "He wanted me to fly down South and buy a car to run in the Permatex 300, the sportsman race. He wanted me to call the shots, and I really didn't like that. I said, 'Gene, if *you* spend your money, I'll go. But I'm not going to be the one to spend your money.' I just didn't feel comfortable doing that.

"Well, I guess he took that the wrong way, because later on Gene told his brother-in-law, 'That sonofabitch Hoag thinks he's too good to drive for me.' I got wind of that, and I called him right up. I said, 'Gene, it's just that I wouldn't spend my own money like that, and I won't spend yours that way, either.' Then he understood what I meant."

By then, the window of opportunity had passed for them to get together for that Daytona event, and the two men did other things; Hoag raced and won with the Turner Brothers, and DeWitt raced and won with a few drivers, among them Ronnie Lux, a New Yorker tipped for Indianapolis greatness before he was killed in a 1966 sprint car crash in Tulsa.

In time, the casual acquaintance between Hoag and DeWitt began to deepen into a genuine friendship. It became a partnership late in 1967, after Hoag shocked the modified world by walking away from the Turner Brothers team on the highest possible note: after winning the Race of Champions at Langhorne. It was Hoag's fourth Langhorne win, but the first for the Turners.

Hoag still grins at the memory: "Ray said after the race, 'I finally got what I always wanted.' I said, 'Good. I'm glad I was able to get you what you wanted. I guess we'll quit now. I'll build my own car for next year.' We parted that day, as friends. I built a car of my own for the next year, and Gene was with me then."

Hoag and DeWitt had what Dutch calls "a hell of a good year in '68," and he wasn't kidding. Among assorted other major victories was Hoag's fifth score in the Race of Champions.

For the better part of three seasons, the DeWitt-sponsored blue #7 coupe, Donald "Dutch" Hoag in the wheelhouse, was one of modified racing's toughest combinations. And they finally did manage to get to Daytona together, running the Permatex 300 in 1969 with a Dodge that DeWitt purchased from legendary NASCAR mechanic Ray Fox.

"The car was a big, square box," Hoag says, "but we did all right."

Yeah, they did. Hoag and the B.R. DeWitt Dodge qualified a strong

Gene DeWitt (second from right) with Dutch Hoag in victory lane at Langhorne, 1968. *(Ray Masser photo)*

fourth and finished a stunning second behind LeeRoy Yarbrough, easily the hottest superspeedway shoe of the day. (Yarbrough, in fact, scored a weekend sweep, blitzing to victory in the next day's Daytona 500.)

The whole story behind the Daytona trip speaks volumes about the kind of casual, supportive sponsor Gene DeWitt always was. Hoag says, "We'd had a hell of a good year in '68, and at the end of the year I went to a banquet over in Buffalo. A bunch of guys there were talking about Daytona, and that got me thinking. The next day I went to Gene's place, and I said, 'You still want to go to Daytona?' He said he did, and that was that."

Today, just the mention of the relationship brings an easy smile to Hoag's weathered face. "The only agreement I ever had with Gene DeWitt was a handshake. He said, 'You run the operation *how* you want to, you race *when* you want to, you race *where* you want to. If I need to know anything, I'll call you.' That's how it was. And we never had a cross word, ever."

Their partnership came to a bizarre end in 1970. By then, Hoag, 43 years old at the time, was admittedly burned out, frazzled from juggling the demands of a growing trucking business—he estimates that he had 35 employees in 1970—and the hours involved in building, maintaining and driving his modifieds. The final straw came that summer, on the last day of July, at Spencer Speedway.

Just four laps into the modified feature, everything went wrong. A coupe driven by Gary Cornelius caught a wheel in heavy traffic; the car jumped into the air, cleared a safety fence and came to a horrific landing in the small set of pit bleachers. Four spectators were killed, and 18 more injured, including Rome's own Cliff Kotary. Among the dead was Bob Petrocci, popular promoter of the Rolling Wheels dirt track, who, according to print reports, was only at Spencer because his own speedway had rained out that evening.

Hoag, not driving that night, saw the whole thing unfold. "That was enough for me," he says. The Spencer tragedy, coupled with the stress of his racing and trucking pursuits, led to what Dutch calls "my nervous breakdown." He decided to hang up his helmet; the retirement proved only temporary, because Hoag later raced off-and-on until 1978, but for a while one of the greatest short-track stock car drivers in the nation faded into the margins.

Gene DeWitt respected Hoag's decision, and sat on the sidelines for a while himself. Ultimately, though, DeWitt couldn't resist the pull of his hobby. By 1972 he had begun to ask around about other interesting sponsorship opportunities, seeking the quiet counsel of friends he respected. One of those friends was Bill Wimble, who had been so impressed by the "bull-dogged" determination and fairness he saw in a young Richie Evans in that race-long fight for third place at Albany-Saratoga. Remember how Wimble put it? *This guy has got something that most drivers don't have …*

Wimble, who had retired at the close of the 1960s to launch a trucking company—and who remained around the stock car scene for a time as a Utica-Rome official—remembers the whole thing as if it happened only yesterday.

"Once I got into the trucking business, one of the things we did was haul liquid asphalt," Wimble says. "B.R. DeWitt had asphalt plants throughout western New York, so I began to attempt to get their business. Eventually, we ended up hauling all their asphalt in the state of New York. I dealt with Gene's dad at first, and then later, particularly after his dad died, I dealt directly with Gene, who I had known for years anyway because of his association with racing.

"We got much better acquainted because of the business relationship, and one day Gene said to me, 'Do you know of any good, up-and-coming guy I can get to drive for me?' I said, 'Yes, I do. If you can get him, I know a guy who can do the kind of job you want done.' And, of course, I was talking about Richie. We talked for a while about Richie—it was mostly just me telling Gene what I knew about him—and he seemed impressed. He asked me if I would contact Richie to see if he was interested.

"So I went to Rome, to Richie's garage, and visited with him. I told him Gene was interested in him, and was thinking about the possibility of becoming his sponsor. Richie seemed to be excited about that."

It was late in 1972, Buster Maurer recalls, that the most dynamic driver/sponsor combination in modified history began to crystallize.

"We were in a banquet room or a hotel barroom or something like that, and Gene was there," Maurer says. "He come over and talked to Rich, and they went off and had a discussion. Richie came back, and he made the comment that there was a possibility that Gene might want to do something with us.

"I think maybe Richie thought, Hell, that's too good to be true. I don't think he put a lot of stock in it at the time."

But there was a second conversation, and then a third. Clearly, something about this unconventional guy with the silly laugh and the growing reputation for driving fast and living faster appealed to the reserved, businesslike DeWitt.

"Gene always said that Richie was a diamond in the rough," Billy Nacewicz says with a grin. "And he was right about the rough part, in the beginning. But Gene definitely saw something there."

DeWitt himself always seemed to have a tough time explaining exactly what that was. The closest he ever came was probably in 1985, after Richie's death, when writer Dick Berggren quizzed him about why he had been so taken with Evans.

DeWitt said simply, "He had a twinkle in his eye."

Daytona Rookie

THE DEWITT/EVANS MARRIAGE began with what Gene DeWitt always called "a one-race deal," a get-acquainted race, and it was a doozy. DeWitt had never lost his Daytona urges—in fact, his 1969 success with Hoag had only heightened them—and in the winter of 1972 he purchased a superspeedway-ready '69 Mercury Cyclone from Dave Nagle, Maynard Troyer's longtime backer, with the specific goal of running the 1973 Permatex 300. The car had been around some, having run in a handful of NASCAR Grand National (now Nextel Cup) events during Troyer's all-too-brief fling at the big time in 1971, but DeWitt's driver was all new to the superspeedway game.

In those days, the Permatex 300 for NASCAR late model sportsman cars was one of America's most unpredictable, and thus most thrilling, stock car races. Then, as now, the Saturday event at Daytona was ripe for cherry-picking Sunday stars, but it also drew an incredible variety of short-track heroes thanks to one of the quirkiest rules in NASCAR's long history of quirky rules: Any driver who had won a top-division track championship at *any* NASCAR-sanctioned speedway was "guaranteed" a starting spot in the Permatex 300, as long as he could (1) come up with a legal car, and (2) run it above a designated minimum speed during practice and qualifying. Beaver Dragon, the great Vermont late model star who had one of those early-'70s guaranteed spots, remembers the minimum speed being 150 miles per hour.

It wasn't necessarily a sure thing, but it was a pretty good trump card to have up your sleeve. And Richie Evans, as the 1972 modified champion at Utica-Rome Speedway, held such a card.

In retrospect, Richie's first trip to Daytona was a mirror of every

It's February of 1973, and Richie Evans, Daytona rookie, is gearing up for the Permatex 300. *(Ray's Racing Photo/Lynn Evans collection)*

racer's first trip to Daytona, especially in those days when everything was less predictable, from travel—crewmen Buster Maurer, Wilbur Jones and Teddy Knipe were marooned for three days at the famous South of the Border tourist trap by a freak Carolinas snowstorm—to inspection procedures.

"I was really psyched up to get out there," Evans told writer Pete Zanardi. "I went down and expected to get out on the race track but we couldn't because of technical problems. So I just sat and waited for four days."

Which only meant more time for the usual rookie butterflies to make laps around Richie's stomach. There has yet to be born the race driver who stands in a firesuit for the first time at Daytona and tells himself, with any real certainty, "I can do this." He might *say* he can, and he might even *think* he can, but he doesn't know for sure, because no amount of 35-lap victories in Cedar Rapids, Iowa, or Malta, New York, is adequate preparation for Daytona's 31-degree banked turns, its scary tri-oval bend, or its will-it-ever-end back straightaway.

Even Richie Evans, never short on confidence, admitted to finding the track a bit daunting once he was finally turned loose for practice.

"I remember I was chewing gum when I went onto the track," he explained to Zanardi. "All of a sudden, I realized I was no longer chewing gum. My teeth were clenched. I was gritting my teeth."

This was no exaggeration, says Wilbur Jones. "Richie told me, 'All those guys who talk about this track being so easy that you can chew gum all the way around, they're full of shit. I was halfway down the backstretch before I remembered I even had the gum in my mouth.'"

Ron Bouchard, another modified guy who was just beginning to dip his toe in the big-track waters, remembers, "When Richie first ran Daytona, he wasn't really hepped up about going that fast. I think, at first, the speed bothered him. But, you know, he got the hang of it."

Yes, he did. Just as he had when he felt the wind blowing his tall coupe to and fro on the Trenton frontstretch in 1971, Evans sucked it up and learned Daytona in a hurry. And he was quick, much more than just respectably quick and far better than play-it-safe, guaranteed-starter quick.

Wilbur Jones says, "It's hard to believe this, maybe, but when people ask me what his best track was, I think I'd say Daytona. From the first time we went there, he could handle it. A lot of people were afraid of that place, but Richie wasn't. He had fear—respect—but he wasn't afraid. And he did good there."

After a couple of frightening practice moments—one day Denis Giroux popped an engine directly in front of Evans, and on another "Tiny Lund kinda slowed up in the middle of the track and Rich about lost the car," Buster Maurer remembers—things settled down a bit, and Evans qualified a surprising sixth.

Come the Permatex 300, Evans did a curious thing. "When the race started, I remember he dropped to the bottom of the track and fell back quite a few spots," Maurer says. "We thought, Maybe he's not going to be able to do this after all. But he [ran] a couple laps on the low side, and, all of a sudden, away he went.

"I think maybe at the start, he didn't know how to react to all the cars on that type of track, because he'd never been put in that environment. I guess he just wanted to see what everybody was going to do, and pick a comfortable spot to ride in until he could start racing his way. And then he started to pass cars. In fact, he passed a *lot* of cars."

Yeah, he did. By 40 laps—100 miles—the scoreboard showed the #61 in second spot, trailing eventual race winner Bill Dennis but ahead of late model sportsman greats Sam Ard, Red Farmer and Jack Ingram. The 1972 Utica-Rome Speedway modified champion was riding in some pretty fine company.

"I believe the car was good enough, and that Rich was doing a good enough job, that we'd have been a top-three or top-five," Buster Maurer declares.

Alas, there was no glass slipper for the Cinderella story in the orange and blue Mercury. Evans ended up falling out with a blown head gasket and was scored 34th in the final rundown. One spot back in 35th, incidentally, was another young man with some promise, a late model whiz out of Kentucky by way of the old Nashville Fairgrounds half-miler. His name was Darrell Waltrip. They would one day meet again at Daytona.

It was a long trip and a long week for a short run at glory, but Maurer says nobody in the DeWitt pit was hanging his head when the sun set that afternoon.

"I think Richie left there with the confidence that he could do this," Maurer recalls. "You know, that he could race on that big track."

 A Title Won

DAYTONA, APPARENTLY, left a favorable impression on Gene DeWitt. His "one-race deal" for the Permatex 300 blossomed into an agreement to sponsor Evans's modified operation. There was no way to know it at the time, of course, but together they were setting out on an adventure which would span 13 seasons and hundreds of victories.

Through all of that, Gene DeWitt was always a sponsor rather than a car owner. That got confused sometimes over the years, because often "B.R. DeWitt" was listed as the team owner in press releases and race reports. There is a simple explanation for that: For years, entry blanks for most major short-track events asked for only the driver and the car owner to be listed, and Evans, looking to take care of his friend and benefactor, simply wrote in his sponsor's name rather than listing his own name twice. Thus, a track announcer was likely to talk about Richie Evans driving for Gene DeWitt in the same manner that he would describe, say, Fred DeSarro driving for Lenny Boehler. But Boehler was a genuine car owner, a guy who hired his drivers and maintained his cars and hauled them up and down the highway; Gene DeWitt's role with Evans was a lot like his role with Dutch Hoag: supportive, yes, but also casual, low-key, and hands-off.

"In the beginning," says Buster Maurer, "what Gene did was take care of the motor bill and give us a credit card for the gas and the motels. And as the season was just getting started, Gene upgraded his support, you might say, by giving us Dutch's old hauler, a Chevrolet with a sleeper cab. It was blue, and we painted it orange.

"Everything else, Richie did on his own. He had his own deals, he paid his own bills. He still owned his own operation, basically."

The arrangement worked for both Gene DeWitt and Richie Evans, and for that reason it never really changed. It was never the open-checkbook sort of sponsorship many of their rivals, perhaps out of jealousy, often wanted to believe it was. Although, if you listen to insiders, it could have been, had Evans been greedy.

"Gene absolutely loved Richie," says Donny Marcello. "I mean, right from the start, he'd have done anything for him."

But, insists Maurer, "Rich was the ultimate fair guy. He treated Gene's money just like it was his own."

So the backing from DeWitt didn't exactly put Richie Evans on Easy Street, but it sure did make his road a little smoother. Long gone were the days of dipping into the till at the gas station, or hitting up trusty old Fred Ulrich for travel money; "Once Gene came along, Richie didn't need my help like he did before," Ulrich said. "Oh, I still helped him a little bit, but Gene had more of that green stuff than I did."

With Gene DeWitt at the far left and Buster Maurer steering, the Evans Pinto rolls to the grid at Trenton in 1973. *(Buster Maurer collection)*

Wilbur Jones says, "Nothing really changed down at the garage. The work still had to be done, and Rich worked just as hard. But it was a good feeling not to be so short of money all the time."

And if money was the only thing stopping him from going after a NASCAR national modified championship, from chasing a dream, well, there was nothing stopping him now. As soon as the deal with DeWitt was secure, Evans began to plan his assault.

"The truth is," Evans told Pete Zanardi, "I like to race and I like to travel, so running for the title was a natural. I never had enough equipment or money to do it before. Now we have."

You can almost see that familiar just-short-of-cocky grin on Richie's face as you read the next thing he said to Zanardi: "I've geared up for this a long time. I'm not what you'd call a newcomer."

Clearly, these were exciting times for everybody at 608 Calvert Street.

"Rich and I sat down one night and discussed how we were going to go about this," Buster Maurer says. "I mean, it was a new thing for us, sure. But Richie didn't want to finish second; he wanted to win that championship. He said, 'If somebody touches a nut on that car, you touch it afterwards and make sure it's tight. Anything anybody does, you're responsible for checking it.' And that's basically the way we handled it. If somebody did something, I had to check it. That was a big motivation for me."

And Maurer had another motivation: Bill Payne, a local running buddy who had been the best man at Maurer's wedding and was his closest friend, happened to work on Jerry Cook's pit crew. Even before the first green flag waved, the two men were exchanging barbs about the long season ahead.

"Bill and I were in a bar one night, and one thing led to another," Maurer says. "Well, Bill said to me, 'You know, you guys will never win that championship. Nobody wins it the first time.'"

Payne had some history to back up his words. Before rattling off his three straight NASCAR championships from 1967-69, Bugsy Stevens had paid his dues with a runner-up finish behind Ernie Gahan in '66. And Payne's man Cook had run second to Stevens in 1968 and Fred DeSarro in '70 before winning his titles in 1971-72. But on this night, a few frosty brews into their discussion, Buster Maurer was in no mood for logic.

"I was mad, I remember that. I said to Bill, 'I'm telling you right now, we're going to win that thing. I have my faith in Rich, and if anybody can win it the first time out, he will.' Of course, the bar was full of people, and they all knew us. I think it was the first time anybody ever saw us arguing, because we were such good friends."

In those days, the NASCAR modified schedule was set as much by Mother Nature as by anybody at the sanctioning body's headquarters in Daytona Beach. Places like Utica-Rome and Albany-Saratoga might still be covered with snow come March, but 600-odd miles to the south there was the high-profile opener at Martinsville, and also early-spring shows at tracks across Virginia and North Carolina: "Caraway, Callaway, Hickory ..." Maurer muses.

"Richie loved it down there," Wilbur Jones says, "and the people seemed to really like him. The other racers would always let us use their shops; I remember working at Paul Radford's shop when he drove that Clarence's Steak House car."

So the battle began. Evans came out of the box strong, finishing second in a pair of Martinsville features, one a 100-lapper in which he chased Radford to the line and the other the modified half of the rain-delayed Dogwood 500, in which Evans was runner-up to Cook.

Closer to home, in April, Evans ran sixth in Stafford's 80-lap Spring Sizzler, trailing Ed Flemke, Fred DeSarro, Maynard Troyer, Radford and flamboyant Canadian Guy Chartrand.

And then they got to the heart of the fight, played out as it was in those days in literally hundreds of events at dozens of points on the modified compass. There was no organized 22- or 25-race tour back then; instead, every feature run at any NASCAR-sanctioned oval awarded points toward the national championship, although those points could be earned in a variety of ways. Point-chasing had a language all its own: There were "regular" shows, "double-points" shows, "special" shows and "national championship" (NC) shows, each paying wildly different numbers of points.

It was about as goofy as arithmetic could get, and today nobody can explain exactly why things were set up that way, but, well, there it was. Check it out: a regular show paid 50 points to win, so a double-points show ought to offer 100, right? Wrong. For some reason, there was a 16-point bonus involved in those events, so double-pointers were actually worth *more* than double the points. And how can you explain the fact that on the very same weekend, a 100-lap special at the Callaway Speedway in Franklin County, Virginia, awarded its winner 66 points, while a 100-lapper at Islip awarded 50? National championship events, meanwhile, theoretically paid unlimited points, the actual number being apparently determined by the purse, the race distance, and the alignment of the moon and the stars. Maybe the winner would get 591 points, maybe he'd get 673, maybe he'd get 915.

And, in those pre-Internet days, it was just about impossible to keep close tabs on the standings at any given moment. It was one thing for Evans to know where Cook stood, and vice versa, because one essentially shadowed the other. But it was something else altogether to know immediately if there was a big points gain made by, say, Bugs Stevens, who joined Evans and Cook at Albany-Saratoga and Utica-Rome most weekends but then split off to Stafford on Saturday nights. For a long time, the '73 NASCAR season looked like a three-way fight thanks to Stevens, and so everybody involved was kept busy making midweek phone calls to the NASCAR office in search of the latest, most accurate standings.

"Back then," says Wilbur Jones, "you really didn't *know* where you stood until the season was half over and you saw who else was still in it."

The only approach was to pay close attention to the entry blanks, checking the race's points status even before you looked at its purse, and to keep the haulers topped off with gasoline.

"Some of these races paid, like, 800 points to win," said Billy Nacewicz, "so you couldn't pass 'em up no matter how little [money] they paid. It meant an awful lot of traveling."

There was no such thing as a typical week. Friday night usually meant Albany-Saratoga, but that could change if some other track threw up a double-pointer. On Saturday night, a NASCAR points-chaser could choose between Shangri-La, Stafford or Islip, but you couldn't rule out a dash down to Winston-Salem for a national championship race at Bowman Gray Stadium. There was no telling what track might run a special event on Sunday afternoon, and then there was Utica-Rome on Sunday night. And, of course, there was always another promoter anxious to take advantage of the open field offered by a summertime Tuesday or Wednesday night ...

"Richie ran three or four nights a week," says Wilbur Jones, "and sometimes twice in the same day."

It took multiple cars, multiple trucks and trailers, plenty of manpower, lots of street vehicles, even a private plane or two. Jones says, "If there was a big Sunday afternoon race somewhere, he'd get out of there as soon as he could and he'd have somebody ready to fly him up to Utica-Rome."

When everything went right, that sort of points-chasing was a gas. When it went wrong, it could be a major headache. And on at least one Sunday in that 1973 season, it was both. Evans was grinning a winner's grin late in the afternoon, buzzed on the adrenaline of an apparent victory in the Coke 250 at Pocono and preparing for a quick flight up to Utica-Rome, where his second car sat waiting. He pulled aside Wilbur Jones, who planned to help load up the Pocono car and then drive the 200 or so miles to Vernon.

Jones remembers, "Richie said, 'Wilbur, you pick up the money, and bring it up to Utica-Rome.' Fine. So I'm hanging around in the payoff line later, and I finally get up to the front. The guy says, 'What car?' I told him, 'Richie Evans, 61.' The guy says, 'OK, second place. Sign here.'

"I said, 'You're kidding me, right?' The guy told me, 'No, you're second. Bugsy Stevens won.' There had been a scoring dispute. Well, I wasn't going to sign for second-place money, because that would have been conceding the win. I said, ' You might as well hold up the purse. I'm not taking second-place money back to Richie, not when he thinks he won the race. Nope.'

"So the finish was under protest, and I headed back to Utica-Rome. All the heats were over by the time I got there. I didn't want to give Richie the bad news just before the feature, so before I went in, I made sure he was out on the track. He ended up winning the race, and when he saw me back in the pits he said, 'We had a good day today, didn't we, Wilbur?' I said, 'Well, it was *pretty* good.' Then I told him what was going on at Pocono. Oh, was he ever pissed."

But Pocono was just one low spot—if second in a major event can be a low spot—in a dizzying string of successes: 99- and 100-lap scores at Albany-Saratoga en route to a record nine feature wins there; a Fourth of July weekend win at Shangri-La; a pair of runner-up finishes to young Ronnie Bouchard in long-distance races at Stafford, a place where Evans had previously struggled; two more key seconds, one to Geoff Bodine in an Islip 100 lapper and the other behind Bugs Stevens at the Devil's Bowl track in West Haven, Vermont. And eight victories at Utica-Rome, four times as many as Maynard Troyer, the only other repeat winner there in 1973.

No matter how a weekend went, it seemed, everything would get better once the pit gates opened at Utica-Rome. Buster Maurer says, "We had a phenomenal car for that place. We saved it for Utica-Rome, and it was *tenths* faster than anybody there. Obviously, I feel like we also had the best driver in the world, but there was just something about that car. You'd watch people go around that track, and when they'd let off going down into three, Rich could drive right past 'em before he let off."

Utica-Rome promoter Dick Waterman says, "It got to the point where Richie almost had to break down if you were going to beat him."

Maurer chuckles about a night when Cook happened to start in the first couple of rows, with Evans deep in the field. "By the time Rich broke out of the pack, Jerry had about a straightaway lead. He was *gone*. In fact, my friend Bill Payne told me that Jerry said later, 'I looked up going into turn three, and there was nobody in my mirror. I had it made.' Well, two laps later Rich passed him. He drove by Cookie so fast, and went on to win by a lot. While Rich was getting the trophy, Jerry drove into the pits and up on the hauler. He was so mad, he loaded up and left immediately."

By the time the regular season wrapped up in late summer, Evans had picked up his second straight Utica-Rome title and was runner-up at both Albany-Saratoga (behind Cook) and Shangri-La (to Eddie Pieniazek).

It was a giddy time, but also, according to Buster Maurer, a stressful time. First, because the quest for NASCAR points placed a premium on finishing races, there was a ton of maintenance work involved. "Everything had to be checked over and over and over," Maurer says. "B&M built our motors, and Rich pretty much looked after them. But as far as everything else, he wanted that thing taken apart every Monday morning. We took the rear ends apart every week; in those days, you'd have a lot of trouble with rear ends because of all the horsepower those big-blocks put down. They wanted to rip the ring-and-pinion apart."

Second, Jerry Cook wasn't exactly rolling over and playing dead. While every other serious contender for the crown faded away as summer turned to fall—only Stevens, who had slipped to a distant third, could even be considered a longshot—Cook had been pounding along, as always: a ton of seconds and thirds at Albany-Saratoga, Shangri-La and Utica-Rome complementing occasional victories, both close to home and on the road.

It was a see-saw tussle, and for a time it looked as if Jerry's consistency would trump Richie's speed. "We were down maybe 100 points or more," Maurer says, "but then we got running good and we clawed our way back."

Running good? How about running great? That was Evans in August and September, when he notched four huge wins fat with points. "Richie," says Maurer, "went on a rampage."

First came the Permatex 200 at Islip on August 11, when Evans, Stevens and Cook finished one-two-three ahead of all the hot locals. "Islip was a real trip," says Maurer. "I couldn't believe the place was so small. In the big races there, we used to pit in the infield, and if you were smart you stood back-to-back with somebody you could trust. That's how you watched the race, turning around in circles, back-to-back so in case something happened, you'd be warned.

"And, God, did those people party after the races at Islip. I saw a guy drink STP and wash it down with beer."

Then, on the second weekend of September, came Malta's Gold Cup 150, where Evans outran Stevens to the checkers.

But it was on the last weekend of that month that Evans had one of the greatest Saturdays of his career. It began with an afternoon 150 at Martinsville, where he started from the pole and led every lap to beat

September, 1973: Evans in victory lane after beating Bugs Stevens in the Gold Cup 150 at Albany-Saratoga. *(Mike Adaskaveg photo)*

Cook, Stevens and Paul Radford. Then he and everybody else hauled their iron the 80-odd miles down to Asheboro, North Carolina, for a 100-lap nightcap at the Caraway Speedway, where Evans won ahead of Cook, Satch Worley, Stevens and Ray Hendrick.

That August-September stretch put Evans on Broadway. Still, recalls Maurer, no one in their camp was taking anything for granted.

"When you're in the middle of a battle like that, you're so focused on what you're doing day in and day out, because there is no rest," Maurer says. "If your opponent has a breakdown and you get a little cushion, then you *might* get a little confidence. But anybody who's chased points knows that you can have all the confidence this week, and next week it can be shot to hell. So you have to keep your head about you, and not say, 'Well, we've got it made now.' Richie was never like that. We never felt like we had it made, and we never felt like [Cook] had it made."

Evans went into October's Race of Champions, the richest event on the schedule in terms of both payoff and points, with a slim chance of clinching the championship. He'd have to do well, and Cook would have to run into problems, but hell, it was a chance.

"Before we went to Trenton," says Maurer, "we were wound pretty tight."

The Race of Champions had moved from dear, departed Langhorne the previous autumn, but it had maintained its "come-one, come-all" allure with both fans and competitors. The fans came for one last big Northeastern blast, turning the Trenton Fairgrounds and the surrounding motels into a rollicking end-of-term party; the competitors came— 101 strong in 1973—because their local tracks had shut down for the season, because the ROC had the richest purse in modified racing, and because, just like Langhorne, the fast Trenton track presented a challenge they found too great to resist. And if the drivers dug Trenton, the mechanics went cuckoo over it; even 30 years ago they were trying to streamline their boxy Pintos, Vegas and Gremlins with fuller hoods, crude spoilers and windshields, and trying off-beat engine and chassis tricks to get the cars around the oddly-shaped Trenton layout.

For Evans, who always enjoyed working on cars as much as he loved driving them, it might have been the ultimate speedway. He came to the 1973 Race of Champions with a pretty neat trick up his sleeve.

"In that right-hand turn on the backstretch, the dogleg, all the oil ran away from your normal pick-up in the pan," Maurer says. "A lot of people would combat that by putting a kick-out on the [right] side of the oil pan and putting more oil in the motor. We didn't have dry-sump systems; the only guy that had a dry-sump, maybe, would have been Geoff Bodine. Well, Rich came up with this brainstorm of using a [mechanic's] brake-bleeder tank to help keep the oil pressure up. See, the bleeder tank was pressurized, and there was a rubber bladder in it. You'd fill [one side] with oil, put 'x' amount of pounds of air pressure in [the other], and as the oil pressure dropped below a certain amount, the air pressure would force oil into the motor. The tank was mounted inside the car, on the right side. When the oil pressure was going up, it was forcing the oil into the tank to a certain point, but if the oil pressure dropped, the brake bleeder would force the oil back into the motor.

"I remember he asked a lot of people if they thought it would work, and they didn't really know. But it made common sense, so we actually went out and bought a brand-new brake bleeder. A lot of people looked inside the car and thought, What the hell is that thing? But it worked good the whole time we were there."

It might seem in hindsight to have been a gamble on Richie's part, trying something like this with the NASCAR title staring him in the face. In fact, it was more like an insurance policy. Drivers were used to sweating as their oil pressure dropped dangerously low every time they sped through Trenton's dogleg; Maurer says, "You knew a motor couldn't live forever like that." Evans, meanwhile, breezed through practice knowing his big-block had a better than even chance of surviving, because its oil pressure needle was as steady as a surgeon's hand.

The front end of the starting grid for the 200-lap, 300-mile Race of Champions reflected the North/South parity modified racing could boast in those days. Paul Radford had the pole in the Clarence's Steak House Vega, that famous #26, beside the fierce-looking black Mason's Garage #45, a Gremlin with young Satch Worley up; both of them averaged better than 140 miles per hour. Third was Bodine, the defending ROC champion in his blue and white Valiant, with Merv Treichler's maroon Gremlin fourth. Evans started a few rows further back, but was feeling good about his long-haul chances.

As it turned out, he had some terrific luck in the short haul. Just 10 laps into the race, Cook began ducking in and out of the pits with problems under the hood. After 15 laps, he was out of the show. From there, Evans could have eased it home, knowing that even a decent finish would sew up the championship. But, true to form, he gassed it instead.

"Whenever we went to the race track, we went to win," says Buster Maurer. "That's the approach we always took. There was none of this, Let's see if we can finish in the top five. Yes, it would have been the easiest thing in the world for Rich to say at Trenton, 'Well, I can back off and cruise. Cookie's out.' But that was never his style."

So Evans went for the Race of Champions glory.

Early on, the race was between three of the division's brightest young talents, Worley, Bodine and Ron Bouchard, trailed hotly by a couple of its most celebrated veterans, Radford and Steady Eddie Flemke. But by halfway, Evans was well and truly in the mix. Then everybody started following their different pit stop schedules—strategy was still something of a black art to the modified gang—and when it all shook out with 40 or so laps to go, Evans and Bodine were swapping the lead between them like it was just another Saturday night at Shangri-La.

Geoff Bodine gave Evans a run for his money in the '73 Race of Champions at Trenton. *(Ray Masser photo)*

Spicing the plot was the fact that Bodine's fuel situation was questionable. Not only had he pitted earlier than Richie had, but some in the Evans pit, Maurer included, were convinced that the tank on Bodine's Valiant might not have been completely filled on that final stop. Maurer: "Geoff had these [plastic] gas cans, and you could see there was no gas left in them because they were so thin and lightweight." Therefore, if Bodine's crew had dumped in all the gas they *had*, rather than all the #99 Valiant *needed*, Geoff might be in trouble.

"I'm standing there thinking, He cannot go all the way," Maurer says.

Here is how much racing has changed: Buster Maurer, crew chief on the brink of a championship, was not in direct two-way contact with his driver. Oh, the Evans team had a radio link between pit and car, but in those days radios were such strange, newfangled items that plenty of old-schoolers were uncomfortable wearing them.

"I thought, If something happens and Richie has to pit, I've got this bulky old thing on and I can't operate," Maurer remembers with a laugh.

So he instructed the crewman who was willing to shoulder the responsibility of playing radio man to inform Evans of Bodine's situation. With that knowledge, Evans simply kept up the fight. "The longer Bodine stayed out there," he later told *Area Auto Racing News*, "the less I had to worry."

Geoff seemed to cop a reprieve on lap 182 when Ronnie Bouchard, a bullet all day in Bob Johnson's purple #17 Pinto, threw a right-front wheel and brought out a short caution. Incredibly, though, Bodine did not pit. He and his crew were banking on the fact that whatever gas they had on board was enough.

Seven laps later, Bodine coasted down that long Trenton frontstretch, pit-bound, his engine having literally died of thirst.

Richie Evans won the Race of Champions by a bit more than six seconds over Flemke, Roger Treichler, Buzzie Reutimann (in a coupe!), and

Evans pulls into Trenton's victory lane, having earned his biggest win to date and his first NASCAR title. *(Shippee-Dugas photo/courtesy of Speedway Scene)*

Don LaJoie, king of Connecticut's closed-clique, members-only Danbury Racearena.

"Rich made the comment later that he owed that win to his crew," Maurer says. "That was special."

There was no getting around how important the win was. It was the biggest payday in Richie's career to that point, something on the order of $11,050 plus a nice pile of lap money; it was his 25th victory in 62 NASCAR starts that season, and his 27th of 78 overall. Most importantly, it put the title mathematically out of reach for Cook and everyone else. The Cardinal 500 season finale was still a couple of weeks away at Martinsville—and it was won, incidentally, by Cook—but Buster Maurer's barroom boast nine months earlier had come true: Richie Evans was the 1973 NASCAR modified champion.

That fact dawned slowly: "When we were fighting for the lead with Geoff, all we knew for sure was that we were in good shape [in the points]," Maurer says.

Crowning a champion: Richie Evans sews up the 1973 NASCAR national modified championship. *(Ray Masser photo)*

But it dawned big, for the crew and for everybody who had known Richie from his earliest days at Utica-Rome: "When we all ran over to victory lane," Maurer grins, "Sonney Seamon leaned in the window and give Rich a big kiss."

Not surprisingly, Evans and company kicked the normally festive post-ROC partying into another dimension. Billy Nacewicz, not yet an official member of the team, had shown up to root for his local hero, and got in on the action. "Trenton had a bar under the grandstands," Nacewicz says, "and it got a little wild in there. Somebody—I think it might have been Mikey Loescher—brought a goat in there. *A goat!* And, of course, a goat will eat anything, and this one did. I remember they were feeding that goat money!"

Donny Marcello says, "I think we partied for three days, in Trenton and back here in Rome." But when he has trouble coming up with many specifics, his wife Rita chips in with this: "To tell you the truth, I don't think anybody who was there could remember very much of it."

Ask Buster Maurer. "You know, nothing sticks out in particular from after that race in Trenton," he says, laughing. "There might have been too many Cream Ales."

But one fellow stayed clear-headed enough to carry the memory for the next 30 years. Not surprisingly, it was old Fred Ulrich, who never stopped keeping a watchful eye over Evans and company.

Ulrich said, "The feeling I had, for Rich and for all of us, was: This is what you worked for, and here it is."

A Title Lost

THERE WAS NEVER ANY DOUBT that Evans, his 1973 crown a comfortable fit, would pursue the championship again in '74. Winning is an intoxicating thing. His core crew looked a little bit different—Buster Maurer, one-for-one as a title-chasing crew chief, took a job at a Rome machine shop and could not make all the races—but most of the usual suspects were still floating around, joined more and more frequently by Billy Nacewicz. It was a solid group.

"Richie always had a lot of free help," Nacewicz says, "and they were good guys, guys you could trust."

The late Fred Ulrich said, "We all kinda knew what needed to be done."

There were the normal Southern events at the front of the season, and immediately Evans and Cook showed strength. Martinsville hosted its traditional 250-lapper in March and April's Azalea 150; Bugs Stevens won the longer race with Richie second and Jerry fourth, and on the return trip, Evans won with Cook third.

Then came a North Carolina NASCAR modified tripleheader: Metrolina Speedway outside Charlotte on Friday night, Hickory on Saturday night, and Caraway Speedway near Asheboro on Sunday. Evans won the Friday show over Harry Gant, Cook and Paul Radford; at Hickory, Radford topped Gant, Johnny Bryant, Cook and Evans; at Caraway on Sunday, Gant beat Radford, Cook and Evans.

It was a terrific run of points-scoring finishing for both Rome drivers. In those five Southern shows, Evans was second, first, first, fifth and fourth; Cook was fourth, third, third, fourth and third.

In April came the Stafford Spring Sizzler, which in '74 was an interesting little sidebar to the Evans/Cook war. See, adding to the general championship confusion caused by the various ways NASCAR awarded points was the fact that in some races, the teams weren't all racing out of the same rulebook. If he chose to, a promoter could designate a race a NASCAR-blessed "open competition" event, which essentially meant a "run whatcha brung" kind of field, although cars meeting NASCAR specs would earn points toward the title. The Race of Champions had been one such race in '73, but with so much on the line there was no way either Evans or Cook was going to be anything but legal on that day; in the early-season Spring Sizzler, however, they were apparently thinking more about the Sizzler's fat purse than about points, because both men showed up with fuel-injector stacks atop their big-block rat motors. It wasn't exactly a winning decision for either: Cook finished fifth (behind Stevens, Ron Bouchard, Merv Treichler and the outlandish Pinto of open-competition specialist Ollie Silva), while Evans fought an overheating problem and dropped out after three laps.

And then, as always, the chase got down to business. This time around, however, it was going to be a two-man fight; Stevens and his veteran car owner Sonny Koszela (who had won the 1970 NASCAR championship with Fred DeSarro on board) decided to cut back on their traveling, and nobody else seemed prepared to step up in their absence to bring the fight to Cook and Evans.

But that didn't necessarily make things any easier, according to Buster Maurer. "I really don't think a lot of people who race today understand what it took to run full-time back then. If there was a points race *anywhere*, [Richie] went. Jerry, of course, was doing the same thing. If that meant running 70 races, 80 races, that's what you did. It'll take your breath away just thinking about it."

From a distance, the 1974 season was points-chasing as usual: the regular weekly shows, the special events, the NC shows that could send both drivers scrambling up and down I-81, or back and forth on I-90.

But viewed from close to home, meaning close to *Rome*, things sure did look a lot different. Lancaster Speedway, which in hindsight had as spotty a relationship with NASCAR as any Northeastern modified track ever did, was under the Daytona Beach banner in '74. Meanwhile, Utica-Rome promoter Dick Waterman was in an experimental mood, giving

Evans gave it the old college try in 1974. In the Permatex 200 at Islip, he won with a broken front end by horsing the car around for the last 15 laps. (B&G Wurthmann photo/courtesy of Speedway Scene)

up his track's traditional Sunday schedule to try his luck on Fridays, with Fulton Speedway boss Bub Benway eagerly accepting the Sunday NASCAR sanction. The big loser in the deal was Waterman, because Utica-Rome suffered seven rainouts while Fulton got wet only three times that season. But the big winner was unquestionably Evans, who won three features (and his third track championship) at Utica-Rome, one in his limited visits to Lancaster, and eight (and a third track championship) at Fulton. Cook, on the other hand, was winless at Fulton, had just one score at Utica-Rome, and was shut out at Lancaster.

Ironic, wasn't it, that Fulton and Lancaster, two tracks which had played such vital roles in Evans's "outlaw" phase in 1970-71, should now prove important in his quest for a second NASCAR championship?

Overall, though, 1974 looked a lot like 1973: Evans winning, winning, winning, and Cook grinding, grinding, grinding, the two of them kept close because Jerry's stream of top-five finishes would offset whatever missteps Evans made.

"I talk to people who were around back then," Jerry Cook says, "and we wonder how we ever pulled some of it off. We ran 70 races a year just for the championship, and on top of that we ran a bunch of other races, too. We were up in the 90s [in total races] every year. I had one week where I once ran eight races in six days."

It was a tight title fight all summer long, but come autumn things got a little bit sideways for both men. In September, Evans ran out of gas in the last five laps of a Martinsville 150, dropping from second to eighth while Cook—grinding, grinding, grinding—finished fourth. That same night, over at Callaway for another 150, things got even zanier. Evans was running second to Paul Radford on lap 101, when the lapped car of Buddy Picard lost an engine in turn one. Phil Smith, writing in *Speedway Scene*, described what happened next: "Radford got into the oil and spun into the wall, suffering front-end damage. While trying to avoid the mess, Richie Evans rode over somebody's wheel and traveled an estimated 50 feet in mid-air. Evans came down with a thud, driving his right-front frame rail back about eight inches ... Evans kept going, losing only one spot [to] eventual winner John Bryant, who was running third before the accident ... Once the race restarted it was Bryant all the way, followed by Evans."

They say it's better to be lucky than good. Evans, bent chassis and all, was both on this Saturday night. But so was Cook, who finished third despite having a water-pump pulley break on the last lap. Another few laps, and he'd have burned up the engine.

Then Evans loaded up and gunned his hauler northward toward Islip, and a 50-lap special event the next day. Cook, in a very atypical move, skipped that NASCAR show in favor of the Schaefer 100 on the dirt mile at Syracuse, canceling his official entry in a Saturday afternoon phone call to Islip's Dick Corbeil. It was a roll of the dice for Cook, but an understandable one because he was a very accomplished dirt racer; he was the 1968 track champion at Fonda, where he won seven career features. Wilbur Jones says, "Most people probably don't know how great a driver Jerry was on the dirt. In fact, I think he was even better on dirt than he was on asphalt." But on this particular Sunday, Cookie rolled snake-eyes and missed the qualifying cut at Syracuse, while Evans started 20th at Islip and carved his way through the field to finish third behind Long Island aces George Wagner and Jim Hendrickson.

Heading into the early-October Race of Champions, Evans led Cook by 627 points. But this was a national championship modified event with a giant purse, so while the points gap *looked* huge, it wouldn't mean a thing if Evans stumbled at Trenton.

Which is exactly what ended up happening.

What most modified folks remember about the 1974 Race of Champions is its incredible finish, Fred DeSarro nosing out his friend Bugsy Stevens by a matter of inches. But the event's big subplot began to take shape at the halfway point, when Evans coasted dead-stick into the pits while Cook soldiered on to an eventual eighth-place finish.

In the final ROC boxscore, the "reason out" column beside car #61 listed "blown engine." But there was more to it than that.

Wilbur Jones administers a bit of homespun first aid on pit road at Trenton. *(courtesy of Speedway Scene)*

"The thing that had helped us win that race in '73 ended up costing us in '74," remembers Buster Maurer. "Our brake-bleeder tank broke. We had taken everything apart on that car before Trenton, except for that tank, because we had only used it once. Well, sitting in the store room for that whole year, the [residual] oil had dry-rotted and softened that rubber bladder. In the race, as the bladder worked back and forth it developed a crack, and the air and the oil mixed together. So, obviously, whenever Rich went through the dogleg, he didn't have oil pressure."

Before long, he didn't have an engine, either.

When they left Trenton that evening, Cook led Evans by 170 points. Do the math: the Race of Champions marked an incredible *797-point* swing in the chase for the 1974 modified crown. *Speedway Scene*, noting that one year earlier Evans had sewn up the title in the very same event,

A bad day all around: Evans (here leading Kenny Bouchard's #35 and Dick Caso's #55) lost the 1974 point lead by blowing an engine at Trenton. *(Ray Masser photo/courtesy of Speedway Illustrated)*

ran a photo of a disconsolate Gene DeWitt and a caption telling the whole story in six words: "Trenton giveth, and Trenton taketh away."

Mathematically, Evans was still in the hunt. Psychologically, he was wounded. He later told writer Andy Fusco, "I knew I couldn't win. I felt the hurt after Trenton. I was already prepared mentally to lose."

When they headed back to Martinsville for the Cardinal 500 season finale—well, the apparent finale, as we shall see—Cook basically needed to just keep Evans in sight; if he finished within eight spots of Evans, the championship was his. Rich Benyo, covering the event, wrote, "It looked like that [points] spread was all that was on the mind of Richie Evans." Indeed, Evans charged throughout the entire 250 laps, swapping the lead all afternoon with Geoff Bodine, Bugs Stevens and Ronnie Bouchard, and ultimately finishing second to Bouchard. But Evans couldn't do a thing about Cook, who finished sixth and ended the day with a 93-point bulge, enough to put the championship in his pocket. Jerry had taken just two wins in 71 NASCAR starts, but his knack for finishing had rewarded him well.

There was a crazy postscript to the 1974 NASCAR modified season in the days following Martinsville. The Cardinal 500 was run on Sunday, October 27; officially, the NASCAR points-collecting season didn't end that year until Sunday, November 3. The week in between was filled with rumors and gossip, speculation and supposition.

First, somebody in the Martinsville pits claimed to have heard Evans asking Vinnie Morabito, promoter of Long Island's Riverhead Raceway, if he was interested in running a NASCAR race on the weekend of November 1-3. That started off a bit of a tempest in the NASCAR modified teapot, because Morabito and Evans were pals and because such a race would likely favor Evans, who was always fast at Riverhead. Interviewed by Andy Fusco, Evans didn't deny that he asked Morabito about a November race. "Sure, I guess I asked Vinnie, 'You going to run another one for me,' or something like that," Richie said. "But I was kidding. Just busting him, you know?"

The rumors flew anyway, first that Riverhead would schedule a double-points show (worth 116 points to the winner) and then that Morabito—egged on, supposedly, by Evans—would book a national championship event (worth, remember, an infinite number of points, depending on the payoff) on November 3, the last day of the season.

After denials all around, the Riverhead rumor died. But conspiracy theorists quickly replaced it with a wild one claiming that Freeport Speedway's Don Campi had chosen November 3 for the 11th-hour resurrection of his track's Cremosa 100, a double-pointer that had been rained out twice during the summer. The theory was that Campi, a flamboyant type whose family ran the Cremosa Cheese company the event was named for, wanted Freeport to grab all the publicity which would go with his track determining the NASCAR modified championship. Evans and Gene DeWitt were said to be pressuring Campi to run the event, a charge Evans hotly denied. He told Fusco, "I don't know how these things get started."

And so everybody's cars went up on jackstands back in Rome, and the haulers got a well-deserved break, and there was celebration at the Cook shop and head-shaking in the Evans garage on Calvert Street.

Meanwhile, on November 1-2, in the final hours in which NASCAR-sanctioned tracks were eligible to award modified points, the roar of the engines could still be heard more than 900 miles to the south, at a pair of half-mile dirt tracks. Both the Golden Isles Speedway in Brunswick, Georgia, and the North Florida Raceway in Lake City, Florida, were NASCAR-sanctioned, and among the divisions they ran was a local modified class, a collection of chopped-up, lightweight cars, many of them coupes. Because they had to be categorized as *something* when it came to awarding national points, NASCAR lumped them in with its regular modified troops. And so when a Tallahassee hotshoe named Harvey Jones swept the weekend, winning both the Golden Isles and North Florida features, he collected a total of 100 NASCAR points, six more than Evans needed to unseat Cook as the national champion.

Andy Fusco, who unearthed that dandy little bit of information, wrote this in the aftermath of the Florida doubleheader: "Richie Evans didn't know about it, but then neither did Jerry Cook or Pete Hollebrand or Gene DeWitt." Fusco quoted a "stunned" Evans as saying, "What can I say? I would have gone if I had known."

Still, as Fusco pointed out, that would have been a little too far out. After all, wrote Fusco, "the Associated Press carried stories on the modified action at Martinsville. To my knowledge, for the first time in the history of the division, NASCAR modified news went coast to coast. The first paragraph of the Monday article on October 28 described how Jerry Cook had clinched a national championship in Martinsville, Virginia. How many Associated Press stories do you think would have been written if Cook had lost the title in Lake City, Florida?"

Work Hard, Play Hard II

"YOU KNOW WHAT I REMEMBER?" Wilbur Jones says with a sudden laugh. "Back in '73 or '74, when Roger Treichler was sponsored by Genesee, Richie tried to buy a tractor-trailer load of beer from them. He was going to keep it in the garage, and then take some to the races as we needed it. But they wouldn't sell it to him. I guess they couldn't sell that much beer to somebody who wasn't a distributor."

Across the 1970s, Evans seemed to do everything he could, although not always intentionally, to solidify his reputation as NASCAR modified racing's ultimate good-time guy. Some of that just came naturally, and maybe some stemmed from the rebellious satisfaction he must have derived from always managing to come out OK no matter how much stuff the world stacked against him.

Think about what Evans's life had been like between, oh, 1968 and '74. He had been dead-ass broke, "running junk," but he brushed himself off and won like never before. He had been bounced out of NASCAR, essentially given a heavy jail sentence for the same misdemeanor racers had gotten away with for years, but he took his lumps, hauled trophies out of every unsanctioned track within driving distance of Rome, and then fought his way back into the organization's good graces and won its championship the first time he ran for it. He had tanked at marriage and been through a divorce, easily one of life's messier dramas, and while it was all going on he was having the best years of his career to that point.

All that can make a free-spirited guy, well, downright rambunctious, and so it went with Richie Evans. If you didn't like the way he sometimes lived his life—and there were those who didn't, among them his old friend Eddie Flemke, who "did not condone that lifestyle whatsoever," according to Ed Flemke Jr.—that was all right with Evans, as long as you didn't expect him to apologize for it.

He was, to spin a current-day term back about 30 years, living large.

Bobby Summers, who oversaw Firestone's modified interests in that tire-maker's heyday as a short-track force, remembers traveling from his Connecticut home and going to Spencer Speedway with Evans. "It was just him and I," Summers says. "We went up there and he won the race, and then we came back to Rome. I was staying at his place; this is when he lived above Coalyard Charlies. I said, 'I'm tired. I think I'll go to bed.'

He said, 'OK. I'm going downstairs.' Well, they had a band down there, and they were so loud that the pots and pans and flower vases and everything else was shaking. I figured, Hell, I might as well go down there and join the party."

And just how long did the party last? "Until daylight," says Summers.

"Around Richie, there was never a dull moment," says Billy Nacewicz. "You never had to think: God, what am I going to do in the next five minutes? Something was always happening."

"Everybody," Pete Zanardi wrote way back in 1973, "has a Richie Evans story."

There were Richie Evans stories about late nights and barrooms ...

"We used to get going pretty good at a place called the Rose Garden, out near Buffalo, after the races at Lancaster," says Wilbur Jones. "They stayed open until four o'clock, which gave us plenty of time. A lot of the racers went there: Maynard, Bobby Hudson, Marvelous Merv Treichler. Richie would let his hair down in there pretty good."

Treichler says, "Things were a lot different back then. People were just a lot more, uh ... *relaxed*. We were more relaxed about certain things."

"Win, lose or draw, we had to go to the Rose Garden," says Buster Maurer. "We had a ritual there: When we won, they'd give us a bottle of Cold Duck. We'd drink it there, then we'd bring the cork home and nail it up over the bathroom at the shop. I remember we had, like, 23 of them lined up over the shithouse door.

"We wouldn't leave the Rose Garden until closing time, and then we'd go have breakfast, and we wouldn't get on the road home until morning. Everybody would be sleeping, and I'd be coming through Syracuse as the sun was coming up. The good thing was, we only had to go to Utica-Rome the next night, so you could go home, catch some sleep, and be back to the shop by noon or so."

Rita Marcello: "My husband had a habit of saying, 'Oh, we might be having some company tonight.' And then he'd show up with Richie, Wilbur Jones, Billy Nacewicz and everybody else from the garage, plus [Long Island modified driver] Teddy Wesnofske and anybody else who happened to be around. All I'd hear was that 'Richie and the gang are coming,' but that could mean *anything*."

There were Richie Evans stories about silly things that happened with street cars ...

"Oh, Christ," says Joe Jones. "Richie, boy, he was a crazy bastard. One time he came up to my garage, and he wanted me to go downtown with him to get something. Well, he drove on the street just the same way he drove on the track. He started right down the Boulevard about 70 miles an hour, in and out of traffic. I said, 'Come on, Rich, this is a little too much here.' He drove *fierce* out on the street. But he was good at it. He was a natural."

Brothers in arms: Evans with Bobby Summers. (B&G Wurthmann photo/courtesy of Speedway Scene)

Ted Puchyr remembers ringing down the curtain at Coalyard Charlies, and getting a lift back to Evans's shop. "We get back to the garage, and Richie does a 180 [degree spin] and backs it into this parking spot! You put a gear shift and a steering wheel in his hand, and he was just unbelievable."

"We were working in the garage one day, Richie and I," says Donny Marcello. "He says, 'Let's go have a little lunch.' We took my car, that 1949 Pontiac. We went and had some pizza and couple of beers. We walk back to my car, and he says, 'I'm driving.' So he drives back, and on Calvert Street you could only park on one side of the street. Well, there's cars everywhere. I mean, there is no place to park, except for one spot that was barely longer than my car. We're going down the street on the opposite side, and Richie—I swear to God, and on my father's grave—he hits the brakes, slides it around, and he puts that car right into that little hole without touching anything. I still cannot believe how he did that! I mean, he spun that car around, got it right between those two parked cars, and put it up next to the curbstone like he had all the room in the world. Like I said, this space is barely longer than my car.

"I said, 'Rich, how the hell I am I going to get *out* of here?' He says, 'Don't worry about a thing. I'll show you.' He goes next door to another shop, and he comes riding out on a forklift. He slides those forks under that 1949 Pontiac Catalina, and he picks it right up! He says, 'See, we can get you out when it's time to go.' Oh, God, we laughed so hard. When he lifted up that car he wrecked the exhaust and the muffler, but it was just so funny, I didn't care."

There were Richie Evans stories about silly things that happened with snowmobiles …

"Richie always had the baddest, meanest, fastest snowmobile made," Puchyr remembers.

Marcello says, "We had a big snowstorm one winter, a really bad one. This was while he was living upstairs from Coalyard Charlies. There I am one night, working in the kitchen, and out the window I see this snowmobile roaring down the street. I mean, *flying*. It's Richie. A minute later, I see a couple police snowmobiles zoom by. Obviously, they're chasing him. Well, he went way past Coalyard Charlies, and somehow he lost them; they couldn't pick up his trail. He parked his snowmobile way back down by the old coal bins that used to be near the canal, and then he ran back home. But he didn't walk in the door, like usual. He snuck around the side of the building, climbed up on a Dumpster, jumped onto the roof, and went into his place through the window.

"The cops had a pretty good idea who they were chasing, so after they lost him they came straight to Coalyard Charlies and knocked on his door. After a while, here comes Richie in his pajamas: 'What do you guys want?' They said, 'Come on, Richie. We know it was you.' He said, 'Hey, I've been home all night long.'

"The cops looked around, and they didn't see any footprints in the

These officers were escorting Evans to his post-race interview at Trenton in 1973. No, seriously. Honest! *(Nelson Ivins photo/Lynn Evans collection)*

snow except their own, because Richie had gone around the side of the building and through the window. So finally they said, 'All right. Goodbye.' And they left."

Different tale, different night, maybe different cops: As Millie Hatch tells it, Evans had two Rome friends named Bill and Sally Page, and they owned a bar. One night, Evans and some pals parked their snowmobiles just outside the bar, hurried in through the front door, and inquired with some urgency about whether or not there was another exit. "Well," said Sally Page, pointing, "you can go out through that door, but there's only a little alley there." So Evans and company made their exit just as the boys in blue, having spotted the snowmobiles they'd been chasing all night, walked into the tavern. While the officers worked their way through the crowd, looking around for the culprits, Evans and company had already jumped back onto their sleds and ridden off into the night. They stashed their rides, Bill Hatch recalls, at a nearby body shop owned by another Evans ally.

In a Spring Sizzler souvenir program, Toodi Gelinas wrote of the time when Evans and his buddies were stopped for riding unregistered snowmobiles; tickets were written, and the sleds confiscated. "The snowmobiles were lodged in a barn by the police," Gelinas wrote, "but it wasn't long before they were scratching their heads. Somehow, someone blew the door off the barn and made off with all the evidence. To this day, Richie just smiles and says, 'I still don't know whatever happened to those machines.'"

There were Richie Evans stories about gags and practical jokes and the kind of stuff you did only on a dare ...

"He loved to pull jokes on people," Rita Marcello says. "One night we were down at the old Holiday Inn in Rome—it's the Quality Inn now—and there were a bunch of us having cocktails in the lounge. Well, Rich gets started with his Loctite tricks. First, he goes out and glues a

Work Hard, Play Hard II

quarter to the front desk, just so we can watch people trying to pick it up. Then he squirts some onto the floor, right next to my feet, and as I move around my sneakers end up stuck to the floor and I fall over backwards. Now he goes walking down the hallway, and he's putting Loctite on the guest-room doors. Well, just as he's doing this, a pizza-delivery guy comes in and knocks on one of the doors he just glued. Naturally, the people inside can't get the door open, and the pizza man is trying to help them. Oh, it was hysterical. It was an entire night of Loctite: Loctite on the bottom of your glass, Loctite between the chair and the floor, Loctite everywhere."

Wilbur Jones says, "You never knew what he was going to pull. If we were staying at a hotel, he'd pull down the covers on your bed, soak the mattress with water, and make the bed up again. You get back to the room late and jump into bed and … *Awwwwww!*"

At Connecticut's Thompson Speedway in 1977, Evans had a lousy result in the big Thompson 300, but that hardly made it a bad weekend, as writer Bruce Cohen noted: "Richie Evans, the fearsome competitor from Rome, New York, lost 13 laps in the 300 with a broken left-front ball joint, but won the first 'Little T 25.' It seems as though Evans and some unnamed associates noticed that there was a covey of golf carts next to the clubhouse. With the ingenuity which carries him to feature wins wherever he runs, Evans discovered that a well-placed quarter made an excellent substitute for an ignition key. Within seconds, 15 golf carts roared off to the adjacent quarter-midget facility [dubbed the 'Little T' in deference to Thompson's 'Big T' nickname]. The race was on, only to be black-flagged by an irate rent-a-cop. While it lasted, it was more fun than the shopping cart races at Langhorne."

The most famous "I dare you" story, no question, is the one about the rented Pinto in Daytona during a mid-'70s Speedweeks. Dick Berggren wrote, "His friend Dick Fowler was riding along with Evans as they drove down the beach. 'Evans,' said Fowler, 'this car is junk. They shouldn't rent cars like this. If you had any balls, you'd drive this thing right into the ocean.

"Evans said, 'Right.' And then he drove the rental car straight into the Atlantic. Incredibly, Evans came up with a story the rental agency believed, and they gave him another car."

Bugs Stevens says, "I wasn't there, but I wish I was. I can picture that crazy bastard revving up that engine and running straight into the waves, laughing all the way. Richie and I had a lot of good times together. We had so much fun. But sometimes I had to stay away from him. I was afraid I'd wind up in jail, and I didn't want any of that shit."

That wasn't exactly foolish thinking on Bugsy's part. On one early-'70s Martinsville weekend, Evans spent the night before the race in the Martinsville lockup after some over-the-top rowdiness at the Dutch Inn. He was sprung only after Martinsville Speedway owner H. Clay Earles posted his bail.

"That time, even Richie realized he had gone too far," Dick O'Brien says, "because Clay Earles was not happy with him. Clay told him, 'I should throw you right out of here, but I'm gonna let you race. But I don't even want you walking through the pits. Stay in that hauler until the race comes, and as soon as it's over I want you to get back in that truck and go home.' I know that embarrassed Richie."

There were Richie Evans stories about … well, you name it.

"Let's face it, a lot of the partying stories got blown out of proportion," says Wilbur Jones. "I mean, here's a guy who worked in the shop until midnight or later almost every night. That doesn't leave a whole lot of time for partying."

Evans himself said as much to Pete Zanardi in 1973.

"Some of the Richie Evans stories get magnified," he declared. "I have a good time. I live a good life. But the way some people talk, I wouldn't have time to race."

Cookie

REMEMBER THAT BEER-CHARGED pre-season barroom spat in 1973, the one between Buster Maurer, pumped-up Evans crew chief, and his pal Bill Payne, a Jerry Cook man?

Payne: "You know, you guys will never win that championship. Nobody wins it the first time."

Maurer: "I'm telling you right now, we're going to win that thing."

That wasn't the only line drawn in the sand that winter over the impending duel between the two drivers from Rome. Dick Waterman, the Utica-Rome Speedway promoter, happened to be tight with Cook. "I was friendly with both of them," Waterman says, "but I was closer to Jerry. Put it this way: When my wife and I had our 25th wedding anniversary, Jerry and his wife were invited to the party. We were that close. Richie and I were *not* that close." And so one night, when Waterman found himself wrapped up in similar tavern talk, he did the admirable thing and stuck with his friend Cook.

It ended up costing him $100, he laughs today, thanks to what he now calls "a foolish bet."

Waterman says, "It was with a local bartender. I said Jerry was going to be the national champion, and he said Richie was."

That's the way it was in 1973. You were either for Cook, or you were for Evans. And nothing much changed for the next, oh, 10 years or so, as they handed the NASCAR modified crown back and forth.

There is no scientific way to know how these things start, or why, on the other hand, some match-ups never heat up; for example, over the course of his career, Evans likely had more head-to-head battles with both Maynard Troyer and George Kent than he had with Cook, but nothing smelled of a blood feud in either of those cases. And in the exact same time frame we're dealing with here, 1972-74, promoters over in New England would have loved to drum up a war between the two guys winning everything, Bugs Stevens and Ron Bouchard. But although it had many of the same elements of Cook vs. Evans—a former national champ versus a rising challenger—there was never a "one or the other" flavor to Stevens vs. Bouchard. They ran first and second on countless nights, particularly at Stafford, but Bugsy and Ronnie remained two very popular drivers who got along quite well and didn't care who knew it.

Meanwhile, Richie Evans and Jerry Cook forged one of the most passionate rivalries in the history of American short-track racing. And, says writer Andy Fusco, "their rivalry was very real, and not some PR fabrication to sell tickets."

Dick Waterman recalls, "It led to a lot of arguments between those of us around here who happened to be involved in racing."

Cook believes that the public perception of the relationship between him and Evans "would have been a whole lot different" had he remained in his native Lockport and never moved east to Rome. Richie, Cook points out, "was born and raised [in that area], and I moved into that town when I got married. Because of that, I think he had more of the 'hometown favorite' thing behind him than I did."

That might have been a tough break for Cook sometimes, but if you're a fan of racing rivalries, you ought to be thanking the heavens it happened just that way.

Viewed through the corrective lens of time, Richard Ernest Evans and Gerald Ronald Cook actually had quite a bit in common. They were fairly close in age—because Cook got to the top sooner, it always seems to surprise people to hear that he was younger than Evans by a couple years—and each of them was by all accounts a brilliant mechanic.

Both ran tight operations, lean and mean. Cook generally traveled with just one or two very solid helpers—over the years, Mike Ray, John Davis, Jerry Bear, George Colwell and Bobby Miller among them—and so did Evans, although Evans generally seemed to have a larger band of volunteers ready at each modified port-of-call.

And both were cunning racers, ready, willing and able to do whatever it took to meet tonight's goals and then hit the road toward tomorrow's. Says Steve Hmiel, who in 1978 put in a tour of duty chasing NASCAR modified points with Cook, "Around Richie and Jerry, you learned an awful lot about surviving. Those two guys knew how to race with next to nothing. They knew about working hard. They knew about driving trucks down the highway late at night."

Yet, in so many other ways, they were miles apart.

You can start with their racing styles. Once Evans truly got rolling in the late 1960s, he was always good for 15, 20, 25 wins a season, and while he quickly developed a reputation as a smart driver, he was still very much a gasser. Buster Maurer on the early-'70s Evans: "If he was leading, he wanted to lap the field. And if he did lap the field, he wanted to have a second lap."

Cook, on the other hand, was methodical, a points-producing machine. In 1974 he won only two features in 71 NASCAR starts, so he didn't necessarily show up in the headlines a lot, but if you scanned the race results you noticed that Cook was always *there*, someplace in the top five or, on an off night, the top 10.

The contrast between their victory totals led to allegations that Cook was a "stroker," a guy whose goal was to stay out of trouble and cruise, more concerned with points than checkered flags. At a glance, sure, that was an easy conclusion to draw. But to fully appreciate Jerry Cook, maybe you had to do more than glance.

Thirty years ago, there was some very real prestige attached to the NASCAR national modified championship. The sanctioning body only had four divisions in those days—Grand National (now Nextel Cup), late model sportsman (now the Busch Series), the modifieds and the old Winston West series—so you can argue that the 1974 modified title gave a racer a bigger pop than the 2004 title. And the money, in relative terms, might have been better, too; in addition to the champion's check for between $5-10,000, there was a $10,000 bonus waiting from Firestone, and 15 or 20 grand was an amazing season-ending payday in early-'70s dollars. Jerry Cook loved the championship trophy and he loved the championship money, and if consistency was his way of bringing it all home, he was unapologetic about it.

"I run the races the way I think is best for me," Cook said in a Martinsville Speedway souvenir program profile in 1974. "I'm in this to make a living and the NASCAR championship is worth enough that it's one of the main things I go after. You have to finish high most of the time to win it. You can't do it by tearing up cars half of the time and maybe winning a fourth of the time. You can go broke doing that."

Those last few sentences were the essence of Cook, a driver who used his steering wheel to put groceries on his family's table. That meant always looking out for the dollar, and if Cook was conservative in comparison to Richie Evans or Bugsy Stevens—and there's no "if" about it, he surely was—well, so what? The guy made conservatism pay off better than anybody this side of Ronald Reagan. Cook estimated his 1974 season earnings at between $40,000 and $50,000, not a bad slice of pie in those days.

His approach was perfect for the longer races, which, not coincidentally, paid the most money and awarded the most points. In 1969, on his way to finishing second to Stevens in the NASCAR national standings, Cook won a 500-lapper at Martinsville, his first win at the Virginia track; he won six more times there between 1970 and 1979, four of them 250-lappers. And there's no telling how many 100- and

150-lap shows the man totaled at places like Spencer Speedway, Albany-Saratoga, Utica-Rome, Shangri-La.

Anytime the modifieds ran an endurance-type race, you had to worry about Cook.

And check this: The guy did finish either first or second in the NASCAR standings *every season* from 1969-1980, which is remarkable. And in 1981, when he finally fell out of the top two, Cookie didn't fall far; he ended up third that year behind Evans and John Blewett Jr.

Nobody lucks his way—or strokes his way—into *that* much success.

In 1974, Cook told writer Rich Benyo, "I may not have been able to set my car up to run as fast as some others, or handle as well, but my record of top finishes is one of the best. You don't run in the top five by stroking, and no one has ever won a championship by stroking."

Dick Waterman says, "Richie and Jerry were two different kinds of drivers. Just telling it like I saw it, Richie's reactions were a hair sharper than Jerry's. You'd see Richie come up on a situation and he'd fly right by it, where it might take Jerry five or six laps. Of course, Jerry might have done it a little bit more cautiously than Richie did, but I think they just had different styles.

"People always talk about this driver or that driver being a stroker. I don't agree with that. I don't think too many drivers are out there stroking; I think they're driving to the best of their ability. But one's ability might just be better, sharper, than another's."

And if they were different men on the speedway, they were even further apart off it. Cook himself says it best: "We lived different lifestyles."

Jerry, the private guy, was closed up, closed off, always a hard man to read. Part of that was just because he was a quieter person to begin with; way back in 1970, writer Les Deuel proclaimed, "As a person, Jerry Cook is sometimes a victim of his own moods. He can be terse, uncommunicative, sullen if things have not gone quite the way he wanted."

Richie, of course, was a party guy long before he made it big, and no amount of victories and championships was going to change that; in fact, his success may have actually emboldened him in that regard. After all, it would have been one thing to criticize his pub-crawling and hell-raising if he was struggling to make the feature on Saturday night, but who was going to tell Richie Evans, with his trophy collection now bulging with hardware, that he needed to change his ways?

In the vernacular of that whole bellbottom era, Cook was Establishment, Evans was Counterculture. Cook was the New York Yankees, Evans was the Oakland A's. Cook was Johnny Unitas, workmanlike and by the book, and Evans was Joe Namath, damning convention. They looked different—Cook often sported a crewcut, Evans had hair that seemed perpetually at war with itself, fleeing in every direction—and they certainly acted different.

"Jerry was a very, very family-oriented man," says Dick Waterman. "After the race, you'd see Jerry with his kids on his shoulders and Sue at his side, and they were going home. Meanwhile, Richie would be with a whole bunch of his cronies, heading out for the night. His evening was just beginning."

Billy Nacewicz says, "Jerry's shop was right there at his house, so when he stopped working on the car at night all he had to do was walk a few feet and he'd be home. You didn't see him out much, because he really had no *need* to go out. In Rich's case, his shop was downtown, and at various times in his career he was, um, between family situations, and that freed up his time somewhat. So he'd get out of work and go out and have a couple cocktails."

Cook had it right: They just lived different lifestyles.

Waterman again: "Everybody has heard the stories about Richie and his guys and their escapades. Well, I just can't *imagine* Jerry Cook ever trashing a motel room, or driving wild on the highway, or anything like that."

The contrasts between them were so sharp that you almost had to choose a side. You rooted feverishly for one to out-drive the other, out-last the other, out-smart the other. Every little battle seemed so ... *important*.

You even wanted one to out-connive the other.

At the height of their points-chasing years, Evans and Cook were both deeply into the kind of fakes and sly double-crosses that made championship battles so much fun to watch in the days when every race counted. Richie might publicly announce that he was going to Islip, but head instead to Stafford; Cook might talk about skipping a long haul to, say, Winston-Salem, but come Saturday morning he'd be halfway there. It quickly got to the point, says Andy Fusco, where "each man greatly distrusted the other." Before long they were literally spying on each other, posting crewmen around Rome and even on the highways leading out of the city, the lookouts trying to decode every move made by an orange Evans truck or a red Cook hauler on a race day.

Fusco recalls things getting really crazy when New Jersey's New Egypt Speedway went to a Wednesday-night NASCAR program, threatening to derail a Canadian gravy train that had been kind to Evans and Cook over the years. Ever since their coupe days, the two men could count on the Capital City Speedway outside Ottawa to put a few dollars in their pockets; Fusco remembers it as a "lucrative" arrangement, because "both guys were getting decent money [from the Ottawa promoter] just to show up, and inevitably they'd run one-two in the feature." Ottawa, nearly 200 miles from Rome, wasn't an easy haul, but it was a picnic next to the run down to New Egypt, a six-hour tow which involved skirting the heavy traffic in the New York City metro area and northern New Jersey.

"Neither really wanted to go to New Egypt," says Fusco, "but if one went there for the points, the other was forced to follow. So now they faced a dilemma: tow to New Jersey for a shit purse and NASCAR points,

A rivalry for the modified ages: Richie Evans and Jerry Cook at Stafford, 1974. *(Eugene Frankio photo/courtesy of* Speedway Scene*)*

or continue to milk the Capital City cash cow? Evans and Cook held a summit. They agreed they would stay at Capital City and that neither would go to New Egypt."

The agreement lasted, oh, about as long as you'd expect it to.

"On the first Wednesday of the truce," Fusco remembers, "Cook planted a spy along Route 26, the road north from Rome toward Canada. As soon as the spy saw Richie's hauler go by, he was to call Cookie's garage, so Jerry would know it was safe to head to Capital City himself. The informant did his job, and Cook headed for Ottawa. But as he drove north, Jerry spotted Richie's rig parked at a roadside restaurant. He smelled a rat. Jerry noticed that the modified on board was Richie's backup car, and did a 180.

"Cookie made it to New Egypt in time for the first heat race. Evans, of course, had already been there for hours."

Laughing, Billy Nacewicz says, "Richie and Cookie both pulled that stuff. They'd have a car at one track, and they'd be at another track with a different car."

Such stories would make the rounds in pit areas and modified garages throughout the Northeast, and it was impossible not to get wrapped up in it. Even if you were a Ronnie Bouchard fan from Worcester or a Roger Treichler fan from the suburbs of Buffalo, it was always fun to hear that Cookie had pulled a fast one on Richie, or vice versa. And the rivalry deepened.

Did it ever get personal? Hell, yes. Fusco brings up a time in the mid-'70s when he and his wife Andrea were strolling through the pits at Albany-Saratoga, and Evans gave her a #61 T-shirt. "Andrea promptly put it on, and paraded around the pits," Fusco says. "Cookie was pretty cold to me for a couple of weeks, and I asked Pete Hollebrand Jr. what was bugging the guy. Pete said, 'Jerry's still pissed off that Andrea was wearing that Richie Evans T-shirt at Malta.' Go figure."

Still, for the most part, the principles remained civil.

"There was never really animosity between the two teams," Billy

Nacewicz says. "It was a friendly rivalry, I'd say. The guys who worked on the two cars got along real well; it was kinda like the way guys from different teams get along on the Cup or Busch circuits today. Jerry's guys used to stop by our shop, or maybe we'd bump into each other somewhere after work and socialize a little bit. There was a good rapport there. In fact, some of Jerry's guys—George Colwell, Jerry Bear—ended up coming to work for Rich as the years went by."

Wilbur Jones says, "We didn't go out of our way to go see Jerry, and he didn't go out of his way to come and see us. But every once in a while, Cookie would stop in at the Rusty Nail and have a beer with Richie, and the two of them would shoot the shit. Sure, on the track there could be some animosity sometimes, but off the track there were no problems."

"The world made a lot bigger deal out of that rivalry than they did," Steve Hmiel says. "Richie was cool about it. Cook was cool about it."

Cook backs that up. "We got along pretty good together," Jerry says. "Of course, at different times that was *strained* somewhat, depending on what happened. But there were times when one of us needed something, and we [knew we] could always go to each other for it. We basically had our own parts supplies stocked on shelves, because we couldn't sit there and call somebody and wait for what we needed. He could drive outside of town to my place, or I could drive downtown to his place."

In 1981, Evans told Dick Berggren, "We're only 10 minutes apart here, so we see each other. We've had our problems before, but we do OK now."

It sounds almost fraternal; Cook and Evans could drive each other nuts, sure, but come any kind of crisis one could always count on the other. Wilbur Jones remembers that back in '73, when Evans had lost Pocono's Coke 250 to Bugsy Stevens in a controversial scoring flap, "Richie's first phone call on Monday morning was to Jerry, and Jerry sent his wife Sue [an expert scorer] down to the garage. Sue and Richie spent I don't know how many hours in the office going over the scoring sheets."

Billy Nacewicz says, "As far as Rich and Jerry went, they might not have been close, but they definitely got along. I think there was a mutual respect there. I know that Rich understood how hard Jerry worked, and Rich was a guy who *appreciated* anybody who worked like that."

So much alike, so many miles apart.

Dick Waterman is of the opinion that it wasn't racing that divided the two men, but Mother Nature, meaning their personalities. He thinks that even if the pair had worked in the same department at some factory in the city—say, Revere or Rome Cable—"they would never have been very close, in my estimation. There was absolutely no way they would have ever palled around together, because they had entirely different lifestyles."

Between them, Jerry Cook and Richie Evans won every NASCAR national modified championship from 1971-85. *(courtesy of Speedway Scene)*

Wilbur Jones puts it in the simplest possible terms. He points to a floor lamp and a wall lamp and says, "Those two things are both lamps, but they're different. Richie and Jerry were both race drivers from Rome, but *they* were different."

And if they couldn't be great friends, fate seemed to say, why not make them great foes?

"It was tough competition," says Jerry Cook, "but it was fun."

"The Capital of Modified Racing"

"I'LL TELL YOU WHAT," Dick Waterman says. "Looking back on that whole period, the 1970s, it sure was a fun time to follow modified racing if you happened to be from Rome, New York."

But even some of those who were there admit that they sort of missed it at the time.

"Sometimes when you're in the middle of something, you don't realize how special it is," says Billy Nacewicz. "I grew up in Rome. Rich had spent most of his life there. Jerry had moved there from Lockport, but he was definitely part of that Rome scene. Then you had the Kotary family; the Kotary brothers had won a lot of races at Utica-Rome and some other tracks, and Cliff Kotary had won the State Fair race at Syracuse six years in a row, so those guys were all very famous right around that area. And Bill Wimble had moved to Rome later on in his career. So it was definitely a town that had a racing *feel*.

"But when you grow up around all that stuff, you just think it's a normal thing. I mean, when I look back on it now, I think of all the races that were won by guys in that town, and all the championships Richie and Jerry won, and it's incredible. It makes me think back to when guys like Bugsy and Ernie Gahan and Don MacTavish and Pete Hamilton were winning NASCAR national championships; I used to picture them living in these little towns in New England, and I'd wonder what those towns were like. And I'm sure that while we were winning all those championships, people were thinking that same way about Rome, like it was the capital of modified racing."

Of course, you forget that even while all that is going on, sometimes a hometown is just a hometown. Rome is essentially a small city that feels more like a large town. It was special to the modified world 30 years ago because of all the magic Evans and Cook were making, but to those guys it was simply home.

"Richie and I were having a beer together one night," says Dick

Waterman, "and he told me how much he enjoyed going out in Rome, because everybody knew him and he could just be himself."

Cute little hometown sidebar: Jill Evans, third daughter of Richie and his first wife, Barbara, happened to be the same age as David Cook, son of Jerry and Sue; the two shared several classes together as schoolmates.

"It was like we had our own little rivalry," Jill smiles. "He was always telling me that his dad was going to win the race, and I'd be like, 'Get out of here! *My* dad is going to win!' We ended up being friends, but it was funny."

Billy

SMACK IN THE MIDDLE OF THE 1970s, with his ambition to race as often as possible burning a hole in him, Richie Evans was fighting one major obstacle: the man-hours required to meet the grinding schedule he had set for himself. Buster Maurer had been gone, on a full-time basis, anyway, since the end of 1973, and Evans was relying mostly on part-time volunteers. Now, voluntary help is what makes the short-track racing world turn, but anyone who has spent any time at all in the sport will tell you that an all-volunteer crew is hell on a full-time racer. There are nights when there's more than enough help, and nights when you're on your own.

That was when Billy Nacewicz showed up. Born in 1949, he had been on the fringe of the Evans team since the gas station days, and by 1973 and '74 he was hanging around more and even traveling some to watch Evans race. He had been groomed for a racing life. "My brother was seven years older than I was," Nacewicz says. "He had gone to Utica-Rome Speedway when it first opened up back in 1961, and he came home all excited. He said, 'There's this guy named Rene Charland, and you have got to go see this guy race.' So I went to Utica-Rome, and Rene was there. In fact, I believe he won the feature that first time I saw him. Anyway, I became an instant fan of Rene's. And for many years—right to this day, really—I hold a lot of very fond memories of Rene and all his antics. For a fan, he was good for the sport, and so much fun to watch."

So young Billy Nacewicz watched Charland every chance he could at Utica-Rome, and then began to follow his hero's travels in the racing papers he bought at the track. "I really paid attention to the Eastern Bandits, Rene and Eddie Flemke and Denny Zimmerman and those guys."

A "hippie-ish" Billy Nacewicz (right) in a mid '70s shot from the Calvert Street garage. *(Lynn Evans collection)*

In the next dozen or so years he got more immersed in the sport, and while attending an automotive technical college he dabbled in pit crew work with Dick Clark, a New York driver who was a threat to win on both dirt and asphalt in the 1960s and later became a blacktop specialist. Back in Rome, his brother was chumming around with Richie Evans a bit, giving Billy Nacewicz a racing connection in his home town. By 1974 he was, he says, a "hippie-ish type" kid with a job working construction. That winter, as is customary with so many construction laborers, he found himself laid off just when Evans found himself looking for a full-time crewman.

Nacewicz hired on for the '75 season, and the fun started immediately. "For me," he remembers, "it was all very exciting. I was in my early 20s, and I was going to all these places: Trenton, Martinsville, New England. We raced at Daytona. We raced at a lot of tracks in the South."

They ended up being together for 11 seasons and eight consecutive NASCAR national modified championships and literally hundreds of victories.

Always, they made an interesting pair, because when he had his race face on, Billy Nacewicz was as buttoned-up and taciturn as Richie Evans was outgoing; "moody" was a word you heard a lot when people talked about him. That presented an interesting paradox: At most tracks, people tended to congregate in the Evans pit because it was generally a fun place to hang around, but Nacewicz, by his own admission, was not always a welcome-wagon kind of guy.

"I'm sure there were probably times when people might have gotten mad because they thought I was ignoring them," he says. "But, you know, sometimes you've just got to get your work done."

Even Evans could feel the chill when Billy Nacewicz went into his all-business mode. Friend and rival car owner Mario Fiore says, "They used to argue a lot, him and Billy. But Richie knew better than to argue with Billy too much. Eventually, Richie would always give in."

But over time their bond deepened, and to watch the two of them communicate—whether through hand gestures in a noisy pit area or in a quiet corner of some tavern after another feature win—was to understand how truly close they were. These were two men who didn't waste a lot of words; Evans knew Nacewicz, and Nacewicz knew Evans, and there were a thousand times when a nod or a grunt or a half-completed sentence was all either one needed to get his message across.

"It never really got to where we had a boss-employee type of relationship," Nacewicz says. "Rich had the final say on anything that was really important, and if I ever had a question about something big I'd clear it with him. And it should be like that, because it was his ass in that seat. But it never really felt like he was the boss and I was the worker. We were basically just two guys working on this race car, and one of them was the driver."

In the late 1970s, writer Toodi Gelinas did a story on Nacewicz for the Stafford Speedway souvenir program. She quoted Evans as saying, "Billy's a super mechanic, and much of my success is due to his talent." It was short praise, but sweet. Some years later, upon Richie's death, Gelinas went much deeper in a poignant column she wrote for *Speedway Scene*.

"When I talked to Richie about Billy," Gelinas wrote, "he got very serious. 'I'd be nothing without Billy,' Richie said. 'He keeps everything together for me and he's always there at my side. He's more than my mechanic, he's a best friend ... Of course, I don't want you to print all that, because I can't have my main man getting a big head ... Just put down that he is the best, and one day you can tell him what I really said about him.'"

Change of Focus

OFTEN, THE PERIOD BETWEEN 1975-77 gets overlooked in reviews of Richie Evans's career. That's understandable, falling as it did between his titanic NASCAR title fights against Jerry Cook in 1973 and '74 and his remarkable string of eight straight championships from 1978-85. But the information gap is mostly due to the fact that Evans spent an awful lot of time in that period running outside NASCAR, and the Daytona Beach sanctioning body and its member tracks have always been better at keeping records than most independent speedways.

Still, it's a bit of a crime to think of 1975, 1976 and 1977 as Richie's lost years, because he sure wasn't losing much.

What led Evans in 1975 to begin backing away from the business of chasing Jerry Cook up and down the East Coast was something he apparently kept to himself. He seemed to be hot on the NASCAR trail early in the season—and in fact finished an arm's-length second to Cook in the final standings—but it was clear by late summer that he had lost interest in pursuing the title. He even skipped several extra-points events, including the September 150 at Martinsville. Here and there over the years, there has been speculation that Evans was upset with NASCAR about one thing or another, but nothing stands out in the minds of those around him at the time.

"I don't know exactly *why* Richie stopped chasing points," says Wilbur Jones. Like everyone else in the Calvert Street camp, Jones did not ask a lot of questions. They raced when and where Evans wanted to race, and that was fine with them.

Was it economics? Had Richie crunched the numbers and decided that, dollars-in vs. dollars-out, the points thing wasn't making sense? Or was it maybe a lifestyle matter; with his personal affairs in a constant state of disarray, had he perhaps decided to control the one thing he *could* control, his own racing schedule?

One thing is certain to everybody who knew Evans: It wasn't a burnout thing, a case of all that travel in '73 and '74 taking its toll. Billy Nacewicz says, "The extra travel [of chasing points] wasn't an issue. I don't think traveling was ever a big issue for Richie, especially once he'd established himself as a guy who could be competitive with the other top drivers who showed up at *his* tracks, like Albany-Saratoga and Utica-Rome. If you could beat the top drivers—say, Bugsy Stevens and Freddy DeSarro, who had been national champions—you knew you could go and race anywhere. Let's face it, winning builds confidence, and he had that early on, even in the coupe days.

"I mean, if he had won just two or three races at Utica-Rome, and that was the only place he'd ever won, maybe he'd have thought, 'Geez, I don't know if I can run against the best guys anywhere else.' There were guys from Utica-Rome who didn't even like to go to *Albany-Saratoga*, because there were a lot of New England cars there. But Richie had become a guy who could win 20 races a year, and who was competitive wherever he went. He was already at the point where nothing intimidated him. He wasn't afraid to go down South and race against Ray Hendrick, he wasn't afraid to go to New England, he wasn't afraid to go wherever you had to go to chase points.

"Besides," adds Nacewicz, "we ran as many races in those years when we didn't chase points as we ever had. I think Richie just went through a period when he decided to run closer to home when he could."

The best on-the-record, horse's-mouth explanation about the whole thing—while admittedly vague—may be one Evans gave *Area Auto Racing News* writer Pat Singer: "We decided … to stop chasing NASCAR points and to just settle down and race where we could win and have some fun."

And he did have fun, some of it unexpected. Evans opened and closed the '75 Stafford season by winning the Spring Sizzler in April—run that year under a controversial 13-inch tire rule—and the Gobbler 150, a one-shot event on Thanksgiving weekend where part of the winner's haul was a pair of live turkeys. (At Evans's request, Bill and Millie Hatch brought them back to Rome, Richie's sister Sandy remembers. And what became of the birds? "Well, they were *good*," Sandy's son Bob laughs.)

Those Stafford successes thrilled Evans—"That first big win there, he was so excited that he jumped out of that car and kissed me," Fred Ulrich recalled—because the flat Connecticut half-miler had been a thorn in his side prior to '75. Its layout, distinguished by a deceptively sharp first corner, tripped up a lot of outsiders, including Geoff Bodine, who prior to moving to New England and becoming a Stafford regular

In 1975, Stafford's small-tire rule added up to big bucks for Spring Sizzler winner Richie Evans. (courtesy of Speedway Scene)

(and 1975 champion!) had never struck gold there. Evans once described the place to radio interviewer Arnold Dean as "a fast track [where] you can get in a lot of trouble," and trouble was what it usually gave him.

"When Richie first came to Stafford, he went quite a long time without doing anything," remembers Ronnie Bouchard, the Boy Wonder of Stafford's early '70s heyday.

Bugs Stevens, who won more NASCAR modified races there than anyone, recalls an exasperated Evans telling him, "There's something you're doing in that first turn. I'm gonna follow you around."

Billy Nacewicz says, "In the early '70s, Stafford had been a frustrating place for Richie. He hadn't figured that place out, and we struggled there. It wasn't our favorite place to run, that's for sure. But once Rich won the Sizzler and that Turkey race, he was OK there."

Better than OK, according to Stevens, who says Evans became "a hard sucker to beat there."

And he remained a hard sucker to beat everywhere else, shining in both NASCAR events and open-competition shows at tracks like Albany-Saratoga, which pulled in great fields for its short-lived Friday-night small-block programs. Evans and his one-time mentor Sonney Seamon dueled for a pair of track championships in New York, Sonney nipping his younger friend at Fulton and Richie turning the tables at Shangri-La.

Rhode Island writer and historian Phil Smith's notes from 1975 included this: "Richie had a busy Labor Day weekend. Saturday, 8/30, Shangri-La ran twin features. First one was Richie, Troyer, Sonny Seamon. Second one was Troyer, Seamon, Richie. Sunday, 8/31, Richie blew up at Pocono; Bodine won it, Satch Worley second and Ray Hendrick in a Bodine/Armstrong team car third. Richie [hauled] to Fulton where he took the win over Seamon and Cook. Monday, 9/1,

A mustachioed Mike Joy interviews Evans after his Gobbler 150 win at Stafford in 1975. In the cage: Thanksgiving dinner! (Burt Gould photo/courtesy of Speedway Scene)

Change of Focus **107**

Bugs Stevens whistles around Evans in 1974 at Stafford, a place Richie had a hard time figuring out. *(Eugene Frankio photo/courtesy of Speedway Scene)*

Troyer won the Stafford 200 followed by Richie, Bugsy, Cook and Fred DeSarro."

His autumn was marked by a couple of close-but-no-cigar finishes at places where he had earlier tasted success. Evans ran fifth (behind heavyweights Ray Hendrick, Merv Treichler, Bugs Stevens and Charlie Jarzombek) in the Race of Champions at Trenton, and fourth (to Geoff Bodine, Stevens and Satch Worley) in the Cardinal 500 at Martinsville.

Over the winter of 1975-76, there was some big short-track news out of his home state. Five New York tracks—Lancaster, Spencer, Fulton, Shangri-La and Chemung—had banded together to form an organization called NEARA, the Northeast Auto Racing Association. The idea was to cultivate a spirit of cooperation among the member tracks and grow modified racing in the area. Lancaster boss Jim Vollertsen was named NEARA president, with Fulton's Millard "Bub" Benway as vice-president and longtime area official Fran Gitchell serving as executive director. The club announced a $30,000 point fund for the '76 season, and signed on several popular drivers, among them Maynard Troyer and Richie Evans. In those days, Troyer and Evans were ticket-money in the bank for a New York promoter, so NEARA held more than a small amount of promise.

Evans wasn't in agreement with *everything* the NEARA brass outlined; its one-tire rule and its gear rule, for example, weren't things he was wild about. But he liked the idea that the tracks planned to work together on the scheduling of their biggest races, and it gave him the non-NASCAR alternative he seemed to be looking for.

"He'd had his little tiff with NASCAR, whatever it was about," says Nacewicz. "Now he was going to prove his point, which was that he could go out and win races anywhere, with NASCAR or without NASCAR. Richie was kinda stubborn that way."

His regular 1976 stops were Spencer on Friday nights, Shangri-La on Saturday nights, Fulton on Sundays. It's a sad fact that today, some 30 years later, these three tracks are unfamiliar places to an awful lot of modified racers, but in the mid-1970s they were New York hot spots visited at one time or another by every big name in the division.

George Kent, then just a pup coming into his own, calls Spencer Speedway "a small Martinsville, just two straightaways and tight, hairpin turns. And it's awful flat. You need a fair amount of brake there, and a lot of horsepower." Fulton, Kent says, "was really nice. It was a third-mile, or a 3/8ths, or whatever they called it, but it was banked pretty good and it was real wide." As for Shangri-La—where he is now the all-time winner, with 99 victories by the close of 2004—Kent describes the place as "a flat half-mile with a *lot* of corner. You're turning all the time, because they're long, sweeping corners. There ain't much of a straightaway there. It's a tough place, tougher than it looks and tougher than a lot of people think it is."

Lacking a single major championship to chase for the first time in three years—the overall NEARA title was unlikely, since he planned on skipping out of the area for the biggest NASCAR events or open shows—Evans set himself another goal: 30 feature wins for the 1976 season. Pat Singer quoted him later as saying, "I told the crew early in the season that when we won our 30th race of the year, we'd take off and have a big party."

Billy Nacewicz thought his boss's plan was a bit optimistic. A number of modified drivers in that period enjoyed seasons in which they'd won 25 races, or 28, but 30 seemed to be a fairly high hurdle. In hindsight, there were just so many good drivers around at the weekly level—New York had names like Troyer, Kent, Seamon and Treichler, New England had Bouchard, Bodine, Flemke and Stevens—that the victories tended to be divided up. Nacewicz says, "Bodine won 50 not long after that [in 1978], and so did we [in '79], but for some reason 30 just seemed to be a major number right then."

Evans started well enough, racking up a February win in New Smyrna's first annual modified meet, then a five-night series, and following that up with March scores in a NASCAR national championship show at Hickory and a very early, and very chilly, Fulton Speedway opener. Then he began to rack up victories at his three weekly tracks and a May 40-lapper at Lancaster.

On Memorial Day weekend he took two cars to Stafford for the twice-postponed Spring Sizzler. The plan, one Evans used often over the years, was to keep his brand-new car on the trailer as a backup, trusting only a tried-and-true piece for a race as important as the Sizzler. But when his faithful Pinto couldn't quite keep pace with the best cars there —he told writer Herb Dodge that it "just wouldn't go no faster"—he had Nacewicz and company back the new one off the truck. With it, Evans won his qualifying heat and led all 80 laps of the main event, beating the gleaming red Dick Armstrong tandem of Geoff Bodine and Ray Hendrick. It was Richie's second consecutive Sizzler victory.

Change of Focus

In 1976, Evans won the Spring Sizzler ahead of Armstrong teammates Geoff Bodine (right) and Ray Hendrick. (courtesy of Speedway Scene)

And the wins just kept piling up: two this weekend, three the next, and a handful of midweek specials across the Canadian border, at Capital City. The Ottawa track was still attractive to New York racers like Evans, Cook and even rising dirt modified star Bob McCreadie because it was often the only place running on Wednesdays.

"The only bad thing about Capital City was that the mosquitoes were *large*, about the size of your fist," Nacewicz laughs. "But it was a crazy, crazy place. Those Canadian fans really enjoyed their racing. They treated it like it was one big party. Hell, they used to let the fans sit right there on the wall in turn one. In fact, one night when we were there, a fan fell right onto the track and they had to red-flag the race to get him off. I guess he'd had a few too many cocktails."

And it was in that wild-and-woolly environment that Evans picked up his 30th victory of that 1976 campaign. That presented a dilemma. All year long he had pumped up his troops about the "big party" they'd have when they reached that milestone, and even an average bash for the #61 group tended to be a hardcore affair. Nacewicz says, "We had always joked that this party would be so good, we'd have to take the rest of the season off." But on the next night, a Thursday, New Egypt was having a Race of Champions qualifier.

Clearly, if the beer started flowing hard in Ottawa, it was going to be tough to revive everyone for the New Egypt event. What to do?

"I gave the crew their choice," Evans later told Pat Singer. "Have the party, or go racing?"

The smart money was on the party. They had just reached a major goal, after all, and there was no great incentive waiting for them at New Egypt. The purse wasn't big enough to make it a must-do race, and Evans had already won two ROC qualifiers, at Shangri-La and Spencer, so it's not like he needed the guaranteed Trenton spot. On top of all that, the driving time alone—Ottawa back to Rome, Rome to New Egypt—would have added up to about nine hours.

"We discussed it a little bit, but not for long," says Nacewicz. "We all said, 'Hell, we can't quit now. We've got to keep going. We'll party after we win the next one.'"

So they headed home, and after a quick turnaround blasted out for New Egypt. Where, of course, Evans promptly upped his victory tally to 31. Partying after that win wasn't much of an option, because they had to run Spencer on Friday, so …

"For the next month or so," grins Nacewicz, "we kept telling ourselves we'd save the big party until after the *next* win. But it always seemed like when we won, we either had too much traveling to do or too much work. Eventually, we decided we'd just do it at the end of the year."

Just as well, because by then they had more to celebrate, including a huge month of September marked by three major triumphs. At Stafford, Evans, sporting a supermod wing he'd borrowed from Nolan Swift, grabbed a "run whatcha brung" show called "Modified Madness." At Islip, he captured the All Star 300 (his first of six straight wins in that prestigious event). And at Lancaster, some 6200 fans saw Richie's normally-orange Pinto—carrying "lots of red oxide primer and shoe polish numbers from collision work necessitated by a wreck at Spencer," wrote John Bisci—dominate the Genesee 200, lapping everyone but second-place man George Kent.

Evans won 39 times in 1976, and very nearly ended the year with number 40. In the modified half of Martinsville's Cardinal 500, Evans was the only man able to pass eventual winner Geoff Bodine, but ended up dropping a cylinder; he finished the day third, behind a one-two Armstrong sweep of Bodine and Ray Hendrick.

And then?

"As soon as the season ended, we stood on the gas," Nacewicz recalls. "Oh, man, did we party that winter!"

Evans had an extra reason to celebrate as 1976 rolled into '77: the Utica-Rome Speedway, which had recently fallen on hard times—running just one modified race in 1975 and never opening in '76—was revived by a pair of young would-be promoters named Mike Talerico and Steve LoPiccolo. The duo leased the facility from Dick Waterman and promptly signed on with NEARA, giving Evans a convenient Sunday evening track.

It was also in 1977 that Evans-watchers began to take notice of a relationship which, in time, grew to be one part friendship and one part rivalry. Richie and George Kent had been acquainted since George's early-'70s modified beginnings at Shangri-La. But, says Kent, "it wasn't until about '74 or '75 that I was in a league where I could run with him." In the NEARA years, Kent says, "Richie used to come over and tell me things, little bits of advice. I'd started running good, and I was building my own cars, and I think he and I kinda related that way." In time, you could make the case that Kent—along with Jerry Cook, Maynard Troyer and perhaps Lou Lazzaro—was one of the drivers with whom Evans fought most, but in '77 he was just hitting his winning stride.

"We had so many fierce battles during that NEARA period, Richie and I, especially at Shangri-La," says Kent. "It was dog-eat-dog racing. Whichever one of us got to the front first usually won, so it would be crazy coming up through the pack."

And in those dog-eat-dog races, they developed a mutual admiration which lasted through the rest of Evans's days. "Way back when I was first starting to run good at Shangri-La, they had an Oswego [Bud 200] qualifying race," Kent recalls. "I chased Richie all night, but I finished second. They had me at the start/finish line with him, because he had already won an Oswego qualifier someplace else, so I got the guaranteed spot. Well, they used to give out those nice silver bowls to win those races, and he walked over to me and said, 'Take it.' I kinda hesitated, and he said, 'Don't be a prick. Take it. You deserve it.' And he just shoved it into my hands."

It ended up being another high-flying year for Evans. He won big both with NEARA—including five features at his beloved Utica-Rome—and on the road. In a single week in July he won two NASCAR national championship events, one at Islip (on the 23rd, his birthday) and the other at Holland. And in April he threw a Stafford Speedway performance that folks still talk about whenever the Spring Sizzler rolls around. For much of the 80-lapper, Evans shadowed Maynard Troyer in a riveting two-car fight. Then, under a caution period on lap 67, Evans pitted to change a deflating left-rear tire. In the remaining 13 laps, he sliced his way through the pack to finish third behind Troyer and Bob Polverari.

Clearly, Evans enjoyed the independence his 1976-77 schedule allowed, skipping in and out of NEARA and chasing the big-dollar shows when he felt like it. But there was trouble in paradise.

Across the 1977 season, NEARA showed signs of unraveling. Despite their limited numbers and the obvious benefits of mutual cooperation, the member promoters just could not seem to play well together. On Sunday, May 1, the organization sanctioned an afternoon race at Fulton and a special evening program at the Evans Mills Speedway outside Watertown. The NEARA brass apparently didn't see the 70-mile driving distance between the tracks as an obstacle, and in a best-case scenario it wouldn't have been. But the Fulton program dragged on, and by 7:00 p.m. only two NEARA modifieds had signed into the Evans Mills pit area. "The [evening] program was cancelled," wrote Andy Fusco. "So was NEARA's affiliation with the Evans Mills Speedway."

Then, in July, a squabble over whether the Sunday-night NEARA modified sanction should go to Utica-Rome or Fulton was resolved in favor of the latter track, not entirely surprising given the fact that Fulton was owned by NEARA vice-president Bub Benway. That decision pretty much stuck a knife into the backs of Utica-Rome promoters Talerico and LoPiccolo, infuriating Evans, who appreciated the hard work they had sunk into his local track.

"Here these kids are trying to do something good," he told Fusco, "and NEARA goes and screws them."

But the straw that broke the back of the camel called the Northeast Auto Racing Association dropped on Labor Day weekend. In 1976, Lancaster's Jim Vollertsen had promoted a NEARA-sanctioned event in direct opposition to the rich Budweiser 200 at Oswego; while Oswego still attracted its usual share of big names, the Bud 200 car count was down dramatically. Seeking peace, the Oswego brass invited NEARA to sanction its five modified events in 1977, the whole deal hinging on the organization's other tracks giving the Bud 200 lots of elbow room. Then, for reasons clear only to him, Vollertsen decided, one more time, to directly buck the Oswego show with a Saturday-night Lancaster program. Vollertsen's show flopped, drawing 11 modifieds and a reported 1100 fans, while Oswego pulled in 64 cars and a huge crowd, so there was indeed some justice in the modified world.

But not enough to suit Maynard Troyer, who, according to Fusco, vowed "never to run another NEARA show for the rest of his life."

And certainly not enough for Richie Evans, who told Fusco, "I'm fed up with NEARA, and you can quote me. The organization stinks all the way through."

And maybe, just maybe, he was getting fed up with something else, too. In 1976 and '77, Cook had cruised to the NASCAR championship virtually uncontested. Oh, there was some noise from the Dick Armstrong/Geoff Bodine camp about chasing the title in 1977—in '76 they had dominated New England and won twice at Martinsville—but that threat ebbed when Bodine hit troubles early in the year and Armstrong opted to stick closer to home. Cook won that '77 title by more than 1100 points.

You have to wonder how all that felt to Richie Evans, late at night, when his head hit the pillow.

Shop Talk

BILLY NACEWICZ SAYS, "You know how in some houses, there's furniture nobody ever sits on? Well, there are race shops like that, too. But ours wasn't one of them. Every machine and every square foot of space was used for something. The building wasn't pretty and the equipment wasn't all shiny and brand-new, but it was very *usable*."

The garage at 608 Calvert Street became, over time, a reflection of the man who owned it: basic, uncomplicated, utilitarian. Dick Berggren

Inside the Evans shop at 608 Calvert Street. *(Val LeSieur photo/courtesy of* Speedway Scene*)*

chose another adjective: *spartan*. "There are no fancy new tools," Berggren wrote of the place. "There aren't even any fancy old tools ... there was nothing in Richie Evans's garage that would indicate that this was anything but a hand-to-mouth operation."

Evans read that description, and said to a mutual friend, "I guess Dick didn't like my shop, huh?" More likely, the place just struck Berggren the way it struck so many who stopped there. It was a surprisingly plain-Jane shop, out of which rolled the most successful modifieds any single team ever had.

Inside the overhead door, there was a large open work area straight ahead, complete with a pair of lifts Evans had installed; all those years at the gas station, he said, showed him that a man didn't need to bend over all day to work on his race car. In that main bay was enough room for a couple of modifieds, and even the truck and trailer if necessary. To the right were a small office, the bathroom, a couple of storage rooms and a refrigerator with a "Willie Nelson for President" sticker on its door. Just behind the work bay was a heated room where tires were kept, so they wouldn't harden up on chilly New York nights. Out back, there was a cold-storage area. To the left of the main bay, through an opening in the wall, was a fabrication room complete with a chassis jig.

"Richie did a lot of work on that shop," Nacewicz says. "We added the chassis room off to one side by laying down concrete in a place where there had been a dirt floor. It wasn't fancy like Troyer's, maybe, but it was good enough for us."

It was, really, a logical sort of workplace. What it *wasn't* was the least bit pretentious. In fact, one quick tour around the place was enough to suggest that it was deliberately *un*pretentious: no walls hung with newspaper clippings, no congratulatory banners celebrating this victory or that championship, no glittering trophy room. Berggren reported coming across a plaque "so covered with garage dust that its face [was] almost illegible." Upon closer inspection, he wrote, the plaque read: *Richie Evans, 1980 NASCAR Modified Champion.*

"I was at Richie's shop one day," says Dick O'Brien, "and he and I stepped into his office. He takes off his hat, and tosses it onto his hat rack, but his hat rack is the Bud 200 trophy! Most modified guys would have that thing in their living room, with a spotlight on it. Richie's got it sitting in the corner with hats hanging on it."

Well, plaques and trophies—however grand the accomplishments they represented—weren't going to get the work done. Better to worry about that stuff, Evans figured. And, as anyone who has spent time around a race team knows, that's plenty to worry about.

"Rich was always juggling," Lynn Evans says, "but somehow he kept everything balanced. At that shop, he was his own bookkeeper, he was his own secretary. And, of course, he wanted it that way. Like with the telephone; he answered the phone at the shop a lot. He could have leaned on people, but he wanted to be in control of everything."

That's a pretty accurate description—"in control"—if you listen to the Calvert Street regulars. But all are quick to add that Evans led by example.

"He worked hard," says Donny Marcello. "I mean, he would bust his ass from the time he came in until the time he left."

Wilbur Jones says, "Rich worked until the work was done. Period. I think a lot of people who didn't really know him might see him come into the shop at 9:30 in the morning, and think, 'Well, this guy can't work all that hard.' But, see, he'd be there until after midnight, working on that race car."

"There was no such thing," says Nacewicz, "as set hours."

In a 1979 radio conversation with Arnold Dean, Evans declared, "You've got to work a lot of hours. [The car] will never win a race if you just take it home every week and leave it on the trailer." Besides, he told Dean, "I like to work on the cars. It's a challenge. I enjoy working on the cars as much as driving them."

That, he always insisted, was one of the keys to his success. Evans told writer Ron Hedger, "I can race the car Friday, Saturday and Sunday, and I'm there Monday morning working on it. I can relate back to every lap and what the car did." Even the best mechanics, he continued, "can't relate the same way. They can watch the car and be real clever, but they weren't in there. They didn't feel it in their rear end."

Then there was that business of setting an example. Throughout his career, Evans got by with one or two full-time helpers and a band of volunteers who by day held jobs outside racing, but by night headed over to Calvert Street and pitched in. The best way to keep those guys fired up, Evans understood, was to be very visibly fired up himself.

"There's no man working at my garage an hour that I'm not there

"There's no man working at my garage an hour that I'm not there working with him," Evans said in 1982. (Val LeSieur photo/courtesy of Speedway Scene)

working with him," he said in a 1982 interview with Winston representative Roger Bear. "I think that makes the guys work better. I don't just pop in the garage and say, 'Why the heck didn't you do this or that?' And I think they feel that if I'm that committed, they should be that committed."

And he was smart enough to motivate the troops in other ways, too. Marcello remembers that if the workload on a given night was exceptionally heavy, "Rich might go out and come back with four or five pizzas for the guys." And Nacewicz says, "Richie used to be big on keeping the refrigerator stocked with beer, so anybody who came in and helped for free could have a beer later on."

That last bit of employee relations, Evans once explained to modified owner Ralph Solhem, was a lesson learned the hard way. "I was up at his place once," Solhem recalls, "and when I opened the refrigerator there were, like, a zillion bottles of beer in there. I asked him if he was getting ready for a party, and he told me this story. He said that early in his career he'd always had beer at the shop, but eventually there were some guys who'd just hang around and get half-looped. Finally, he decided he'd just get rid of the beer. Well, some time later, he was all by himself, trying to load up his race car. He said he concluded right there that it was better to have a bunch of guys hanging around, because at some point you might need 'em. He filled the refrigerator back up, and before long the same people got back into the routine of stopping by for a cold one."

On any evening across those years, the lights burned late in the Evans shop, and the revolving workforce—Buster Maurer, Billy Nacewicz, Wilbur Jones, Anthony Evans, Danny Morgan, Kenny Tomasi, Don Marcello, Max Baker, Jim Small, George Colwell, Jerry Bear, Bondo Clark, Tony Pettinelli, Fred Ulrich, Art Newman and more, some paid, some incredibly skilled volunteers—rolled up its collective sleeves and went to work. Everybody had his own job to do. "Richie was very organized that way," said Fred Ulrich.

By the tail end of the 1970s, that consistency had made the shop run very smoothly.

"Richie and I used to lay out a plan," says Nacewicz. "We'd look at what we had to accomplish that week, and we'd say, 'OK, I'll do this and you do this.' And whoever showed up as far as free help, I'd make sure they had something to do."

Tony Pettinelli, just a teenager when he signed on, says, "Richie and Billy really had things under control. They had these lists, and whenever the car got back to the shop on Monday we knew exactly what had to be done.

"We had a system. When the car got back, we'd roll it off the trailer, wash it and put it in the shop. Then we'd wash the truck and trailer and park it out of the way. I was the low man on the totem pole, so I'd clean out the inside of the truck and straighten out the back [compartment]; you know, replace whatever had been taken out as far as parts and stuff like that. Then we'd throw the car on the scales, air up the tires —Richie always wanted it scaled with the tires he'd run last—and weigh it. If it was in the era when you ran a big-block at one track and a small-block at another, we might have to start pulling a motor. Then we'd all start doing whatever our own little jobs were.

"Richie could be a hard boss. If he asked you to do something, he expected you to do it right. If you didn't know how to do it, he expected you to ask. He was very big on that; he used to say, 'If you don't *know*, you *ask*. Don't do it if you're not sure.' And he wasn't bashful in telling you when you did something wrong. At the same time, though, he'd tell you when you did something good. He was an excellent teacher.

"Obviously, there were things that only Richie or Billy handled. Billy did a lot on the fabricating side, like if he needed to make spare parts because Richie's car had gotten banged around. If there wasn't a lot going on, I'd help him by making up some brackets or motor mounts or whatever he needed.

"Bondo was always around, taking care of the bodies and keeping everything looking right, and there were different guys that showed up at night. If we ran out of things to do, Richie kept a little to-do list over by the coffee pot. We'd cross things off as we got 'em done, and add new things as we thought of 'em. Then he and Billy would look it over as the week went along."

When all of the to-do tasks were caught up—a rarity, given the schedule—or when autumn signaled an end to racing, much of the shop's focus shifted to the chassis room, where Nacewicz and ace welder Dick Abbott turned steel tubing into frames and roll cages. "Having the jig there allowed us to build our own cars and repeat anything we liked," Nacewicz explains. "Every year, we liked to build at least one new car for ourselves, and we would also build and sell a few cars every winter.

Riverside Park, 1978: Evans races against one of his first "customer cars," the Fiore 44 of Reggie Ruggiero. (courtesy of Speedway Scene)

Mario Fiore was one of the first people to buy a car from us [in 1976], and he and Reggie Ruggiero won a bunch of races with it. That helped us sell some more cars.

"The way Richie looked at it, in the off-season he had no racing income, so this was a way to pay the heat and the light bill."

In time, there were Evans cars winning races for drivers around the Northeast: Don Howe on Long Island, Marty Radewick, Bruce D'Alessandro and Mike Murphy in New England, Tom Green and Barney Truex in New Jersey, Ruggiero everywhere.

The chassis business helped the Calvert Street balance sheet, and the boss had other angles, too, other deals. Which leads to one of the funniest stories—well, at least funny in hindsight—to come out of the old headquarters.

In the mid-'70s, few short tracks offered racing gas for sale, so many competitors relied on high-octane Sunoco pump gasoline. Others went to great lengths to get their hands on the hot stuff used in the big leagues. Evans, by then a champion whose name had some clout, forged some sort of an arrangement to procure Union 76 racing gas in bulk. He came up with the bright idea of sinking a huge tank in the ground behind his shop, and every so often dispatched one of Gene DeWitt's tanker trucks to a Union Oil depot in Dover, Delaware, to bring him a new load. The tank was, shall we say, not exactly in compliance with Rome's zoning codes, but, hey, what did that matter? Once you've driven rental cars into the ocean or gone bar-hopping around your hometown in a modified coupe, a little something like a building ordinance wasn't likely to intimidate you.

Unless, of course, something went wrong, which it did one spring.

"It had been raining pretty good for a few days," Wilbur Jones remembers. "At about 11 o'clock one night, Richie asked me to go out and 'stick' the tank to measure how much fuel we had left. Well, I'm out there in the dark, and for a minute I thought I was seeing things; I'm looking right at the tank. It's sitting right there in front of me! See, the ground back there was all clay, and the water just filled up that clay hole and popped the tank out of the ground.

"I went back into the garage and said, 'Jesus, Richie, we've got a little problem.' He said, 'What's that?' I said, 'I can't stick the tank.' He asked me why not. I told him, 'Because it's *on top* of the dirt.' He came outside with me, and he just couldn't believe it."

The tank, its neck broken off on its journey out of the earth, was pouring its contents out. The next morning, Mario Fiore, in town from Massachusetts, came driving up. He turned the corner from Arsenal Street onto Calvert, and noticed something out of the ordinary.

"Gasoline was running down the street along the curb," Fiore says. "It was all you could smell. And, let me tell you, Richie was some worried. He was trying to get everything cleaned up, because he knew he might be in big-time trouble. You didn't see him get that way very often, but he was really, really nervous."

Wilbur Jones laughs. "Nervous? Oh, *yeah*. I mean, you have to have permits for things like that. Our story, if somebody had ever discovered we had the tank, was always going to be, 'Well, this place used to be a dry-cleaning shop. It must be one of their old tanks. We don't know nothing.'"

That might have been a hard sell with racing gasoline spilling down the block.

"Luckily, we had that thing fixed the following day," says Jones. "Richie called up a cousin of his, and the cousin came down to help us. We pumped the water out of the hole, poured some concrete, put the tank back in there, strapped 'er down and covered everything up again."

By the way, Fiore just happening by was nothing unusual. People, from out-of-town racers ducking off the Thruway to say hello or locals just checking in, were always dropping around.

"There were times when it was hard to get things done," Billy Nacewicz grins, "because we'd have a lot of people stopping by. All day, all night, somebody would pop in. Especially, like, the retired racers in the area; the Kotary boys would stop in, and they liked to chew the fat and see what we were up to."

Normally, Evans was a genial host.

"Unless something was super-pressing, where we had to get something done right now, he would be very polite when people stopped in," Tony Petinelli says. "He wouldn't ignore anybody; he'd ask 'em what they'd been up to, stuff like that. And if he was busy, he'd still be good about it. He'd basically say, 'Look, I'd love to sit and talk some more, but we've gotta get some work done.' He understood why they came, and he was good with those people."

Wilbur Jones says, "You know what it was? I think it was pride. Richie was very proud of everything he had, including that garage, because there was a time when he didn't have much. And nobody *gave* him anything. What he had, he earned."

The shop wasn't just a place to work, a place for the race cars to sit. The shop was a large part of the man Richie Evans had become.

His friend Corky Stockham, who published the Syracuse-based *National Parts Peddler* tabloid which served as a printed clearinghouse for new and used racing components, once wrote of an occasion when he needed to verify the contents of an advertisement Evans had placed. The problem was, it was a holiday. Stockham called the Calvert Street shop anyway, thinking he might get lucky and catch someone. The phone seemed to ring for five minutes, Stockham reported. When Richie himself finally answered—he was there, he said, rebuilding a transmission—Stockham, also working alone, suggested that they shared a similar problem: No help on the holidays.

"Don't blame them," Evans replied. "We are just greedier."

Stockham reflected, "He wasn't talking monetarily … He meant that to be successful at what you do, to be number one, you must be willing to pay the price."

R-E-S-P-E-C-T

IT WAS ALWAYS A TOUCHING SCENE: Richie Evans standing in the pits at Oswego or maybe Spencer Speedway, a warm smile spreading across his face as he looked up to see Dutch Hoag approaching. Hoag's son Dean was a driver himself by then, and so Dutch was still around, still a towering figure to those who knew him and knew what he had done. Evans was in that group, of course, and he always had time for his old rival.

"Whenever I saw Richie at the race track," Dutch Hoag says, "we'd always be battin' the breeze."

And to witness those conversations was to see something very unusual: Richie Evans looking vulnerable. Childlike, almost.

"Rich had a lot of respect for the generation that came along just before he did," said Fred Ulrich. "If he saw one of those guys at the race track, he'd never ignore them."

With Evans, "those guys" carried a whole lot of weight. Though he never talked about it much for the record—there aren't many printed stories in which he goes into any real depth about his greatest racing influences—he was clearly a fellow who had heroes, men whose fingerprints can be seen all over his career.

Wilbur Jones says, "Richie looked up to a lot of guys, and Eddie Flemke was number one. Why? Because Eddie was the master. When he pulled into the pit area back then at Utica-Rome or Albany-Saratoga, he was the man to beat and everybody else was running for second.

Another guy he really looked up to was Lou Lazzaro. He and Rich spent an awful lot of time together; Louie used to come to the garage quite a bit, and those two would talk forever."

It was no great surprise that Evans would put that pair on pedestals. In his formative years, at the places which shaped him, Flemke and Lazzaro were gods. Try looking at it through Richie's eyes: In 1964, his final year in the hobby cars at Utica-Rome, Evans saw Flemke set Utica-Rome records for the most modified wins in a single season (11) and the most consecutive wins (five); two years later, Flemke was the Utica-Rome champion. Lazzaro, meanwhile, won the Utica-Rome title in 1963, '70 and '71, and in the days when the New Yorker 400 was actually a twin-200 format with an overall winner, he topped *all four* segments in 1968-69. And as Evans began to hit the road for real in the late '60s, he found Lazzaro wherever he went, and Louie was winning: he was the All Star League champion in 1968 and '71, NASCAR's New York State champ in '69, '71 and '72, the Albany-Saratoga track champ in 1969.

The all-time Utica-Rome pavement modified win list shows Richie Evans first with 33 features, Lou Lazzaro second with 28, Ed Flemke third with 24; in races over 100 laps there, Evans and Flemke top the charts with 10 wins apiece, followed by Lazzaro with nine. The Albany-Saratoga rundown shows Evans leading with 17 features, followed by Lazzaro and Flemke, tied at 16. A hero and *his* heroes, one-two-three.

Flemke and Lazzaro were different men, and they seemed to give Evans different things.

Steady Eddie Flemke was the thinking man's racer—"a real psychologist," Bugsy Stevens called him—who studied his sport and had it all down cold: he knew his cars, his rivals, the tracks, everything. He had natural ability to spare, that much was obvious, but Flemke won more with his head than with his hands.

"Richie," said Fred Ulrich, "picked up an awful lot from that man."

Ed Flemke Jr., says, "Every Monday or Tuesday, there would be a marathon phone call between Richie and my father. That happened a lot in the early '70s, but it actually went right into the late '70s. It's funny, but if you were at the shop back then, you always knew when Richie was on the phone because my father would sit down to talk with him. Most of the time, he'd stand there or pace back and forth when he was on the phone. But with Richie, he would sit right down, like he knew this was going to take a while."

"Richie," says Pete Zanardi, "always saw himself as one of Eddie's boys. He told me that. I remember him saying, 'I am one of Flemke's guys.' I recall, distinctly, him going out of his way to express that debt."

Lou Lazzaro was a gut-level racer, more heart than head. That's not to say that Lazzaro wasn't a smart driver; he won far too much to leave any doubt that he had a quick brain. But he was certainly a lot more, well, casual about it than a guy like Flemke was. Lazzaro was likely to

Lou Lazzaro was held in very high regard by Evans.
(Feuz collection)

show up halfway through warm-ups, his car still crying for attention to last night's wounds, and hope for the best. Fortunately, he was talented enough that it all seemed to work out. And there was this: Lazzaro, a full-time racer from the early 1960s, supporting a family on what his coupes took in, always appeared just a few laps away from being broke. Maybe Evans, having been so desperately short on funds in his own coupe days, saw in Lou Lazzaro a guy just like himself, only one who never caught the right breaks.

"I think Rich thought of Louie as his big brother," says Buster Maurer. "They traveled a lot together, and we'd stay in the same hotels. Louie didn't have anything. He'd come to the race track after he'd been fishing all afternoon, and he couldn't qualify through the heat race because he didn't have tires that were any good. Rich would tell us, 'Take those tires down off the rack, and let's put 'em on Louie's car,' just so Louie could make the show. Unbelievable. And this was before we were sponsored by Gene [DeWitt], or had any big tire deals."

In their "FONDA!" book, Andy Fusco and Lew Boyd recount a moment which summed up Evans's devotion to Lazzaro. It occurred in a 1971 All Star League event at the Rolling Wheels Raceway, where Richie was making a rare dirt-track start: "A wreck halfway through the main collected Evans, and the race was red-flagged. Realizing his friend Louie had not one decent tire on his car, Richie ran over and offered the four tires off his own wrecked racer. Junior [Bianco, Lazzaro's crew chief and right arm] changed them in a flash and Louie restarted at the back. Upstairs he went, calmly and deliberately powering by Will Cagle for the win on the last lap."

A hero and his heroes.

"And there were others," says Wilbur Jones. "Dutch, Bill Wimble, Bugsy, Rene Charland, Ernie Gahan. And even though they weren't that far apart in age, Richie really respected Maynard Troyer. Maynard was a hell of a driver and he worked really hard on his equipment, and Richie thought a lot of him. And he definitely looked up to Ray Hendrick, because Ray had won everywhere. Those guys were running up and down the Eastern seacoast winning races when Richie was just getting going. They were on top when he was nobody, and Richie never forgot that."

Billy Nacewicz says, "Rich wasn't born with a silver spoon in his mouth, by any means. He worked hard all his life to achieve everything that came his way, and he never forgot how hard it was for him to chase all those guys. He *knew* how good they were, and he had a great, great respect for them; in fact, I think he had even more respect for them as time went by, because by then he had a better understanding of what it had taken for them to be on top. How could he not respect guys like Flemke and Bugsy and Bill Wimble and all those people who set the standards? Those guys set the bar so high, and he knew that.

"As wild and as crazy as people thought Rich was, he was still very

There were certain foes Evans always had time for, men like Maynard Troyer (left) and Ray Hendrick. *(courtesy of Speedway Scene)*

humble inside. He still had that good, solid work ethic, and he knew those guys hadn't been handed all the races and championships they won."

Buster Maurer, who saw that admiration in his friend's eyes many times, says, "Because they reached the pinnacle before Rich did, I think that in his mind, they were the guys. And I think if Rich was alive today, he'd *still* say, 'They were the guys.'"

And wouldn't that be something? Wouldn't it be something to listen to Richie Evans talk, all these years later, about Lazzaro and Flemke, Hoag and Wimble, Charland and Gahan? Wouldn't it be something to *hear* what those people meant to him, instead of having just the memory of that warm smile he gave them?

Ed Flemke Jr. says, "I just wish I could sit down today with both of them, Richie and my father, and ask them what they saw in each other." That chance disappeared when a heart attack took Steady Eddie Flemke in March of 1984. Evans drove to Connecticut for the services, and as he stood in the chapel that day, paying his respects, he looked ... well, vulnerable. Childlike, almost. And when he won the very next race he ran, at Riverside Park, a subdued Evans quietly dedicated the victory to his old friend.

Even heroes, it turns out, have heroes.

Family Man III

LYNN KREUSER, she of the Milwaukee Kreusers, was working in the '70s as a flight attendant for Mohawk Airlines, and was based in Utica. Some friends of hers knew the area well, and were always trying to drag the Midwestern girl along on some of their misadventures.

"I had a roommate who used to go to the Rusty Nail," Lynn says, "and she would say, 'You ought to come with me.' But I was kind of reserved, and I didn't like hanging out in bars. Anyway, she told me about the people she knew there, and about this guy Richie Evans who was a race driver."

Back home she had a brother who'd raced motorcycles, but she had no interest in race cars or the men who drove them. Still, the roommate kept it up, and, what the heck, a night out was a night out, and so off to West Dominick Street they went. Sure enough, that Evans fellow, the race driver, was there.

"He looked like he had just come straight from the garage," she remembers. "But we talked, and he asked if he could buy me a drink. I said no, and I think that perturbed him. I think that really got to him."

It was just a meeting, but it was the start of something. Lynn Kreuser and Richie Evans talked by telephone, occasionally at first and then more often. As it happened, in one such conversation he mentioned that he'd be racing at the Shangri-La Speedway, outside Binghamton, on a particular Saturday night. She didn't know a thing about the race track, but Binghamton was familiar to her; sure enough, her schedule had her making a layover there on that same Saturday. Hmmm ...

And so, come the weekend in question, the flight attendant talked a Mohawk Airlines baggage handler into driving her from Binghamton to Shangri-La, where she bought a ticket and took a bleacher seat to watch the first modified stock car race she'd ever seen.

"I was sitting there," she laughs, "and I didn't even know which car was his. I had no idea. I remember thinking, What color did he tell me his car was? Did he ever mention a *number?*"

It seems like a lot of trouble to go through for a guy who, in that Rusty Nail meeting, had made that straight-from-the-garage first impression. But there was something, the flygirl from Wisconsin caught herself thinking, about this Richie Evans. "His personality was what attracted me to him," she says. "He was just too cool."

They got together after the races that night, and dated a bit in the weeks that followed, her finding him increasingly "cool" and trying to gauge his interest. Which, to her chagrin, he demonstrated one night in classic Evans prankster style.

"I had some friends, guy friends," Lynn says, "and for a long time I didn't have a car, so if I was going to show up somewhere I'd have to catch a ride with one of these friends. There was this one particular friend I had, and Rich wanted to make sure he was *just* a friend.

"Rich actually went out and had 200 tickets printed up, and had somebody call and tell me that they were having some sort of a party at the Rusty Nail. I can't remember what the circumstances were, but the big thing I was told was that everybody was going to be wearing white to this party. I wasn't sure what to make of that, but I was up for anything, so I put on a white outfit.

"Well, I show up there, me and this guy friend of mine, and I don't see anybody in white except me. Rich is standing there, holding a beer, and he's got that shit-eating grin he always had. What I didn't know was that he had arranged for this mock 'wedding' to take place between me and this guy who was just my friend. Rich signals this guitar player to start playing 'Here Comes the Bride,' and then he comes up with this bottle of champagne, and there's an announcement that we're all here for 'the wedding of Jack and Lynn.' This guy Jack was so perturbed with me—because he thought I was in on all this—that he took the champagne and poured it on my head."

Mr. Evans and Miss Kreuser survived that little bit of foolishness, and certainly a few more, and in time they were clearly on the brink of a serious relationship. There was some talk, just exploratory conversation from both sides, about maybe getting married. Trouble was, at that point in his life, Richie Evans seemed to view being on the brink of a serious relationship like being on the brink of a cliff. He hadn't been divorced long, and by all accounts his full-throttle racing life had helped spoil his first marriage. He had already achieved a great deal, but he was not yet the big success story he became later. Did he really need a major change in his life just then?

To listen to Lynn discuss those days is to sense the turmoil in her man's head: "I think Rich was really confused, and when I look back I can honestly say that I understand it ... He wasn't where he wanted to be, financially ... I think getting married again was the farthest thing from his mind ... I didn't want to force him into something that he didn't seem real sure of ..."

It went on like that for a couple of years, anyway. And then, in the middle of all that indecision, Lynn discovered she was pregnant. It was an extra bit of pressure neither of them needed.

Each of them had a pretty full plate. She was working as a flight attendant, living mostly on her own, looking after her pregnancy, and worrying about her relationship. He was, well, busy being himself: winning races, working hard, playing hard.

They talked about the upcoming birth, and what they might call the child. Evans steered the conversation toward girls' names; he was simply playing the odds. "Rich, of course, had already had four daughters," Lynn says. "On my side, my mother comes from a family of eight girls, three boys, and there are four girls and a boy in my family.

"I kept saying to him through the pregnancy, 'If we have a boy, what are we going to name him?' He said, 'Well, we won't have to worry about that.'"

She went into labor on the day before Easter in 1976. "I couldn't find Rich," Lynn says, and in those pre-cell phone days that was hardly out of the ordinary with a rambler like Evans. And so, in one of those developments that seems incredible in hindsight but simply wasn't any big deal back then, Lou Lazzaro drove Lynn Kreuser to the hospital to

Two guys named Richie Evans, one a Utica-Rome winner and one a toddler, in 1978. (*courtesy of* Speedway Scene)

have Richie Evans's child. Lou's wife Roseanne went along to be her birthing coach.

The baby didn't come that night. Evans finally showed up at 10:00 a.m., and was greeted with less than a warm welcome. "At that point I was pretty much in heavy labor," Lynn recalls, "and I didn't really want him there."

At 3:00 on the afternoon of Easter Sunday, she delivered a baby boy. She remembers, "When I gave birth to a son, Rich was like, *'Holy cow!'*"

Before long it dawned on the new parents that, in their conviction that the child would be female, they hadn't ever really discussed boys' names. Lynn asked the father what he thought he'd like to name the newborn.

"Rich said to me, 'Whattaya mean, what are we going to name him? *Richie!*' Like, no question about it."

And that was that. Richie Evans now had a Richie Jr. to go with his four girls. And, while it took some time, he was finally to wrap his head around the idea of trying matrimony one more time. He and Lynn Kreuser tied the knot on November 20, 1976.

Three years later came another child, daughter Tara.

That made Evans a self-employed husband with six kids in two households and an occupation requiring unending amounts of sweat, concentration and time. Try keeping everybody happy under those conditions.

"He worked all day," Lynn recalls, "then he'd come home for dinner, play with the kids a little bit, and go right back to the shop. But he wasn't a wind-up doll; he had to take some time. So sometimes after dinner he might fall asleep on the couch for an hour or two, but then he'd be right back out the door, heading to the shop."

Richie Jr. and Tara, though very young, saw a pretty good bit of their dad, but the four older girls had to settle for less.

Generally in cases where divorced parents split time with the children and the mother has primary custody, the father ends up seeing his children on weekends, because that's the easiest way for the average Joe to schedule things. But Richie Evans didn't lead an average life; his job obviously required him to work weekends, often hundreds of miles from home. Somehow, he managed to work things out. Fortunately, he and Barbara did not live far apart, making possible quick hellos and sometimes even longer last-minute visits if a race happened to rain out. But, for the most part, he had to be a dad when he wasn't being a racer.

"Everything kind of revolved around racing," remembers Janelle, daughter number two. "You know, whether he could be at a birthday party, or at a graduation, all that depended on where he was racing."

Jodi, the oldest, says, "He spent time with us when he *had* time. Holidays, of course, and weekends in the winter."

As the years rolled on, Jodi and Janelle spent some time living with Richie and Lynn at the home Evans bought up by Delta Lake, just north of Rome, while the youngest two, Jill and Jacki, stayed with their mother closer to town. And when time allowed—always, that fight with time—he would try to get the kids together, taking them, as Jill remembers, "to this one pizza place a lot" or to his house, where, in Jacki's memory, "we'd go up there and swim, or go out on the lake."

Things got a bit easier when, after the usual bit of early discomfort so common in situations like theirs, Lynn and Barbara grew friendlier. "The children did spend a lot of time with Rich and Lynn," says Barbara, "and it was just easier that everybody got along." Together, they made the best of the balancing act that was the Richie Evans version of a two-household family.

Says Jacki, "I thought my mom was awesome about it. I mean, I'm sure she was lonely a lot of times, because whenever my dad was around she'd let us go see him. And Lynn, too, she was great to take us all with her to the races; after she had the babies, that meant bringing six kids!"

Ah, the races. When Lynn could go, naturally the youngest Evans kids, Richie Jr. and Tara, went along; Tara was in the Oswego grandstands at just *two weeks* old, attended to by Lynn with the aid of Richie's mother, Satie. And the older kids? Well, in the beginning going to the races may have just been a way to spend more time with their father. But in time it became something even better: It was *fun*. Why not? By that point, their dad was reaching peak form, running up front on a regular basis and often winning, and so whenever Evans was racing in the area—Utica-Rome, Oswego, Fulton, Spencer, Shangri-La—the whole clan enjoyed turning out to watch. Says Jodi, "I remember sitting in those stands, rooting for him: *'GoDadgoDadgoDad!'* We were pretty loud."

Utica-Rome was an obvious family favorite. For many seasons the speedway had an old Evans #61 mounted high on its entrance sign, quite a thrill for his kids in their impressionable years. And, of course,

Richie Evans Jr. and Tara Evans gave their pop a second crack at fatherhood. *(Val LeSieur photos/courtesy of Speedway Scene)*

(left) Richie's wife Lynn at New Smyrna in the late 1970s, with his daughters Jodi, Janelle and Jacki. *(Val LeSieur photo/courtesy of Speedway Scene)*

(right) (Left to right) Lynn Evans, Tara Evans, and Richie Evans Jr., enjoy life on the road. *(Val LeSieur photo/courtesy of Speedway Scene)*

as a local driver who had gone on to score national championships and major victories at all the big modified strongholds, Evans was a Utica-Rome hero. The bleachers were awash in orange.

"They used to have 'Ride With Your Favorite Driver Night' at Utica-Rome," Jodi says, "and of course we'd get in line to ride with my dad. It seemed like all the kids at the track wanted to ride with him, but he'd take us first. We'd all pile in there together, hanging on."

"Everybody knew we were Richie Evans's kids," says Jill. "That was kinda cool."

One at a time, it dawned on each of them that their dad was something of a celebrity.

"We'd go to the races and I'd follow my sisters around, and everybody was talking about my dad," says Jacki. "Then we'd see him in the pits later on, and I remember trying to get his attention, because so many other people would be talking to him. It was exciting."

They felt it at the New York tracks, and they felt it whenever they were lucky enough to go on a long-distance trip. The Evans girls recall pulling up to the Safari Motel in Daytona Beach and seeing the words "Welcome Richie Evans" on the marquee out front. They even felt it during the week, in the classroom.

"All through school, everybody looked at my dad as being somebody famous," Jill says. "I was on the yearbook staff in junior high, and he let our whole staff come down to the garage and interview him. I didn't think he'd want to—in fact, he blew me off a couple times because he said he was too busy—but finally I talked him into it. I was like, 'Dad, my teacher wants to know when we can come. I need a date.' So we ended up going down there, and he was actually very good about it. Me and my teacher interviewed him about racing, and we took pictures of the cars and stuff. My friends thought it was really neat."

Again, it wasn't a normal Ward Cleaver-style fatherhood, but you

(left) Daughter Jill's high school yearbook staff visited the Calvert Street shop for an interview. *(courtesy of Jill Evans)*

(right) Richie's pontoon boat, which played a prominent role in his daughter Jodi's "Party Barge Incident." *(Val LeSieur photo/courtesy of* Speedway Scene*)*

get the impression that Evans tried to make it as close as possible. Come December, he'd load all the kids into his pickup truck—or onto snowmobiles if the winter was especially bad—and haul them up Gifford Hill to harvest one of the Christmas trees he'd planted in his own youth. "He'd let us pick one out," says Jodi, "and he'd cut it down."

Lynn says, "Richie loved his kids. I mean, yes, he sacrificed his family life because, to him, the racing came first. But he really, really loved his kids."

The older girls suspect that because his hours with them were limited, he tended to be what Jodi calls "the good-time dad," trying to make up for lost time. He could be, they say, a bit lax in the area of laying down the law. But, Jill points out, he had a way of establishing who was boss: "He never really disciplined us in any way, but he had this *look*. It's hard to describe, because I've never seen it in any other man I've known. It was a look that said, like, *Behave*. He didn't yell, and he didn't have to, because he had that look."

It was probably Jodi, the senior Evans girl, who tested his mettle most often. In her high school years, she pulled all the normal late-teen stunts, from minor stuff like changing report-card grades to bending his favorite red pickup truck in a wreck. He nicknamed her "CD," short for "crash and destroy."

It was Jodi who starred in what has come to be known in family circles as "the Party Barge Incident." Like so many lake-dwellers, Evans owned a pontoon boat, a homemade special he used—though not nearly enough—as a floating rec room. When Jodi was "16 or 17," she got the devilish idea that she and some friends could take the thing for a slow spin around Delta Lake, and dear old dad, as busy as ever at the shop, would be none the wiser.

Big mistake. "We hot-wired the party barge and went for a ride," she says, laughing. "One of the guys had a keg of beer, so naturally we brought that with us. Everything was going fine, but then some people at the place where my dad used to park the boat called him and said,

'Rich, someone just stole your boat.' Well, he drove up there and got on another boat with a couple guys and came *flying* out there. Imagine his surprise when he saw me!

"He was *livid!* When I look back at it now, I think he was more worried than angry. We had all that beer with us, and we really didn't know what we were doing. He said, 'Do you realize what could have happened if someone had gotten hurt?' I remember him grabbing this guy I had been dating, because this guy admitted to helping hot-wire the ignition. He couldn't swim, and I remember my dad telling him, 'I ought to throw you in!' This guy was like, 'No, Mr. Evans, please, I'm so sorry!' I'm sure he thought my dad was going to drown him."

Thankfully, incidents of that magnitude were rare. Mostly, the visits had a lighter feel, sometimes leaning toward the mischievous. Jill says, "Not too long before he died, he took me and Jacki fishing. That was right out of the blue, because we never fished. Well, this boy I liked happened to be fishing at the same spot with some of his friends. I was freaking out; I didn't want him to see me *fishing*. Well, naturally my dad had to go right by those guys, just to break our chops. Jacki ended up falling in the water and got her hair soaked, and she was so embarrassed because those guys saw her. She ran back and sat in his truck, but he wouldn't leave for about two more hours."

More mischief: If the girls needed money in their teen years, he'd tell them to come down to the garage, which was intimidating because the shop was "gross, like a *guy* place," Jacki says. "Everything was greasy, dirty." Then he'd tease them as if they didn't have a chance of getting what they'd come for. Janelle says, "He loved to make us cry, especially if we were with our girlfriends, to embarrass us." In the end, reports Jacki, "he'd give you what you wanted, *plus* some."

Today, there is a suspicion that the tough-guy chop-busting was a front, a shell to wrap around a soft heart. Jodi remembers things: her dad having "a really hard time" when Boot Camp, the family German Shepherd, passed on … or the day her sister Janelle moved out of the lake house, when her father "came outside begging her to stay, and he had tears in his eyes, crying."

Barbara Evans says flatly, "He was a good father."

Lynn Evans, meanwhile, thinks about all the time she and her husband spent apart, him off at a race and her off on a flight, and believes that in many ways it strengthened their marriage.

"I think that, to Rich, I had the ideal job," she says, "because this way he had his own space. And, you know, I tried to give him a lot of space even when I wasn't gone. That was part of why I didn't travel with him much. First of all, there would have been a lot of extra expense involved in that, and, don't forget, this was how Rich made his living. For me to go, and for the kids to go, it would have cost him a lot more. We're talking about six kids, which means more hotel rooms and a lot more meals. He also used to point out—and I can see how true this was

—that it wouldn't have been fair to the other guys who worked on that car for me to go when *their* wives or girlfriends had to stay home. He could see how maybe that would cause some jealousy.

"Plus, you know, the racing was *his* thing. When I did go to the track, I was never the wife who would run out to get into the victory lane pictures. That was Rich's win, and the team's win, not mine. He worked for it, he and the guys, and they deserved that moment.

"When I saw him after he'd won a race, he'd always give me that little smirk he had, and that's all I needed."

 # 1978

THE FACT THAT NEARA was in the process of crashing and burning didn't mean that Richie Evans necessarily *had* to go back to chasing NASCAR points in 1978. He could easily have tweaked his 1976-77 schedule just slightly, hitting the major spring and fall events as always and then peppering his summer with the biggest shows he could find, sanctioned or not.

Looking back, '78 would have been a great time for that, because there were several solid open-competition tracks running special events on a fairly regular basis, Oswego and Thompson among them. And a number of New England speedways had banded together to host midweek small-block modified events as part of the Yankee All-Star League, a knockoff of the old All Star League which had helped make Evans a region-wide name. Evans could have taken off in any direction, chased dollars rather than points, and returned home on Sundays in time to kick ass and take names in the Sunday-night events at Utica-Rome, back under NASCAR sanction in 1978.

But long before the snow started to melt in Oneida County, it was clear to the gang on Calvert Street that Richie Evans had another NASCAR title on his mind.

"I always had the feeling that Gene DeWitt might have said something," Wilbur Jones suggests. "You know, something like, 'Hey, Rich, let's get us another championship.'"

Billy Nacewicz believes that it might have gone a little deeper than that.

"While we'd been sticking close to home, running NEARA, Jerry Cook was racking up those NASCAR national championships," Nacewicz says. "Of course, being from that same town, we heard a lot about that. People would tell Richie, 'Geez, Cook's a *four*-time champion now,' or 'Hey, Rich, Cook's got *five* championships. How many more are you gonna let him win?'

"The NEARA circuit was basically an upstate New York deal. Don't get me wrong, it was a good circuit, and we still ran against some quality cars. Any time you're going up against a guy like Maynard Troyer or anybody else of that caliber, you've got to put your best foot forward. But there was no real attention paid to it, at least compared to the attention you'd get if you won the NASCAR championship. And I think Richie just reached a point where he decided he wanted to take that NASCAR championship back."

Whatever it was, off they went, Evans and Nacewicz and a fleet of orange trucks, trailers and modified stock cars, back on the NASCAR championship trail.

Their chase began with a new engine program for the #61. For years, Evans had been faithful to B&M, and for the longest time that Rochester shop had produced the baddest ground-shaking big-blocks in the Northeast. But come 1976 and '77 there had been something of a revolution in asphalt modified racing. Small-block engine technology had improved to the point where many weight-conscious racers took a fresh look at the age-old "pounds per cubic inch" modified rule. They drew two conclusions: (1) that a small-block modified could still out-handle the heavier big-block cars, which had been true all the way back to the old "sportsman" days in the coupes, and (2) that the small-block cars were now capable of beating the big-blockers down the straightaways, too. Geoff Bodine and car owner Dick Armstrong had blitzed a lot of big-block fields in 1976 with a 368-inch Jack Tant Chevy, and Bugsy Stevens had dominated Stafford in '77 aboard Sonny Koszela's Pinto, powered by a small-block Ford built by Tommy Turner at the Holman-Moody complex in Charlotte. By the dawn of the 1978 season, high-revving small-blocks were phasing out the old 427-based rats. The little engines brought several new builders into the division, and Evans tried his luck with a couple, among them the legendary Daytona Beach eccentric Smokey Yunick and an engine shop operated by famed North Carolina chassis man and ex-driver Banjo Matthews.

In February, Evans headed to Florida for the annual modified series at the New Smyrna Speedway just south of Daytona. Eager to get the bugs worked out, he showed up for the nine-night grind well-stocked with screaming small-blocks.

And then a bad thing happened. All of his high-revving small-blocks started slinging parts all over Volusia County. Despite his own considerable skills as an engine tuner and his hard-knocks ability to piece together whatever parts *didn't* break, Evans had gone through his last powerplant by the eighth night.

"Rich was not in a good mood," Fred Ulrich remembered. "Basically, he was out of options."

Well, not *completely* out. He did have one option left. During that week in Florida he had chatted with an Ohio engine builder named Ron Hutter, an experienced drag-racing hand who was beginning to dabble in oval-track stuff, building Chevy small-blocks for a late model pal named Kenny Adams. Hutter had come highly recommended, his name having been dropped in the past by Stahl Headers proprietor and Evans confidant Jere Stahl.

"Jere's a talker," Hutter says, "and whenever he gets excited about something—whether it's headers or carburetors or an engine builder or whatever—he's the kind of guy who'll talk it up to everybody he runs into. I guess he had mentioned me to Richie a few times. Well, at New Smyrna, Richie had pretty much expired everything he had, and he decided it might be time to talk with somebody else."

The two met at the Safari Hotel, Daytona headquarters for the Evans clan, on the morning of the final New Smyrna race. In the parking lot, Hutter recalls, "Richie made a point of showing me everything that had gone wrong. Like, 'This motor blew up *this* night, this motor blew up *that* night, this other motor had the rear main pulled out of it.' I guess he had gone through three or four motors that week."

Together with Nacewicz and the rest of the team, they yanked the most recent small-block fatality out of the Pinto and slipped in one of Hutter's fresh engines, intent on trying it out that evening. Evans finished only sixth but liked the horsepower, so he asked Hutter if perhaps he could rent the engine for the season's first two NASCAR modified events at Hickory and Martinsville. The pair reached a deal, with the rental fee being a percentage of whatever Evans won in those two races.

It ended up being a pretty slick business deal all around. Evans went to Hickory and won; he went to Martinsville and won again. Faced with writing a pretty fair-sized check to Hutter based on their percentage agreement, Richie went instead to Gene DeWitt, whose sponsorship arrangement included providing the engines. Between them, DeWitt and Evans figured that with so much money already invested in this one, they ought to just go ahead and buy the damned thing and give all their business to Hutter.

After a February of uncertainty, Evans was now confident that he had the kind of solid engines a man needed to chase NASCAR points in those days. Fred Ulrich recalled discussing the situation after the Martinsville race: "I said to him, 'Rich, what did you think of that motor?' He said, 'Holy Christ, does that thing have some power.'"

Back on Northern turf, Evans won the Dogleg 200 at Trenton after a stirring battle with Bugs Stevens was cut short when Bugsy's fuel tank ran dry with two laps left. Then Richie finished third in Stafford's Spring Sizzler, behind two men about to make big news of their own in 1978: winner Maynard Troyer, going it alone with his first Troyer Engineering house car after years of partnership with Dave Nagle, and Geoff Bodine, who had designed and built a brand-new car for Dick Armstrong and was just beginning a 55-win season with it. Richie had no real complaints over ending up third in the Sizzler; "It was loose all day, but we're not complaining," he told writer Mike Adaskaveg. "All the wheels are still on the car."

Daytona Beach, 1978: Evans and Nacewicz swap engines, again, in a motel parking lot. *(Val LeSieur photo/courtesy of* Speedway Scene*)*

It was the kind of thing a serious points-hunter might say.

Evans did some winning as the season deepened—a couple of features at New Egypt, three of the first four Sunday shows at Utica-Rome, a 150-lapper at Islip—but he also stuck to that points-gathering creed. Over the Independence Day holiday he ran third in a Catamount Stadium NASCAR special event won by John Rosati and then chased Charlie Jarzombek to the checkers in a double-pointer at Riverhead.

A few things had changed since Evans's last do-or-die title run in 1974. The schedule had gotten a bit more streamlined, with fewer conflicts between double-pointers and special events and national championship events, those points-rich "NC shows." Richie Evans and Jerry Cook weren't traveling any less, but at least it was slightly easier for them—and everybody else—to figure out where they'd be next weekend. Steve Hmiel says, "It was a very straightforward points race. Everybody's heard the stories about how Richie and Cook used to sneak off and try to get in an extra race on the other guy. But [by '78] that stuff was pretty much over. If we went down to Caraway, Richie and his guys went to Caraway; if we hauled ass to Bowman Gray, they went to Bowman Gray, too."

But a few other things had *not* changed. Even though NASCAR sanctioned only one modified division, its competitors were still obliged to race out of a rulebook which was cloudy enough to be printed on gray paper. Some items, like the engine-displacement weight rule, were carved in stone, while others—tire widths, maximum engine sizes, etc.—were essentially left open to a promoter's whim. As a result, there were still enough kinks to make a wandering modified racer batty.

In 1976, the Riverside Park Speedway in Agawam, Massachusetts, had shed its long-held independent status and joined the NASCAR fold as a Saturday-night track. The Park's management, however, was concerned that teams which had supported the track might be overrun by big-dollar outsiders, so they insisted on keeping the Park's one-of-a-kind 340-cubic-inch engine cap. This wasn't any big deal at first, because any serious NASCAR points-chasers still had lots of Saturday options. Hell, Stafford, where the engine rules were much more conventional, was just 25 miles down the road. But once Stafford switched to Friday nights in '77, Riverside became a place teams *had* to consider if they had any designs on the NASCAR title. In the days when every race counted toward the points tally, every *track* sure counted; if Riverside Park happened to be the only Saturday-night NASCAR speedway not threatened by rain on a particular weekend, a points-chaser had better be ready to head for Agawam, rules be damned. Which is why in 1977, Dick Armstrong, a championship on his mind, popped for a hot Tant 340 for his man Bodine, who won six times at the Park that summer.

And which is why, come '78, both Jerry Cook and Richie Evans got their own hands on 340-inchers. Cook's came from veteran Connecticut engine man Bob Brunneau, while Evans tracked down a used Hutter

mouse previously owned by Pee Wee Griffin in Florida, where 331-cubic-inch engines were all the rage in late model racing. Special events elsewhere meant that neither man ran the complete Riverside schedule, but they were there often enough that it was common to see them yanking out their Friday engines and plugging in their little 340 mills on Saturday afternoons, Evans at Agawam racer Marty Radewick's shop and Cook in the Riverside Park parking lot. Evans won the first two features of the Riverside Park season, and won three more as the year rolled along.

Interestingly, the tiny Riverside engines weren't the only new thing Evans and Cook faced as they got into the meat of the 1978 season. Firestone, which had been a force in asphalt modified racing forever, had lost its grip on the division in 1976 and '77, while Goodyear-shod guys like Bodine, Maynard Troyer and Bugs Stevens and M&H Racemaster drivers like Ron Bouchard were showing a decided speed advantage on tracks of all sizes. Firestone's regional distributor, popular Bobby Summers, kept the Firestone ship afloat, but by the summer of '78 the only name drivers he had left were Evans and Cook. With the championship at stake, they could only hold on so long. By July, both men jumped ship and went with Goodyear.

All of that was a prelude to perhaps the wackiest event of the 1978 NASCAR modified season: the last Riverside 500 ever held.

Conceived in 1952, when the idea of a single jalopy-style modified running that distance seemed absurd, the 500 was a "team" race. The entrants paired off in two-driver squads and qualified through time trials the previous week, combining their fastest laps. Come race night they ran the 500 laps in shifts, with their crewmen and pit equipment crammed into every nook and cranny of the figure-8 course in the Riverside infield. One car would run, say, the first 100 laps, then its driver would signal his teammate that he was ready for relief; the first man

Evans stayed loyal to his friend Bobby Summers and Firestone's troubled modified tires, but jumped to Goodyear in mid-1978. At this Riverside Park event, Richie ran a Firestone decal but Goodyear rubber! (courtesy of Speedway Scene)

would pull off the track at a designated exit point, and his teammate would re-enter the race via another designated path. For years, the first driver would actually pull in and tap his teammate's bumper to make the transition official, but that practice was abandoned, longtime Riverside car owner Mario Fiore recalls, after "somebody came flying in and slammed into his teammate and almost wiped everybody out." Because of concerns about something similar happening, a driver had to only get within 20 feet before his teammate could leave. There were strict penalties for violating the ins and outs of infield protocol.

It was a nutty race, and its day had probably come and gone, but it was such a traditional part of New England racing that it had just sort of lingered on.

Over the years, the Riverside 500 had been won by some lofty combinations: Buddy Krebs and Jocko Maggiacomo in '52, Eddie Flemke and "Moneybags" Moe Gherzi in '56, Dick Dixon and Danny Galullo in '62, Billy Greco and Bob Stefanik in '69 and '72, and Bob Polverari and Ron Wyckoff in '75 and 76. In 1977, Stefanik had won it again, teamed with Park newcomer Geoff Bodine; they paired up again, not surprisingly, in '78.

Cook teamed with Polverari, who was riding a wave of three straight Riverside track championships. Evans paired up with Reggie Ruggiero, who was driving Fiore's Evans-built Chevette.

"That was something we were really proud of, having Richie for a teammate," Fiore remembers. "That was a big deal, because we were small-time compared to him."

Here, Fiore laughs. "But it ended up getting really crazy. We practiced in the afternoon, and each of us was doing his own deal. Our car was practicing, Richie was practicing, and we were concentrating hard because we were both new to Goodyear; Firestone had been good to our team, and obviously to Richie, but they just didn't have a good tire anymore. Richie had dabbled with Goodyears a couple weeks earlier, but it was the first time for us, and I was really concerned because the tires were so different.

"Well, in the middle of all this, Richie comes over and taps me on the shoulder. He says, 'What do I do now?' I didn't know what he was talking about. He says, 'I just blew the engine.' Now, normally Richie would have a spare motor at every track, but Riverside was the only place he'd ever need to run a 340, so he didn't have another one. Luckily, Billy Greco happened to be standing there. Greco was sort of an alternate for the 500; he didn't have a teammate, but he had his car there in case somebody had a problem and couldn't start the race. He said, 'Richie, you need a motor? I'll take care of it.' He went over and talked to his car owner, and they started pulling the motor out to give to Richie.

"So now he had an engine, but it was getting close to race time."

At the moment, Evans had too much on his mind to worry about trivial outside matters. Like, say, race procedures. While the rest of the drivers were getting last-minute instructional reminders about proper pit entrances and exits, Evans was rolling up his firesuit sleeves and helping Nacewicz and the crew pull out their broken 340.

Fiore: "Reggie started the 500, obviously, while Richie and his guys were changing engines. They were working really quick, but they ran into a problem fitting his headers onto Greco's motor; there was a different bolt pattern or something, and of course Greco's header's wouldn't fit on Richie's car. Well, Richie knew he had an adapter in his truck, but we're all in the infield and his truck is in the regular pit area [outside the backstretch]. Somehow, he was able to get the word across the track—I don't know if he signaled somebody, or what—and as the race was going on, somebody actually flung those adapters over the fence and across the track, into the infield. I'll never forget that; the cars are out there running around, under green, and they're throwing parts across the race track! But he had to get that thing together.

"Meanwhile, our car is struggling. The Goodyears had more grip than we figured, and we really missed on the setup. The car pushed so bad, it just ripped up the right-front tire. Reggie got lapped a couple of times, and I'm just waiting for Richie to get his car running. He finally got it fired up, and he yells to me, 'OK, I'm ready.' He climbs in his car, and we signal Reggie to come in.

"Well, as soon as Reggie starts to head in, Richie blasts out. I mean, Reggie wasn't anywhere *close* to being within 20 feet, and off goes Richie. That's a one-lap penalty. Then he pulls out onto the track the wrong way, and that's another one-lap penalty. So we're two *more* laps down.

"But Richie's out there now, and he's flying. I mean, he was just so fast, and I was thinking we might still have a shot to make up that

Keystone Kops! With the Riverside 500 team race underway, Evans hustles through an engine swap. *(Shany Lorenzet photo)*

ground because it's such a long race. Then, probably not 30 laps later, that [borrowed] motor blew up, too. The yellow flag came out because of all the smoke pouring out. The rule there was, if you had a big problem like that you didn't have to pull into the pits; you could just stop on the track, and your partner could get back into the race. Well, Richie pulls into the pits instead, the wrong way, and we get *another* penalty. We were actually seven laps behind Geoff Bodine when Reggie got back in the race."

They got a reprieve when Bodine, the fastest man on the track, blew an engine. Ruggiero, driving virtually the entire race, hauled his team back onto the lead lap. In the end, Evans and Ruggiero were scored second behind Cook and Polverari, who'd had problems of their own: Cook, starting for his team, broke early, leaving Polverari to put in an iron-man driving stint 483 laps long.

Evans did the only thing he knew how to do after a night like that one. He laughed, he had a beer, and, according to Fiore, "he gave his end of the purse to the guys he'd borrowed the motor from."

Then he focused again on the big picture: Cook and that NASCAR championship. Bodine's hot season didn't leave many spare trophies lying around, but Evans was fast, too. One week in July he won New Egypt on Wednesday night, ran second to Bodine at Stafford on Friday, beat Stan Greger and everybody else at Riverside on Saturday, and grabbed a Utica-Rome win on his way home Sunday night. In August he had a similar week, winning a regular show at New Egypt, a 200-lap special at Islip on Saturday, and a 30-lapper at Utica-Rome. That Islip 200 was the first of *five straight* Evans wins in national championship events; next came New Egypt, Islip again for the All Star 300, Monadnock in New Hampshire, and another at New Egypt.

The anchor to his season, really, was Utica-Rome. Richie Evans won nine features there in 1978, and *seven* of them were races in which Cook ran second. They finished that way in the track title fight, too, Evans over Cook by just four points. The last of Richie's nine scores came in a Labor Day weekend 200 which capped off another solid points-producing week: there had already been a 100-win over gritty Long Islander Freddy Harbach and Cook at New Egypt on Wednesday, and then a runner-up finish between winner Charlie Jarzombek and third-place Tom Baldwin in a Riverhead 100 on Friday.

Still, there was no shaking Cook, because you *never* shook Jerry Cook. On one September Saturday he showed his hang-tough colors, finishing second to Satch Worley in an afternoon Martinsville 150 while Evans ran eighth, and that night finishing two spots ahead of Evans in a Franklin County top five of Paul Radford, Worley, Cook, Brian Ross and Evans. (The next day, in the non-NASCAR Race of Champions at Pocono, Evans exploded an engine and in the resulting oil fire suffered first- and second-degree burns on his shoulders, back and legs, but he didn't skip a beat in the points battle.)

Richie bags a national championship win at New Hampshire's Monadnock Speedway, 1978. *(Burt Gould photo/courtesy of Speedway Scene)*

It is interesting to note that both Evans and Cook scored 57 top-five finishes in NASCAR-sanctioned races that season, and therefore it is absolutely clear that the difference between them was in the win column. Evans won 25 of his 75 NASCAR starts, with Cook in victory lane just five times. And of the 19 points-heavy national championship shows run that year, Richie won seven.

It had been a great points chase, a clean fight—"They never ran into each other, all year long," Steve Hmiel says—but by October it was obvious that it would take a major collapse by Evans for Jerry Cook to have a chance. And Richie Evans did not collapse.

Cook tried, as always. In an NC event at Kingsport, Tennessee, he finished third behind winner Ron Bouchard in the Judkins #2X and Evans; Harry Gant, in one of his increasingly rare modified starts, was fourth in the Mason #45.

That made the Martinsville finale almost an anticlimax, although a failing spur gear which had Evans in and out of the pits all day added some suspense. But the drama ended when Cook lost an engine on lap 135. As Geoff Bodine cruised to yet another major victory in the best year of his modified career, Evans wrapped up his second NASCAR national modified championship.

The gear troubles in the #61 Pinto had made things close—the final gap was 110 points—but close didn't mean much to Cook. He told writer Andy Fusco, "There's only two places when it comes to running for points: first and last. This year, I was last."

It was a special winter for Billy Nacewicz. "Standing at the NASCAR banquet and getting that plaque as the championship crew chief, that meant a lot to me. I remember thinking of the people who had been up there before me, whether it was Lenny Boehler or Sonny Koszela's team or whoever, and thinking that they were all people I had looked up to."

And it was a special winter for Evans, too. "Wrestling that championship away from Cook was a big, big thing, especially around Rome," Nacewicz grins. "We did some partying."

Here, the smile fades, and 25 years later Billy Nacewicz's race face pokes through.

He says, "But the partying only lasted for a while. See, pretty soon, everybody said, 'OK, Richie, that's two. Are you gonna go for number three?'"

 # Shifting Sands

IF EVER A SMALL-TOWN SPEEDWAY should have been successful, Utica-Rome—in its original configuration as an asphalt bullring—was the place. The little oval on Route 5 in Vernon just seemed to have everything going for it.

It had a nice location, not far off the New York Thruway, an easy drive from both the cities it was named for. It had a great layout, small enough to keep victory within reach for the low-dollar guys who couldn't afford big-track horsepower even as it drew some of the finest equipment in modified racing. It had hometown heroes aplenty, and, thanks to its Sunday-night schedule, a regular invasion by region-wide stars looking to pile up NASCAR points; for years that produced great theater, pitting Vernon Center's Sonney Seamon, New Hartford's Dick Fowler and Canastota's Bernie Miller against New Englanders like Fred DeSarro, Gene Bergin and Bobby Santos, not to mention Long Island's Fred Harbach and Canada's Denis Giroux. It had track champs named Wimble, Flemke, Lazzaro and Bodine.

And Utica-Rome had a distinction no other Northeast racing facility had ever been able—or will ever be able—to claim: it was the hometown track for the NASCAR national modified champion, *eight years running*. From 1971-78, local fans could drive down local roads to their local track and hear one of two local guys, Jerry Cook and Richie Evans, introduced as the premier modified driver in the land.

And yet somehow, the Utica-Rome Speedway was in trouble, struggling for crowds and therefore struggling at the bottom line. Dick Waterman, who had been part of the place almost since the beginning, says, "I don't think the fans really appreciated what they had."

Nor, perhaps, did the local merchants, too few of whom had yet to see the value of being associated with weekly short-track racing. Waterman grouses, "In those days, it was hard for a promoter to get any [sponsorship] help. If you went to your beer distributor—the guy you sold hundreds of cases of beer for every week—and asked him for a free can of beer for the drivers after the race, you'd have thought you asked him to cut his arm off. Today, he'll pay the purse for you."

But the biggest factor was probably the shifting sands upon which stood all of stock car racing in upstate New York in the late 1970s. Once dirt modifieds and pavement modifieds became distinctly different animals, the two sides fought a kind of turf war, dividing up the tracks and the stars. For a time, they seemed to be on equal footing: dirt fans had Fonda, Orange County, Lebanon Valley, Weedsport, Rolling Wheels, Will Cagle, Jack Johnson, C.D. Coville, Tommy Corellis, Lou Lazzaro … the asphalt set had Albany-Saratoga, Utica-Rome, Lancaster, Shangri-La, Spencer, Maynard Troyer, Geoff Bodine, George Kent, Jerry Cook, Richie Evans.

But by the second half of the 1970s, things were looking different, more brown and less black, as dirt-track racing began to get the upper hand. In retrospect, it is hard to say for sure if dirt—or DIRT, Glenn Donnelly's Drivers' Independent Race Tracks group—simply had momentum, or if asphalt blunders like the NEARA saga and NASCAR's on-again, off-again relationships with several tracks had caused pavement fans to throw up their hands. But dirt was clearly on the rise, and blacktop modified racing in the Empire State was in decline.

Among the places hardest hit were three joints where Evans had once been the big man on the modified campus. First C.J. Richards, a veteran Vermont-New York promoter, bought Albany-Saratoga and covered it with clay for the 1977 season. Next, Fulton's Bub Benway announced late in 1978 that his speedway, too, would be converted to dirt. But surely the most personal blow for Richie Evans came when Utica-Rome lay stagnant for a time in 1976 and then, two years later, Waterman decided he'd had enough and sold the place. Its new ownership declared that the blacktop oval would be razed and replaced by a bigger dirt track.

Evans won 42 modified features at Fulton, 33 at Utica-Rome, and 17 at Albany-Saratoga. Add it up: 92 checkered flags. When they covered those three tracks with dirt, they buried a whole lot of one man's history.

And it wasn't just the fact that he had been so successful at those places. For so long they had been the three pavement modified tracks closest to his home, and now they all belonged to the other side.

By the time the snow flew in 1978, it was clear that Evans's future was going to look nothing like his past. From that point on, Friday nights were going to mean Spencer Speedway out Rochester way, or Stafford Speedway over in Connecticut, or Riverhead Raceway on Long Island, or New Egypt Speedway clear down in central New Jersey. Saturdays were another toss-up, this time between Shangri-La just west of Binghamton, Islip on Long Island, and Riverside Park outside Springfield, Massachusetts. And Evans could forget forever the notion of salvaging a tough weekend with a great showing at home; instead of Utica-Rome just down the road, Sunday nights were going to belong to

Richie Evans, 1978. *(courtesy of* Speedway Scene*)*

Thompson Speedway, 250 highway miles to the east, tucked into the corner formed by the borders of Connecticut, Massachusetts and Rhode Island.

Never again was Richie Evans going to be a local racer, and never again would he have so intense a local following. He belonged less to Rome now, and more to modified racing in general.

"That meant a lot more traveling for a lot of people," says Wilbur Jones, "because so many of Richie's fans went wherever he went. It used to amaze me the way we'd see so many of the same faces everywhere. Down to Owego, out to New England, anywhere we went.

"But, of course, not everybody could travel. So the guys down at the mill, they always wanted to know, 'How's Richie doing?' If he had gone to Florida or Martinsville or New England or wherever, they wanted to know what he was up to."

In the spring of 1981, writer Dick Berggren visited Rome and quoted a sentimental Evans admitting, "We lost a lot by not running near town." Then the two of them drove out to Utica-Rome, which had floundered as a dirt track and was sitting idle.

Wrote Berggren, "Richie Evans stood at what was once the pit entrance … and looked intently at the weeds growing up high into the unpainted bleacher seats. 'It's a damn shame,' he said. 'This used to be a really good race track.' He shook his head and began to walk away, stopped, took another look at the abandoned speedway, shook his head again, and got back into his car and drove away without ever checking his rearview mirror as he left."

PART FOUR
Richie!

Mike Adaskaveg photo

"Where Modifieds Belong"

NOBODY IS QUITE SURE just how it all got started, although everyone seems quite sure that all involved had the right intentions. At some point in the early and middle 1970s, there began a quiet, determined and multi-faceted attempt to make the modifieds into something they were not, and those who raced in the division had little choice but to go along for the ride. They built special cars, or at the very least drastically altered the cars they had, and they found themselves traipsing off to all kinds of strange locales, and nobody—not even the winners—seemed to enjoy the whole thing very much.

"Insanity," was Richie Evans's terse summary to writer Andy Fusco.

First came the road courses. Daytona ran the modifieds on its infield road course during Speedweeks from 1974-76, with Bobby Allison winning the first and last editions in aerodynamically sleek, full-fendered short-track late models and Merv Treichler copping the '75 race in a Monza modified with a pointy nose up front and bulging, air-deflecting IMSA-style fenders on the rear. All three races were lousy—especially for Evans, who fell out each year—unless you enjoyed the sight of great modified drivers reduced to looping through the Daytona infield (or maybe you had the exclusive rights to sales of spare clutches and transmission parts.)

It didn't stop there. Up in the leafy hills of northwestern Connecticut, Lime Rock Park boss Jim Haynes and Stafford Speedway owner Jack Arute staged a 1973 modified test at Lime Rock, persuading car owners Bob Judkins and Sonny Koszela to haul their iron to the historic road course so Ed Flemke and Bugs Stevens, respectively, could try out the place.

The 1974-76 road-course modified events at Daytona went badly for Evans, who fell out of all three. *(Lynn Evans collection)*

And in 1975, the sweeping fast turns of the Watkins Glen road course, a venue which in those days was best known for hosting the Chardonnay-and-brie Formula One crowd every autumn for the United States Grand Prix, threw open its gates for the Budweiser-and-burgers modified folks when Lancaster's Ed Serwacki organized an event there. Evans won the pole but broke a brake line during the race, won by Treichler in that Monza over Jerry Cook, Maynard Troyer and Bobby Vee.

Promoters everywhere seemed to want in on the act. In May of 1977, Charlotte ran something called the Patriot 300, a curious mix of Camaro-type late models and short-track modifieds and cars whose bodywork absolutely defied description. Richie Evans stayed home. He did, however, turn up that same season at Dover, which ended up attracting a similar tossed salad of aero-sleek one-offs and Saturday-night specials, some running on 10-inch Goodyear Cup-style tires and others on the traditional modified steamrollers from Firestone and M&H. Maynard Troyer appeared with a swoopy Mustang so superior that, after Maynard fell ill and decided he couldn't complete the race, a sidelined Geoff Bodine jumped in and made up *four laps* to win the thing. The margin of victory said all anyone needed to know: the Troyer/Bodine missile finished nine full seconds ahead of Paul Radford's short-track Pinto, whose only concession to the high speeds was a full windshield installed by veteran Virginia car owner Wayne "Speedy" Thomas. (Radford, bless him, had won a 200-lapper at Bowman Gray Stadium the previous night.) Evans ended the Dover event two laps down, in fourth, with his plain-Jane Pinto.

Even Pocono's three-cornered 2.5-miler, with the longest straightaway in all of American racing, was deemed suitable for modifieds originally constructed to run at tight little pens like Islip and Albany-Saratoga. There were open-competition modified races there in 1974 and '75, again dominated by tricked up cars: Ray Hendrick won in '74 with a full-nosed Dick Armstrong Pinto, and Armstrong won again in '75 with a Mustang streamliner wheeled by Geoff Bodine. Evans was a 1974 Pocono no-show, and when his car broke during morning practice in '75 he promptly loaded his gear and headed 200 miles up the road to the friendlier ground of Fulton, where he beat Sonney Seamon to win the feature that evening.

In 1977, with the Trenton Fairgrounds on the skids and apparently headed for the wrecking ball, the Race of Champions moved to the big Pocono tri-oval and stayed there through '79. The tri-oval was both good and bad for Evans: he ran third in 1977 behind Troyer and Bodine, spectacularly blew his Mustang's engine and suffered burns in '78, and won in 1979 aboard a short-track Pinto loaded with various deflectors and wind-catching doodads. Those three races drew fine crowds, but Evans insisted that this was an endorsement of the *event* rather than the long-track modified concept. He told Fusco in '77, "This is the Race of

Champions. Langhorne, Trenton, Pocono, it really doesn't matter. They'd come if this race was held in the parking lot out back."

Most of the other superspeedway and road-course modified races held in the 1970s came perilously close to making a mockery of the division, because the very definition of the class grew more clouded by the month. The cars didn't look like modifieds, the events didn't draw many of the day's top modified stars—Stevens, Flemke, Ron Bouchard, George Kent and others were often absent—and they simply lacked a modified feel.

Reporting on the 1977 Daytona Modified 200, Rich Benyo was clearly astounded by what he found: "A walk through the modified garage area," he wrote, "became a walking tour of aerodynamic theory from the Wright Brothers to the NASA Space Shuttle."

One of the weirdest of the weird creations on hand for that show was a gorgeously crafted, long-nosed Camaro belonging to Pee Wee Griffin, an ex-Jersey dirt modified star who had moved home to his native Miami earlier in the decade. The car, a tan number 72, had a Banjo Matthews chassis, a Smokey Yunick powerplant, and a driver named Richie Evans, who had first crossed paths with Griffin when both men ran coupes in the All Star League. It looked like a team full of talent and potential, and yet it did absolutely nothing worth remembering. In fact, it may have been the ultimate case of a bunch of smart people being way too smart for their own good.

"We didn't have anything to do with preparing the car," Billy Nacewicz says. "We worked on it some while we were down there, but not prior to Daytona. We did go down [to Miami] and fit Richie for the seat, and we did test with it at Daytona. The car wasn't right in the test —it had way too much downforce on the front end, because the nose was so long—and Rich told Pee Wee that he needed to change that, but he neglected to do it. So it still had all this downforce on the front end and almost none on the back, which made it way too loose for Daytona."

And at superspeedway speeds—the pole position lap that year was over 186 miles per hour, run by Ohio late model shoe John Anderson— driving anything "way too loose" was not much fun at all. Nacewicz says, "Rich wasn't happy, but he'd committed to run the car, so we'd show up in the garage area early every morning. We were running New Smyrna at night, so we'd pull our modified truck and trailer in through the [Daytona] tunnel and park it in the infield. Then we'd just walk in through the garage gate, and Richie would check on how his ride was doing."

Most mornings, it wasn't doing too well.

"The car wouldn't run fast, mostly due to the aerodynamics, but Pee Wee thought it was because of the motor," says Nacewicz. "Rich would go out every day to practice and he'd be a second off the best cars, so Pee Wee would pull the motor out and take it back to Smokey's shop [in

(left) Pee Wee Griffin's long-nosed Camaro was Richie's 1977 Daytona 200 ride. *(Keith Smith photo/Lynn Evans collection)*

(right) Evans pits the Griffin 72, ending a week full of troubles. *(courtesy of* Speedway Scene*)*

Daytona Beach] so Smokey could work on it overnight. We'd come into the garage area in the morning, look under the hood, and if there wasn't a motor in the car we'd just walk out and work on the New Smyrna car. The motor would usually show up from Smokey's after lunch, and then Richie would do some laps in the afternoon."

With the tan Camaro wagging its tail on the high banks, Evans qualified eighth. The race itself didn't go much better. He slip-slid his way around for a while, logging laps and hanging on.

"We weren't up to speed with [eventual winner] Harry Gant and the other top guys, mainly because the car wasn't anywhere close to aerodynamically balanced, but it still could have been a decent day," Nacewicz recalls. "Then the thing broke a fan belt. Rich came into the pits, and I looked under the hood and hollered to the guys on Pee Wee's team to get a belt. Well, they had one back in the truck, over in the garage area, but they didn't have one in the pits. That was going to take some time, so Rich said, 'Let's park it. This operation is not where it needs to be.'

"Pee Wee wanted everything the best," Nacewicz says, "but he just didn't go about it the right way."

Which, really, might have been the theme for the entire test run of modified races on road courses and superspeedways. Lots of important people wanted the best, wanted things to work out, but they just didn't go about it the right way. The whole thing seemed to be a mess from the start.

"You just can't expect short-track drivers with short-track cars to put on a decent superspeedway show," Evans told Andy Fusco in the winter of 1977-78. "And likewise, you can't expect us to go out and spend [lots of money] for a big-track car which we can only use a few times a year. A lot of people are risking a lot of money to make this superspeedway thing work. I just wish they'd take some of the money and put it into the half-mile tracks. That's where modifieds belong."

By the end of the 1970s, Richie had essentially gotten his wish. Well, sort of. The part about the money getting redirected toward the short tracks apparently didn't pan out, but the big-track specialty modified was, for all purposes, a dead animal. The Race of Champions was switched to Pocono's 3/4-mile infield track for 1980. Charlotte and Dover gave up long before that. Ed Serwacki lost a reported $80,000 on the Watkins Glen race, and there was no return date. Sure, there was still a Daytona Modified 200, but—as with the old infield road races—that show always seemed to be more about helping fill up a Speedweeks Friday than about boosting the modified class. Once again, modified racing was a matter of tripping up and down the East Coast to the half-miles, thirds and quarters that had put the division on the map.

And getting back to basics happened to trigger maybe the most exciting period in Evans's long career. He had always been one of those "one-name" racers, the sort of popular driving star who didn't need a complete introduction; his first name was enough. Well, along about 1979, that changed a bit.

Up until then, he was Richie.

For the next several seasons, there was more excitement attached to the name just about every time somebody spoke it.

Richie!

"There was an aura about Richie, a mystique," says Steve Hmiel. "If you happened to be out eating dinner in the same place he was, and Richie came by and goofed with you, that was really, really cool."

 ## Fun in the Sunshine State

SOME OF THE TRACKS WHERE Richie Evans was a statistical giant come as no great surprise. Check the numbers at the back of this book, and you might not bat an eye at his win totals for Shangri-La (66 features), Spencer (49) or Fulton (42). It probably won't even come as much of a shock, given how dominant Evans was in New England between, say, 1979 and '81, to note that he won a combined 102 modified features at Stafford (38), Riverside Park (32) and Thompson (32).

But the number that really jumps out comes from the New Smyrna Speedway and its annual multi-night World Series program, run since 1976 in conjunction with the Speedweeks goings-on at nearby Daytona. Though he ran only 74 modified features there—the first two World Series schedules consisted of only five or six events, and rain always seemed to wipe out a race or two once the track went to its nine-night format—Evans took home an incredible 39 New Smyrna trophies for a 53 percent win rate.

Yes, Richie Evans sure did have some fun in the Florida sun, and under the Florida moon.

He had been a Speedweeks racer since that first Permatex 300 with Gene DeWitt in 1973, and in '74 he was thrilled with a sixth-place finish—albeit two laps down—in that same event. Truth be told, by then DeWitt's Mercury was a tired old girl. He and Evans brought it to Daytona twice more, in '75 and '76, but both years the car lacked speed in qualifying and reliability in the Permatex, falling out twice. Woven in among all that were those three miserable modified events on the road course, none of which left Richie smiling.

But once New Smyrna imported the modifieds in 1976, pairing them with the late models in those World Series marathons, Florida became a very happy place for Evans. He immediately fell in love with Clyde Hart's fast, banked, brightly-lit half mile; that very first year, he told Dick Berggren that it was "the best track I have ever raced on, bar none."

A sixth-place run in the 1974 Permatex 300 was a Daytona high point for Gene DeWitt's old Mercury. *(John Bisci collection)*

It turned out to like him an awful lot, too. Six times—in 1977, '79, '80, '81, '83 and '84—Evans was the World Series modified champion. And when he didn't win the title, he was generally the stiffest competition for whoever did. Evans won three times in 1978, but that was the year he kept popping engines, so the title went to consistent Ron Bouchard; in '82, in a World Series dominated by six-time winner Greg Sacks, Evans captured the only two other features run; and in '85, Jimmy Spencer was the New Smyrna champion after a series in which he and Evans both won three events.

Boy, what times Richie Evans had there. In '77, he finished second in *five* straight races, and then won the finale on night six. In 1979 he'd gone six-for-seven, losing only to Merv Treichler; Evans sat out the Wednesday night action that year to attend the NASCAR champions dinner, but did arrive just in time to watch his old friend Sonney Seamon steer the #61 to a runner-up finish behind Bouchard. In 1980 he did the banquet thing again, trusting Mike Loescher to qualify his New Smyrna car, but skipped out of the ceremony in time to show up and win the feature; "Richie's only instruction," recalls crewman Ray Spognardi, "had been, 'Don't touch a bolt.' Then, with no practice, he

For a few years, Evans brought lots of artillery to Florida. This shot from '76 shows a late model sportsman car and multiple modifieds. *(Lynn Evans collection)*

Mike Loescher (right) qualified Richie's Pinto for a New Smyrna feature in 1980. *(Val LeSieur photo/courtesy of Speedway Scene)*

annihilated the field." And Evans won six straight at New Smyrna in 1981, went five-for-eight in '83, and six-for-seven in 1984, when only Charlie Jarzombek and a broken fuel pump could stop him.

"The best thing about going down there," says Billy Nacewicz, "was that it let us see where we stacked up against the other top cars. At New Smyrna, you might have only had half a dozen really good cars in a given year, but they were usually the best teams at that given time."

Billy is absolutely right. To run down the list of men Evans faced at New Smyrna, year by year, is to trace the ebb and flow of modified talent in the last 10 years of his career: Maynard Troyer, Freddy Harbach, Jerry Cook ... Fred DeSarro, Geoff Bodine, Bouchard ... Treichler, George Kent, Doug Hewitt ... Jarzombek, Jamie Tomaino, Brett Bodine ... Sacks, Reggie Ruggiero, Spencer. It really was, as Nacewicz suggests, "a great way to gauge where you were at, early on in the season."

It was also a crusher, particular for a multi-tasking racer like Evans. Says Wilbur Jones, "That was hell week, anytime we went to Florida. You'd be at New Smyrna every night, but sometimes you also had to be at the big track every morning because for years Richie was running something there, too. They'd throw us out of the Daytona pits at five o'clock, then we'd grab a quick hamburger and get over to New Smyrna."

What made the whole thing worthwhile—in addition to all those checkered flags—was the relaxed atmosphere so pervasive on most of those World Series nights. Most of the features were 25-lappers, with the odd 50 or 100 toward the end of the week. The prize money was good, but not great. Free from the constraints of chasing points, able to experiment with engine and chassis tricks they wouldn't dare try in a major race back home, and, certainly not least, away from the New York and New England snows, most modified folks looked at New Smyrna as a good time.

And, thanks to their shared pits in the confines of the infield, they also got to mingle with and often befriend some of the best late model teams in the country. Depending on the year—indeed, depending on

Sun, surf and a race car! Daytona Beach, 1981. *(Lynn Evans collection)*

Assume the position: Richie and his troops strike a familiar New Smyrna pose. *(Lynn Evans collection)*

the night—a guy like Evans might be pitted beside Michigan's Mike Eddy, Canada's Junior Hanley, Florida's Gary Balough, or a red-hot teenager from Arkansas named Mark Martin.

Then, of course, there was Dick Trickle, the Wisconsin legend reputed in those days to be America's winningest short-track driver. Trickle and Evans became fast friends, regularly kibitzing during the drivers' meetings and often re-running their respective features over a cold beer later on. Theirs was a kinship full of laughter and pranks. Many nights ended late, with Evans and Trickle flipping a coin to determine who'd pick up the breakfast check at a Daytona Beach diner; *Speedway Scene* publisher Val LeSieur recalls Trickle losing so many of those flips that for years afterward he suspected Richie had been using a trick coin.

Speedweeks, in the Evans years, had that kind of feel.

Rick Jarzombek, whose brother Charlie had been a regular New Smyrna player—in addition to having dominated a short-lived modified series at the tiny Daytona Memorial Stadium in 1976 —recalls the whole atmosphere as being rather loose.

"Back then, everybody used to play tricks on one another, silly stuff," Ricky says. "You might wake up in the morning, and the soda machine from down the hall was blocking your doorway. But if you did something like that, you'd better do it in such a way that you wouldn't get caught, because the paybacks were going to be a lot worse than what you'd done.

"We'd usually all stay down there a couple days after we were done [at New Smyrna], and this one night we were racing bumper karts on the boardwalk. My brother and I had to leave the next morning to come home, and Richie was making fun of us because he was going to stay another week. He was going to take his rental car south to see some friends, and just goof around. Well, that hurt our feelings; here's our *friend*, making fun of us! Anyway, when we were getting ready to leave, I looked over and said, 'Oh, my god, there's Richie's rental car, parked right next to us!' So I took the lug wrench out of our trunk, and spun all

Fun in the Sunshine State

the lug nuts off that car except for one on every wheel. The one lug I left on, I backed off until it was hanging on by maybe one thread. Then we headed home.

"The whole way home, I was thinking, Boy, if Richie ever finds out about this, I'm in big trouble. But then I kinda forgot about it. Well, some time later—maybe a year, maybe two—I heard these two guys in a bar laughing and telling a story about Richie Evans. Turns out they'd seen him leaving with that rental car. 'Something's wrong with this thing,' he said. Somebody else said, 'Yeah, the wheels are loose.' Well, he took off and drove it until the wheels fell off!

"This is the first time I've ever told that story. My wife knew about it, and my parents knew about it, but we never told anybody because we knew that if Richie found out, we'd never be safe. That guy has been gone almost 20 years now, but if I ever find the wheels loose on my rental car in Daytona, I'll know Richie is up there laughing at me."

 # "That Orange Camaro"

ALL THAT MISERY EVANS SUFFERED at Daytona in 1977 at the helm of Pee Wee Griffin's temperamental Camaro had an upside. It frustrated him enough to decide that if he was going to tackle Daytona at all, he was going to do it properly.

"He knew he could run better than that," Nacewicz recalls. "Rich knew he could run with those guys. So we talked it over with Gene DeWitt, and decided to do it ourselves in '78."

DeWitt, still more than a little bit obsessed with Daytona, gave Evans the OK to purchase a NASCAR-legal Camaro from the Banjo Matthews shop in Asheville, North Carolina. The car, says Nacewicz, "was a really nice piece. Banjo's guys built the chassis and did the rough work on the body, then we brought it back to Rome and finished it up in our own garage."

The end result was one very slippery superspeedway modified, with a sculpted nose, a laid-back windshield, and a fat black stripe running across the hood and down the car's orange flanks, and then—with a very '70s strobe-type effect—slashing up and over the roof. Under the bubbled hood was a 460 cubic-inch B&M big-block which put out, grins Nacewicz, "a *lot* of horsepower." To service it on race day, Evans recruited a crew led by Bill Seifert, a journeyman Grand National driver from North Carolina who'd begun to build a reputation as a savvy pit-road guy.

It was, they guessed, a combination that could win them the 1978 Daytona 200. And, but for a twist of fate and a questionable call from the official's tower, it might have done just that.

Richie's orange Camaro, twice a Daytona winner. *(Dorsey Patrick photo/Lynn Evans collection)*

Evans had locked himself into a race-long duel with Darrell Waltrip, then the hottest rising star in the Winston Cup series, where he had won six times in '77. (It's worth noting that Darrell—just a few days past his 31st birthday—was some five and a half years younger than Richie.) He was driving a green and white #88 Camaro fielded by Charlotte's Robert Gee and sponsored by Gatorade, which also backed Waltrip's big-league efforts with DiGard Racing. They swapped the lead back and forth, two strangers sort of feeling each other out; though they'd shared the track in some Permatex 300s and a couple of superspeedway modified events, this was the first time Richie Evans and Darrell Waltrip had ever truly squared off.

And in the closing laps it looked like Evans, glued to Waltrip's rear bumper, had the upper hand. In those days of unrestricted engines, second place was the catbird's seat at a place like Daytona; the leader was a sitting duck in any shootout between equal cars, because the guy behind him could basically draft right past on the run to the checkers. And even when Waltrip seemed to slow the pace a bit, all but begging Richie to take the lead, Evans wasn't budging.

"I tried the old slowdown tactic," Darrell remarked later, "but he wasn't about to go for that."

Evans said, "I wasn't going to lead the race and have him behind me."

"Richie was just riding there," sighs Nacewicz, "waiting for the last lap."

Then, as the pair approached the two-laps-to-go point, Merv Treichler had a problem on the back straightaway and pulled his car into the infield, way over against the berm that served as a barrier between the track and Lake Lloyd. Normally in those days, cars sitting in that area were deemed to be out of harm's way and were left alone; check the old films from any Daytona 500 or Permatex 300, and you'll see a half-dozen bent or broken machines parked there. But this time the caution flag was waved, and Evans never got the chance to mount his planned charge. As the yellow light blinked on, Nacewicz says, "Darrell just kept the hammer down, and he beat us [to the line.]"

Evans checks out the, uh, scenery after his 1979 Daytona score. That's lovely Linda Vaughn on the right. (Val LeSieur photo/Speedway Scene collection)

The final two circuits were run at caution-period speeds, with Evans staring hard at the tail of that Gatorade 88. "It's tough," he later admitted, "just sitting there and knowing you can't do anything."

Waltrip was gracious about the whole thing, telling the assembled media that he was "impressed with Evans. If we'd had to race to the checker, I don't know if I could have won it." And Richie played the good loser, keeping to himself any ill feelings he may have had about the yellow-flag decision. But he admitted to having breathed the accelerator for an instant when he first noticed that last yellow light blink on, and fretted quietly that this lapse might have cost him the win.

"We felt really bad, losing on that caution," Nacewicz says. "We thought we had the dominant car, and Darrell was just getting to the peak of his career, so to beat him would have been really nice. Richie wasn't happy, but he said, 'That'll never happen again.'"

And it never did. Evans never again gambled on a last-lap strategy at Daytona, never again played a waiting game, and never again finished second there.

"For the next two years," Billy Nacewicz grins, "they didn't see anything but the back of that Camaro."

No, they didn't. In both 1979 and '80, it strained every driver in the joint—and the Daytona 200 continued to draw a handful of Winston Cup regulars—just to stay close enough to get a whiff of the B.R. DeWitt Camaro's draft.

Yet, strangely enough, neither victory was anything resembling easy. Whatever speed advantages Evans had were countered by problems which, had they happened on different days or to different people, might have led to defeat.

In 1979, Evans, having qualified second to Anderson, was waltzing off with the lead in the race's early stages when something—a wheel weight kicked up by another car's tire, he guessed—came rocketing into his windshield, leaving behind a small hole. He immediately relayed the situation to Nacewicz, aided on pit road this day by longtime Winston Cup crew chief David Ifft and his tire-changers from the Benny Parsons team.

"The hole was directly in Richie's line of vision," Nacewicz remembers. "He came on the radio and said, 'I've got a problem. The windshield's broken.' We had a spare in the pits, just in case, but it takes time to change a windshield, especially under green. Luckily, David Ifft had been to Daytona a hundred times. David told me to ask exactly where the hole was. Rich said, 'Right where I'm looking.' Then David had me ask him if it was caving in. Rich said no. So David said, 'Well, tell him to stay out there until it does!'

"We ran almost the whole race that way, and luckily that windshield hung right in there."

Their only real on-track challenge came from Neil Bonnett in the Griffin 72, having shed its anteater look in favor of a much more con-

Neil Bonnett, in a much-reconfigured Griffin 72, found "that orange Camaro" to be too strong on the big speedways. *(Larry Riveland photo/Bones Bourcier collection)*

ventional nose. Bonnett, with five Winston Cup victories under his belt, used every ounce of his superspeedway savvy—and Neil was acknowledged as a drafting master—to hang in there, particularly after restarts. But Evans always managed to pull away. He won by an astounding margin, something a bit over 30 seconds.

"That orange Camaro," Bonnett proclaimed to the media, "was just too strong." Finishing behind Evans and Bonnett were Harry Gant, Ron Bouchard (in a Bob Johnson Firebird) and Joe Thurman.

"I've tried 10 years to get here," a joyous Gene DeWitt told everyone who stopped in the winner's circle to shake his hand.

Nacewicz says, "One of Gene's big wishes, forever, was to stand in victory lane at Daytona. When we finally got him there, that made Gene so happy, and it made Rich really happy to have him there."

In February of 1980, the Evans Camaro, powered now by a Ron Hutter 460, was even more dominant. The entry list was weak, just 24 cars—weak enough, in fact, to doom the Daytona modified show forever—but there were enough heavy hitters on hand to create a bit of a buzz. That died down a bit, however, when Evans qualified some three miles per hour faster than his front-row mate, Gant. His pole speed was 196.807 miles per hour, "faster than any stock car driver in Daytona history," Dick Berggren pointed out. (The pole man for that year's 500, Buddy Baker, turned a 194.009.) In fact, more than a few stopwatch junkies claimed to clock Richie on practice laps of over 200 MPH. Alas, the modified event and its speed-demon polesitter got little attention. Nacewicz recalls being dismayed to find that their blazing qualifying run had earned "about four lines in the Daytona paper, on, like, page 12 of the sports section, next to the ice skating or some other stuff."

One more time, Evans looked to be on a trouble-free run toward the checkered flag. One more time, looks were deceiving. In this Daytona 200, the culprit was a defective radio.

"We could hear Rich, but he couldn't hear us," Nacewicz says. "So he had no real way of knowing how many laps he had run, because it's not easy to read the pit board at that speed and he couldn't see that little digital scoreboard they used to use. The biggest problem with that was, he needed to know when to pit, or he might run out of gas."

Maybe once you've gotten used to battling through traffic at places like Utica-Rome, Islip and Riverside Park, you develop a knack for quickly solving any dilemma that comes up. At Daytona, Evans used his one-way line of communication to ask his crew to hand him a pen and a strip of duct tape on his first stop. As he roared off pit road, he slapped the tape against his left thigh.

"And for the rest of that race," says Nacewicz, "every time he came past the pits he'd put another scratch mark [on the tape]. He did it in groups of five: *one, two, three, four, slash … one, two, three, four, slash.* He was left-handed, so he'd just scribble with his left hand and drive with his right. He figured that when he got to the number of laps when he knew he needed fuel, he'd come in."

Their closest competition, interestingly, came from Doug Hewitt, an up-and-coming New York driver and a quasi-teammate of Richie's in that they shared the same sponsor. *His* DeWitt Camaro was also a Banjo Matthews piece, and Hewitt had it in what looked like a secure second spot until he lost an engine with 50 miles left.

In the end, Evans beat Gant and Bonnett for the win, the operative word being "beat" because Evans had cuffed them around all afternoon. The only hope for Gant, who broke a valve spring, was through drafting well, and he sure did that; he was able to slingshot past Bonnett with three laps to go as they raced back to a caution for Dick Trickle's blown engine, and the green never reappeared. And the crafty Bonnett, as expected, tried every sly gimmick he knew.

"At one point," Nacewicz recalls with a smile, "the yellow flag came

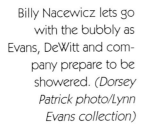

Billy Nacewicz lets go with the bubbly as Evans, DeWitt and company prepare to be showered. *(Dorsey Patrick photo/Lynn Evans collection)*

out, and Neil passed Rich and took the lead as they got to the line. That was legal, but kinda questionable. Richie wasn't very happy about it; he came on the radio and said he was all through playing around.

"There was a restart later on, [with Evans leading] and he noticed that as they came through turns three and four before the green, Bonnett was dropping way back. He said, 'Neil's going to try a flying start. He thinks he's going to blow by me on the restart.' Well, just when he figured Neil had dropped back about as far as he was going to, Rich stood on the gas and just *left* him.

"Neil told us later, 'When Richie took off on that restart, I didn't see anything but two black strips of rubber on that track.'"

And to the press, Bonnett was more blunt: "Richie made spectators out of me and Harry and the rest. It was a total mismatch, probably the biggest one I've ever been in."

How lopsided was it, really? Well, Ed Flemke, spectating from high in the grandstands, had noticed something peculiar while watching his one-time pupil's car. Evans would come through the fourth turn's banking high against the wall on one lap, and right down near the apron on the next; on his third time by, he might be smack in the middle of the track. When Eddie asked about it later, Richie responded that between the lack of chatter from the pits and the fact that he had no real pressure, he'd gotten bored.

"I was just playing," Evans told Flemke.

Reporters asked Evans about the strip of tape on his leg. He pointed out the ink marks, and explained, "Well, I had no radio, so I stuck this on my leg and used it to keep track of the laps." Even some of the most seasoned men in the Daytona press corps shook their heads in amazement.

The swan song for the Evans Camaro came just under three months later, in May of 1980, not in a modified event but in a 300-mile Talladega race for NASCAR's struggling Grand American division. Richie entered the event for the simplest of reasons: with the superspeedway modifieds dead and the Grand Americans on the ropes, it was probably going to be his last shot to run a car he had come to love.

Changing classes meant changing the car a bit. Out came the big-block, and in its place was installed a Grand American-legal Hutter-built 368-inch small-block. "And NASCAR made us put on a more conventional Camaro nose," Nacewicz recalls. But that wasn't likely to slow it down much, and everybody knew it. Said Bonnett, who had entered the race with Griffin's car, "I told the guys to bring me a bullet to Talladega. It'll take something that fast to keep up with Richie Evans."

Another Grand American interloper that weekend was a Missouri kid named Russell "Rusty" Wallace. Just 23 years old in that spring of 1980, Wallace had been tearing up the ASA and assorted other Midwest circuits, and had made several successful runs in the United States Auto Club's old stock car division. But the really fun thing about Rusty

February, 1980. Gene DeWitt joins Richie and Lynn Evans in celebrating a second straight Daytona score. *(Dorsey Patrick photo/Lynn Evans collection)*

Wallace back then was that he was liable to show up at any mixed-bag, wild-assed stock car show he could find. A Grand American race at Talladega, then, was right up his alley.

"I ran my USAC car, which Pete Hamilton had actually helped me design," Rusty remembers. "It had leaf springs in the back and a Stock Car Products snout on it. It ran everywhere, from the one-mile dirt track at DuQuoin, Illinois, to the Milwaukee Mile. And when we took it to a place like Talladega, we'd fix it up with these big ol' humped-up front fenders so we'd have more tire clearance. My car and Richie's Camaro, those were awesome-looking cars."

Wallace won the pole, no small accomplishment given that the field included superspeedway sleepers like Bonnett and Gant. Those guys, both of whom crisscrossed the country racing occasional late model events, were familiar to Wallace. Evans, on the other hand, was a guy he barely knew, but sure knew a lot *about*. Wherever you go in this sport, winners seem to study winners.

"I hadn't ever had a whole lot of interaction with Richie," Rusty says, "but I'd had a few conversations with him and Dick Trickle. He and Trickle were always good buddies, and they'd had a lot of fun racing at New Smyrna every February. I always had a lot of respect for Trickle, and through him I had a lot of respect for Richie, too. I knew he was just an all-around great racer."

That point was underscored for Rusty Wallace come race day at Talladega. Gant and Bonnett both ran into mechanical trouble, and the fight for the Grand American 300 trophy ended up involving just Wallace and Evans.

Actually, it might not have been much of a fight if Evans hadn't had some trouble of his own. "We had a one-lap lead over everybody, including Rusty, who was second," Nacewicz recalls. "Then Rich picked up a bad vibration; he thought it was something in the left-front corner, but he hadn't done enough superspeedway racing to pinpoint exactly what it was."

A loose wheel? A bad tire? Evans didn't see any sense in taking chances. He ducked down pit road, under green-flag conditions, for a four-tire stop. Again, David Ifft and his Winston Cup tire-changers were manning the Evans pit.

"They got the right-side tires changed," Nacewicz says, "and when they pulled off the left-front, you could see right away what was wrong. In those days, everybody ran double shocks on each side up front, and one of those shocks was just hanging there. Well, there wasn't much we could do to fix that in a hurry, so they just took a look around to make sure everything else was OK and then they put the tire back on.

"Once Richie knew what the problem was—that it wasn't a wheel about to fly off or something like that—he was fine. He still had to deal with that vibration, but he was back up to speed."

In truth, calling it a vibration is downplaying things a bit. Evans said, "The wheel was bouncing so much that the tire was digging in under the fender and blowing smoke up through the hood. Every time that tire smashed up into the fender, it was like, *wham, wham, wham!*"

Nacewicz says, "Even with that broken shock, he ran a lot of laps at over 200 miles an hour; we actually had [him clocked at] laps of 202. But [when Richie pitted], Rusty had unlapped himself and taken the lead. From that point on, it was a two-car race."

Wallace remembers it as "a great run, a great battle," with him out front and Evans trying to reel him in. Time was in Rusty's favor; speed was in Richie's.

"Toward the end of the race, Rusty was leading but we were catching him," says Nacewicz. "Rich finally got to him right at the end. It looked like he *might* have a chance to slingshot past him for the win. Maybe, maybe not. But coming down toward the checkered flag, our motor blew. So Rusty won, and we were second." Wallace headed for the podium, and one of the biggest celebrations of his life to that point.

"I've still got some great photographs taken after that race," Rusty says. "At that time, victory lane at Talladega was just a big patch of dirt with a plastic sign. I pulled in there with my crew sitting all over the hood of the car. Fun times, man."

Evans, meanwhile, headed back toward the garage area.

"We rolled the car over to the scales," Nacewicz says, "and as we were standing there, Bobby Allison walked up. He'd been following the race pretty good, and he knew about the broken shock and all that. And Bobby said, 'Man, that was a heck of a try on that last lap, Richie. I thought you might get him.'

"Rich said, 'I think I *could* have, if the motor hadn't blown.'"

The look on Allison's face, Nacewicz recalls, made it plain that he didn't completely buy that blown-engine explanation. Which, of course, is not totally surprising. When you've been around racing as long as Bobby Allison has, you hear a million such excuses. The winner has a bottle of champagne, everybody else has a sad story.

According to Nacewicz, "Bobby said, 'Come on. No way that car blew a motor, as close as you came to winning.' So Richie reached in and hit the starter button, and all you could hear was *clang-clang-clang-clang*.

"Bobby just smiled and shook his head."

The whole day is a fond memory for Wallace, and not just because he won the race. "I always read about Richie, and I'd watch him whenever I could," says Rusty. "And to have run with him at Talladega, that's extra-special."

The short, spectacular run of "that orange Camaro," as Neil Bonnett called it, was done. "Here's something to think about," says Billy Nacewicz. "We ran that car four times: three at Daytona and one at Talladega. We ran it with a B&M big-block, a Hutter big-block, and a 368 [Hutter] small-block. It won twice, and finished second twice.

"That car was never out of the top two."

On the Road Again

THERE IS SOMETHING ABOUT being hundreds of miles from home and having the unexpected unfold—for better or worse—that gets into a man's veins. Some are put off by that sort of chaos and opt for the safety of the *known*, living calm, centered lives. Others are curious, turned on, and keep heading out looking for the next great adventure.

Early on, Richie Evans landed in the latter camp. It probably wasn't any one single trip that hooked him, but rather an accumulation of the way everything looked different when he and his race car were four, six, eight hours down the road.

Such as ...

"The first time we ever went to Martinsville [in '68], Richie wanted to get a beer," Ted Puchyr remembers. "We'd been working our butts off on that coupe, and we felt like we deserved a break. So we started looking around, but everywhere we went, they told us, 'You can't buy beer here. It's a dry county.' We stopped in this one grocery store and they said, 'No, you gotta go to North Carolina if you want a beer.' *The next state!* So we drive down to North Carolina, get a case of beer, and come back. We drank a couple beers in the motel room.

"The next day, we're in the pits, talking to some guys from down there. Richie said, 'This is pretty bad, this being a dry county.' They said, 'Why don't you come to the turkey shoot tonight?' Richie and I looked at each other. He said, 'Come *where?*' They said, 'The turkey shoot.' Anyway, they give us directions, and that night we go down this Godforsaken back road. At the end, there's this little wooden hut with a fire in it. They're making moonshine! They're shooting at targets, and the prize is hooch. We're saying, 'This *can't* be. This is the '60's. Nobody's making their own whiskey anymore!'

"The very next day, we're at a gas station. This car comes in, and it's got what we used to call a 'California rake.' That's where the nose is really low, the tail really high. I said to a guy in the gas station, 'Where we come from, that style of hot rod went out in the late '50's, but that's the second or third car I've seen like that down here.' The guy said, 'What are you talking about, hot rod? That's a tanker, a moonshine hauler. See, we don't outrun the cops any more, we outsmart 'em. They fill the back of that thing up [with home-brewed whiskey] and it levels right out. Then the guy puts his wife and two kids in the car and they're out for a nice Sunday ride, and nobody knows about all that hooch.'

"Richie and I are sitting there saying, 'This is *not* happening.'"

It was certainly not something Evans was likely to see on a side street back in Rome, or up near Plattsburgh on the way to Airborne Park, or in the flat farm country around Spencer Speedway. He was curious about the unknown, turned on. You just know that seeing this tanker car had him laughing all afternoon. And it was that sort of incident that helped make him a highwayman for life.

"He loved to travel," says his old friend Wilbur Jones. "God, how he loved that road."

It wasn't until the early-'80s that Willie Nelson recorded "On the Road Again," a number Evans would play anytime he got close to a jukebox, but by then he had been living its lyrics for years. He was one of that special breed who could handle anything the highway life threw at him; he not only didn't fear the unknown, he seemed to appreciate its challenges.

Another Martinsville trip, from late in the coupe days: "It was me, Danny Morgan and Richie in the truck," Jones recalls. "Of course, Richie didn't want to leave until about two or three o'clock in the morning. We went up to the Rusty Nail and had a beer, and then we hit the road. We made it until we were just outside of Harrisburg, Pennsylvania. Richie had his foot right to the mat, and the motor blew up. We were one mile from an exit, and I remember him coasting off the exit, around the corner and into a gas station.

"By now, it's daylight. He called Rome, and he talked with Junior Carpenter, who worked for him at the gas station. Richie said, 'Take the motor out of that yellow Camaro that's sitting there. Put that motor in the back of Freddy Ulrich's pickup, and get down here.' While we waited for him, we took the motor out of the truck. Once he got there, we put the Camaro motor in, buttoned it up, and went on to Martinsville."

The road had plenty of potential pitfalls, to be sure. In April of 1985 —just months before Evans's death—Richie, Billy Nacewicz and Tony Pettinelli Jr. were heading south for a doubleheader weekend, Friday night at "either Calloway or Caraway," Pettinelli remembers, and Saturday afternoon at Martinsville. Pettinelli was driving, Evans and Nacewicz napping. They were somewhere in Virginia. The mile markers were flying by, and the tires were humming, and, well, things got a bit hypnotic for Tiger Pettinelli, just like they do for every long-distance wheelman at some point. Before he knew it, he had joined his two bosses in Slumberland.

"I woke up just as the truck was heading off the left side of the highway and into the median," Pettinelli remembers. "Well, it bounced around pretty hard, and stuff started flying everywhere. Billy's in the front seat and he's bouncing around, and Richie's in the sleeper with stuff falling on him from the upper bunk. It would have been no big deal—just a trip into the ditch—but about five feet from me getting it completely stopped, one of the front wheels hit a guardrail post. That broke the steering box.

"They shut down the highway while a big tow truck pulled us out of there. Richie got in touch with a guy he knew who had a trucking outfit not far away. The guy said, 'Bring it here. We've got a big yard, and you can use whatever tools you need.' We went over there, and I pulled off the broken steering box while they went and found a new one. We bolted the new box on, and everything worked fine, except for one small detail: When I turned the steering wheel to the *right*, the wheels were turning to the *left*. What happened was, we had a front-steer truck and this other steering box was a rear-steer. It would have been funny, except we're still going to try to get to this Friday-night race.

"Billy says, 'Hell, I'll drive it just the way it is.' We all told him there was no way; if something happens, your natural instincts kick in, and maybe you'll end up steering toward something you want to avoid. Billy says, 'I can do it.' So he jumps in to try it out. Now, this is about a ten-acre parking lot, and it's empty except for one little guard shack in the middle, but Billy couldn't drive around that place without almost cleaning out that shack a half-dozen times. He finally admitted that this was a bad idea."

They missed the race.

Of course, given the miles they traveled, Evans and any number of his modified competitors were lucky that the only real misfortunes were the occasional lost events.

There was the return trip from Oswego when one of the Evans trucks—a cabover monstrosity nicknamed "Big Orange," a tag eventually applied to Richie's cars and team, too—ended up on its side in a ditch beside a rural two-lane. Thankfully, there were no injuries.

George Kent, who led and followed Evans up a lot of interstate highways, says, "We raced one night at Shangri-La and didn't get out of there until midnight or one o'clock. The next day, there was a modified race at North Wilkesboro, North Carolina. Off we went. And I'm telling you, we were going down the road at 90 or 100 [MPH], which was as fast as my truck would go. George Colwell was driving Richie's truck, and we couldn't catch him. *God*, that Ford of his would run.

"Richie told me later that he sat up in the sleeper one time and looked at the speedometer, and he couldn't even see the needle. He said he just laid back down and went to sleep."

So the life had its risks. It also had its share of cheap hotels and greasy-spoon restaurants. When you're racing short-track cars for a living, the bottom line is important, so Evans and his troops slept and ate in no-frills places, particularly on a typical weekend when the wives and girlfriends stayed home. For example, he spent many post-Riverside Saturday nights in a West Springfield motel that had long since transitioned from "quaint" to "seedy," and in most race towns he was an even-money bet to dine at a pancake house or a sandwich joint. There was little luxury in the highway phase of things, even for a mega-time NASCAR modified champion.

"I'm sure it tired him out at times," Lynn Evans says. "But if it did, he never complained about it."

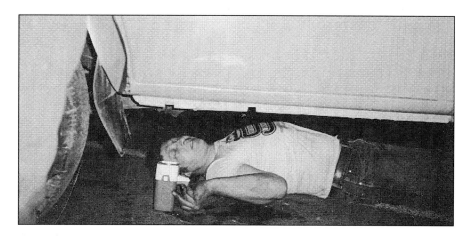

Ah, life on the road! Billy Nacewicz plays truck mechanic in the early 1980s. *(Val LeSieur photo/courtesy of Speedway Scene)*

The hook was the romance of the whole thing, the allure of the road, waiting to see exactly what that next great adventure was going to be.

Billy Nacewicz says, "It's funny, because as a kid I had followed the Eastern Bandits and the way they traveled, and to me that was amazing. But later on, with Richie, it felt like we were kinda like the Eastern Bandits. Running for those championships took us *everywhere*. The only difference was, we usually had only [Jerry] Cook out there with us, and there wasn't the friendship between us that there had been between, say, Eddie Flemke and Denny Zimmerman. So we didn't travel down the road with Jerry, even though we'd always show up at the same places.

"But if we'd been racing 15 years earlier, we'd have been right out there on the road with Flemke and the rest of 'em. Because we *enjoyed* traveling."

Evans saw his Rome base as an advantage in all this. While some championship-chasers over the years—say, the Massachusetts team of Bugs Stevens and Lenny Boehler, based virtually on the Atlantic shore—had to rack up incredible miles to get beyond their local tracks, for much of his career Richie was surrounded by a considerable number of paved modified speedways.

"I'm sitting here where I can go either west or east," he told radio host Arnold Dean.

Some on-the-road weeks were easy ... relatively speaking, of course. Early on, his all-New York weekends—whether Malta/Plattsburgh/Utica-Rome or Spencer/Lancaster/Fulton—were never very taxing from a travel standpoint. And in the late 1970s and early '80s, Evans often spent entire weekends in New England, running Stafford on Friday nights, Riverside Park on Saturdays, and Thompson on Sundays. Though the run to Stafford, Evans told Dean, was "three and a half hours, with the hammer down," once he got out there his longest haul, Riverside-to-Thompson, was less than 90 minutes.

"I enjoyed those New England weekends," says Nacewicz. "I didn't necessarily like being away from home that long"—by now, Billy was

On the Road Again   **163**

also married—"but I liked running those three tracks, all of them so close together. And sometimes we could go to Long Island and run Riverhead and Islip, or Freeport and Islip, on the same weekend."

Other weeks were a bit trickier. "When you were chasing a championship," Nacewicz says, "sometimes that meant passing up a race close by for another race several hours away that paid the same money, just because the second race offered more points." And so there were a number of Friday nights at Stafford followed by a 270-mile westward haul to Shangri-La for a Saturday show and then a 300-mile pull right back to Connecticut—passing right by Riverside Park in the process!—for Thompson's Sunday afternoon program.

Then there were the wild-card shows to fit in, some of them NASCAR-sanctioned and others well-paying open-comp events: New Egypt or New Hampshire's Star Speedway or maybe Westboro, Massachusetts, on a Wednesday night, even Catamount on a Tuesday if it happened to be, say, the Fourth of July.

"The toughest trip was probably New Egypt, just because it was six hours down and six hours back every Wednesday night," says Nacewicz. "The guys who helped us on their own time couldn't do that trip very often, so a lot of weeks it was just me and Rich." (For a brief time in the late 1970s, Evans simplified the New Egypt hassle by flying to Newark—at a discount rate, thanks to wife Lynn's airline connection—and driving a car he'd sold to Jersey veteran Tom Green, a man whom "Rich thought the world of," Lynn says.)

And some weeks were just plain insane. Imagine a weekend consisting of Stafford on Friday night, Bowman Gray Stadium in North Carolina on Saturday night, and Thompson Speedway on Sunday. Both Richie Evans and Jerry Cook could tell you all about that, having done it more than once. Approximate highway miles for those three days, leaving from and returning to their Rome shops: 1955. With, of course, the small matter of three races to run, the Bowman Gray stop being a 200-lap national championship event.

"Richie would come down to Bowman Gray for the 200-lapper," says Bobby Hutchens, then a Stadium regular. "He'd miss qualifying on Friday night because he was up North racing someplace else, then he'd show up on Saturday.

"Now, Bowman Gray is a tough, tough place. I've watched a lot of good drivers come in there and not do a thing. It doesn't look like much —just a quarter-mile around a football field—but it's a place where setups are very important, and it's the hardest track in the world to get around. Richie would get very little practice, if any, and he probably hadn't seen the place since the year before. On top of that, they usually had some wacky tire rule he wasn't used to running on. Yet he'd roll that car off the truck, start wherever, and if he didn't win he'd end up in the top two or three. Then he'd load up and head back to New York or New England, chasing more points."

Of course, adding to the fun of all this highway stuff was the fact that anything was subject to change at any time, depending on the skies above.

"We always kept a really close eye on the weather," says Nacewicz. "Richie had a little weather-radar radio deal that Lynn had gotten him, and 24 hours a day it would give you the weather within a 200-mile radius. Don't forget, at that time there was no Weather Channel or anything like that, so this was kind of a trick piece. We kept that thing in the truck at all times. It might be Friday afternoon and we'd be headed to Stafford, but if we checked that radio and it looked like Connecticut seemed shaky because of rain, we'd turn around on the Thruway and head back toward Spencer Speedway."

George Kent, who didn't have a fancy radio like Richie's, used a simpler method for a while. On cloudy Saturdays, he and his brother (and car owner) Ron would leave their Horseheads shop early, and sit a spell in Albany. "Then," says Kent, "we'd decide whether we should keep going [east] toward Riverside Park or head back [west] on I-88 toward Shangri-La." Eventually, Kent found a method that proved much more accurate: whenever possible, he simply followed Evans!

"This one particular Saturday, it looked like rain everywhere," says a chuckling Kent. "We decided to go on toward Riverside, but then I spotted Richie's truck heading the other way on the Mass Pike. I said to Ronnie, 'Turn around and follow him.' When we saw him in the pits at Shangri-La, boy, Richie was hot. He said, 'I'll *never* let you catch me on the fucking road again. I'll find different routes, and you'll never know where I am.' Oh, he was bitching."

Billy Nacewicz says, "I'll tell you how well we had that weather situation covered. If there was a forecast of bad weather all over on a Friday night, we might send one truck to Spencer and send the other to Stafford. At the same time, we'd leave a passenger car right there at the Thruway exit in Rome. That way, if it rained out late wherever Richie was headed, we just got that truck back to Rome as quick as we could, then he'd jump into that car and haul ass—I mean, 100 miles an hour down the Thruway if he had to—to the other track."

Not everybody could switch plans so easily. Millie Hatch, Richie's fan club president, says she and her husband Bill "got stung a couple times that way. One week, I called him and said, 'Where are you racing this Saturday night?' It was his birthday, and we were going to bring a cake for him. He told us he was going to Shangri-La. Well, we were there with the cake, but he ended up going to Riverside Park."

The funny thing was, Richie actually missed a lot of the highway life he's remembered for. "His only weakness was driving the truck," Nacewicz says. "And he didn't do much of it." Anybody who ever traveled with him seems to have the same story: Somebody else was driving while Evans himself covered a lot of miles with his eyes closed.

"We used to have a deal," Wilbur Jones says with a smirk.

"Everybody drove for one tankful of gas. Well, somehow Richie's tankful never lasted as long as anybody else's."

Over the years, the cast of characters who shared the wheel, the navigation and the madness continued to change. When guys like Buster Maurer and Danny Morgan jumped off the road, that left room in the tow rig for, say, George Colwell and Jerry Bear and Dave "Carter" Best, a Canadian wrench; later on, their seats were filled in turn. Scott Findlay, a Rome-area kid, did his share of seat time in those orange trucks during the '80s. "Of course, Tiger went with us a bunch, and Bondo, too," says Nacewicz.

Tiger Pettinelli was "16 or so, still in school" when he signed on with the Evans team, working afternoons and evenings for a while and then joining the full-time roster. "My dad was out someplace, and he ran into Richie. I guess he asked my dad what I'd been doing. Richie said, 'Have him stop over and see me.' I had just picked up an old street stock and I'd been dickin' around with that in the back yard, so I guess he figured I was into race cars. I dropped by the shop, and he asked me if I wanted to go to work for him. That was in 1979.

"It was cool to go to all these places I'd only heard about. Like, we'd work all winter, and all of a sudden we're off to *Daytona*. Then we're going to *Martinsville*. But, you know, those guys used to break my balls pretty good. See, until I got with Richie I'd never done any traveling, to speak of. We might have taken one or two family vacations, but nothing major. Now, here I am, going on the road for the first time with these guys, and I've literally got all my clothes shoved into a brown paper grocery bag. They all said, 'What the heck is that?' I said, 'It's my luggage, man.' They suggested that I get something a little more durable."

Bondo Clark had been on board since '73, as mentioned earlier. He recalls being 15 years old when Evans "gave me a handful of quarters and told me to take the truck and the race car down to the car wash and get it cleaned up. He explained to me how to drive a standard shift, and away I went. A driver's license didn't seem to matter much at the time." He studied auto body work in trade school, shot an awful lot of "1021 orange" paint on Calvert Street, and went from "sneaking into the Utica-Rome pits in the sleeper of Richie's truck" to riding in the front seat all over the Eastern Seaboard. He says, "Looking back, it was neat going traveling like we did, because I was still pretty young."

And then there were all the scattered crewmen who either chased the Evans bandwagon up and down the concrete trail, or stood by ready to lend a hand when the bandwagon rolled to a stop at their local track. Bay Stater Ray Spognardi lived something like 275 miles east of Rome, but he hooked up with Evans and Nacewicz on countless road trips. "Then we had Steve Krupski and Ronnie Jarvis from Albany, who went to an awful lot of races and helped us," Nacewicz says "We called them 'the Albany Connection.' And we had 'the Holland Gang,' three terrific guys who helped us every time we were out in Western New York; one of 'em was actually a police chief, so I'm not sure what he was doing on our crew! And none of those people ever asked for anything, not even a pit pass. They'd pay their own way, and they'd do whatever they could to help."

With all those folks, from the regular travelers to the more casual camp followers, Nacewicz says the commitment was unstated but understood: "If you need us, we'll be there."

Of course, it wasn't all toil and drudgery. The road had a way of promoting zany behavior, perhaps as a natural counter to the milepost monotony.

Andy Fusco remembers heading west on the Massachusetts Turnpike in 1970 in the company of *Gater Racing News* columnist Mike Monnat, the two of them making their weary way home after an All Star League swing into New England.

"Merv Treichler pulls alongside us in the passing lane, honking as if to challenge us to race," says Fusco. "All of sudden, here comes the Evans hauler on the right side, making it three-wide on the shoulder."

Monnat and Fusco glanced over. Evans, in a rare stint behind the wheel, was "laughing like a hyena."

Fusco says, "Imagine that: racing on the Mass Pike, with Richie Evans flying by in the breakdown lane."

And Lynn Evans brings up another bit of highway tomfoolery involving her late husband. On a trip home from a Pocono Race of Champions, Richie was snoozing in the passenger seat of their car as she tooled along in the middle of a convoy of his trucks, trailers, crewmen and fans. On a quiet stretch of Pennsylvania interstate, Lynn saw another car enter the freeway from an on-ramp and dart in and out amongst them. "The guy was playing games," she says. "I was concerned about his trucks and the guys, so I woke up Rich and said, 'You'd better pay attention to this.' He watched for a few minutes, and then he said to me, 'Slide over.' We'd done that before—you know, changing drivers while we were moving—so I got out from behind the wheel and he took over. Well, he caught that guy, and the next thing I knew that car was off the road, out in the wild. Rich said, 'They won't be bothering us anymore. Now slide back over here.' And down the road we went, with me driving again.

"Eventually we all stopped to get something to eat. A lot of our gang had seen what happened, and as they got out of their cars they were saying to me, 'Gosh, Lynn, maybe *you* should drive race cars. You really took care of that guy.' Rich loved that. He just quietly motioned to me, like, *Ssshhh!* He kept it a secret."

And at least one Evans road trip ended up creating an international incident.

Anytime an American team crossed into Canada to compete in a race, it was customary for the officials at the border crossing to take a complete—and often invasive—inventory of all cars, engines, parts and tools. This was in an effort to stem the common practice of Yankee teams quietly off-loading their used equipment to Canadian racers, with nobody worrying about governmental trivialities like exchange rates or sales tax dollars or trade tariffs. Ted Puchyr says, "They'd actually tell you, 'No matter how bad you wreck, bring back your tires, bring back your rims. Do not leave *anything* in Canada.'"

Well, on this one particular night back in the coupe days, Evans was rolling home from a midweek show up in Ottawa, and he got a little impatient when, to his surprise, there was no attendant at the border crossing. Maybe the guy had gone off for a fast bathroom break, maybe he was napping in a corner. Either way, Puchyr remembers Evans snapping, "We ain't waiting. Let's go."

Two days later, the phone rang at a Shell station in Rome, New York. The proprietor, a Mr. Evans, picked up. Canadian Customs was on the other end.

"They had a record of us crossing into Canada," Puchyr says, "but they had no record of us coming back. They said, 'When are you going to get this car out of here?' You know, meaning out of Canada. Richie said, 'Get *what* car out of here?' They said, 'You guys went across the border the other day, and according to our records you never brought that race car back out.'

"Richie said, 'You mean the one sitting right here next to me?'"

The man from Customs thought that was a joke. So, according to Dominick Street lore, Evans fired up the engine and goosed the throttle, thus proving conclusively that his race car was indeed nearby.

"They weren't too happy with him," Puchyr laughs. "In fact, we didn't go back to Ottawa for a while."

Yeah, but that was all right. The United States had enough all-night diners, flophouse hotels and race tracks to keep Richie Evans fed, rested and happy.

 Top Gun

NOW, HERE ARE A COUPLE OF weekend itineraries for the travel-hungry NASCAR modified racer. How about a pair of early-April 100-lappers, one on a Saturday night and the other on Sunday afternoon, the first in Hickory, North Carolina, the second in Seekonk, Massachusetts? Sound a little too stiff? Well, then, we'll build in some spare time for this next one; let's say, 100 laps at Stafford, Connecticut, on an October Friday night, and then maybe 250 laps on Sunday afternoon in Kingsport, Tennessee? Saturday can be a driving day. Did we mention that it's only 765 miles?

Evans was always up for those sorts of challenges. Heck, he might just take you up on both tour packages. And he might, as he did in 1979, go right ahead and win *all four* races.

That was Richie's top-gun season, 1979, his most lopsided year in a career full of lopsided years. He won 52 of his 84 starts, won from Florida to Quebec, won the Race of Champions at Pocono and the 200 at Stafford and the Port City 150 at Oswego, won his second straight—and third overall—NASCAR modified title, just plain *won*.

He started with six victories in seven New Smyrna starts, and he just refused to slow down. By the time he left Seekonk on that April Sunday—having worked his way past Jerry Cook, Bugs Stevens, Leo Cleary and Ron Bouchard to win on a track he'd never even seen—Evans had been triumphant in 10 of the 13 races he'd entered that season.

And then he got serious. Twice in the middle of April, chasing (and being chased by) Cook on the NASCAR points trail, the Evans rig rolled out of Rome and picked up I-81, southbound, toward doubleheader weekends in Dixie. You could call both trips successful. On Saturday, April 21, he won Martinsville's Azalea 150 in the afternoon and backed it up that night by grabbing a national championship show at Caraway Speedway in Asheboro, North Carolina. The following week, he captured a Friday-night 100-lapper at Franklin County in Virginia, then skipped across the state line to Winston-Salem to pick off a Bowman Gray 200 by passing leader Satch Worley on the final lap.

When the Northeast season opened, he won wherever he felt like winning: Stafford, Riverside, Shangri-La, New Egypt. In late spring he won big at a brand-new modified place, the Duex Montagnes Speedway near Montreal (in a 100-lap score over Worley, Cook and Ron Bouchard), and at a familiar one, Oswego (topping Ohio late model convert Mark "Captain Sizzle" Malcuit, Cook and George Kent in the Port City 150).

In the first week of June came a New England hat trick: Stafford on Friday night, Riverside Park on Saturday night, the Yankee 100 at Monadnock on Sunday.

Yes, it was looking like 1979 might be a pretty decent year for the Rapid Roman.

"I can't pinpoint any particular reason why that was such a good period for us," says Billy Nacewicz. "I guess you could say we were sort of refining our package. Even though we had built new cars that winter, they were basically the same stuff we'd been running, chassis-wise. And it was our second year with Ron Hutter's engines, which definitely helped us with both power and reliability. And the team we had at that point had been together a while, which helps."

The core of the DeWitt #61 squad was Evans, Nacewicz, Ray Spognardi and Kenny Hartung. Spognardi was a Massachusetts veteran who had labored on race cars dating back to the days of the old Norwood Arena, outside Boston; Hartung, a Long Island guy, had been a Freeport Stadium late model competitor. Alongside Nacewicz, they gave Evans perhaps the deepest team he'd ever had, mechanically. Where in the past he might have had one solid wrench like Buster Maurer and a few helpers, or Billy Taylor and a few helpers, now he had a crew of mechanics who could reliably divide the routine trackside work and handle whatever crises came up.

"Until you have that stability," says Nacewicz, "even a little thing like getting a tire mounted becomes something you have to worry about."

Speaking of tires, they played a role, too, in refining the Evans package in 1979. It was his first full season with Goodyear after his mid-'78 jump from Firestone. Now, just as had worked so closely with Bobby Summers at Firestone, he got tight with the right Goodyear folks, from Phil Holmer and Dick Dimmig on the corporate side to local dealers like Dave Lind in New England and Red Kosinksi in Central New York.

It is impossible to overstate how deeply Evans delved into the hows-and-whys of racing tires. Steve Hmiel, who'd watched this from across the pit area in his time with Cook, says, "Richie would get out of his car and go straight to his right-rear tire, and study it. Yeah, you see a lot of guys do that—looking at the tire, feeling it—but Richie actually knew what he was looking at. He really understood tires."

Bobby Summers remembers that even in the early 1970s, "Richie had a real interest in tires. I think he'd done some different things, through trial and error, that showed him how important tires were. He had what he called his 'wine cellar,' where he kept his tires. Not a whole lot of people got to go back there, but he'd let me in, and in that room he had every tire marked by date, race track, and number of laps. His theory back then—which was probably correct—was that the more age the tires had, the better they were. There were a lot more different tire compounds and constructions back then than there are now, but his theories seemed to work out very good. As a matter of fact, he would tell me things we needed to do to improve the product, and we did 'em. He was a real sharp character when it came to tires."

Maynard Troyer once told Dick Berggren, "Reading tires is an art all its own. I've seen Richie Evans pull a tire off the right-front, saying it's not working. He puts another one on—identical compound, same pressure, same everything—and it works much better. He puts the one he just took off on the rack, and he'll remember what it's like. Maybe a month from now, that tire will be just what he's looking for."

So by 1979, Evans knew exactly what he had in the way of tires, in the way of engines, in the way of his chassis, and in the way of personnel.

"That stuff *all* helped," says Nacewicz. "Plus, I think probably Rich was at the point in his career where he had a lot of maturity and confidence as a driver."

Mario Fiore, who spent a lot of time around Evans in that stage, says, "He was always thinking, 24 hours a day. It was just go, go, go. I don't know where he got his energy."

In mid-June, Richie Evans—going, going, going—won four races in five nights, beating Charlie Jarzombek and Cook at New Egypt; Ron Bouchard and Eddie Flemke at Stafford; Cook and Ron Wyckoff at Riverside Park; and Reggie Ruggiero and Cook at Monadnock.

By the end of that month he was an astonishing 29-for-40, and many were calling him a bet-the-farm cinch to eclipse the 55-win modified standard Bodine had set the previous season. Evans claimed to have no interest in Geoff's mark per se, telling Toodi Gelinas in June, "I'm not looking for any records. I just want to win as many as I can. That's what racing is all about."

Bodine had pretty much walked away from modified racing that season, focusing instead on his Winston Cup and NASCAR late model sportsman aspirations. But when he did turn up, it was as if he had never left. In July of '79 he came to Oswego with a jet-black Troyer-built car owned by New Hampshire's Lee Allard, an ex-supermodified shoe. Bodine and Evans ended up staging what Dick O'Brien called "the best modified race in Oswego history," and O'Brien saw them all. The two men ran side by side, Bodine low and Evans high, for virtually the entire race, with Geoff coming out on top.

It was a loss, but still a performance about which Evans could hold his head high. And that meant something, because, now that Utica-Rome was topped with dirt, Oswego Speedway—run by the Caruso family, patriarch Harry and sons George, Romey and Doug—was Richie's new home track. He raced four times there in 1979, never finishing lower than third.

If he had a second home that season, it might have been Stafford. He did miss a couple of weekly shows there—sacrificing the track championship to Ron Bouchard as a result—but could usually be counted on to roll through the pit gate late on Friday afternoon. In many ways, that was a puzzling choice for a points chaser, because Stafford was certainly the toughest Friday-night stop on the NASCAR modified circuit. But Evans had taken a liking to the place, and so had his crew chief.

"It would have been much easier for us to race at Spencer on a Friday night than it was to go to Stafford," Billy Nacewicz says. "At Spencer, even if we were off a little bit, we were going to run in the top five. But at Stafford, with that field as strong as it was, you couldn't *be* a little bit off. I mean, think about how tough that place was back then; you had Bugsy, Flemke, Ronnie and Kenny Bouchard, John Rosati, Bob Polverari, Ray Miller ... where do you want to stop?

"That place on a Friday night was just so exciting. Every week, just before the feature, they'd play that song—the theme from the movie 'Shaft'—and it would send chills up my spine."

John McMullin, then Stafford's director of public relations, says, "I believe that on any Friday night, we had the best modified racing in the

Two of the best, Evans and Ron Bouchard, slug it out at Stafford in 1979. *(Howie Hodge photo/courtesy of Speedway Scene)*

country. Actually, I think we had the best racing of *any* kind. We had the big stars of that time, and they were all starting in the back in a 30-lap feature. In fact, the problem we had at Stafford back then was that whenever we had a big show, it really wasn't much different from our Friday-night show but the [ticket] prices were higher. The fans didn't like it, because they already saw the best show in the world every week."

Evans won 10 times at Stafford in 1979, including eight scores in those exciting Friday-night 30-lappers. In July he won the open-competition Modified Madness event, piping normally-outlawed nitrous oxide into his small-block Hutter. "Some of the cars had 500 cubic-inch engines, and alcohol [fuel], and injectors, and so on," Evans explained to Arnold Dean. "I ran a 368 cubic-inch motor, which is 140 cubes smaller than some of the other motors. The rules said [using nitrous oxide] was OK, so I did it."

And on Labor Day, NASCAR-legal once again, he outran Mark Malcuit and Maynard Troyer in conquering the traditional 200. It was win number 46 for the season.

Runner-up Mark Malcuit (left) and third-place man Maynard Troyer flank the 1979 Stafford 200 winner. *(Mike Adaskaveg photo)*

Thompson starter Dick Brooks (left) and legendary driver/official Bill Slater (right) congratulate Evans on his 50th win of 1979. *(Paul Bonneau photo/courtesy of* Speedway Scene*)*

The next week, Evans went to Islip and took the All Star 300 for a fourth straight time. That was the 10th NASCAR national championship event Evans won in '79; he ended up winning exactly half of the 24 run, on the way to boosting his NASCAR numbers that year to 37 wins in 60 starts.

And elsewhere, his overall total just kept rising ...

He won the Race of Champions on the 2.5-mile Pocono tri-oval, brushing off a Troyer scoring protest; "There's no question in my mind that I won the race," Evans told Dean. "Maynard, from all the sources I heard, really had no complaint."

The magical 50th win came in the Thompson World Series, over Dave Thomas (in the Allard 66, having taken over for Bodine) and Charlie Jarzombek. Number 51 came in Stafford's twice-postponed Fall Final, in which Evans beat a very tough Jerry Cook and Bugs Stevens.

And Richie's 52nd and final victory of 1979 came in that Kingsport 250—two days after Stafford, on the last crazy road trip of the year — when he led Cook and Satch Worley across the stripe.

Evans didn't end the year on the highest note, but he came close. At Martinsville, Evans stuck Ronnie Bouchard into his backup Pinto— "Bobby [Judkins] didn't have a car ready for me, for some reason," Bouchard recalls, "and Richie said, 'Hey, you need a ride?'"—and the pair had a great Cardinal 500. Bouchard, shadowing eventual winner Jerry Cook with eight laps to go, actually waved on a faster Evans, who had the freshest tires of the top runners. So Evans and Bouchard, one-shot teammates, ended up second and third on a day in which Richie locked up the NASCAR championship.

One week later, Evans was edged in a Shangri-La special by George Kent—an 11-time winner there in '79—and then he called it a season. To the surprise of many, he passed up the Turkey Derby at Wall Stadium on Thanksgiving weekend.

Maybe by then, he'd simply done enough winning.

There were those cynics who suggested that had he won Martinsville and Shangri-La, and thus had a shot to tie Bodine's mark,

A fine way to end a season, with victory number 52 at Kingsport, Tennessee. *(David Allio photo/courtesy of* Speedway Scene*)*

"Go on, boss." Ronnie Bouchard in the backup #81 Pinto waves on Evans late in the 1979 Cardinal 500. They finished second and third behind Jerry Cook. *(Balser and Son photo/courtesy of Speedway Scene.)*

Evans would have made the haul to New Jersey without batting an eye. Others insisted, as Evans was doing way back in June, that Geoff's 1978 numbers were irrelevant to Richie in 1979.

Billy Nacewicz remembers he and his boss just being thrilled to have had that kind of a season.

"It was an outstanding achievement," says Nacewicz. "I know Geoff did it the previous year, and I know he outdid us by a few. But we honestly didn't care. I mean, it's a rare thing to get 50 feature wins.

"Oh, yeah, we were pretty satisfied."

 ## The Natural

AT THE 1976 Cardinal 500 at Martinsville, the oft-married actress Elizabeth Taylor and her fiancée, former Secretary of the Navy—and later Virginia Senator—John Warner, turned up to campaign for the Republican presidential ticket of Gerald Ford and Bob Dole. They chose to stick around and watch a bit of the race.

During the modified feature, wrote Al Pearce of the *Newport News Times Herald*, "Warner noticed that Richie Evans was making a strong run at the front. He pointed out Evans to Miss Taylor, and together they began to exhort him onward. On three occasions they stood and cheered as he made daring moves to pass leader Geoff Bodine. Miss Taylor waved her arms frantically one other time as Evans dipped low and tried unsuccessfully to pass the leader. 'This is fabulous,' she yelled to a reporter …"

As it happened, Evans didn't win. Neither, of course, did the other team Liz backed that autumn; Ford and Dole surrendered the White House to Jimmy Carter and Walter Mondale.

The point: It didn't take a seasoned fan to understand that Richie

Charlie Jarzombek, his "cowboy boot stuck right inside that carburetor," puts some body English into chasing Evans at Thompson. *(Kevin Hodge photo/courtesy of Speedway Scene)*

Evans was fun to watch. Even an aging movie star and her suave politico boyfriend got *that* right away.

"There was something about the way he drove," Tom Baldwin once said of Evans. "It was fantastic to watch."

And yet his racing style was tough to pin down. Not all the great ones were that hard to figure out; some of their nicknames gave it all away. Steady Eddie Flemke, the psychologist, won with his head; Chargin' Charlie Jarzombek drove, in the words of Thompson Speedway announcer Russ Dowd, with "the toe of his cowboy boot stuck right inside that carburetor."

Evans was somewhere in the middle, his methodology flexible. Says Billy Nacewicz, "Richie was aggressively smooth, if that makes any sense. He was aggressive in the sense that he could always get to the front, but he was so smooth, so relaxed.

"Sitting in that race car, waiting for the feature to start, he'd look so comfortable. Some other drivers would look nervous, hyper, but Rich looked like he was getting ready to drive down to the store to get a loaf of bread. It was like he and the car were one unit."

"Aggressively smooth" is how Billy Nacewicz describes Richie's style, and that shows in this green-flag shot of Evans made by a remote-control camera mounted on Bob Polverari's roll cage. *(Marc Rohrbacher photo/courtesy of Speedway Scene)*

The Natural

Maynard Troyer puts a lot of it down to pure genetics— "I guess the biggest thing Richie had going for him was that he was just naturally good"—and that's a hard stance to argue against.

"He was as natural a driver as anybody I've ever seen," claims Ron Hutter. "I mean, I probably didn't realize it at the time, because working with Richie was really my first experience dealing with a circle-track guy. But over time, I came to realize how natural a talent he was."

Nacewicz says, "You can't overlook the God-given talent Rich had. Money can buy a lot of things, but it can't buy whatever it is that gets you from 20th spot to first in a 30-lap feature."

No, it can't. That comes from someplace else.

In the racing flick "Winning," the fictional driver Frank Capua—played by Paul Newman, who actually raced a modified against Evans in the 1974 Daytona road-course event—mutters, "You gotta learn to trust *something*. It might just as well be the seat of your pants." And much, indeed, has been made of the seat-of-the-pants feel Evans possessed.

"It was uncanny," says Buster Maurer. "Anybody can feel a car twitch; with Richie, it's like he could tell when that car was just getting *ready* to twitch."

And over the years he trusted that feel enough, and then had that trust rewarded enough, that he developed a quiet-but-strong belief in his own form. Evans had an unorthodox way of holding the steering wheel; while most drivers rely on the conventional "10 and two" grip, both of Richie's hands were a bit closer to the top of the wheel, in something of an "11 and one" configuration. Asked about it once, he shrugged and said, "It works for me." He saw no need to examine the issue any further.

According to Mario Fiore, "Richie had a lot of self-confidence. He knew he was a good driver. I mean, he might not *say* it, but he'd never give you the impression that he thought somebody else was a better driver than him."

And so night after night, feature after feature, here would come that bundle of talent and confidence, guiding that orange #61 toward the front. "He was like the bulldog that won't let go of the bone," Maurer grins. "Once he focused on something, he really went after it."

In one of his most-repeated quotes, Evans declared to Pete Zanardi, "A good racer is one whose head is in communication with his balls." If you read the words too quickly, focusing only on the profanity, you can almost hear that goofy Evans giggle. But this was no laughing matter. He saw that balance of brains and brawn—all right, head and balls—as being absolutely critical.

"You can't have too much either way," Evans told Zanardi. "You have to find a perfect balance."

Brawn: "Think about all those races he won, the 30-lappers where a guy really had to crank it up and go," says Dick O'Brien. "He was obviously extremely brave."

Brains: "Richie was a smart driver, a heady guy," insists Bugs Stevens.

Brian Ross can't recall where he read it, but says, "I saw a study about how many minor and major decisions a race driver makes in a minute, and it was just an incredible number. Well, Richie was a quick thinker, witty, in and out of the race car. And, you know, I think that was a big part of his success. You've got to be a quick thinker—a tremendously quick thinker—to be a good racer."

"He was very good at not *over*-driving the car," says Nacewicz. "He always knew what he had, and he always knew exactly how much time he had to work with, and he didn't rush things. He knew he had to go from the back to the front, and he knew he'd have to pass the best guys in the business, but he also knew he could do it."

Baldwin used to tell a funny story about that. "This one night at Riverhead—it was a 100-lapper, or 150, whatever—I was really on my game. I'm leading the race, and my son, Tommy Jr., comes on the radio: 'You've got 'em all covered, Dad. Just take it easy and don't kill the car, and we're gonna win this thing.' But I'm looking up ahead, and there's Richie. I'm thinking, 'I'm gonna *lap* Richie Evans! Oh, am I gonna bust his ass about that later!' So I start driving harder and harder; Tommy Jr. is telling me to relax, but, hey, I'm gonna go up and lap Big Orange.

"Richie's taking a nice wide line around the place, saving his stuff. I'm driving it *in* hard, driving it *out* hard, going crazy. Well, naturally, I burn off the right-rear tire, and anybody who knows Riverhead will tell you that once you lose the right-rear, you might as well get a gun and put yourself out of your misery. Now I'm sideways, and there's nothing I can do. I start falling back, falling back, and before you know it I see Richie coming up behind me. He catches me, smokes right by me for the lead, and wins the race.

"And instead of me being able to bust his ass about lapping him, it all gets turned around, and I've got to put up with him: 'You really shouldn't drive so hard, Baldwin.' Oh, he was laughing."

Greg Sacks knew the feeling. In his formative years, running the same Long Island bullrings where Baldwin competed, Sacks had his share of nights when he allowed himself to believe he had Richie Evans covered. "We'd be [running] the Islip 300, and you wouldn't even see him for a while," Greg remembers. "It was like he was just out there cruising around." Come the last quarter of the race, everything looked somehow different. Evans, says Sacks, "was cruising around, all right. Cruising around the outside, going to the front!"

Jarzombek, that boot-in-the-carburetor leadfoot, had an interesting take on Evans. He told writer Ron Mentus in 1975 that Richie was "a very cautious driver. We've run side-by-side many times, even three-deep through a corner, and come out of it without crashing. At Pocono in 1973, he got trapped behind a slower car while leading, and I came by and passed him. If it was anybody else, he'd have just turned right into me. But Richie stayed where he was, and not many people would do that."

What was it Nacewicz said? *He always knew what he had, and he always knew exactly how much time he had to work with.* A guy could afford to be a little cautious with all that going for him.

George Kent says, "I've told a lot of drivers, young guys, that what made Richie so good is that he knew when he had a car that could win, and he knew when he had a third-place car. Richie knew enough not to crash trying to get further ahead than his car could take him. And that's something else: He was *really* good at missing wrecks."

Was that natural talent? Brains? Caution? Whatever was behind it, Evans had a knack for self-preservation.

"We once went one whole season, 80-some races, without ever breaking the steering," Nacewicz says. "Those rack-and-pinion setups were pretty sensitive; you didn't have to hit a wheel too hard before you'd break a tie-rod or chip a tooth, but we never had to replace a rack all year."

And when you're that kind to your own equipment, you end up being kind to everyone else's, too. It's hard to find a driver who ran up against Evans at any stage of his career who'll call him anything but a fair racer.

Dutch Hoag, from the 1960s: "We went flat out, but it was always good, clean racing between us, not rubbing wheels."

Ron Bouchard, from the 1970s: "You could run beside Richie *all day*, and he'd never, ever rub you. If he could pass you, he'd pass you. If he couldn't, he wasn't going to hit you to get by."

Bob Polverari, from the 1980s: "I can honestly say that I never, ever saw Richie put a guy out. I mean, in all the years I watched him and raced with him, I never saw him do anything rough or dirty."

Buster Maurer recalls their first-ever trip to Hickory in the early points-chasing days. "Paul Radford was the hot dog down there," Maurer says. "In the feature, a 100-lapper, Rich chased Radford for about the last 60 laps. He tried him inside, tried him outside, and Paul's head was swinging back and forth as he looked around, trying to keep Richie back there. Paul was *really* blocking him, to the point where I was furious. Anyway, Paul won and we finished second, and when Rich pulled up to the truck, he was laughing. He enjoyed that so much, the fact that he'd made that guy so nervous.

"The people who came into the pits afterwards wanted to know why Richie didn't just knock Radford out of the way. But Richie said, 'I don't want to win like that.'"

Put it like this: Evans drove the way you wish you could teach every aspiring young short-track kid to drive. "Richie raced to win," Sacks explains, "but not at all costs, ever. He wanted to win it his way, cleanly, by out-driving you, out-preparing you, and maybe even out-foxing you. It was never a bull-in-a-china-shop, knock-'em-out-of-the-way thing. It was always clean racing with Richie. He never wanted it any other way."

Nacewicz says, "He felt really strongly against dirty driving. He didn't like it being done to him, and he wouldn't do it himself."

"Richie," says Merv Treichler, "would never get you into a situation that was going to hurt either one of you."

Now, none of this necessarily made the guy a softie. Asked how he would describe Richie Evans, Reggie Ruggiero comes back with a one-word answer: "Selfish." But, anxious to make sure his remark isn't mistaken as an insult, Ruggiero says that *all* the best drivers are selfish. "They just want to win, all the time. I'm that way myself."

"He was *tough*," Maynard Troyer declares, "I mean, we [accidentally] pushed and shoved some nights. But anybody who races hard is going to do that sometimes, and we were really hard competitors. Every now and then things would happen on the race track, and we might call each other an asshole or something. But we'd still have a beer together. It might have taken an hour or two to get over it, but I don't think we ever went home mad at each other. Pissed off, maybe, but not mad to the point where we wouldn't speak to each other."

And George Kent says, "He'd run you the way you ran him. If you raced Richie clean, he raced you clean. But you didn't want to mess with him too much, because he could rough you up. He roughed me up a couple times, but nothing *bad*. And, you know, I accidentally spun him out one night up at Oswego; he wasn't real happy with me. But he always raced me hard, and if and when I could catch his ass, I'd race him hard, too."

Selfish, tough, occasionally rough ... but not unfair. Richie Evans just raced hard and clean, taking the fight to wherever the fight happened to be. Which brings up one other point that can't be ignored in any discussion of the man's talent: his incredibly versatility.

Reggie Ruggiero describes Evans as "selfish," but quickly adds, "I'm that way myself." The best drivers, says Reggie, "just want to win, all the time." (*Val LeSieur photo/courtesy of* Speedway Scene)

It didn't matter much if Evans was at a sprawling track like the Pocono tri-oval, where a driver needed to be silky-smooth to maximize speed, or a tiny joint like New Egypt, where, says Tony Siscone, "you were all hands, feet and eyes." In either case, the guy could produce, displaying a range unmatched in NASCAR modified history.

Think about this: in his blazing 1978 run of five straight triumphs in NASCAR national championship events—at Islip, New Egypt, Islip, Monadnock and New Egypt—the roomiest track on the list was Monadnock, a tight, elbows-up quarter-mile. Just a few months later, the same fellow who put together that amazing bullring streak dusted off Neil Bonnett and Harry Gant at Daytona.

"If he had a weakness, I never saw it," says Billy Nacewicz. "Richie proved himself everywhere: little tracks like Islip, round tracks like Oxford Plains, weird tracks like Trenton, both the superspeedway and the three-quarter-miler at Pocono, and every other kind of track.

"I've never seen another driver adapt so fast to new race tracks. We'd go to a place for the very first time, and by the second warm-up session we were usually up to speed. Then he'd go out and win the race. I mean, we won a *lot* of races at places we'd never been to before."

And all that jumping around, Nacewicz figures, only made Evans better. "The more tracks you go to, the more different situations you get into, the better prepared you're going to be next time you see that same situation develop," says Billy. "Look at Eddie Flemke; that guy was amazing in traffic, and I'm sure that went back to all the traveling he did in the Eastern Bandit days.

"If you just run every weekend at Stafford, you're going to be lost if all of a sudden there's a big race at, say, Lancaster. Hell, you won't even know where the pit gate is, let alone what might happen there in a given situation. With Richie, no matter what happened or where it happened, it wasn't something he hadn't seen before. He'd been there, done that."

And it gave him an almost otherworldly ability to see every race through his own wide-angle lens.

Laughing, Nacewicz says, "He was so good at analyzing things, and he always had a plan of attack. He'd call me on the radio during a caution and tell me what was going to happen on the restart. He'd say, '*This* guy is gonna run into *that* guy, and I'll probably have to go through the infield to miss it.' And, sure enough, it would happen."

Ron Hutter, who listened in on many of those same radio conversations, still shakes his head over Evans's fisheye view. "He pulled some weird stuff," Hutter says. "Like, he'd be in the third turn someplace, and he'd say, 'Did you see what that guy just did going into [turn] one?' I'd be thinking, 'How in the world does he know that? How can he see that?' He was the kind of guy who was always running in the front, setting the pace or at least running in the top five, but he knew what everybody else was doing, too.

"I've worked with a lot of drivers, and there are times when I'll ask, 'What's the tach reading in the middle of the turn? How far down are the RPMs dropping?' Typically, they can't tell you that; they're too busy, because driving those things takes a lot of concentration. But Richie could not only relate back what was going on with his own car, he could explain everything else that was happening, too."

The well of superlatives runs very deep when you get folks talking about Evans.

Six-time NASCAR mod champion Mike Stefanik: "I *loved* racing against Richie Evans."

Brian Ross: "He was the ultimate champ, and the best driver. He set the standards. He's the guy who made us all race so hard."

Bugsy Stevens: "When you beat Richie, you beat somebody."

Gene's Machine II

IT IS SOMETHING OF AN UNDERSTATEMENT to say that Gene DeWitt had a lot on his plate by the early 1980s. The B.R. DeWitt umbrella had widened to cover a variety of construction-related businesses spread across upstate New York. Among the outfits Gene oversaw in his position as the corporation's CEO were B.R. DeWitt, Inc., which produced ready-mix concrete, sand and gravel, and hauled salt and construction materials up and down the East Coast; Cole Sand & Gravel, which excavated and processed sand, gravel and various aggregates; Genesee Stone Products, which owned stone quarries, manufactured and sold asphalt, and dredged and processed sand and gravel; LeRoy Lime and Crushed Stone, whose operations were similar to Genesee Stone's; Potter-DeWitt Corporation, which specialized in road building and excavating, and leased out road-building equipment under state and municipal contracts; Pavilion Truck Sales, which sold new International trucks and stocked replacement parts for trucks of all types; Outlet Tire Sales, which sold and serviced new and recapped tires to trucking operations; and Sampson Hauling Corporation, which transported construction materials and machinery throughout the Eastern United States. The DeWitt banner flew over 18 concrete plants and eight gravel plants and Lord knows how many job sites at any given point.

Gene DeWitt also served as a director of the Pavilion State Bank, the New York State Bituminous Concrete Association, and the New York State Crushed Stone Association, and held a term as president of the Empire State Concrete and Aggregate Producers Association.

He hardly needed more things to occupy his time, or his mind, but the man just couldn't seem to get his fill of stock car racing. DeWitt had been backing the Evans team since 1973, and in '76 he gave himself

Richie Evans and Gene DeWitt at a B.R. DeWitt, Inc. concrete plant. (Lynn Evans photo)

another way to root by sponsoring a young equipment mechanic from his firm who was beginning to make a name for himself in Western New York late model racing: Doug Hewitt. In 1978, Hewitt jumped up into the modifieds, and immediately became a force; he won multiple features at places like Spencer, Shangri-La and Holland, and in no time at all began to look good on the road, too.

So come a Saturday-night modified special at Oswego, or a big show over in New England at Stafford or Thompson, there would be this man DeWitt, in some quiet corner of the pit area. He had been through a double hip replacement after years of suffering from arthritis, so getting around meant using a cane, but any discomfort he might have felt was always masked by a warm smile. If you happened to mention that it was nice to see him again, Gene DeWitt would thank you for the kind words and say something along the lines of: "Oh, I just wanted to come out and see Richie and Doug and the boys."

He used to say that his racing ventures were good for business, although even DeWitt himself had a hard time explaining how. In a 1984 interview for videographer Mel Thomas, Gene suggested that some customers did business with B.R. DeWitt "to some degree because of our involvement ... Maybe they stop in and talk to me: 'How'd Richie do this past weekend?' ... It's a hard thing to describe, but it does bring business ... And the employees, they feel that they're part of the team. Monday morning, everyone's saying, 'Well, what happened over the weekend?' It's just something to cheer about."

That last sentence summed it all up. He didn't hold a steering wheel, didn't change cams, didn't jack up the car on pit stops, and didn't wrestle with decisions about gear ratios or tire stagger, but Gene DeWitt was a racer. Truth be known, he was in it for the sport.

"I think racing was Gene's golf game," says Billy Nacewicz. "With us, he was more of a friend than he was a sponsor."

The man just loved his racing, and he never hid his pride in his lead driver. On that 1984 Thomas video, DeWitt said of Evans, "The fella

doesn't know [the meaning of] 'it can't be done.' He lives, eats, dreams and drinks racing. And when you put that much energy into *anything*, whether racing or playing poker, you're going to win."

Fred Ulrich used to smile about a post-victory conversation he shared with DeWitt in the Oswego infield. "Because he'd had all that trouble with his hips, Gene used to sit on the fender of the trailer," Ulrich said. "Well, he motioned for me to come over and sit with him. We talked a bit, and eventually Gene kinda pointed to Rich and said, 'Fred, did you ever keep track of how much money you spent on him over the years?' I told him I hadn't, but that we'd had a lot of fun in those early days. And Gene said, 'I'll tell you what, Fred. If you knew how much you spent on this guy, I'd pay you back.' I couldn't believe it when he told me that, but that's how much he enjoyed being around Rich and the team." Half of the attraction was the fun, and the other half was the fellowship he took from the modified scene.

"Gene liked coming to certain races," Billy Nacewicz says. "He enjoyed the Race of Champions at Trenton and then at Pocono, and he loved Daytona. I think he liked the races that had kind of a social atmosphere; like, the Race of Champions was a serious race, but it was also a big party weekend that brought together all the teams from New York, New England, Long Island, New Jersey, and down South. And Gene really liked that part of it."

Grinning, Nacewicz adds, "He'd hang out with us, and he'd get right into the party. Of course, you wouldn't catch him out *too* late. He'd stay around until things started getting a little crazy, and then he'd say, 'Tell me tomorrow what I missed.' Then he'd slip away. The next day he'd hear about our antics, and he'd just laugh and shake his head. And if something was *really* wild, Gene didn't want all the details."

For so many, that was always the interesting part of the Evans/DeWitt relationship: the contradiction between the polite, gentlemanly Gene DeWitt and the band of racing rogues led by his man Evans.

(left) Gene DeWitt joins Evans and promoter Joe Gerber in victory lane at Trenton's 1978 Dogleg 200. *(Mike Adaskaveg photo)*

(right) "Racing was Gene's golf game," says Billy Nacewicz. Here, Mr. DeWitt shoots a round in the Daytona paddock. *(B&G Wurthmann photo/ courtesy of* Speedway Scene*)*

Gene DeWitt (right), who loved races with a social atmosphere, takes in a cookout at a Pocono motel. *(Val LeSieur photo/courtesy of* Speedway Scene*)*

Bill Wimble, who had played such a pivital role in getting the two sides together in the first place, says with a smile, "I told Gene right up front about that side of Richie's personality, so he knew about that stuff all along. And he always seemed to be OK with it, for the most part. He did tell me, a couple of times over the years, that he had been less than pleased with some of Richie's antics. But, by the same token, he'd be so doggone pleased by the results of the races that he was willing to put up with it. And, you know, he really *liked* Richie.

"I think Gene looked at it like, As long as this doesn't directly impact the business, it'll be OK. And, you know, I don't think anybody ever directly connected Richie's antics with either Gene's company, or with Gene DeWitt personally. I never heard one iota of that, and *everybody* knew about Richie's antics."

Mostly, Gene DeWitt watched it all—the racing and whatever shenanigans went along with it—from a distance. What he had told Dutch Hoag when they got together in 1967 echoed throughout the Evans years: "You run the operation *how* you want to, you race *when* you want to, you race *where* you want to. If I need to know anything, I'll call you.'"

It was, plain and simple, a grand relationship.

"I couldn't ask for a finer person to be associated with," Evans said in 1980. "Gene has helped me in more ways than just trackside. He inspires rather than demands, and he is encouraging rather than critical ... More than being a perfect sponsor, Gene DeWitt is a man I look up to with real respect."

And that respect was something Evans was never afraid to make public. When he swept both of the front-row qualifying races for the Thompson 300 in the summer of 1985, thus earning his choice of the pole or the outside pole for the big September classic, it presented Evans

A shot Gene DeWitt would have loved: Evans and Doug Hewitt, wheel-to-wheel at Spencer Speedway. (J&H photo/courtesy of Speedway Scene)

an interesting conundrum; the pole certainly carried more pre-race prestige, but at Thompson the outside spot generally gave a man a better launch off the fourth-turn banking. So when track announcer Rich Bonneau asked Evans on the night of his second win which spot he thought he'd pick, it was not an obvious choice.

Richie paused, shrugged and said, "I'm going to have to talk to Mr. DeWitt. He's going to have to tell me."

Brian Ross declares, "There was probably never a guy who was any better with his sponsor than Richie was with Gene DeWitt."

DeWitt used to keep a running tally of the races he had won with Evans. Whenever they passed a significant milestone, a congratulatory ad would quietly show up in the trade papers, something along the lines of, "Congratulations, Richie, on victory number 200 under the B.R. DeWitt banner." After Evans died, someone checked the tally. Between 1973 and 1985, the driver who "lived, ate, dreamed and drank racing" and his "perfect sponsor" won 409 modified features together.

Keeping it Simple

TOM BALDWIN ONCE SAID, "We've seen a lot of guys in modified racing put up some fantastic seasons. Geoff Bodine, Greg Sacks, a *lot* of guys had their great years. Those guys had great talent, yes, but they also had great equipment with all the latest flippers and flappers. Well, here came Richie with his homemade stuff, and year in and year out he was the guy to beat."

Richie Evans very seldom toyed with the "flippers and flappers," the wild gadgets and off-the-wall theories that swept across short-track stock car racing in the late 1970s and early '80s. As a dedicated championship-chaser, he had two very sound reasons for that. First, trick stuff doesn't always work right away, and Evans couldn't afford to be slow; second,

A dedicated points-chaser, Evans stuck with cars that were easy to work on. *(Mike Adaskaveg photo)*

trick stuff sometimes fails, and he certainly couldn't afford to break down. So he preferred to stick with proven components and systems, and made sure that his cars were always built to facilitate a quick fix, just in case.

According to Billy Nacewicz, "Richie's thinking was always, 'Let's not make things too complicated.' You know, if you're running for a championship, you don't need a car so trick that it causes you a lot of extra headaches. Let's say you pit with a problem; you don't want to waste a lot of time pulling off pieces of sheet metal that didn't need to be there in the first place. We tried to keep our car simple, so it could be repaired fast. Any major part, we could get at it right away.

"We could change a motor in less than a half-hour, no problem. Some of the other modifieds you saw back then, hell, they'd be taking off body panels for five minutes just to get *at* the motor. We didn't believe in making something fancy if it didn't have to be."

No one on that race team—least of all Richie Evans—would have dared use an artsy term like "minimalism," but that's exactly what was being practiced whenever a new car went together at 608 Calvert Street.

"I think everybody in this shop was a firm believer in the KISS method—'Keep It Simple, Stupid'—and you could see that by looking at the cars," says Tony Pettinelli Jr. "There was nothing fancy. But it was where you put that nothing-fancy stuff, and how you paid attention to details, that made those cars work."

For probably the last 10 years of his career, each new B.R. DeWitt #61 looked like an evolution of the previous year's model. There were subtle revisions, sure, as chassis offsets changed and coil-over suspensions replaced torsion-bar fronts and leaf-spring rears, but George Kent says the basic Evans car—with its twin-hoop roll cage and uncomplicated mounts and brackets—"never really changed much over the years." Evans left the revolution to others.

Maybe that was a lesson learned early, from Utica-Rome teachers like Sonney Seamon and Ed Flemke. "When you look at it, most of the successful people in that era were the ones who kept things simple,"

Eddie Flemke Jr. points out. "They got 100 percent out of everything they had instead of buying something fancy and getting 50 percent. They had a very practical, meat-and-potatoes way of looking at it."

It was, says veteran modified owner/constructor Ralph Solhem, "a blue-collar approach to car-building. Richie had an uncomplicated, basic-needs style."

Maynard Troyer, who by the early 1980s had become the Northeast's most prolific producer of asphalt modifieds, recalls, "Some of us were always trying new things that sometimes worked and sometimes didn't. Richie stayed basically with common sense, with what worked for him. He didn't really dally around like Geoff [Bodine] and I did. We were always looking for a better mousetrap, but Richie just stayed with the same old mousetrap, and won with it."

Says Reggie Ruggiero, who won big aboard Evans-built modifieds for something like 15 seasons, "His cars were very flexible, and very simple. There were no extras on Richie's cars. The best way to say it is, you weren't driving a Cadillac, you were driving a Chevrolet. But it had everything you needed to go fast."

Yet it is wrong, Brett Bodine insists, to merely declare that Evans's cars were uncluttered, bare-bones machines, and let it go at that. Brett, who checked out plenty of Richie's personal cars and then drove an Art Barry-owned Evans modified in 1986, says bluntly, "Richie was one of the best car-builders there was. Yes, his cars were simple, but he was very good at making sure all the components were in the right spots and did their jobs. He was very weight-conscious. After I drove that car for Art, there was no question in my mind that Richie was a much smarter car-builder than he's ever been given credit for."

Not that failing to get that sort of credit ever bothered Evans much. He often pooh-poohed the idea that there was any great science to making modifieds go fast. In 1981, Dick Berggren wrote, "While Troyer is regarded as a technologist—someone who can talk bump-steer, roll couple and Ackerman with the best of them—Richie Evans is exactly the

According to Brett Bodine, here battling Evans in 1984, "Richie was a much smarter car-builder than he's ever been given credit for." *(Steve Kennedy photo)*

opposite. 'You don't need all that shit,' says Evans of the current wave of technology that is sweeping racing. 'It's just not that complicated.'"

Bobby Hutchens remembers "sneaking out into the infield at Martinsville just to measure something on Richie's backup car. To me, he *had* to be doing something really trick. But he wasn't. He wasn't one of those guys who had the latest week-to-week speed secrets."

Actually, he had no secrets, period. That was sort of an unofficial career-long policy with Richie Evans; even when he tried to keep things to himself, he generally failed.

"He always helped out the next guy," says Buster Maurer. "If we had some little secret, he'd tell all of us who worked on the crew, 'Don't mention to anybody that we've got this.' Then he'd be having a beer with some other racer, and he'd tell the guy exactly what he told us not to tell anybody else."

Maurer grins. "Of course, then he'd go out and beat that guy the next week anyway."

Tommy Baldwin could relate. A while back, Baldwin told the story of a long-ago encounter he'd had with Evans on pit road at Martinsville. "I was in the middle of putting together a new car back home," Baldwin said, "and I asked Richie, 'Where do you think I should locate the roll center?' He looked me like I was nuts. He told me he really didn't know much about that stuff. He said, 'Look, we just put these things together the way we think they're supposed to be put together. Then we move the wheels up and down. If everything looks right and nothing binds, we're ready to go racing.'

"I told him he was full of crap. I was actually *mad* at him; I really figured he was trying to keep a secret from me. So I said, 'All right, how about if I measure your front end and draw it right out in the pits?' He laughed and said, 'You can do whatever you want. Draw it out, drive it, I don't give a shit.' And right there, with an audience of I don't know how many people standing there, I measured his car and drew it out on the asphalt. I said, 'OK, now I know where your roll center is at.' Richie just shrugged. That was his way of saying, 'So what? I'm gonna beat you anyway.' And he did!

"But the point is, how many other guys would let you examine their whole cars, and just measure anything you want?"

Brian Ross remembers a number of occasions when Evans said to him, "Hey, here's something you might want to try at Stafford," or "You know, this might help you out at Riverside Park." Says Ross, "I think he just liked sharing things. You know, Richie helped an awful lot of people out that way."

On the flip side of that was another Evans who, says Flemke Jr., "wasn't afraid to run his ideas past you. He might call my father and do that, or he might call Jere Stahl. And it's not that Richie didn't already know what he wanted to do; it's just that he wanted to ask around and get all the information he could. He was smart like that."

Nor was Evans too proud to borrow ideas from time to time. When he bolted a trailer-bar setup under the rear end of his Pintos in 1979 and '80—forming a crude sort of torque arm—it was an idea he had swiped directly from his old pal Lou Lazzaro, who'd been running his dirt modified that way. And George Kent recalls, with a grin, the time when he "finally convinced Richie to use a setup I'd been running. And he actually ran a lot better with it. I should have never told him."

Tony Siscone says, "If you were fast, he thrived on figuring out *why* you were fast." Driving for Dick Barney, whose modifieds had carried names like Joe Kelly and Wally Dallenbach to huge fame in the Garden State, Siscone provided Evans with some incredibly stiff New Egypt competition in the early '80s. At one point, Siscone and the Barney car had the whole pack covered, Evans included; "We were, like, three-tenths faster than *everybody*," Siscone says. Evans, striving as usual to figure out why, narrowed it down to shock absorbers. Barney was running Bilsteins, and by that point the brand had been aboard enough winning modifieds—principally Reggie Ruggiero's in New England—that Evans no longer saw them as exotic stuff. The problem was, he was a Carrera man, on a factory deal.

"So this one night," Siscone remembers, "he was parked right near us in the pits. Richie had walked away for a minute, and we were kinda checking his car out. All of a sudden, Dick points and says, 'Look!' Richie had put on a set of Bilstein shocks, but they had Carrera decals on them! Well, here comes Richie, walking over. I tell him, 'Boy, these shocks look familiar.' He laughs, throws his cigarette down, and puts his fingers to his lips. He says, 'Hey, I had to *try* 'em, right?'"

Generally speaking, that's how it went with Evans: He wasn't afraid of those flippers and flappers, but he saw no sense in bolting them on until he'd seen the right amount of R&D work done by other teams.

In fact, so seldom did Richie Evans try anything different that his few "experiments" still stand out in the memory. The aerodynamic Mustang-bodied car he ran at Trenton and Pocono—it was a Dogleg 200 winner in '78—was quite a departure from his utilitarian Pintos. And in 1983, in a radical departure for Evans, he shipped one of his modified frames to Wisconsin, where chassis builder Dennis Frings welded on a front clip employing the hottest late model geometry of the day.

"One night at Shangri-La, I drove that car with the late model front end," says George Kent, "and it was *fast*. Richie got out front in the feature, and I chased his ass all night. I caught him, and I would've gone *by* him if it wasn't for this flimsy-type gas pedal he ran. I pushed it so hard I bent the damn thing, and after that I only had about half throttle. Shangri-La is more of a handling track than a horsepower track, so I was still right there; I could drive right alongside of him through the corners, but he kept beating me down the straightaway. I told him after the race, 'If your chintzy throttle hadn't bent, I'd have beat your ass with your own car!'

Mike Stefanik, in Richie's wild straight-axle car, battles alongside John Rosati in the 1980 Thompson World Series. (Howie Hodge photo/Stefanik collection)

"But you know something? Richie *hated* that car. It was fast, but it drove funny; it had a lot of body roll, kinda like a late model. He told me later he was hoping I wrecked it, so they could cut that front end off."

And then there was perhaps the wildest contraption ever to carry the #61. In 1980, Evans enlisted the help of supermodified chassis builder Kevin Reap—a quiet, pleasant fellow from Syracuse whom friends called "the Professor"—in the design of a modified unlike anything found in a NASCAR pit area. Its narrow frame rode on a straight-axle front end, and beneath its steeply-raked Pinto skin was an internal wing meant to create huge amounts of downforce. The trick tunnel-like tinwork gave the machine its nickname: "the Laundry Chute." But for all its bells and whistles, Richie never felt completely comfortable in it, nitpicking about everything from its "different" steering feel to its high rear-end bodywork. "I remember him telling me he couldn't see out the back," says Mike Stefanik, who drove the car at Thompson in its only memorable appearance. Evans sold the car without ever having given the thing the old Roman try.

It was just easier, he seemed to figure, not to waste time playing around.

"As long as your car works," Nacewicz says, "why trick it up by hanging all kinds of things on it?"

That philosophy extended from the technical to the cosmetic. "Richie's cars were a little on the rough side," says Rusty Wallace, who remembers checking out Evans's short-track stuff in the pits at New Smyrna. "Just orange and black, not real polished, no chrome. But they also looked *mean*."

Billy Nacewicz says, "In the late '70s and early '80s, we were running against a lot of pretty cars: Dick Armstrong's cars, Maynard's cars. But Richie didn't worry about pretty. He worried about *fast*. Plus, Rich wasn't one to waste money. He couldn't see spending the extra dollars to chrome the nerf bars when a can of flat-black spray paint would do the same job. Chrome doesn't put you in the winner's circle, and Richie knew that.

"He always admired Lenny Boehler, and Lenny's cars weren't exactly red-carpet beauties. But, you know, Lenny's cars sure ran. I'm sure there were a lot of nights early on when Richie looked at Lenny's equipment and thought it might fall apart before it got onto the track. Then, in the feature, he'd look up and see Lenny's car going right by him. After a while, we *all* figured out that Lenny was smarter than a fox; his car might not have had nice bumpers, but it had good brakes and a good motor and the right suspension."

No flippers, no flappers, just practicality and speed.

"I remember going to Martinsville every spring," says Ralph Solhem, "and the cool thing about that trip, especially in the '70s, was that you got to look at everybody's new cars. The hot modifieds you wanted to check out were Maynard Troyer's and Charlie Jarzombek's. You couldn't wait to see them, because Maynard always had some beautiful creation he'd built over the winter, and the Jarzombeks always had something wild-looking. When everybody still built their own cars, some people would just lock themselves in their garages and come up with this cool stuff, and Maynard and Charlie always had the cars you *had* to look at."

But as you walked down pit road, Solhem recalls, the contrasts were striking: "Maynard's car was always slicked-out and shiny. Richie's frame was just flat black. I'll never forget that the first time I ever saw rack-and-pinion steering on a race car, Maynard and Richie [both] had it at Martinsville. Maynard's rack looked like a surgeon had attached it, because everything was so polished. Richie's looked like it had been on that car forever."

Robin Pemberton, who has applied wrenches to everything from low-dollar dirt coupes to clear-coated Daytona winners, sums the whole thing up with a smile.

"Richie's cars weren't always the cleanest," Pemberton says. "And they weren't always the nicest. But they hauled ass."

Evans and Nacewicz with Kevin "the Professor" Reap, the wizard behind Richie's radical straight-axle modified. *(Mike Marrer photo/courtesy of Speedway Scene)*

 ## "Bo Diddley"

NOT LONG AGO, GEOFF BODINE—"Geoffrey" these days—was standing in the paddock of a NASCAR Craftsman Truck Series event, talking with an acquaintance about old times. Geoffrey, it seems, is in the process of tracking down and restoring some of the more significant cars he has raced, and naturally the discussion turned to his modified days.

After a while, the acquaintance brought up Richie Evans's name. Bodine smiled a wide, unforced smile; it was the kind of warm, open expression he wears when he is absolutely at ease.

"Lotta good races," Geoffrey Bodine said softly. "Lotta good *memories*."

Geoff Bodine leads Richie Evans at Pocono in 1972. Evens ended up in victory lane. *(Ray Masser photo)*

Ah, it really was pleasant once ...

"Geoff burst onto the scene in the very early 1970s," recalls Billy Nacewicz. "That's when he was driving the T.K. McLean number 99, that Valiant. He was young, and he was fast, and right away he was putting a dent into the hold that Richie and Maynard Troyer had at Spencer, Fulton and Shangri-La. But you've always got to accept it when somebody new comes along and goes fast, and Richie *did* accept it. In the early parts of their careers, he and Geoff always got along."

Barbara Evans remembers Geoff's young face among the crowd that squeezed into The Nutshell for drinks and a bite to eat after those long-ago Utica-Rome features. It's interesting to picture the two of them there, shooting the bull: Bodine, always with his head in the game, studiously focused on his cars and their problems, and Evans, every bit the same dedicated racer but a fellow with a much wider social streak.

Brett Bodine, just barely edging into his teens back then, says, "For a while there, Geoff and Richie were actually pretty friendly. They sort of hung out a little bit.

"A lot of people won't remember this, but Geoff actually *drove* for Richie. This was back in the very early Pinto days, when Richie's cars were still built by Sonney Seamon. Richie was interested in trying coil-over front suspension, but he had never worked with it. Well, Geoff had always worked with coil-overs; he was probably the first guy to use 'em in the modifieds. Anyway, I don't remember why Geoff didn't have a ride at this particular time—he and T.K. McLean might have been on the outs—but Richie asked him to run one of his cars at Fulton."

Things went pretty much that smoothly for a big chunk of the '70s. "We raced hard with Geoff for many years with no problems," Nacewicz says, "even later on when he was out in New England running for Dick Armstrong."

Bodine hooked up with Armstrong early in 1975, and before long he had moved from Chemung to Bellingham, Massachusetts, and was running the show at the Armstrong shop in nearby Franklin. He built and

In 1978, Evans and Geoff Bodine were fierce foes, but not yet the combatants they became later. *(Mike Adaskaveg photo)*

drove the Nu-Style Jewelry Pintos—always a rich blood-red, always boldly numbered 1—for four seasons, and in that time established a remarkable résumé. With Armstrong, Bodine won the 1975 and '77 Stafford track championships; won three of the first four Thompson 300s; won five times at Martinsville; won the 1978 Race of Champions; won multiple weekly features at Seekonk, Westboro, Riverside Park and Utica-Rome; won special events at New Smyrna, Waterford, Monadnock and more; and had a season for the ages in 1978, winning 55 modified events. And that's just scratching the surface.

In that time, he banged wheels with Evans a time or two, but it was certainly never anything out of the ordinary; a rub at Utica-Rome, a bump at Stafford. No big deal. Bodine's racing then was centered around New England; from 1975-77, Evans was mostly doing the upstate New York thing, and in '78, back chasing NASCAR points, he was all over the map. They were not weekly rivals, never mind nightly rivals.

And yet somehow, Geoff Bodine ended up being the biggest adversary Richie Evans had since … well, maybe ever. Those in the Rome area tend to view Jerry Cook as Richie's number one rival. Outside Oneida County, though, many would grant that distinction to Geoffrey.

If anything like that was going on in the Armstrong years, it never showed on the Evans side. The two didn't appear as close as folks said they'd once been, yet Richie never revealed any real hostility. About the most he'd do, publicly, was refer to his foe as "Bo Diddley," a nickname popular among the growing anti-Bodine camp in New England. But every now and then, Geoff seemed to be drawing battle lines. In a 1977 interview with Dick Berggren, he kicked things up a notch; Berggren reported that Bodine ranked "himself as the best modified driver, Evans as second and Troyer third."

Well, there you had it. If he was calling himself the best driver in the division and labeling Evans second-best, how could this *not* be a rivalry?

And even after he began dabbling in Winston Cup racing in 1979—showing flashes of brilliance with Jack Beebe's Connecticut-based Race Hill Farm team—and was catching on with Southern late model sportsman owners, Bodine sometimes appeared eager to stoke the fires beneath his simmering rancor toward Evans. That year, Evans was the hottest man in modified racing, on his way to winning 52 features and

Left to right: Ron Bouchard, Richie Evans and Geoff Bodine at Trenton, 1979. *(Lynn Evans collection)*

already having won the hearts of the division's fans in a way that Bodine hadn't managed to do in his amazing years with Armstrong. And yet when Bodine beat him that summer in an Oswego thriller, Geoff couldn't resist flashing a small sign someone had handed him in victory lane: "Home of the Orange Crush."

It was a slap, an outright taunt, and maybe the Evans vs. Bodine rivalry became real on that night at Oswego. And if that's correct, maybe Modified America owes a debt of gratitude to Mr. Bodine. After all, he and Evans had fans streaming through the speedway gates whenever and wherever they appeared together for the next few years.

"The fans build on stuff like that," says Billy Nacewicz. "It's like when one football player puts a tough hit on another football player; for the rest of the game, you're watching that match-up."

In 1980, Bodine joined forces with a new team owned by Phil Taylor, the head man at Phil's Chevrolet in Ellenburg Depot, tucked deep in that far up-country corner of New York which has Lake Champlain to its east and Canada to its north. The connection between owner and driver was Phil's brother, Billy Taylor, whose mechanical pedigree already included stints with Bodine's "best three" modified shoes: He'd spun wrenches on Richie Evans's coupes, on Maynard Troyer's Pintos, and on the Armstrong #1 cars in Bodine's glory days there. The Taylor car ran a busy but selective schedule; really, it showed up only when Geoff and Billy wanted to go racing, and it always showed up ready. It was a cutting-edge "Bo-Dyn" design—a collaborative effort between Geoff and the Connecticut-based Chassis Dynamics duo of Bob Cuneo and Bobby Vee—and it carried a Ron Hutter engine.

It was in his time with the Taylor machine—a gleaming #99 Pinto dubbed "the White Tornado" by Connecticut scribe Brian Danko —that Bodine and Evans really began to press each other. They clanged bumpers and rubbed wheels all week in the season-opening New Smyrna series, in which they each won four times in the first eight races

Geoff Bodine and Richie Evans, hard at it during a 1981 Stafford Speedway feature. *(David Allio photo)*

and then nudged each other out of the top two spots in the finale. Once racing resumed in the Northeast, their intensity did not diminish.

John McMullin, who in addition to his Stafford duties often attended other tracks as a fan, says, "Richie and Geoffrey had some unbelievable races, and not just in the big shows. Even in the weekly features, they really raced each other *hard*."

It's safe to say that Richie Evans lifted Geoff Bodine's game, and Bodine returned the favor. Around each other on the race track, the two men seemed to reach just a little deeper into their personal sacks of tricks. The result was some incredible modified competition.

"One of our most spectacular wins was one a lot of people might not remember," says Billy Nacewicz. "It was at Thompson [in a 40-lapper in August of 1980], and it involved Geoff. Richie and Geoff got together and spun [with 11 laps to go], and they both had to go to the rear. Well, the two of them came through the pack, but they were running out of time. When they got the white flag, it was John Rosati leading, George Kent second, and Geoff third. Rich was fourth."

Heading down the long Thompson backstretch, Bodine, with a great head of steam built up, poked his nose to the inside of Kent; it was his bad luck that at that same instant, Kent ducked low himself, looking for a way past Rosati. But crafty John was having none of that, and entered turn three lower—and thus slower—than usual. It looked like a winning move on Rosati's part, because Kent had to climb on the brakes, and Bodine had to do the same, and the blue Rosati #73 was at the head of a three-car train as they hit Thompson's third turn.

But here ... came ... *Evans!* He had the outside lane—traditionally Thompson's fast groove—all to himself, and he poured his Pinto deep into turn three. Almost before the crowd had time to comprehend the move, much less applaud it, he was beside Bodine, then beside Kent, then beside Rosati, and then, out of turn four, he was leading.

"With those guys all bottled up on the bottom and Rich up top, on the banking, he just drove around all three of 'em," says Nacewicz. "That had to be about as wild a win as you could get, to go from fourth to first in less than half a lap without a wheel being touched."

Back in the pit area, a semi-circle of fans maybe a dozen deep ringed the B.R. DeWitt hauler. Nacewicz says, "I have never, ever seen a bunch of fans more excited than they were that night. They were all gathered back at our pit, and it was like a parting of the sea when we brought that car back in."

But there's no getting around the fact that the key round in the Evans/Bodine slugfest occurred in March of 1981, in the modified half of the Dogwood 500 at Martinsville. After that day, nothing was ever the same between them, like the nasty breakup of a high-school romance in which so much emotion flows and so many bad things are said that there's no chance of parting as friends.

It started as a dream weekend for Bodine. On Thursday he set quick time for the late model sportsman race, driving for Virginian old-timer Emanuel Zervakis. The next day Bodine put the White Tornado modified on the pole with a lap nearly two miles per hour quicker than Ron Bouchard, who qualified second in the Armstrong #1. "We came down with the car right," Billy Taylor told Dick Berggren. "We haven't touched a bolt all week." Evans, complaining of wheel-hopping chatter in his car's rear end, settled for fifth.

Next, to open up the Sunday program, Geoff mounted a terrific late charge to pass Sam Ard for the sportsman win.

And then came the cage match.

Everybody with even a passing interest in asphalt modified racing remembers the 1981 Dogwood 500 as the day when Geoff and Richie spent the last two laps trying to crash themselves out of the show. Everybody remembers them clouting the concrete out of turn four with the checkered flag waving a few hundred yards down the track. Everybody remembers Evans winning the thing with his car in pieces, having shed wheels and parts as it rode the frontstretch wall, engine screaming. Everybody remembers Bodine's car plowing into the inside pit wall after the finish line, a battered second.

What folks tend to forget, thanks to the famous sloppy finish, is that the first 248 laps were as good a modified show as you could ever hope to see.

Bodine led from the start, but Evans—having fixed his wheel-hop with a Saturday redesign of his rear suspension—clearly had the best long-run setup. He was glued to Geoff's tail like a bumper sticker; the two of them raced together, lapped slower cars together, pitted together, and then raced together some more.

"It was a pretty scenario," wrote Berggren, "the two of them threading their way through traffic … a symphony should have been playing in the background."

Their ballet hit a bit of a speedbump on lap 194, when they spun in tandem entering turn one after an attempted inside pass by Evans. Later on, still revved up from the final crash, each pointed a finger at the other for that bobble. In truth, it was probably as close as two men could come to staging the perfect "that's racing" sort of incident. Richie thought he was far enough under Bodine to have rights to the lane, Geoff thought it was still his—six of one, half a dozen of the other—and they touched. No harm, no foul.

"What happened earlier in the race," Nacewicz says, "was really no big deal."

What happened later on was a *very* big deal.

Bodine and Evans had long since made their way back to the front of the pack by the time a late caution flag waved. The restart came with exactly 10 laps left. Geoff was leading, Richie second. Behind them were lined up John Blewett and Jerry Cook, and then the lapped cars of Maynard Troyer and Roger Treichler.

The Motor Racing Network was broadcasting the event. Mike Joy was the achorman, with Dick Berggren serving as color analyst in the booth. Eli Gold was stationed in turns three and four. Dr. Jerry Punch and Charlie Roberts—the latter a New Jersey racing fixture and an Evans pal—were patrolling the pits. Even today, you can listen to their excited call of that 1981 Dogwood modified race, full of rising voices and urgent inflections, and be left with chills.

When the green waved, Joy said, "Here goes Bodine. And Evans goes *right after him* coming down the homestretch and into turn number one."

Joy again, three laps later, as the leaders barreled through turn one: "Evans goes up to the high side, and pulls up just as far as the right-rear fender of Bodine's car … and no closer."

Berggren chipped in, "And, boy, he was right out *sideways*, Mike, when he came off that turn. Richie Evans is just hanging it out for all he's worth. This is the time when there's no such thing as strategy. The only possible thing Richie Evans can do now is just stand on the gas … and be as brave as he possibly can."

"And Bodine," Joy replied, "is not a driver that is easily psyched out."

The caution waved again with 244 laps complete, for a chunk of exhaust pipe at the end of the homestretch. Instead of deflating the tension of a highly-charged struggle—and a highly-charged broadcast—the lull only intensified things. The always observant Joy, in recapping the lap leading up to the yellow, said, "Richie Evans was right alongside in the backstretch. But going up into turn number three, it looked like the track may have been a bit slick."

Their jousting resumed after the final green flag, Evans constantly lunging to Bodine's outside, Geoff squirting away exiting the corner. Berggren observed, "Boy, it's just got to be very, very tough on both these guys. They're both *intensely* competitive race car drivers …"

There was, for all purposes, no one else in the race. Blewett was a distant third, and Cook wasn't close enough to threaten him.

"There are only three laps to go," Joy announced. "Evans takes it in hard ... *Bodine hits the curb, and Evans slams into the back of Bodine!* That was a judgement error on Bodine's part, the first one we've seen today. They're up in turn three."

Eli Gold picked it up from there: "Geoff pulls away by a half-car length, as Evans comes charging to the high side. Bodine stays down low. Single file it'll be, off the turn, with Evans pushing Bodine for the lead. *Two laps*."

Joy: "Evans has Bodine a little bit rattled. Geoffrey hit the curb coming into turn one. Evans goes to the high side ... can't make it work. But he's *hard* on the throttle, and jumps *underneath* Bodine on the backstretch!"

They were half a lap from the white flag.

Gold: "Looking to the inside, Evans tries to draw alongside, gets the nose *there*. But Bodine shuts him down ... *He spins! Bodine! Gathers it back in!* Evans goes underneath him. It'll be *Evans* off turn four with the lead, Bodine second ... as Evans took advantage of a sideways move."

Those few seconds in turn three were the race's pivotal point. The crux of the whole thing was the cause of Bodine's slide. Geoff claimed Evans nerfed him out of the lead; Richie vehemently denied that, telling Berggren later, "When [Bodine] went into the corner, I was 10 feet away from him. I did not even touch him going into the corner. The track was covered with oil and water, and Geoff just plain lost it ... I didn't make him slip. He did it on his own."

One impartial observer, Troyer, backed up the Evans version of things. "I know for a fact there was water on the race track," Troyer said to Berggren, "because I saw steam coming off the tires, which is what happens when you run over a wet surface ... There was definitely water on the race track. No question about it."

Most eyewitness accounts also supported Evans. In Bodine's defense, though, he had little time to think things through. He had gone into the third corner leading, his fiercest rival hot on his tail, and, just like that, he was sliding up the track. Now he was second, and he was as mad as a hornet. And Geoff Bodine had a plan for Richie Evans.

"My intent," he later told Berggren, "was to spin him out."

All day long, Bodine had appeared to have the second-best car. Once Evans got past, he should have driven right off with the lead. But as they roared down the back straightaway for the last time, Geoffrey was closing furiously.

"Three car lengths," said Eli Gold. "Down to two ... down to one ..."

Evans admitted to Berggren later than his own concerns about the track allowed Bodine to catch up. "Knowing that turns three and four were covered with oil or water," he said, "it was my turn to not go through there and not [screw] up when I'm going for the checkered. So

I went through there very carefully, because I'd seen [Bodine] slide for life the lap before. I looked in the mirror going down the back chute and saw that I had a sizable lead, so I could be real careful going through three and four. I mean, it's payday."

Not quite. Geoff caught Richie as they rounded turns three and four, and drilled him good. Evans got sideways. They came together again out of turn four, angling the Evans car nose-first into the outside wall. Richie later told Berggren, "I came off four, and he just smashed right into me. I felt like I could almost feel him cut the wheel. All of a sudden I was turned into the wall. Then I knew, *This sonofabitch is trying to kill me*. I just pressed 'er on the board and said, 'I gotta get to the white line.'"

From that point on, Richie always claimed, he never backed off the gas until the car stopped.

Gold: *"Off the turn, sideways goes Evans! Here comes Bodine! They bump! Bodine is in the wall! Evans, high in the wall! He crosses the line first!"*

As the two cars ground to a halt, every last person in the pits seemed to surge toward the frontstretch; it looked, as much as anything else, like a super-sized version of one of those bench-clearing baseball brawls where an entire team rushes the mound. The Evans crew ran to check on Richie; the Bodine crew ran to check on Geoff; everybody else ran to rubberneck.

"I didn't know what kind of condition Rich was in," Nacewicz says, "because he'd hit the wall awfully hard. I ran over to the car not knowing what I was going to find."

Here, Nacewicz laughs. "I leaned in and said, 'Are you all right?' And the only thing he answered back was, 'Did we win?' Unbelievable."

Naturally, each blamed the other, and each talked tough.

Bodine: "It's very obvious that Richie Evans just doesn't know how to lose. I've never done [anything dirty] to him, but things just might start changing."

Evans and Bodine slam the Martinsville concrete, and Richie's car careens wildly toward victory in the 1981 Dogwood 500. Note the empty wheelchair! *(photos by Mike Purcell and Mike Wray/Martinsville Bulletin)*

The battered DeWitt Pinto is towed out of victory lane at Martinsville. *(courtesy of* Speedway Scene*)*

Evans: "Whatever games he want to play, I'll play."

Later, once he'd had some time to cool off, Evans wasn't backing down. He told Berggren, "[Bodine] can say that I'm a dirty sonofabitch, but that ain't how it was. I am not at fault in the slightest. My conscience is clear. Hell, he must have closed the door on me 50 times [during the entire race]. I didn't hold that against him. He was the leader. But he was the one who slid in the shit [on the next-to-last lap]. I wasn't even near him when he slid. I went by him a hell of a lot nicer than he ever went by me.

"The guy's sick."

Mike Joy drew parallels to the 1976 Daytona 500 finish, in which David Pearson limped his crippled Mercury across the finish line first after a wild last-lap tangle with Richard Petty: "Two titans in their own area of the sport, coming off the final turn of the final lap, crashing together, spinning down to the start-finish line …"

But Martinsville promoter Clay Earles would brook no comparisons. "That," he declared in the moments after the '81 Dogwood 500, "was the greatest finish of any race, anywhere."

For all that day's drama, it also managed to produce three very funny memories.

The first came when NASCAR briefly chose to stick with the usual post-race procedures despite the decidedly *un*usual finish. That meant, among other things, that both the Evans and Bodine cars needed to report for the mandatory weigh-in.

"Our car is basically one big pile of junk in victory lane," Nacewicz remembers, "and this official comes over and says, 'Don't forget, you've got to take this thing to the scales.' They were actually getting ready to tow it over there with a wrecker. I'm telling the officials, 'How can you weigh this thing? Hell, half the car's missing. The right-front wheel assembly might be up in the grandstands, for all I know. There are parts *everywhere.* Are you serious?' Meanwhile, the cops are trying to keep the Evans fans and the Bodine fans apart. The whole thing is just chaos."

Richie, quick on his feet, ordered his crewmen to grab every part they could find on the frontstretch, even if they knew it hadn't come from his car, and toss it into the cockpit. The absurdity of the whole thing may have been made clear to the officials when it was noted that between what was still hanging from the chassis and what was laying in the seat, the Evans car now had *five* shock absorbers.

"Finally, they said we could forget about the weigh-in," says Nacewicz.

The second bit of humor wasn't evident until later, back in Rome, when Evans and his pals were checking out photo sequences of the crash in the papers.

Wilbur Jones says, "In one photo you can see a guy in the grandstands, down low by the start-finish line, sitting in a wheelchair. Then you see Richie's car climb up on that wall. By the time he goes by and wins the race, the wheelchair is empty. We used to say, 'What did the guy do, get up and run?'"

The third funny thing was that the customary Martinsville photo of the modified and late model sportsman winners posing together—a tradition which dated back to the beginning of those grand doubleheaders so many years earlier—was delayed a bit. The Martinsville brass, led by Earles and crackerjack PR man Dick Thompson, wisely decided that it might not be a good idea to ask Evans and Bodine to shake hands and make nice for the cameras just then. So the official victory lane photograph from the 1981 Dogwood 500, which was featured on the next year's souvenir program, was actually taken at the 1981 *Cardinal* 500 in October. By then, the pair was behaving civilly enough to smile and, holding a Confederate flag, stage a mock tug-of-war as the pictures were snapped.

Northbound fans leaving the speedway after the Dogwood 500's finish passed by the Collinsville Holiday Inn, for many years the Martinsville headquarters for the Evans gang. Out front, its marquee read: "Richie, You're Incredible."

Seven months later, after Geoff ran away with the modified portion of the Cardinal 500 while a broken-down Evans sat on the sidelines, that same sign read, "See Ya in the Spring, Bo Diddley ... Love, Richie." It was posted by the hotel management, and Evans had nothing to do with it, but to some it brought back memories of Geoff's "Orange Crush" placard at Oswego two years earlier. Neither message was designed to do anything but rile up the other guy.

The interesting thing is, any and all of these little barbs were thrown from a distance. Nobody remembers a night when an angry Geoff got in Richie's face, or the other way around. Try as each of them might to crank up his opponent, neither of them ever let things get out of hand. The thought occurs now that, way down deep, the two men didn't dislike each other nearly as much as the rest of us—fans, promoters, media types—sometimes wanted them to. Maybe their shared background, from those early battles at Shangri-La to the laughs at The Nutshell to the time Bodine drove for Evans at Fulton, got in the way of all that.

"It was a bitter rivalry, but I wouldn't necessarily call it a feud," says Billy Nacewicz. "Feuds are something the press like to build up, and, let's face it, they're good for the sport. But we didn't hate Geoff, and I'm sure he didn't hate us. Yeah, we had some fierce on-track battles, but, from our side, most nights we'd go down the road and not think about it until we got to the garage and somebody brought it up.

"We always took Geoff Bodine very, very seriously, and I *know* Richie respected Geoff. How could you not respect a guy who could win 50 races in a season, who could win all the big races, and who had the knowledge and the driving ability Geoff did?"

In the wake of their two signature seasons in 1978 and '79— when, respectively, Bodine won 55 of 84 starts, and Evans took 52 of *his* 84 starts—there was a huge debate among their more rabidly partisan fans about how those two years stacked up. Bodine's supporters pointed to his slightly higher winning percentage; the Evans crowd suggested that since he was chasing points, Richie's schedule was tougher. Both sides missed the point. Looking at these two *on paper* was no fun at all; the only real fun of Evans vs. Bodine came in watching them slice through traffic, anywhere, each trying to beat the other to the front. Heck, when Thompson Speedway owner Don Hoenig paired them in a 1980 match race—led all the way by Bodine—the thing was a colossal bore; it was only in a real race that these two real racers excelled.

Richie and Geoff, Geoff and Richie. Lotta good races. Lotta good memories.

What a pair they were; so fast, and yet such opposites.

One of them, Evans, was the consummate people's champion, a guy with a circle of friends and fans that seemed to include his entire division. He wanted everybody to be in on the fun. At the "Racerama" trade show just a week before that crazy Martinsville finish in 1981, Richie had pulled five bucks from his pocket, plopped it on a table set up by the Geoff Bodine Fan Club, and bought himself a membership, just to get a rise out of the club's officers.

Bodine, on the other hand, was modified racing's perpetual outsider. For a long time, Geoffrey always wanted to blame that on the New England press and the New England fans and their overt affections for regional heroes like Bugs Stevens, Fred DeSarro and Ronnie Bouchard. But it went beyond that; in 1977, Bodine himself told Dick Berggren, "I've never been popular. I can't understand that. I've never won a popularity contest."

Then, curiously and tellingly, he added this: "Richie Evans can win [them] every year. He raises hell. When I'm at a race track, I'm there to do a job. I do a job, and I'm serious about it."

Richie's response to that was best summed up by a remark he made in 1978. "I work just as hard as Bodine does," he told writer Toodi Gelinas, "but I have more fun."

 On a Roll

ON MARCH 25, 1980, they threw a little party in Rome for their three-time NASCAR modified champion and two-time Daytona winner. Mayor Carl Eilenberg declared it "Richie Evans Day," with a number of friends and area dignitaries showing up for dinner and a ceremony on a downtown plaza. Richie, figuring there was no sense in receiving the key to the city unless the thing came with a little power, immediately banned mufflers on all street rods and declared the city's motorcycle helmet law null and void.

For that one day, Evans was the toast of his town. For the first two years of the 1980s, he was the toast of his division.

Sure, on paper it might have looked like he backslid a bit in '80; he won "only" 45 times in 87 starts. But he had a spellbinding season in New England, where he centered his activity that year. So tough was Evans in the spring and summer months, the weekly-feature guts of the season, that he captured Friday-Saturday-Sunday track championships at Stafford, Riverside Park and Thompson despite missing at least one feature at each of those tracks.

How did it stack up in his own mind compared to 1979, a *Speedway Scene* columnist wanted to know? Richie hemmed a bit, hawed a bit, and finally decided it was "sort of a tie."

For Billy Nacewicz, the team's 1980 success is as tough to dissect as 1979's. "It's a very simple thing, and yet it's hard to explain," he says. "Sometimes in racing, you just get on a roll."

They had come out of New Smyrna fired up, having grabbed the World Series title in a week marked by scuffles with Bodine. Richie and Geoff had been in their own league during Speedweeks, and now, with Bodine spending most weekends racing late models in Virginia and North Carolina—and winning more than two dozen features there—Evans didn't seem interested in taking prisoners.

He was past the 20-win mark by the middle of June, and returned to victory lane with such regularity that when a weekend actually passed *without* an Evans victory—July 10-12, 1980, you can look it up!—it was big news in the race-paper columns. (Still, even in that "bad" week he finished fourth at Stafford, fourth at Riverside, and third at Thompson.) A Thursday-Friday romp at Holland and Stafford on the first weekend in August pushed him past 30 victories. That same month, Evans set a new

Rome Mayor Carl Eilenberg tries out the seat of the orange Camaro on "Richie Evans Day" in March of 1980. *(Jodi Meola collection)*

Ron Bouchard, Evans and Greg Sacks at Stafford, 1980. *(Paul Bonneau photo/courtesy of* Speedway Scene*)*

Riverside Park record by becoming the first man in the track's 30-odd year history to win four straight features; the mark lasted only a week before he pushed it to five.

The NASCAR national points race lacked its usual zing, with neither Evans nor Cook logging the atlas-shredding miles they had in the past. In fact, they probably saw less of each other in 1980 than they had in years, with Jerry spending his Fridays and Saturdays at Spencer and Shangri-La while Richie played in New England. Only at Thompson did they regularly face off.

Nacewicz, meanwhile, was having the time of his racing life.

"I had always been a big fan of New England racing," Billy says, "because as I was growing up, that's where all the champions were from. That's where most of the big-name drivers were. So I looked at it like, those are the guys I want to beat.

"There were some great drivers in New York, of course, and at places like Spencer and Shangri-La you had to run against some really good teams. The top five guys at those places could hold their own anywhere. But the modified racing in New York wasn't as strong, top to bottom, as it was in New England in that period.

"In fact," says Nacewicz, "when we won our first Stafford championship [on the strength of 10 feature wins], I thought that was a great honor."

Evans beat Ron Bouchard for the Stafford title, Bob Polverari for the Riverside crown, and Cook for the top laurels at Thompson. And check this out: though he'd made only a smattering of 1980 appearances at Shangri-La, he also cracked the top 10 there, finishing ninth in a points column topped by George Kent.

Early in September, Richie went to Islip Speedway for the All Star 300, an event he hadn't lost since 1975. That didn't happen this time, either, although it took some fastastic luck on his part—and some terrible luck on Charlie Jarzombek's—to steer Evans into victory lane.

Stafford promoter Ed Yerrington congratulates 1980 Stafford champs Evans and Nacewicz. The latter called that title "a great honor." *(Howie Hodge photo/courtesy of Speedway Scene)*

Throughout the 1970s, Chargin' Charlie had essentially crowned himself king of Long Island's modified bullrings. He was the toughest guy at Freeport Stadium on the New York end of the Island, the toughest guy at the more central Islip Speedway, and the toughest guy at the Riverhead Raceway out toward the eastern tip, where the Jarzombek clan made its home. One of modified racing's most-told jokes in those days went like this:

Q: How can you tell if it rained all last weekend on Long Island?

A: There are no victory shots of Jarzombek in this week's racing papers.

If anybody was going to give Charlie a tussle, it was generally a Long Island regular: Fred Harbach, Wayne Anderson, Don Howe, Tom Baldwin, or this hot young guy, Greg Sacks. Rarely did an outsider come in and get the job done at, say, Freeport or Islip; Jerry Cook had done it, and so had New Englanders Flemke and Stevens, and so, with impressive frequency, had Evans, who had 20 career Long Island victories.

So the pre-race favorites for the 1980 All Star 300—bastardized a bit that season by being trimmed to 250 laps, with a 50-lap support show for street stocks—were Jarzombek, the toughest local guy, and Evans, the toughest invader. Everybody sensed that. Whenever Richie stepped onto Charlie's turf, it was magic.

"Those guys ran *hundreds* of laps together at Islip Speedway within two feet of each other," Ricky Jarzombek says, "and I can honestly say that they never rubbed wheels. Richie never ran into Charlie, and Charlie never ran into Richie. They just had such a respect for each other."

The shortened All Star race threw everybody a setup curveball. There were two tire choices available, a hard compound and a soft one. In a 300 lapper, the decision would have been a snap: hard, hard, hard. But if a guy really knew Islip Speedway, and really knew his tires, maybe a gambler could get lucky on the softer rubber …

"We had run a couple of 100-lappers on the soft tires," Ricky recalls, "and they'd done OK. So we figured we'd try 'em in the All Star race. That day, Richie came over and said, 'What are you gonna do about tires?' Charlie told him, 'I'm running the soft ones. I'm gonna go as fast as I can for as long as I can, and then I'll just hold on and see what happens.' And Richie said, 'Well, if you're gonna run 'em, I will, too.'

"Then the two of them went out there and ran together all day, with Charlie leading and Richie on his bumper, or Richie looking outside, or Richie sticking his nose inside but never getting there. It was beautiful to watch."

It sure was ... for 246 laps. Then, as they were halfway through the 247th, smoke poured from the tail of the Jarzombek Vega, and both Charlie and Richie went sliding.

"Our motor blew up," Ricky says. "We got in the oil and hit the wall, and Richie crashed into us. We were done, obviously. But Richie got going again, and he limped around under caution and won the race."

And Evans sewed up two more huge victories before the 1980 season was out.

In the Race of Champions—run for the first time on Pocono's infield track—he and leader Ronnie Bouchard (in the Armstrong #1) locked horns in a thrilling battle, nose-to-tail and side-by-side. So absorbing was the fight that almost nobody noticed a closing Geoff Bodine, Evans included. "My radio wasn't working, but my [crew] motioned to me that Geoff was closing," Richie told *Gater Racing News* columnist Bruce Ellis. "I figured, If I don't get out of here now, I'm gonna be third." So he got out of there, passing Bouchard with 13 laps left and never looking back. That gave him two straight ROC victories on two very different Pocono tracks; "The big track was mentally harder," said Evans, "and the short track is physically harder."

And in the Cardinal 500 at Martinsville, Richie took the checkers ahead of Bouchard, Bodine, Brian Ross and Jarzombek. It was his 37th victory in 65 NASCAR starts, and his sixth in the 17 national championship events run that year.

And it officially gave him his fourth modified crown.

But after 1979 and '80, the smart thing to do was to stop watching the numbers Richie Evans put up, and just watch Richie Evans.

When he saddled up again in 1981, Evans wasn't as jazzed about the idea of chasing points as he had been. The previous season's championship fight hadn't been a fight at all. He told one columnist that the whole thing just wasn't as much fun without a stiff challenge; "I'd rather see a couple more guys going gung-ho after it," Evans said. New Jersey's John Blewett was dropping some hints about running the whole NASCAR trail, but he hadn't done anything close to that kind of traveling before and wasn't seen as the same kind of a threat that Cook had always been.

There was some gab floating around that Evans might not pursue the '81 title, but that situation basically took care of itself. By the first of April he had won Martinsville's Dogwood 500—the checker/wrecker fandango with Bodine—and Thompson's 81-lap Icebreaker, and there he was, leading the NASCAR standings for, oh, about the billionth time.

"We looked at the NASCAR points the same way every year," Nacewicz remembers. "Rich would say, 'We'll see where we're at by the end of March. If everything looks good then, we'll go for it.' I'm sure that if we got off to a really bad start, Richie would have decided to forget the points and just run for the money. It's just that we never got off to that bad start."

After Thompson came Stafford's Spring Sizzler, where Evans was as spectacular in defeat as he'd been in victory at Martinsville. He set fast time on Saturday afternoon, which, thanks to the inversion policy that weekend, lined him up 10th in the 80-lap Sizzler on Sunday. He followed second-quick qualifier John Rosati to the front, then hounded leader Maynard Troyer in a tremendous two-car duel before finding a way past midway through the event. But under reduced caution-flag speed with 53 laps complete, Evans sensed that his right-rear tire was losing air and pitted for a replacement. In the 23 remaining laps, he knifed back through the pack, and was sitting third on a restart with three circuits to go; a melted clutch had done in Troyer, leaving Bob Polverari and Reggie Ruggiero in the top two spots. Evans disposed of Ruggiero on the restart and, on the final lap, made a brave lunge inside Polverari as they dove into the third turn. They were even off turn four, but Polverari, the outside lane's momentum on his side, gassed it and took the win by maybe a yard. It was the first big win of Polverari's long career outside his home track, Riverside Park. In the old newspaper clipping, both winner and runner-up are beaming broadly in victory lane.

"Even though I had been racing for years," Polverari says today, "I really hadn't run the half-mile tracks very much. Certainly not as much as guys like Richie had. It was just great to run with the best, and to beat him. Later on, Richie told me he was happy for me. I think he was proud of me, because he'd taught me a lot about racing at places like Stafford."

Evans had his usual fine spring, but with an unusual twist. He came to New England in late May sporting a scraggly beard and a miserable scowl, plagued by a nasty case of chicken pox and burning with fever. He won Stafford's Manchester Oil Heat 100 anyway, and backed it up with a 50-lap Riverside score the next night. Then he went straight home to Rome, "to get better," he told everyone. But the next week, he looked just as bad; the beard was fuller, the scowl still there. This time, he won Stafford again, won Riverside again, and then a Sunday 81-lapper over Ron and Kenny Bouchard at Thompson.

Then came a Riverside 200 victory and an Islip 150 score and a Wednesday-night triumph in an 81-lapper at Monadnock. And in-between, as had become his custom, Richie Evans just piled up the weekly-feature wins.

Gracious in defeat, Evans (right) congratulates 1981 Spring Sizzler winner Bob Polverari. *(Paul Bonneau photo/courtesy of Speedway Scene)*

Evans, a course beard covering up a nasty case of chicken pox, scores at Stafford in '81. *(Howie Hodge photo/courtesy of Speedway Scene)*

He made a lot of those weekly conquests look easy, and in a way he had some help with that. Nacewicz says, "I don't want to say that everybody else was intimidated by Richie, because there were a lot of great drivers in the modifieds at that time. But sometimes when you're really fast—like we were in that period—a guy might give you a break just because he looks up in the mirror and says, 'Well, here *he* comes again.' It's not like the guy just pulls over, but the smart drivers will usually cut you some slack in a tight spot if they figure you're going to get by 'em anyway."

And that '81 season, it seemed like Richie Evans was always likely to get by 'em anyway.

He won his second track championships in a row at both Stafford and Thompson, having thrown away any shot at a Riverside repeat by running off so often to Shangri-La, Islip and Oswego.

More and more often across those weeks and months, engine builder Ron Hutter was flying in from Ohio on the weekends for Eastern modified events. For one thing, his customer base in the division had grown from one to more than a dozen; "Richie really helped us out there, because now everybody knew who we were," Hutter says. For another thing, he had gradually become a cog in the Big Orange wheel, often serving as part of the Evans crew.

"Richie and I just kinda hit it off," Hutter says. "Our personalities were way different, but we both liked racing, and we both liked running up front. Anyway, I ended up being a part of the team as much as the engine builder; I'd change tires on pit stops, or whatever they needed. I don't know how that happened, but it was fun for me because it was a way to be involved in the race rather than standing around watching."

In September came another All Star blitz at Islip. The '81 race had been shortened further, to 200 laps, and that was probably just as well. Evans led the entire way in beating John Blewett—who, by the way, was still hanging in there in his quest for points—and might have lapped the field under the old 300-lap distance.

Engine man, throttle man: Ron Hutter and Richie Evans. *(Val LeSieur photo/courtesy of* Speedway Scene*)*

"Richie was just so good at Islip," said Tom Baldwin. "He taught me a great lesson there. He said, 'Listen, you're trying to drive by everybody in the corner.' What did I know? I thought that's how it was done. I'd bury it down into the corner, turn it, slide around, go all crazy like a wild man. But Richie said, 'That ain't the deal. Watch what I do.' So I'm following him, and he's smooth as glass, but he's passing cars every lap. He would run down into the corner nice and easy, just hard enough to get outside a guy but not hard enough that he'd ever get out of shape. That way, when it was time to come out of the corner, poof, he was gone. *Gone.*

"He didn't waste the horsepower going *into* the corner. He didn't waste the brakes. He did it all coming *out* of the corner. He'd just hold that inside guy down—if they rubbed, they rubbed, no big deal—and blow him off when they came out of the turn. Boy, he was the master."

It was a curious sort of season when it came to unexpected highs and lows in special events. Evans blew an engine in Oswego's Bud 200. Then, in the very first lap of the Race of Champions, he noticed his car revving so highly that for an instant he thought he'd been too busy to shift from third to fourth; instead, his car's spur gears had been installed upside down. He dropped out after eight laps, finishing dead last. At Martinsville in October, a busted master cylinder had him loading up even earlier, after just *two* laps. In the Turkey Derby at Wall, Richie drew the pole position and lapped almost the entire field before he pulled into the infield with a punctured left-rear tire.

But maybe that was just Dame Fortune evening things out. In August's Winston 100 at Stafford he had been running a decent fourth, nothing special, behind Geoff Bodine, Reggie Ruggiero and Ray Miller. Then, with 82 laps complete and a caution flag waving, a wild chain of events took place. Bodine was black-flagged for spewing water; Ruggiero felt something amiss in his chassis and pitted with a broken strut rod; and Evans, sensing an opportunity to make chicken salad from chicken shit, scooted past Miller on the restart and held him off the rest of the way.

In the space of a few weeks toward season's end, Richie took a Shangri-La special, the Fall Final at Stafford, and the Thompson World Series.

All right, if you *must* have the numbers: Evans won 38 of his 71 NASCAR starts, eight of the 15 national championship events run that year, his fourth straight modified title and his fifth overall. John Blewett had given it a hell of a run for a first-time points-chaser, but ended up so far back that he'd have had to dial a "1" just to give Evans a congratulatory phone call.

The winter of 1981-82 could, then, have been a joyous time on Calvert Street, but it hardly seemed there was *any* joy in Modifiedville in those months. No matter which direction you turned in, there was some level of upset and confusion.

Santa Claus, played by Bob O'Rourke, congratulates 1981 NASCAR mod champ and Islip Speedway banquet guest Richie Evans. (B&G Wurthmann photo/courtesy of Speedway Scene)

On a Roll

NASCAR had completely revamped its modified points structure for '82, announcing that in addition to the traditional title, the division's drivers would compete in a new Winston-backed system which broke the country into different regions with the goal of creating a national NASCAR short-track champion. (Evans, while publicly supportive—"Anytime we've got a company like Winston that's put up this [extra] money, I'm pleased"— was wary of how it all might work, as were many competitors.)

The sanctioning body had also mandated a rule limiting modified engines to carburetors flowing no more than 390 cubic feet per minute, down a substantial chunk from the big 650 and 750 CFM breathers the troops had been using. (Evans hated that one.)

Meanwhile, over in New England, where Richie had made so much hay from 1979-81, the promoters at four tracks—Stafford, Riverside Park, Thompson and Seekonk—had gotten together with the New England Drivers and Owners club to introduce a one-brand modified tire rule for the '82 campaign. (The brand was a Hoosier, and Evans, now a Goodyear man who was rarely spotted without the Akron manufacturer's blue cap atop his head, *really* hated that one, threatening to do the bulk of his racing elsewhere if the NEDOC tire mandate went into effect.)

And when you look back on it now, this turmoil—and his reaction to it—may have cost Richie Evans more than it cost anyone else, in terms of results.

Out of sorts over all the changes—particularly the ones messing with his rubber and his horsepower—Evans broke a pattern he'd held to for several seasons. "We always figured that a new car was worth a couple of tenths right out of the box, just by improving a little bit on what you had," Nacewicz remembers. "So most years we'd generally start with one new car and one older one, maybe even two new ones. But that year, we hadn't built a new car over the winter. We decided to run the '82 season with the '81 cars." They swapped the sheet metal on one to a Chevrolet Cavalier, keeping up with the latest trend, leaving the other one clad in Pinto tin for a while.

"We had won a lot of races in '81, and we were super-fast everywhere," says Nacewicz. "So we figured our cars were still good enough. Maybe we got a little lazy. If that was it, we paid for it. Because Greg Sacks showed up at New Smyrna with a new car, new motors, and a new team, and they just rocked everybody."

Did they ever. Sacks and a couple of Long Island neighbors, Ernie Wilsberg and his son Jamie, had one of those dream weeks in Florida. Every afternoon they'd roll a gleaming white Troyer Cavalier—striped in red and numbered 5—out of their trailer, and on six nights out of eight at New Smyrna they loaded it back up as a feature winner. If Sacks set fast time and started up front, he won; if he set fast time, lost the traditional New Smyrna coin flip, and lined up sixth, he won anyway.

"To go by Richie on the outside," Greg said, "is a great feeling."

Over at the #61 truck, things weren't nearly as cheery, and they wouldn't be for quite some time.

"That wasn't a good year for Rich and I, personally," Nacewicz recalls. "We started out in Florida on a bad note. We had a little problem between us—nothing I want to talk about, just a disagreement over ideas—and we parted ways for a while. It happened while we were running New Smyrna, but I stayed through the week basically because I needed a ride home."

When the Northeast season opened, Evans was without Nacewicz for the first time since 1975, and some folks noticed the difference. Not necessarily in his performance, mind you—because Evans had lots of company in being outrun by Sacks—but in his attitude. Tom Baldwin said, "The most I ever saw Richie get shaken up was when he lost Nacewicz for a while. Oh, you couldn't live with him. He was like an old lady, whining about not having Billy around."

By the time the two old friends and teammates patched things up at the end of April, Evans had watched Sacks win twice more, at Martinsville in March (where Richie ran second) and in the Spring Sizzler (where he had engine trouble). But the reunion was a good one; they captured a victory in the Thompson Icebreaker, run that season on the final weekend in April.

That Thompson win, however, was a bit misleading. Sacks had blown a left-rear tire while out in front. When he didn't hit trouble that year, he was all but unstoppable. *Speedway Scene* writers John Brouwer and Dave Shippee labeled him "Superman," and nobody—including Evans—seemed able to get their hands on any Kryptonite.

"Greg had put together a dynamite combination," says Nacewicz, "and we knew we didn't have what it took to beat him. To us, it was like we had brought a knife to a gunfight. Rich couldn't make up for what the car was lacking. We could get close, but that was it. All we could hope for was to be, like, best in class."

Come the regular season, Evans made good on his threat to avoid Stafford and its Hoosier rule, instead making New Egypt his Friday-night home, and he ran Shangri-La most Saturdays. But he did haul into New England for the Sunday shows at Thompson, which, like Riverside, had backed out of the NEDOC arrangement.

Sacks was the hottest man wherever he chose to race—cleaning house at Stafford and also scoring at Oswego and Thompson—but elsewhere Evans kept punching away. He grabbed an 80-lap biggie at Spencer, won some at Shangri-La, and was especially tough at New Egypt, where in the space of two months he'd won the opener, a Winston 100, a Bud 150 in June, a 100-lapper in July, and another Bud 150 in July. His toughest competition on the Jersey quarter-mile was Tony Siscone, who topped Evans in a number of features that year, but there were more.

Victory Lane at Riverside, 1982. From left to right are Tony Pettinelli Jr., Evans, Billy Nacewicz, Kenny Hartung and Ray Spognardi. (*Rich Carlon photo/courtesy of Speedway Scene*)

(left) Greg Sacks had Evans, and everybody else, for that matter, covered in 1982. (*courtesy of Speedway Scene*)

"There was a period in the early '80s when New Egypt was as tough a place as there was," Baldwin said. "It was such a tight little bullring, flat, and you had a lot of talent there: Evans and Siscone, yes, but also Bobby Park, Fred Harbach, John Blewett, Wayne Anderson, Jerry Cook in the big shows, and you can keep going."

New Egypt was certainly the ace up Richie's sleeve—by July he'd already won five times there—but it's not exactly like he was foundering everywhere else. By mid-July he had taken three main events at Thompson, two at Shangri-La, two more at Riverside, and one each at Spencer and Holland. Figure in his two New Smyrna wins and an April 150 at Martinsville, and he'd won 17 features by time the weather had even gotten sticky.

"In a sense, it has been an off year," he told a *Speedway Scene* columnist. "But I'm sure there are a lot of guys who'd love to be in the rut I'm in."

Really, the only guy who had his number, consistently, was Sacks. Whenever they paired off, the new Wilsberg #5 was still more than a match for the old DeWitt #61.

Nacewicz says, "We knew all along what the problem was, but it's hard to start building new cars when you're racing as much as we were. We were racing Fridays, Saturdays and Sundays, and even a lot of Tuesdays and Wednesdays, so we weren't home enough to put new cars together."

Then, along about the middle of the year, they got a new car—sort of—in a rather unexpected manner. A Thompson crash had kinked his Cavalier just enough that Evans decided it needed overhauling. They stripped the car and set it on the frame jig, where Nacewicz and Dick Abbott torched off the front snout and welded on a new one. Instantly, there was an upturn in the car's feel.

Richie Evans, 1982. *(John Grady photo)*

"You've got to crash these things once in a while," Evans told writer Ron Hedger, only half joking. "That way, they get a new snout on them and they think they're a new car."

He led every lap of a Riverside Park 200, went back to Thompson and stole a pair of Sunday-evening 30-lappers, and won both Spencer's regular-season finale and its big post-season 200.

In the Bud 200 at Oswego, Evans ran a so-so fourth behind Sacks, Roger Treichler and Maynard Troyer, and in the Race of Champions at Pocono he finished second, trailing Sacks yet again. Greg still had the fastest gun in town, but at least Evans had closed the gap a bit.

And September did end with some highlights. Evans beat George Kent to win a NASCAR national championship event at Maine's Oxford Plains Speedway, and sewed up the track championship at Shangri-La. And his season-long tussle with Tony Siscone for the New Egypt title

Evans collects the 1982 Budweiser champion's trophy from Ned Jarrett (left) and NASCAR president Bill France Jr. *(Lynn Evans collection)*

ended in Richie's favor when Tony blew a tire in the season-ending 200.

NASCAR's twin-championship system had puzzled Evans a bit—he acknowledged that he had completely misunderstood the regional format—but in the end he cashed both checks, one from Winston and the other from Budweiser signifying his national title. George Kent, saying that "Richie was the one who convinced me to chase points," was the only man to give Evans a serious run for the national honors. And Evans was a player in Winston's country-wide tally, ending up third in a best-average-finish scale topped by Iowa dirt-track racer Tom Hearst.

The Budweiser title, incidentally, made Richie the first man in NASCAR history to win five straight championships in any division.

He'd been right: *some rut.*

There was another bit of interesting news that autumn concerning NASCAR modified champions. After the 1982 Cardinal 500 at Martinsville, Jerry Cook had put his helmet on the shelf and announced that he was taking an official's job with NASCAR. Even though many saw it coming—in '82, most of Cook's racing was done aboard cars owned by Ed Cloce and Wayne Miller, with the familiar Cook 38 a noteworthy absentee—the decision still hit like a thud.

Cookie had simply been around forever, and sometimes he seemed as much a part of Evans's career as orange paint. Sure, Cook said, "there were weeks when [Richie] chose to run at Stafford on a Friday night and I chose to run at Spencer. But there were many, many more times when we both wound up at the same place. There was usually at least one night a week when we'd see each other."

At least one night a week for, what, 15 years?

It was just one more thing for Evans to think about at the end of a long, hard 1982, a year he conceded had taken more than the usual toll.

"You figure, we've run over 80 races," he told *Speedway Scene.* "Over the summer, we [were] averaging 30 hours a week in the truck, just traveling to and from the races."

Those numbers weren't far out of the ordinary. But this one was: It was the first time in four years that he ended a season with less than 40 wins. And on some days when he'd been beaten, he'd been beaten *badly.*

"It was," he admitted, "the hardest year I've ever had."

The days since then—and probably all the success they had later on —have provided Billy Nacewicz a kinder, gentler perspective. "Yes, we lost all the big shows [in 1982]. Sacksy killed us at Martinsville, Oswego, the Race of Champions, the Spring Sizzler, the Thompson 300 ... you name it, those guys won it, all the marquee events. Golf has the Grand Slam, and modified racing has those big races, and Sacks had a grand-slam year while we pretty much got our fannies slapped. That hurt. But, you know, we still won 25 or so races, and a couple of track championships. That ain't bad."

No, it sure ain't.

Nacewicz says, "I'll never forget something Gene DeWitt did that year. He got us aside just after the season, and he said, 'Look, everything is OK. You guys did what you did, and Sacks did what he did. But Greg had all new stuff this year; next year, his stuff won't be as new, and you'll have fresh cars to run. And we'll be fine.'

"And, you know, Gene was right."

Most Popular

"GOD," SAID EVANS to Pete Zanardi way back in 1973, "I don't know what I would do if I was ever booed at a race track. I wouldn't know how to handle it."

Almost from the very beginning, he had been a hit with fans. Ted Puchyr remembers that in the coupe days, "There were caravans that would go down from Rome to Malta on a Friday night. I mean, *caravans* of people who wanted to watch Richie race."

But his popularity spread like crabgrass once he started traveling on the NASCAR trail. In 1973, his first points-chasing season, he was named the modified division's Most Popular Driver by vote of the sanctioning body's membership; the NASCAR record book noted that Richie had edged Bugs Stevens, who'd accepted the award in 1971 and '72.

In '74, Evans won it again—edging Jerry Cook and Stevens—and then he made it three straight in 1975. While Richie was off running NEARA in '76-77, the NASCAR laurels went to Cook and Harry Gant, but once Evans returned to the fold he essentially took all the suspense out of the annual balloting, coming out on top every year from 1978-83.

That made nine Most Popular Driver plaques he could hang above his nine NASCAR national modified championship trophies. And in weighing up his legacy, there are those who consider the plaques more important. He was his division's Pied Piper; where he went, the fans went, too, and when he was done with his work they all seemed to want to gather around him.

Lee Osborne, who saw that in Evans early on, thinks he has an explanation. "If you look around," Ozzie says, "there are a lot of *good* drivers, but there's not many *great* drivers, guys who can take a car with a front end that's all wanged up or a motor that's missing and still win the feature. Richie had that kind of ability. Everybody wants to be around a driver who wins, but when he's also just a good, fun guy, it makes him even more popular. Everybody knew Richie because of his personality."

Linda Holdeman—who was Linda O'Brien in the days when she and her husband Dick both worked at Oswego, Linda in the front office and Dick on the officiating side of things—had a long, wisecracking sort of

(left) Evans shares a pit-side laugh with Fred DeSarro and mechanic Clyde MacLeod at Stafford in the mid-'70s. *(Bones Bourcier collection)*

(right) Surrounded by well-wishing youngsters after a Thompson Speedway victory. *(Paul Bonneau photo/courtesy of* Speedway Scene*)*

friendship with Evans. "I think people enjoyed the *whole* of Richie," she says. "There was the racing—the incredible talent—but there was also that guy who was just such a fun person."

Ex-hubby Dick O'Brien says, "He was always at ease after a race. He'd have a few beers with his fans, and he'd be holding court. That's what he was like, a king in his court. And I think that's when Richie enjoyed himself the most."

Dutch Hoag remembers Evans making post-race conversation with older fans while also "making time for the younger people, the kids." Crewman Ray Spognardi says, "That was something that impressed me when I first started working with Richie, the fact that he really took the time to talk to any kids who approached him."

Maybe the key to his cross-generational appeal was this: By the early 1980s he had been driving stock cars for 20 years and winning for 15, so he had lots of old-school fans, but he was also young at heart, cool, and so teenaged fans liked him, too.

"The thing about Rich was, he was just charismatic," says Buster Maurer. "If somebody wanted an autograph, he'd sign an autograph, just like you've always heard about Richard Petty. He would stay in the pits until the end."

Dick O'Brien says, "If you were a fan, you got to chit-chat with Richie Evans for an hour, two hours. Really, Richie would be there until *you* wanted to leave. It might be two or three o'clock in the morning, or whenever the beer ran out, or when the cops kicked you out."

And, Lord, the tales you'd hear if you hung around the Evans hauler, the metaphorical Big Orange campfire, after a race. There was the one about the night when Billy Nacewicz, having momentarily taken his eyes off the #61, missed seeing it tangle with another car and sail off the track. Noticing the yellow light blink on, Nacewicz keyed his radio microphone and barked, *"Caution, caution, caution!"* And even though they'd each told the story a hundred times, both driver and crew chief always cracked up when they recalled Richie's response: "I *am* the caution, you asshole."

Then there was the one that went back even further, to the years before radios, when Evans was in the middle of an extra-distance race and wanted to know how far along the event had gotten. He tried asking for the lap count through hand signals, but his message wasn't getting through; his crew could only shrug in response. Finally, Richie had a brainstorm. He pointed repeatedly and theatrically at his wristwatch, as if to implore, "Time? How much time have I got left? Time?" The next time around, Evans recalled with a laugh, he saw a crewman holding up a pit board. It read, "9:30."

Hearing that stuff, a casual fan could almost feel like part of the group. And if he came around a few more times, before long he might actually *be* part of the group.

"Richie was a package deal," says Maynard Troyer. "And I don't know if you could ever put one part of that package above the other, because if you took away one part, you wouldn't have had that same package. If he had been a hell of a racer, but a snob, he wouldn't have been Richie."

Pete Zanardi, who has given this matter a great amount of thought, believes that Evans's superstar status owes much to the fact that he came along at just the right time. "No matter who we're dealing with, the times make the man," Zanardi says. He points out that the modifieds had only gained true national acceptance in the racing generation just ahead of Evans—through the successes of Northeastern drivers "like Flemke, Charland, Bill Slater, Fats Caruso, Ernie Gahan, Bugsy"—and that conditions were ripe for spawning a legitimate division-wide hero. Places like Trenton and Martinsville were still staging a number of Civil War-type modified races, crowds were booming, and the class was getting unprecedented media attention.

Zanardi declares, "We were looking for somebody who could come in and say, 'Here I am.' That's what the Roman did in the '70s, when you still had a national modified scene."

The result, says Zanardi, is that "everybody 40 years old or above can tell a Richie Evans story." And it doesn't really matter where they're from. That's saying something, because even at the high point of its national acceptance, modified racing's fans remained a parochial bunch, most devoted to drivers from their own particular regions. It wasn't easy for even the biggest names to gain a fan foothold in a distant parish; "When I first came to New England to race," says Jerry Cook in a perfect for-instance, "I was looked upon as an outsider." That was something Eddie Flemke had felt on his initial trips south in the 1960s, and something Ray Hendrick admitted to feeling when he made frequent invasions north in the early '70s. And yet Richie Evans, this Rapid Roman, seemed to catch on everywhere.

"Down South," he proudly told interviewer Roger Bear in 1982, "I get cheered as good as any Southern guy."

It was the same in New England, a region which, as noted, hadn't

Evans was a fan favorite almost everywhere he went. This is a 1980 Riverside Park scene. *(Jim Squalliano photo/courtesy of Speedway Scene)*

Millie Hatch, who ran the official Richie Evans Fan Club, and a sampling of #61 memorabilia. (Val LeSieur photo, Karl Fredrickson photo)

exactly embraced New Yorkers Cook and Geoff Bodine. By the late 1970s, the same grandstands which once thundered only for locals like Stevens and Ronnie Bouchard also got noisy when this Evans fellow was introduced.

"Once we started running in New England almost full-time, I felt like we were really accepted," says Nacewicz. "Maybe it's because we weren't just showing up when the big money was on the line. We were at Stafford for the 30-lappers instead of just for the Spring Sizzler; we were at Riverside Park for a lot of the regular Saturday nights, and not just for the double-pointers. Same thing at Thompson. Good or bad, rain or shine, we were there. We'd take whatever starting spot they gave us, 16th or 18th or whatever it was, and we'd go racing. And I think the New England racers and the New England fans appreciated that."

Bill and Millie Hatch were hawking "T-shirts and stuff" for Evans in the mid-1970s; by decade's end, they were running his fan club, with Millie as president. They peddled an assortment of #61 memorabilia "just about everyplace he raced," and their testimony is as good as anyone's on the subject of Richie's widespread appeal. "He was always popular at Oswego, of course," Millie says. "But, you know, Thompson was always big for us, too. And Islip; God, at Islip they'd mob us before we were even set up."

Islip, like its lone surviving cousin on Long Island, Riverhead Raceway, could be a clannish place, a hostile environment for intruders. "There weren't a lot of people who got received well when they came to the Island," Tom Baldwin said. "It was hard for Cook to come in; it was hard for a *lot* of guys to come in. But Richie came, and it seemed like he'd been with us forever."

Roger Bear questioned Evans on this topic, telling him, "You weren't always famous, but you're famous now. I mean, when people talk about modified racers—when they talk about stock car racers—they talk about Richie Evans. At what point in your life did you say, 'Well, now I'm famous'?"

Crewman Tiger Pettinelli says Evans "liked people as much as they liked him." *(Howie Hodge photo/courtesy of* Speedway Scene*)*

"I never looked at it that way," Evans replied. "I just went racing every year."

He seemed almost embarrassed by the subject; that sort of question took Evans out of what wife Lynn calls "his environment, meaning the shop or the race track," and she adds that when that happened he could sometimes be "a very insecure person." He absolutely looked like one in his videotaped interview with Bear; Richie Evans was a guy who could deal with fame, who could certainly enjoy fame, yet he was anything but comfortable *examining* fame. So he toed the dirt, glanced around, came up with a couple of false-start answers—"I guess … uh … I've had pretty good feelings [at] all the tracks"—before settling on something very basic: "I think the people enjoy good racing, and I try to race hard."

He did admit to Zanardi back in '73 that he was "very proud that so many people follow my racing." He just didn't want to discuss it much.

Tony Pettinelli Jr. thinks about his old boss winning that NASCAR Most Popular Driver award nine times, and seems almost surprised to admit, "You know, I never once heard him talk about it. In fact, the rest of us never even mentioned it around the shop. I think we just read it in the papers, and we each said, 'Hey, he won it again. Cool.' I don't ever, ever remember a conversation about it. But I'm sure it meant a lot to him. I know it did. Because he liked people as much as they liked him."

Evans told Zanardi, "You have to have people on your side to be successful," and he sure did have a way of *keeping* them on his side. So many drivers, jumping as they do from ride to ride, tend to hang with small groups of running buddies and shifting bands of owners, mechanics and crew members. Teammates are temporary, and lasting bonds therefore rare. But because Richie Evans had always driven his own cars and captained his own ship, associations lasted; you got the sense that his band of crewmen and friends was the closest thing modified racing had to a real brotherhood.

"If you were part of that gang," says Rita Marcello, who belonged, as did her husband Donny, "you were always part of that gang."

Pettinelli says, "The guys who had worked on that car at one time or another, they all still came around from time to time, even if it was just to stop in and shoot the baloney. No matter who you are, things in your life change, and sometimes you can't do things like work on a race team anymore, even if you'd still like to. People change jobs, or they get married and have kids, or whatever. But it seemed like just being a little bit involved with Richie was better than not being involved at all."

Buster Maurer had jumped off the full-time racing road by taking a job at Bartel Machinery in 1974 and taking a bride a year later. But that didn't mean he gave up on his friend, or his friend's race car. Proud of the fact that he and his peers—Wilbur Jones, Max Baker, Danny Morgan, Fred Ulrich and others—had "helped Rich build the foundation for his team," Maurer still kept coming around to Calvert Street. He remembers, "I worked afternoons [at Bartel's], so in the mornings I opened up the garage, got the car off the hauler, took the rear end apart and did the preventative maintenance, just like when I worked for him full-time. I was doing that for him probably until '77 or '78."

That sort of loyalty clearly went both ways. Fred Ulrich said, "If you did something for Rich, he never forgot it. Yes, I helped him early in his career, but for years he looked after me. If we were going to Martinsville, Daytona, wherever, I always had a ride down and back, always had a place to stay. That all went back to him remembering how I'd helped him when he really needed it."

And Joe Jones, half-owner in that first-ever Evans stocker, ol' PT 109, says, "He invited me every year to go to Daytona, and now I kick myself in the ass because I didn't just go. I'll bet he asked me 10 times if he asked me once: 'Oh, come on down and spend the week.' I said, 'Well, next year. I'll work this year.' But, you know, at least once or twice a year I'd go down to his shop and spend a few hours."

Speedway Scene publisher Val LeSieur, who both covered and befriended Evans, says, "Richie was the kind of guy people wanted to do things with, and even do things *for*."

Example: Reporting from the Daytona Permatex event in 1974, writer Phil Smith noted that Evans had "four top drivers on his pit crew: Dick Fowler, Sonney Seamon, Mike Loescher and Merv Treichler."

Another example: John McClellan, a crony of New Jersey dirt modified star Billy Osmun, had met Evans at some long-ago dirt track. An elevator installer by trade, McClellan took to moonlighting in the racing apparel business, marketing his wares under the name Brew Crew T's. Evans shot him some business, and McClellan joined the gang. "It was probably 300 miles from my home in New Jersey to Richie's shop. But if he needed me up there, for *anything*, I'd be up there in a heartbeat. He was just a good guy."

More examples: a friend who supplied Evans with homemade ice

The relationship between Fred Ulrich (left) and Richie Evans showed that loyalty is a two-way street. *(Mary Hodge photo/courtesy of* Speedway Scene*)*

cream, another who handcrafted him countless pairs of Hush Puppy-style loafers.

"There was this one older guy who used to be a customer of Richie's at the gas station," Wilbur Jones remembers. "Well, long after Rich had gotten the shop on Calvert Street, this guy used to drive by at maybe 11:30 at night. He'd blow the horn three times, and he'd leave. By the time you walked out, he'd be gone. But there was a six-pack sitting there in the middle of the street. He just loved Richie."

Smiling, Pettinelli says, "Richie had some great people skills. He could read people; he knew if something was bothering them, and he would try to help. Yeah, he could be very blunt, but at the same time he could also be a very understanding guy. We used to joke that he could tell you to go fuck yourself, and you'd look forward to the experience."

One other Evans strong suit: what onetime Stafford PR man John McMullin calls his "nice way of *acknowledging* you." Seldom did the man let an acquaintance slip past unnoticed, or unappreciated. He had a sort of reverse nod that, even in the middle of the chaos that was so often his life on a race night, he would direct at the friend, and that would be enough.

"He could carry on five or six conversations at the same time," Zanardi recalls. "And if he was talking to someone else and you walked by, he might wink at you or toss a little stone or give you that nod, and that was his way of communicating with you, too. That's all it took."

It was, in essence, a conversation without words.

"It wasn't just your imagination doing that," Zanardi says. "It was a conscious effort on his part that resulted in a reaction on your part. That might have been your only interaction with him all night; you simply walked by. But the next day, somebody would ask you who you talked to at the races, and you'd say, 'Well, I talked to Richie ...'

"He had an extraordinary ability to do that, to communicate with his friends. And you know, for a lot of people, it's still like a badge: They say, 'Richie and I were good friends.' That's a great tribute to him."

And for his good friends, Richie did whatever he could. He got involved in their lives, to whatever extent they wanted or needed him to.

"In a lot of ways he was kinda like a father figure to me," says Tony Pettinelli Jr., "and I think he understood that. There was a time when me and my dad didn't get along; for a while, I wouldn't even speak to him. And if it wasn't for Rich and his people skills, we might never have talked. See, Rich actually came right out and said, 'Look, that's your father. He's always going to *be* your father. You might want to think about that.' Well, I did think about it, and it got me talking to my dad again.

"But it's funny. Anytime I had those sort of talks with Richie, there was never anybody around. If there was, he wouldn't bring that stuff up. It was like he had this image he thought he had to protect, and he couldn't let anybody see that side of him. And that's a shame, because it was a *good* side."

Rita Marcello says, "This is sort of personal, and I haven't told this to many people, but Rich helped out Donny and I financially when we first bought our house. We were in a pinch, and we needed a little bit of help, and he was there. Along the way, I saw him help a *lot* of people, and he never showed it, never advertised it. He always wanted to do the kinds of things he thought you should do for friends."

"Richie did things for people," says Wilbur Jones. "He financed more than a couple of businesses in this town, I know that. You know, friends of his who needed help getting started. And he helped a lot of racers who were broke and maybe needed tires or even a motor. But he was very quiet about that stuff; he never, ever said, 'This guy owes me money,' or anything like that. Maybe it was a private side of him that he wanted to keep private."

And he let his friends get involved in his life, to whatever extent they wanted or needed to. His house up on Delta Lake served as a no-charge bed-and-breakfast for any number of racing folks. Some—like Dave "Carter" Best, a familiar '70s sight in the Evans pits— had signed on as shop help and needed temporary lodging, and others were on overnight stops in Rome. There was always a pillow for a stray mechanic, a wandering journalist, even a rival driver.

"Boy, we had so many fun guests," Lynn Evans says. "Our home was always open, and I think Rich enjoyed that. We always had a house full of people, and in the morning I'd end up cooking in shifts, sometimes for people I didn't even know. Richie loved that."

And yet somehow, in the middle of all this fun, Evans began to run into the one thing he had feared most: God, being *booed* at a race track. When he first began to notice it, what he'd told Zanardi so many years earlier proved accurate: He didn't know how to handle it.

Lynn says, "I remember him coming home and talking about something that had happened at Stafford. Apparently, he had heard a lot of booing there for some reason, and he had never really experienced that. That bothered him."

It happened at other places, too. He was still the modified division's most popular driver, as voted by applause, and its Most Popular Driver, as voted annually by the NASCAR dues-payers. But there was no denying the fact that at places where he once heard only cheers, more and more catcalls were cutting through the air. He'd win a few in a row at Riverside or Thompson, and there was no way to miss the booing.

"I hoped that would never happen," he told Dick Berggren in 1981.

Other drivers, he often said, counseled him not to worry about it. Booing, they told him, went with winning, so it was possible to see it as a good thing. He heard that from Eddie Flemke, from Will Cagle, from Lou Lazzaro, people he truly admired. And yet it always struck a sad chord in Evans when he did get booed. It was as if he couldn't figure out how in the world his racing could bother anyone else when it was so damn much fun for him.

John McClellan, the T-shirt man, says, "You know what Richie got a kick out of? We'd be at a race track, looking up from the pits into the stands, and there would be so much *orange*. Oh, that made him smile."

Work Hard, Play Hard III

BILLY HARMON, A CONNECTICUT DRIVER whose decades-long career driving modifieds up and down the East Coast led to his 2004 induction into the New England Auto Racing Hall of Fame, is one of those guys who has known everybody. What that has given Harmon is a hall-of-fame ability to tell long, funny stories, and he told a beauty in his acceptance speech.

Naturally, it involved Richie Evans. Any long, funny story about the modifieds sooner or later gets around to Evans.

This one concerned a Florida night when Evans, Lenny Boehler, Harmon and the late George Pendergast—a former driver and promoter and himself the star of a million funny stories—had finished up another evening's racing at the New Smyrna Speedway and were unwinding at Edie's Bar in Daytona Beach. The place got a little crowded, so Evans, Boehler and Pendergast opted to take their refreshment on the sidewalk out front.

"Well, drinking on the sidewalk in Daytona is, uh, not allowed," said Harmon. "A cruiser drove up."

The policeman told the three men to climb into the back seat.

Harmon said, "Lenny opened the door and let them both in, then [climbed in] and closed the door behind him. And as the officer drives away, Lenny starts singing [the old Mills Brothers hit]: 'Cab driver, once more around the block … Never mind the ticking of the clock.' The officer was so impressed with Lenny that he started laughing. He turned the car around, drove back to the bar, and asked them to please get out and call it a day. And then [the cop] said, 'By the way, Richie, did you win again tonight?'"

Beautiful.

Edie's, which is gone now, had a short stint as one of those can't-miss bars on any modified fan's list. The beer was cheap and cold, so it met all the Speedweeks requirements. Boehler was generally credited with discovering the place. On a good night there in the late '70s or early '80s, you might also find drivers like Ronnie Bouchard and Merv Treichler, car owners like Bob Judkins and Joe Brady, and any number of mechanics and assorted troublemakers. And Richie Evans became a regular there, which raised the stature of the joint considerably.

"We had a few places that kinda became hangouts," remembers Billy Nacewicz. "See, if you go into places where you're welcomed—where people treat you well— you want to go back. Then you kind of drag your friends in there, whether they're other racers or fans or whatever. And then, as the word spreads, more and more people come."

Nacewicz laughs. "And, you know, for a period of time there, Richie was the center of attention. So wherever we were, people wanted to be, because they wanted to see what was going to happen next. It was almost like we were the draw. Pretty soon, the people who owned those places realized that we were helping them make money, so they started treating us better and better."

The Holiday Inn bar was the Martinsville hangout. At Riverside Park there was Josie's Outpost Lounge, directly across the street from the track. Thompson Speedway had its clubhouse, built for golfers but, as it turned out, tailor-made for racers: good food, a jukebox, and a well-stocked bar. Nacewicz remembers, "We'd stay in that clubhouse until this one particular cop—Pistol Pete, everybody called him—would throw us out. He'd wander up and say, 'Now, Richie, it's time to leave. New York is *that* way. Get going.'"

But a place didn't necessarily need walls, a roof and a liquor license to be a good hangout. In a pinch, a lighted pit area or a track parking lot would do just fine.

"We spent many a night in the Stafford parking lot, partying outside that pit gate until I don't know when," says Nacewicz. "Some good friends of ours from Connecticut, Al and Peg Gaudreau—two great people who had owned race cars for years—would bring these big cookers, and we'd eat steak and drink beer and tell stories until the sun came up."

Islip, where Buster Maurer had once seen a guy drink STP, had one of the greatest trackside party scenes. "As soon as the racing ended, the party would start," said Tom Baldwin. "By the time it was over, the sun would be coming up on Sunday morning. There'd be Richie's guys, my guys, Charlie Jarzombek's guys, Fred Harbach's guys. Just a bunch of people, bullshittin' with a couple beers."

Bill Hatch remembers John Farone—who traveled the modified circuit as "Seymour the Clown" and could always be counted on to liven up any post-race gathering—making the rounds at one such Islip bash with "a fire extinguisher filled with vodka and orange juice."

"With Richie," says Ron Hutter, "it was a constant party. If he wasn't racing, he wanted to be having a good time."

A pause here, for reflection and clarification. The Evans legend includes so many stories involving alcohol and barrooms—from the Rose Garden's Cold Duck after every Lancaster win to that failed attempt to buy a truckload of beer—that it has become easy for people who didn't know him to paint Richie as some kind of a hard-drinking boozehound. Today, you will run into plenty of folks eager to tell you

Two guys who could liven up a party: Evans and John Farone, aka "Seymour the Clown." (Rene Dugas photo/courtesy of Speedway Scene)

about the time they got blind-drunk with Richie Evans on the night before he won the *blah, blah, blah* ...

Most of this is nonsense. For one thing, nobody can drink that much and win that often. And then there's this: Why is it that in all the stories about So-and-so getting blotto with Evans and the guys, it's always So-and-so who passes out, throws up, sleeps in his car, and shows up with a hangover?

Richie Evans might have been the farthest thing from a poster boy for sobriety, but, according to those who really *did* party with him, he knew when to say when.

"If he was drinking beer, he might nurse the same one for an hour," says Wilbur Jones. "If he was having a mixed drink, he'd tell the bartender to only pour in half a shot instead of a full one. He wasn't an angel, by any means, but he was sneaky about it. I think the biggest thing was, he never wanted to be out of control."

Lynn Evans remembers her husband telling visiting friends that if they were going to drink in Rome, they were going to drink Rome-style. "He'd say, 'Around here, we do a shot, and then a beer.'" Before long, the visitor would be walking on his or her elbows, and Evans was still standing straight as a board. "That's because he was drinking shots of water," says Lynn. "He'd have a shot of water and sip his beer, and laugh his ass off."

Ah, that was really the key to the whole thing; once the alcohol got everybody limbered up, the fun started. And if he could do anything to help speed up that process, Evans was happy to lend a hand. Val LeSieur, a teetotaler and thus a more reliable witness than some who partied with Evans, says, "After a couple drinks, Richie would switch to a ginger ale or a 7-Up with a lime in it, something that *looked* like he was still drinking. Then he'd stir things up, and get everybody going."

Steve Hmiel says, "They talk about Richie being such a party guy, but I never saw that man get falling-down drunk. I did see a lot of people *around* Richie get falling-down drunk, and I saw Richie enjoying that atmosphere. But I think he gets mislabeled as being some kind of a wildman himself. He enjoyed people, and he enjoyed people having a good time, but he was more of a spectator in that. He'd get things going, then he'd stand back and watch."

"Richie was an instigator," laughs George Kent, cutting right to the chase. "He'd kind of get the ball rolling, but he was pretty good at getting other people to pick it up from there."

Howard Maseles, a popular product rep who knew Evans well from having worked with manufacturers whose equipment Richie used and/or endorsed, felt the sting of that instigation. One year during Syracuse's Super DIRT Week—the dirt modified world's version of the Race of Champions, and an even bigger party—Evans told a couple of Howard's helpers about a get-together he was having that night in Rome, just a short drive down the Thruway. "They were supposed to be back in a couple of hours," Maseles told Dick Berggren. "But they didn't even make it back the whole next day."

Mr. and Mrs. Dominic Marcello knew all about that instigation, too. When they were married in 1975, Richie and Lynn Evans stood as their witnesses. Rita had spent the previous night at Lynn's house, and the girls were at the church, St. Paul's in Rome, nice and early.

"I'm standing there, a nervous wreck," Rita remembers. "Lynn and I are waiting. And we're waiting. And we're waiting."

Well, Donny? What went wrong? "Rich took me down to this place on Dominick Street called Ye Old Eagle. He said, 'We've got time. Let's have a beer.' Well, one beer turned into a few, and we started goofing around. I remember they had this big jar: cherry peppers, three for a quarter. Richie pointed to me and said, 'Give him three.' I ate those, and he ordered me three more, and then three more. Well, at one point I walked away from the bar, and Richie got his hands on a bottle of Tabasco sauce. He filled one of those peppers full of that sauce. Sonofabitch, was that hot!

"Eventually, we head off to the church. I still remember walking down the sidewalk—OK, staggering down the sidewalk—and Richie opening up that door and waving me in: 'Here we are!'"

Rita says, "A half-hour late, in walks my husband-to-be with Sir Richard, and my husband-to-be is shitfaced. I'm nervous anyway, and my stomach is in knots. Now I'm *steaming*. I mean, just to tell you what kind of shape my wonderful husband-to-be is in, he turns to the Father and says, 'How long is this going to take?' Oh, was I mad. Then, once the ceremony gets started and the Father is reciting his part, my dear inebriated husband-to-be says, 'Have you got this *memorized*, or are you reading it from that book?' The whole time, I was giving Rich these dirty looks. I was even madder at him than I was at Donny, because I knew who was really behind all this.

"But you know something? I couldn't stay mad at him. Nobody could. You couldn't help but love the guy, even if there were times when you wanted to choke him."

Mike McLaughlin says, "Richie would never do anything to hurt anybody. He was just out to have fun."

Billy Nacewicz adds, "It's not like we're talking about really bad things. It was just crazy stuff, nothing you'd get thrown in jail for."

Whoa, whoa, whoa. Hang on just a second. There was a night when a handful of folks, Nacewicz among them, actually *did* end up in the Gray Bar Hotel. It happened in Agawam, Massachusetts, and the group became known, jokingly, as the "Agawam Five," sort of modified racing's version of the "Chicago Seven" radicals jailed during the Vietnam protest era. It was quite a collection in that Agawam cell: Evans, Nacewicz, crewman Kenny Hartung, *Speedway Scene* boss Val LeSieur, and Stafford PR man John McMullin.

Accounts differ as to exactly how the whole thing started. What is certain is that on this particular Saturday night, Evans and some friends bypassed their usual stop at Josie's Outpost Lounge after the Riverside Park feature, and headed instead for a now-dead tavern called the Green Gables, just down the street. "There probably weren't four people in there when we got there," LeSieur remembers. But as usual, where Evans went, a crowd followed. His orange truck in the parking lot guaranteed a good race-night house, so, little by little, the Green Gables began filling up.

Then somebody said something to somebody else—Evans not being either of the somebodies—and one of the bar's management staff apparently got hot. One fellow who was there thinks that was the spark, that this management fellow wanted everybody out and called the cops, claiming there was a disturbance at the establishment.

Or something like that.

"The next thing we knew," says LeSieur, "there were police from Springfield, West Springfield, Agawam, *everywhere*, more cops than you'd see at a political convention. They came in every door. And, of course, they came in thinking they had to break up this supposed fight, so with that attitude they started steering everybody out the door. Well, you know how that gets: They're pushing people to leave, and some of the girls in the crowd start talking back to the cops, and now the guys get mad, too, and pretty soon everyone is wrestling around, pushing and shoving."

Evans left. LeSieur left. McMullin left. Kenny Hartung left. So far, so good.

Then Nacewicz left.

"Billy's outside, and there's a police cruiser sitting there," LeSieur remembers. "So he pulls a valve-stem remover out of his pocket and starts letting the air out of the cruiser's tire, just being a wise guy. Well, one of the cops sees him, and he starts roughing Billy up, hitting him with his club."

McMullin, a polite sort of fellow you wouldn't expect see within six miles of something like this, says, "When they grabbed Billy and handcuffed him and threw him onto the car, I went over there just to try to calm things down. I said, 'Aw, leave him alone. He really wasn't doing anything.' Well, the next thing I know, *I'm* in the back seat of the police car, and I'm cuffed, too."

"Now everybody started getting wild," says LeSieur. "I started walking toward my car to get out of there, and somebody jumped me from behind. I whacked the guy because I didn't know who it was, and it turned out to be a cop. Richie had already jumped in a car and was leaving, but the cops were all hollering that they were looking for Richie Evans. They thought he started the whole mess, and he had nothing to do with it! They stopped him there and pulled him out of the damn car."

McMullin says, "I think [certain members of] the Agawam police were out to get Richie. You know, Richie had done some mischievous things over the years—the things he was known to do, innocent things but the kind of stuff police might take offense to—and I think they were out to get him."

There was, shall we say, a struggle involving Evans and some of the police.

"They were beating on him," says LeSieur. "Oh, they beat the shit out of him."

Somewhere in the middle of all this, Hartung had gotten involved by coming to the aid of his teammates, and he, too, was handcuffed. So, with blue lights flashing, the five of them—Evans, Nacewicz, Hartung, McMullin, LeSieur—were hauled across town to the Agawam pokey. The charge: public drunkenness.

Now, LeSieur hadn't had a drink in 20 years, and, claims McMullin, "None of the rest of us were drunk, either." This absolutely enraged the normally quiet Stafford publicity man. McMullin says, "We're all there—me, Kenny, Val, Billy and Richie—and *I'm* the one who's going bullshit. Oh, I was pissed, because I hadn't done a damn thing and yet they had arrested me."

Laughs LeSieur, "The way McMullin was hollering at those cops, I'm surprised they didn't lock him up for life!"

McMullin's suspicions about the arrests intensified during the booking process. He says, "When they started fingerprinting us, they were trying to egg Richie on. They were calling him names, trying to goad him into doing something. But Richie didn't take their bait. He just kept his mouth shut."

Outside, a large group friends and fellow racers had gathered to see what they could do to help. "Somebody in that group called the police chief," LeSieur says. The chief, Stan Chmielewski, happened to be a diehard race fan himself, and was friendly with everybody in the group. He drove to the station, and calmed things down, and by morning the Agawam Five were released.

Which was a good thing; Evans had to be at Thompson for a Sunday modified program. He showed up with both eyes blackened from the previous evening's rumble.

There was a bit of legal back-and-forth between Evans and the Agawam police over the bruising he'd taken, before the whole matter went quietly away.

"But it was all so silly," McMullin says.

Silly? You want silly? Well, there was the Agawam night—yes, *another* one—when Richie and a group of friends lingered too long in Riverside Park's "beer garden," an expansive refreshment area located back behind the first-turn grandstands in the adjacent amusement park. The Evans hauler was parked only a short distance away, in a lot just across a small footbridge and beyond a gate through which the beer garden crowd had been exiting for years. On this particular evening, as security guards shooed them out of the place in order to close the park, the revelers noticed that the gate was locked. The only other exit was through the park's main gate, which would have added maybe half a mile to their walk.

Mario Fiore remembers, "Somebody said, 'Looks like we can't get out this way.' Richie said, 'Oh, is that right? Billy, get the truck.'"

"I climbed over the fence and brought the truck over," says Nacewicz. "We had an acetylene torch with us, so I cut the chain on the lock. We let about 25 people out, and then we all continued the party in the parking lot."

"You know something?" asks a grinning Fiore. "They never locked that gate early again."

You want silly? How about the night in Martinsville when Fiore and Ralph Solhem were having a wee-hours cup of coffee in a Waffle House on the main drag? "Richie came in, sat down with us, and ordered a coffee," Solhem recalls. "He said, 'Kind of hot in here, isn't it?' We said no, and we all kept talking. Then he said, 'Boy, it really feels hot in here.' Mario and I said, again, that we didn't think it was hot. So the conversation went on, and then Richie said, 'You *sure* it's not hot in here?' I don't know how many times he'd poke in with that, but it was every couple of minutes."

Finally, from the corner of his eye, Solhem noticed a glow outside.

"I turned around," he recalls, "and the Dumpster in the parking lot was just *ablaze*. Richie laughed that little laugh: *Huh, huh, huh, huh.* I guess he had lit up the Dumpster just because he happened to be walking by it."

You want silly? How about the times—on the sands of Daytona Beach, or in the outback of some speedway parking lot— when Evans and one whacko or another filled a giant truck-tire inner tube with acetylene gas and, using yards of gasoline-soaked rags as a fuse, set the thing off? *Ka-BOOM!* Windows rattled for miles, and you could lose a small car in the crater left behind.

You want silly? How about the Friday night prior to the 1983 Thompson 300, when Evans was having a beer with a friend from the track's safety crew who some months earlier had purchased a used Cadillac ambulance? The guy told Evans how he and some friends had taken the thing to Martinsville that spring, and about all the fun they'd had with the car. Richie looked the thing over, asked if he could take the red and white monster for a spin, and then bought it on the spot. His only request: "Fix the siren." By Sunday morning, the ex-ambulance was wearing a fresh coat of paint—yes, "1021 orange"—and was lettered up in fine style. On its flanks were the words "61 Courtesy Car," and over the windshield was the acronym "FUBAR," which, as any military man with some years under his belt can tell you, stands for "Fucked Up Beyond All Repair." That afternoon, just after he'd won the big 300, Evans showed off the car in fine style; he coaxed runner-up Corky

The Evans ambulance, with a fresh coat of orange paint but as yet unlettered, on Thompson 300 weekend in 1983. *(Tim Christopher photo/courtesy of* Speedway Scene*)*

Cookman and third-place finisher Kenny Bouchard into the old Caddy and ferried them, siren blaring, to the press tent for the post-race interviews.

"In a lot of ways, Rich never grew up," says Lynn Evans. "He was like a little kid, always wanting to have fun. But that was one of the things that made him so unique, I guess. He was a kid at heart."

And at one point in the late 1970s, Richie Evans finally found the one ultimate prize every kid wants: his very own clubhouse. He was snowmobiling in the hill country north of Rome with a collection of friends, among them Billy Osmun, the Jersey dirt modified hot dog. The pair had met back in the All Star League days, and their friendship had grown, Osmun remembers, when they'd spent some time together at Syracuse "in '71, '72, somewhere in there."

Says Osmun, "I don't know why we hit it off, but we did. We didn't see much of each other during the summer—I only did a little bit of asphalt racing—but we had a good friendship going over the phone. And in the winter it was party time, and we'd do some snowmobiling."

Osmun would come up from New Jersey, bringing along friends like John McClellan. "We spent an awful lot of time up in Rome," McClellan remembers, "snowmobiling and just hanging out."

On one such trip, they sledded past an old country inn up near Osceola, in an area called Tug Hill. The place was called the Freeman Hotel, and it looked like the ultimate *guy* hangout: rustic, woody, rugged. And, in a crazy twist, it turned out that the Freeman was owned by Chuck Mahoney, the same ex-driver, ex-promoter and "character's character" who had talked Richie Evans into going stock car racing in the first place.

Out there in the snow, Evans and Osmun and their riding mates mused about how cool it would be to have a place like that all to themselves.

Winter at the Freeman Hotel, Osceola, NY. *(Lynn Evans collection)*

For all the fun Richie was still capable of having around Rome, there were more and more nights when he'd feel a bit uncomfortable. Wilbur Jones says, "He always had people asking him about the racing, and, you know, in some ways he was kind of a shy guy. If he was surrounded by friends, he was OK, but he didn't always like the extra attention from strangers." Evans had even taken up Wilbur's suggestion that he join the local chapter of the Elks Club. "He liked that," says Jones, "because he could go to the club and have a beer and not have to play 20 questions."

Well, gosh, wouldn't the Freeman Hotel give him and his pals just a bigger, better blast of that same fraternal feeling? Out there in the snow, it seemed like a hell of a pipe dream.

And then one summer—the years blend together, Osmun laments—Evans called, and there was an excitement in his voice.

"He said that Mahoney needed some money, and that we could probably buy the place," Osmun recalls. "We talked about the price, and decided we'd split it and go from there. 'Send me the money,' Richie said, and I did. We did the whole deal over the phone."

They assumed ownership at the dawn of the 1980s. The place needed a good overall sprucing up, and certain areas required major repairs, but their plan was to work on it a little at a time. There was no need to hurry; this was something for the years that lay down the road.

"We were still young," says Billy Osmun. "We were still racing."

One winter night in the middle of this sprucing-up period, some of the gang was leaving the Freeman, heading back toward Rome, a few guys in Evans's pickup and a few more in Osmun's car.

"It's snowing to beat hell," Osmun says, "but we're running along about 40 or 50 miles an hour. All of a sudden, Rich's truck spins right in front of me. It turns completely around, and on along he goes. I knew what he did; he'd put it in reverse and spun it on purpose. Well, he does it a couple more times. I had one of my car owners riding with me, John DeBais, and I said, 'John, the next time he does that, hang on.'

"Naturally, Richie did it again. As soon as I saw him start to spin, I hit the gas. Just as he got turned around, facing me, I hit him head-on. We were bumper-to-bumper, and I was pushing him down the road backwards.

"We stopped at a bar and had a few shooters, and when he climbed back into his truck and tried to put it into reverse, it wouldn't move. He says, 'Osmun, you blew my transmission!' And so the next day we put a new transmission in that thing. He was laughing like hell the whole time."

Just a kid at heart.

"Evans," wrote Dick Berggren, "was perhaps the ultimate fun-loving stock car driver of them all."

Side Jobs

IF THE MODIFIED 200 at Daytona in 1979 was Evans's favorite win, as he always claimed, there were a couple more he loved to boast about. Like that Daytona victory, these seemed to please him mostly because they happened away from his weekly gig driving pavement modifieds on short tracks. They were side jobs, really. Side jobs that just happened to work out well.

"I've won on dirt," he'd say. "Only *once*, but I still won."

It happened on June 20, 1971 at the Weedsport Speedway, 60-odd miles west of Rome on the New York Thruway.

Thanks to NASCAR's, um, request that he stay away from its member tracks, Utica-Rome was off-limits to Evans. He planned on spending his summer Sunday evenings at Fulton, but, curiously, that track ran Friday nights for the first three weeks of its '71 season. And so Evans talked a little bit with Glenn Donnelly, the young Weedsport promoter whose DIRT empire was still just a vision, about running some of the Sunday-night modified events there.

"Richie disagreed with Donnelly about the way he handicapped cars," says Buster Maurer. "As I remember, they went by the money-won system, but they used your *total* season's earnings instead of what you had done recently. A guy could come in anytime and finish last for two weeks, and on his third week he'd start on the pole because his season earnings would be so low. Rich argued with Glenn that this was wrong; he said, 'That's not the way it should be. A guy could come in and take advantage of your regular runners.'"

The system, Donnelly said, was the system. Evans, deciding that it wasn't really a battle he needed—hell, he planned to bolt to Fulton anyway, once they switched from Fridays to Sundays—abandoned the argument and made up his mind to haul his second car to Weedsport for the first three Sundays in June.

"We went there with the car Eddie Flemke ran for us at Albany-Saratoga," says Wilbur Jones.

In their first visit, something mechanical broke on the car; over the years, neither Maurer nor Jones nor Fred Ulrich managed to retain what it was. But the memory of Richie's second Weedsport outing, on June 13, stayed crystal clear.

Jones says, "In the feature, Richie came off the fourth turn going like hell. Now, down the straightaway, I don't know if somebody else came down on him or if he just got over somebody's wheel, but he went end over end, flipping. I remember throwing the stopwatch one way and running the other way, toward Richie; I mean, I got nervous that night. Richie was upside down, but he was OK."

They loaded up the battered coupe, pounded out the dents, prettied it up as best they could, and Jones and Ulrich hauled it to Albany-Saratoga for an unsuspecting Flemke the following Friday night.

"The top of the car was all primered up from where we'd tried to fix the body up," Jones chuckles. "Oh, it looked terrible. Eddie said, 'How did *this* happen?'"

When it dawned on the Evans gang that they'd likely be starting their third Weedsport feature from the pole—in two miserable weeks there, their take had amounted to little more than pocket change—it became a busy week at the Calvert Street shop.

"We got the best dirt tires we could get," Maurer says. "We put in the biggest motor we ever had, a 454 that was .125 over. Rich said, 'I'm gonna win that race.'"

That was the optimist talking. Evans, still broke enough to be a realist down deep, had a backup plan. He won his qualifying heat, and then confided in his pal Wilbur. "He was going to stay in the bottom groove," Jones says, "so he didn't get in anybody's way."

And that's how it went. "He drove that place just like it was asphalt," Maurer remembers. "Right around the inside."

As it happens, the best groove on dirt is never as certain a thing to define as it is on pavement. Over the course of a race program, the most-used lane of a dirt track can dry out, or even glaze over with spent rubber; when that happens, the sharpest drivers will shift their attacks elsewhere, looking for moisture and the bite it provides. This is all complicated by the fact that some promoters will water and even grade their surfaces several times per night, so a groove that appeared all but spent after the last heat race might be perfect come feature time.

On this night at Weedsport, the bottom lane—Richie's lane—was perfect. He took off from his pole starting spot, and some of the best guys in dirt modified racing gave chase. Chuck Ciprich got close to Evans, but then spun out. Canadian Terry Edwards, daring the high groove, also gained ground before he, too, lost control. That left Dave Kneisel, a seasoned pro on the New York dirt, in second place. But not even the great Kneisel, Weedsport's eventual 1971 track champion, could reel in the orange coupe with the primered roof and Richie Evans's biggest engine under its hood.

"He could catch us in the corner," Maurer says, "but down the straightaway, Rich would draw away."

A grinning Wilbur Jones says, "Pretty soon the 30 laps were up, and Weedsport had a new winner."

The records show Evans beating a dandy crop of Weedsport regulars: third through fifth, behind Kneisel, were John McArdell, Merv Treichler and John Podolak.

Buster Maurer remembers Evans telling Glenn Donnelly, "I told you that handicapping deal's not fair for your regular guys."

And Donnelly had another system Richie managed to beat that night.

"We went over to get paid," Jones says, "and Donnelly peeled off these $100 bills. Richie said, 'Why such big bills?' Donnelly said, 'Oh, a lot of these guys like to flash 'em around.' Rich told him, 'Give it to me in twenties instead, so I can carry it around and spend it.'

"And I remember how he spent *some* of it. We made a flying trip home that night, because Rich wanted to make last call at the Rusty Nail and talk about winning the dirt race. I was driving the truck, and I remember going by a couple of troopers on the Thruway just as fast as that truck would go. When we got back to Rome, we didn't have an exhaust system left on the truck. Blew it right off."

The Weedsport run wasn't Evans's only good result on dirt. Maurer recalls that during the All Star League days, "Rich ran pretty good at the old half-mile Nazareth track, and on the big [one-mile] track at Nazareth he ran *great*. He loved that place. He ran with all the top dirt dogs at that time."

But there were more days, Maurer conceded, when Evans "wasn't very good" on the dirt. "We went to Flemington for an All Star race, and Rich pulled the pole position, but in the feature he ducked into the pits on about the third or fifth lap. We all ran down to change a tire or fix whatever's wrong with the car, and Richie said, 'Don't worry about it.' I said, 'Whattaya mean?' He said, 'I can't see where I'm going, and I can't race when I can't see.' It was real dusty that night. Guys who race on dirt regularly, maybe they get used to that and they know what they're looking for, but he could never see that.

"But what I really remember is, the next thing Richie said was, 'Besides, this looks like it's gonna be a pretty good race. Let's watch it.' And that's what we did. We watched Kenny Brightbill and Sammy Beavers go at it."

On this night, Evans loaded up and left Fonda Speedway before the All Star feature, not comfortable on the tough dirt surface. *(courtesy of Speedway Scene)*

And Ted Puchyr recalls another All Star outing on dirt, this one at Fonda: "Richie wasn't afraid of dirt, but he just wasn't comfortable on it. So we qualified, but we never ran the feature. Richie sold his starting position to one of the [track] regulars who didn't make it, and we loaded up and went home. He said, 'We ain't racing this car. We *need* this car.'"

Evans had his reasons, Puchyr pointed out. "A blacktop modified was not built anywhere near as strong as a dirt modified, and Fonda back then—*any* dirt track—would just put so much stress on a car."

Later, Evans took the same practical approach to another of his side jobs, when he drove a backup car for New Jersey's fabled Statewide Racing Team in the 1976 Schaefer 100 at Syracuse. He was a guaranteed starter—having won that honor by copping the open-competition Modified Madness event at Stafford—and Syracuse had a great purse, so he went. If the track turned hard, as the old fairgrounds mile was prone to do, Evans figured he might have a decent shot to make some noise; but it didn't, and he never really got rolling. He finished 38th.

Dave Lape, who had raced and partied alongside Evans so often in the days before dirt and pavement modifieds became two completely different categories of racing, wonders what might have happened had his old friend been as interested in dirt racing as he was in the blacktop stuff.

"I don't think Richie disliked dirt, necessarily, but it just wasn't his thing," Lape says. "He was an asphalt guy. Dirt wasn't his cup of tea. But, knowing Richie, if he had ever decided that dirt was the way he wanted to go—if he really put his mind to it—he'd have figured it out."

The record book suggests that Lape was probably right on the money, because Evans didn't fail at much.

The race which will likely be remembered as Richie's most successful side job was one filled with tragic irony. On the first weekend in November, 1975, Evans hauled his Pinto to Connecticut to compete in the small-block modified portion of the Thompson Speedway's World Series of Speedway Racing. Just to pad his schedule a bit, he also agreed to drive the famous 10-Pins supermodified owned by Nolan Swift, who was making the transition from champion driver—Swifty was an eight-time Oswego Speedway champion and won the track's International Classic, supermodified racing's premier event, six times—to car owner. Evans and Swift had been acquainted for years, and, hell, Richie was going to be at Thompson anyway. He had never raced a supermodified, but had taken one or two out for hot-lap sessions over the years; "They give you a beautiful feeling because of the rapid acceleration," he told writer Pete Zanardi in 1973.

Nobody much remembers what happened to the Evans modified that weekend, except that it dropped out of the Sunday 50-lapper—won by Fred DeSarro over Eddie Flemke—with some sort of minor failure. The supermodified event, however, is the stuff of regional racing folklore.

There were 47 supermodifieds on hand for the World Series; 42 took time on Saturday. Evans shattered the track record in winning the pole during the unique qualifying session; his total time for two laps around the 5/8ths-mile track was 38.653 seconds. Thompson was overflowing with race cars—there were over 220 modifieds, supermods and midgets on the grounds—so the supers were pitted in the infield, splayed around a raised quarter-mile oval occasionally used for minor events. And so, come race day, there sat Nolan Swift's 10-Pins, about midway down what would have been that small inner oval's backstretch.

It was an atypical November Sunday—*Speedway Scene* writer Gene Rebello termed it "a day of days, [with temperatures] around 70 and no wind at all"—and both the regular pit area and the infield were jammed with folks eager to catch one last dose of racing before the snow came.

Close to the Swift pit gathered a confluence of prominent Northeast racing personalities. Writer Dave Shippee and his pal John Brouwer, whose father had once been a co-owner of Connecticut's Waterford Speedbowl and who was for years an official there, were talking with Waterford promoter Harvey Tattersall III and Bruce Cohen, a New England fixture who had been a writer, promoter and team owner. All four men knew Evans, to varying degrees.

In his *Speedway Scene* column, Shippee recalled, "Brouwer said, 'Let's go look at the 10-Pins,'" and off they went. They stood for a while and watched Evans, in Shippee's words, "thoughtfully taking a mental inventory of the legendary super he was to drive that day."

On the speedway, the second of two consolation races for the small-block modified division was just getting underway.

Then Evans peeled away to join a conversation which included Oswego Speedway's Dick O'Brien and Jim Shampine, the quiet but charismatic New Yorker who had replaced Nolan Swift as king of the supermodified scene.

"The three of us were standing near Swifty's pit, maybe a car or two away," O'Brien says.

And then everything went to hell. Exiting turn two, what should have been a minor jingle produced disastrous results. A modified driven by Lou Funk Jr., a regular at the Danbury Racearena, shot out of the melee and roared into the Thompson infield, headed for that elevated inner oval.

"I was facing the backstretch," says O'Brien. "Richie and Jimmy were facing me, with their backs to what was happening. Anyway, I see this little commotion, and a car comes out of turn two and across the infield."

Funk's modified, wildly out of control and going God knows how fast, sped toward an earthen bank just below the spot where the Swift pit was set up.

Dave Shippee wrote, "Everything had to go wrong for the Funk car to get that far away from the racing surface, and it did. The front wheels were toed out in opposition … the throttle was obviously jammed wide open … hitting the bank simply launched that car to incredible heights, and ultimately into the crowded pit."

O'Brien remembers shouting a last-minute warning to Evans and Shampine. "Then the three of us took off, literally running for our lives."

Close to the 10-Pins, working on the car and obviously unaware of the chaos, stood mechanic John Roberts of Camillus, New York. He was a longtime crewman for Swift and a supermodified devotee who, coincidentally, often traveled to far-flung races with O'Brien and veteran Oswego track worker Eddie Lynch. O'Brien recalls Roberts preaching, "Don't watch the cars that have gone by you. It's the one that's coming that you've got to look out for."

The one that was coming—front end askew, steering gone, no brakes, full of ghastly momentum—smashed down into the Swift pit. It felled Tattersall, who had been standing so close with Brouwer that, in Shippee's report, "one's left arm was touching the right arm of another." The two men had seen the coming carnage at the last second, and Brouwer made a lucky dodge while Tattersall's movements were blocked by the car beside the 10-Pins. Tattersall ended up underneath Funk's modified. He might have been crushed had not the car ended up partially supported by a tool box and other pit equipment; as it was, he sustained a broken wrist, a dislocated shoulder, and assorted bruises and burns.

Shippee wrote, "As the flying modified was still settling on top of Tattersall, Evans was single-handedly trying to lift it off him. Tattersall remembers the car in the air, and he remembers Evans trying to drag him from under it."

Less noticed in the immediate rush to free Tattersall was John Roberts, because, O'Brien says, "the car just clipped John. It didn't land on him or anything." But Roberts had suffered a serious head injury, and as the ambulance carted him off it was clear to everyone on the scene that he was dead.

The beautiful November Sunday had gone all wrong. Around the 10-Pins, there was a terrible, empty confusion. On the track, the consolation events finished and the features were nearing and their friend was gone and they couldn't bring him back.

O'Brien recalls, "Now came the dilemma. 'What do we do? Do we race?' Swifty and co-owner Billy Wright and three or four of Swifty's old-guard helpers talked it over. I stood right there and listened. They asked Richie what he thought, and he said, 'Look, I'm here. If you don't want to race, that's absolutely no problem. I'm going to run my modified anyway. But this was your guy, your friend, so you've got to do whatever you think is right. I don't want you to do something you think is disrespectful, or anything like that.'

"And then Richie said, 'If you *do* want to race the car, I'll run that sonofabitch as hard as I can.'"

They made a quick, heartfelt decision to run the race and donate the car's earnings to the family of John Roberts.

The World Series supermodified feature was 100 laps long, broken into two halves by a planned intermission at 50 laps. In the opening 50, Evans lapped all but the next three men across the line, and they were heavyweights all: Canadian Warren Coniam, hot young Steve Gioia and Shampine. In the last half of the race, Evans really got down to business. He wrung every last ounce of speed from the 10-Pins—John Roberts's car—and lapped the entire field. Not even Shampine, who ran third, and New England hero Dick Batchelder, the runner-up, got anywhere close to him.

He had beaten the best in the first supermodified race he ever ran.

Dick O'Brien, as solid a supermod history buff as there is, says, "Looking back at it today, I'm not surprised Richie could do that. But at

(left) On a tragic day, Evans blitzed the Thompson World Series in his first supermodified start. *(Burt Gould photo/courtesy of* Speedway Scene*)*

(right) Car owner Nolan Swift (right) smiles through the pain, starter Harley Marshall stands by, while Evans looks suitably conflicted after a long, sad day. *(Burt Gould photo/courtesy of* Speedway Scene*)*

the time, it was pretty shocking. That was an era when supermodifieds were a very tight group; you just didn't have outside guys float in and run good enough to win. There were *career* supermodified guys from Ohio, from Canada, from Texas, from New England, and of course from New York, and they were tough, hard-nosed racers. And the cars back then were so lightweight, and they had unlimited engines—500 cubic inches and more—so you really had to hang onto them, especially at a place like Thompson where they'd slide up the banking, turn, and shoot down the straightaway.

"So for Richie to do that, in my eyes it just confirmed the seat-of-the-pants ability he had."

It was years before Evans climbed back into a super with an eye on winning, although he did briefly own one in the late 1970s. That was more of a business deal to Richie than anything else—it was part of a large cache of parts and equipment he purchased from Oswego driver Ronnie Wallace and then sold off, piece by piece—and he never seemed to see it as anything more than a profitable lark. As near as can be determined, he only raced it once, in a midweek event at Star Speedway.

"We were going to run a series of pretty good-paying supermodified races between Star, Oswego and Sandusky [Ohio], like a big 'triple crown' thing," remembers former Star promoter Russ Conway. "I saw Richie someplace and mentioned our race and he said, 'I'll be there. Wait and see. I'm going to bring my own super.'"

Conway blew it off. But come July 3, 1979, sure enough, Evans showed.

"I remember this, clear as a bell," says Conway. "In pulls this number 61 supermodified, Evans orange, the whole nine yards, with 'The Orange Crate' lettered on the side of the wing. And he said, 'See, I told you.' Oh, he was as proud as hell of it."

The car had some minor problems—fuel issues, maybe, or faulty injectors?—and sputtered to an unmemorable finish out of the top five.

A rare shot: Evans aboard his "Orange Crate" supermod in 1979. He owned the car only briefly. *(Clint Lawton photo/courtesy of* Speedway Scene*)*

Later that year Evans warmed it up at Thompson, before unloading it over the winter.

From there, supermodifieds were mostly something he encountered only from a distance during twinbill events at Oswego or Thompson or Star. But then, in the autumn of 1984, some conversation with car owner Skip Matczak got Evans fired up about the idea of going supermodified racing for real.

Matczak, an open-wheel diehard who hauled cars to Oswego from his Connecticut home on a weekly basis, remembers, "We were both signing into the pits at Thompson for the World Series. I had finished second in the Oswego Classic with Dave Shullick driving, and Richie asked me what that paid. I told him—and I don't remember exactly what the numbers were—and I guess it stacked up pretty good next to what he'd gotten [for winning the Bud 200] the night before. You could see it in his face. And, just to bust him because I knew how dedicated he was to the modifieds, I said, 'Well, Richie, the A-main cars always get paid much better than the B-main cars.'

"Later that day, he kept repeating that line to me, the line about A-main cars and B-main cars. But I could tell he was studying the issue. I could see the wheels turning. Then the two of us ended up talking to Dick O'Brien, and O'Brien confirmed the numbers. And Richie said, 'You know, let's try this a little bit.' That's how we got together. I was absolutely thrilled."

They settled on a loose 1985 schedule revolving around Evans's availability: the Oswego mod/supermod twinbills, of course, and whatever else they could make.

They debuted at the Port City event, expanded that year to include 100-lappers for both the modifieds and supermods. Evans won the modified half—nothing new there—but fuel pick-up problems kept him and the Matczak car from showing their stuff. Later that summer, on a night when it seemed certain they *would* show their stuff, a commendable case of sportsmanship on Richie's part kept it from happening.

"We had run a couple shows, but we were not ready to win yet," Matczak told writer Pete Zanardi. "This one particular night, we're ready to win. [Richie] used his patented outside line like nobody else could; he went three-abreast on the last lap to win the heat."

Oswego's finish line is on the far end of the frontstretch, and Evans sure seemed desperate to win that qualifying race; he stayed in the throttle so long that he had the Matczak super hung out dirt-track style, trying to keep it out of the first-turn fence. Dick Macco, a rabid supermodified nut who used to write a wonderfully beery fan-in-the-stands column for *Speedway Scene,* proclaimed in print, "A finer heat race I will never witness."

According to Matczak, Evans declared, "We're going to win the feature tonight."

They were readying for the main event, Matczak recalled, when

(left) Oswego, 1985. Evans sneaks a smoke before pushing off in Skip Matczak's supermodified. *(Bev Ver Straete photo)*

(right) On Richie's best night at Oswego, he handed the Matczak car off after a dynamite heat race victory. *(Rick Nelson photo/courtesy of* Speedway Scene*)*

longtime Oswego favorite Eddie Bellinger walked over to their pit stall. "Bellinger was going for the championship, locked in a torrid battle. He had broken his motor. He needed a car to run, and said to me, 'Is there any chance of getting in the car?'

"I was torn," Matczak told Zanardi. "Eddie is a friend, but here's Richie who tells me he's going to win. You could put money on that one. But Richie, without hesitation, said, 'Give him the car. There'll be another day for you and me.' He truly understood a champion going for points, how important that was."

Evans understood racers, period. He had friends in every division, it seemed, from dirt champions like Will Cagle and Kenny Brightbill and Billy Osmun to supermod heroes like Bentley Warren and Swift and Shampine. He clearly delighted in catching up with old foes who had moved on to other things, whether it was Winston Cup driver Ronnie Bouchard making a cameo appearance in New England or World of Outlaws standout Lee Osborne taking advantage of a night away from the Speedweeks sprint car wars to visit with Evans, Cook, Troyer and Loescher at New Smyrna. And he relished the idea of stepping in and out of other worlds himself, and taking on these brief side jobs; he told Winston's Roger Bear in 1982 that he'd love to fight it out with the other NASCAR regional champions in a series of races, rotating between their various classes of cars and track surfaces.

"How do you think you'd fare?" Bear asked him.

Smiling, Evans replied, "Oh, I'd hang in, one way or another. I'd be up to it."

Connecticut radio man Arnold Dean once asked Richie what type of race car, budget constraints aside, he'd most like to have in his garage. His laughing reply was, "I wish I had a dirt car, a supermodified, a modified, a Grand National …"

Dean said, "You like 'em all?"

"Yes."

But, at his core, Richie Evans was a modified guy.

Dick O'Brien says, "We almost had a deal pieced together for him to run the first ASA race at Oswego [in 1985]. That would have been a big thing for us, to have him there running against those ASA guys, Dick Trickle and Bob Senneker and the rest. But Richie was running for another [NASCAR] championship, and there was a points race at Shangri-La, and we just couldn't quite get the deal done.

"But you know what I remember most about that whole thing? Dick Trickle had called Richie to ask him about Oswego, and Richie had given him all the info: what the track was like, what he thought Trickle ought to run. Well, Trickle goes and wins the show. That night, I'm lying in bed at three o'clock in the morning, and I'm sound asleep; it's been a long day, and I've been geared up all week for this big race, and now I'm worn out. The phone rings, and it's Richie. He says, 'Well, did Trickle win it?' I said, 'You bet your ass he did.'

"We talked a minute, and I said, 'Where are you, still in the pits at Shangri-La?' He said, 'Nah, we're just outside the gate. They threw us out.' And that was Richie. He was having some fun with his modified buddies."

"I Like What I Do"

STEVE HMIEL, WHO STARTED OUT doing grunt work at New York bullrings, chased modifieds up and down the East Coast, moved to North Carolina in 1979 to take a job with Petty Enterprises, crew-chiefed his way to victory lane with a number of NASCAR Cup teams, and in 2004 was working as the technical director at Dale Earnhardt, Inc., not only doesn't forget where he came from, but is thankful for the entire ride.

So it was interesting to listen to Hmiel sigh at a recent Nextel Cup race, and say, "I'm fairly frustrated with every 20-year-old kid who walks up to me in khaki pants and the right golf shirt and says, 'Hello, Mr. Hmiel. I'd like to drive your race car one day.' I'd much rather see a kid who's actually out there winning races at some short track, and everybody's saying, 'Holy cow! Look how fast that kid is!' And that's probably because I remember Richie Evans, and what a racer he was."

In another Nextel Cup garage area on another afternoon, someone mentioned Evans to Bobby Hutchens, who had combined his modified education with some high-falutin' college studies and ended up as an engineer for Richard Childress and a string of terrific drivers, Dale Earnhardt among them. Hutchens took a look around, and said, "I hate that he never reached this plateau, only because I know that most of these guys couldn't have kept up with Richie if he had the right equipment."

Being around Evans in his modified prime was similar to what it must have been like to be around the New York Yankees in Babe Ruth's era. Not everybody is privileged enough to watch the acknowledged best at work, day in and day out, in any sport.

But another analogy from Ruth's sport fits, too. There are a number of baseball scholars who insist that Satchel Paige, the old Negro League star, might have been the single greatest pitcher of all time. If that's true, it's sad for Paige that his color kept him off the Major League stage, and every bit as sad that his color kept so many mainstream fans from seeing him throw his curveball in person.

So it is with Richie Evans. All the right racing scholars seem to know just how good the guy was, but not enough people got to witness that for themselves. He never played in NASCAR's biggest league—largely by his own choice—and therefore never raced before the sport's biggest crowds. And the fear is that, in time, that might cloud the way he is remembered, particularly this Cup-crazy world where every driver's perceived worth is based on what he's done at Charlotte or Chicagoland or in the Brickyard 400. After all, Matt Kenseth is already a much bigger name in his native Wisconsin than Dick Trickle, despite Trickle's years of amazing short-track accomplishments there.

It's hard enough to explain to modern-era fans that not all the best drivers make it to Nextel Cup. It's nearly impossible to make them understand that for years, many of the best ones didn't much care about that.

Was Richie Evans good enough to move up, had his desires run in that direction? Could he have cut the mustard at stock car racing's highest level?

"Oh, there's no doubt about it," says Jerry Cook. "If he wanted to do it, yes."

Bugs Stevens, who had a brief Grand National fling in 1970, says, "Richie could have driven anything he wanted to: Cup cars, Indy cars, anything."

"Richie could have been a good Cup driver," insists Ron Bouchard. "Definitely."

Greg Sacks mocks the very idea of guessing at Richie's big-time potential: "Was he good enough? Come on. We all *know* he was. There's no question about that."

Ray Spognardi uses the same phrase—"no question"—and offers some eyewitness testimony to back up his point: "I saw what Rich did at Daytona. He adapted to that place so fast it was scary. We'd get there, and before he'd go out for the first warm-ups he'd be as nervous as anybody else. I mean, it's *Daytona*. His temples would be twitching. He'd go out once for a few laps, and when he got back in he'd still be the same way, high-strung. But after he went out the second time, he'd be as relaxed as if we were off running at some half-mile. That used to just amaze me."

Bugs Stevens (right, after running second to Evans at Freeport in 1974) is of the opinion that "Richie could have driven anything he wanted to." (B&G Wurthmann photo/courtesy of Speedway Scene)

Right there beside Spognardi, of course, was Billy Nacewicz, who says, "There's no doubt in my mind that Richie could have driven with anybody. As long as he had the right equipment, he'd have gotten the job done.

"There's no big secret to winning in a Cup car, versus winning in anything else. Those guys haven't invented a special way to put their pants on. They're just drivers. The best ones have a lot of talent, yes, but so do a lot of guys all over this country. And so did Richie. It didn't bother him to race against Darrell Waltrip. It didn't bother him to race against Donnie Allison or Harry Gant."

Hmiel says, "The only problem Richie would have had in moving to the next level would have been finding a situation where people listened to him. He knew everything there was to know—*everything!*—about tires, gears, motors, you name it. If he went to a team and just drove, all that knowledge would have been wasted. He would have had to be in an operation where the people said, 'Richie, what do *you* want to do?' He was going to have to run the show, because I believe that running his own show was what made him so strong. That would have been key to him being successful at any level, but it's hard to find race teams that will do that."

Evans himself seemed to understand that. Way back in 1983, he was using 21st-century NASCAR buzzwords like "chemistry," and talking about how the difference between success and failure at the Cup level came down to a team taking the best advantage of its human resources. He told *Speedway Scene*, "If you've got a weak chief, you need a strong driver, and if the driver is missing a little bit, you need a good crew chief."

He admitted to having had a "couple deals" pitched to him at the tail end of the '70s, feelers from folks gauging his interest in moving up, though he never got much into specifics. It wasn't right, Evans said, to talk openly about closed-door discussions, so he wouldn't name names publicly. He was apparently pretty quiet about such things in private, too; even Nacewicz, who spent more hours with Richie than anybody in those years, was in the dark about most of his boss's big-league conversations.

"He did have talks with some Cup team owners, I know that," Nacewicz says. "I guess he talked to the Wood Brothers at some point; I'm not sure if this was just after David Pearson left the team [in 1978], or later on. And there were some other owners who talked with him. I never really pushed him about how serious the discussions were, or anything like that. I do know that he had no interest in going with any of the lower-echelon teams that talked with him."

"Maybe," Evans said in 1983, "I'm just scared of defeat."

And that, Nacewicz says, is a critical point. "Remember, you only had a handful of super-good teams back then. The manufacturers were pretty much out of racing at that point, at least compared to today, and

Different paths: The 1980 NASCAR champions dinner honored Richie Evans and Dale Earnhardt (in background at left), who for years owned their respective divisions. *(Lynn Evans collection)*

there weren't that many big sponsors. So most of the teams were struggling.

"He wasn't going to get into Junior Johnson's car, because Junior still had Cale Yarborough. He wasn't going to get Richard Petty's ride, or Bobby Allison's ride. Those guys were still winning all the races, and they were with the best teams. So what are you going to do? Do you jump into a bad car, or do you wait for one of those top guys to retire? Hell, in a sport where you've got guys racing up into their late 40s and still winning, how do you sit around and hope somebody retires?

"It's easy to say, 'Well, Pete Hamilton went down there, and he won the [1970] Daytona 500.' But Pete was running the second Petty car, and that was the best equipment available at that time. Pete did a great job with it, yes, but he still had a good car to start with."

Evans said, "I just never had anything put together that looked like instant success."

He did daydream just a bit about putting together his own Cup team with backing from Gene DeWitt, who could certainly have afforded to play the sponsor game in those less-luxurious days. "If Rich couldn't go to a team like the Wood Brothers or Petty Enterprises or somebody like that," says Nacewicz, "his first choice would have been to do a Cup deal with Gene. That way, he figured, at least we'd know what kinds of material we were working with."

And DeWitt was more than willing to lend his support. In 1979 he told Andy Fusco, "I'm in modified racing simply because of [Evans], not because of the class of car. If Richie wanted to race boats, I'd do it. If he wanted to take a swing at [Cup], I'd do it."

Dick O'Brien, who knew both men well, says, "I know for a fact that Gene said, 'Rich, let me get you started. I don't know how long I can last [on my own], but at least let me get you started.'"

But the whole idea was a non-starter for Evans. His wife Lynn says, "Rich told me once, 'I respect Gene DeWitt too much to do that to him.' And I appreciated that."

What bothered Evans most was the idea that B.R. DeWitt, Inc., no matter how large it had grown, was still a family operation at its core. Byron DeWitt had hustled hard to start it, and then Gene had hustled hard to expand it, and that made it personal to Richie Evans. This was not Pepsi or Miller Beer or STP; this was a contracting outfit run by people he *knew*, and that weighed on him.

"I couldn't spend that kind of money from a friend," Evans told *Speedway Scene* in 1983. "Maybe I look at my dollars different. If a big company's spending it, that's no problem. But when it's *earned* dollars, you've got to remember that somebody labored for that money.

"A big company, they're going to write it off anyway; somebody else is going to take it if *you* don't. But if somebody, at one time, had to start work at seven in the morning to earn that money, to me that's different."

If the right big-league deal isn't knocking on your door, and you aren't interested in chasing the right big-league deal, and you're not comfortable with your only chance at putting together your own right big-league deal, the right big-league deal probably isn't going to materialize.

It didn't for Richie Evans, and he was OK with that. The truth is, he was happy right where he was.

"He just never had that burning desire to move up," suggests Nacewicz. "He enjoyed that kind of racing, and he certainly proved he could do it, but it wasn't something he *had* to do. He was very content doing what he was doing. He loved the modifieds."

Greg Sacks says, "I talked to Richie about it several times, and he would always say that he liked his life right where he was at. And you know something else? With his attitude toward life, and being a bit of a partier, I think he knew that at the next level—where Corporate America was involved—he wouldn't have been able to be himself anymore."

A relucftant suit-and-tie man, Richie poses with Lynn at the 1980 Stafford banquet. *(Howie Hodge photo/courtesy of Speedway Scene)*

"Richie was never comfortable with the shirt and the tie," says Dick O'Brien. "He wasn't comfortable with the whole corporate deal, being the 'yes' man. He told me often that he didn't want to *have* to be nice to people he didn't like. If you look at all that, you've got the main reason why he never would take that shot. The off-track aspect of big-time racing bothered him, there's no question about that."

Maynard Troyer, who'd taken an early-'70s crack at Cup racing and had his own troubles feeling comfortable with it, agrees that Evans might have struggled with that off-track side of things. "The lifestyle stuff, I think, would have had a bearing on it," Troyer says. "I tried all that stuff, and it was a rough row to hoe. I finally figured out that I was happier coming home, being around people I knew, and winning races. I think Richie probably looked at it that same way.

"In other words, Are you willing to give up winning, and being popular at home, just to say you went to the big time? I just don't think the big time meant that much to him."

Today, the "big time" means everything to short-track drivers everywhere, and clearly much of that lure is financial. The top Nextel Cup drivers make millions of dollars annually on the race track, with the potential to make tens of millions more through endorsements, merchandise sales and appearance fees. Hell, even a moderately successful Busch Series driver will bank more income in a given year than the best modified driver will see in *five* seasons.

But that is a fairly recent development. In many cases, short-track purses have barely kept pace with inflation; the winners of some big modified races in 2004 made less money than those same races paid Evans and Geoff Bodine a quarter-century earlier. Meanwhile, earnings for Nextel Cup and Busch Series drivers have risen through the roof; they can pick up far more money for showing up to sign autographs at a Saturday-night track than that track will pay the winner of its biggest race all year.

It is a very different motorsports economy than the one Richie Evans knew. Cup purses in those days were hardly eye-popping, once you got past the first few finishing positions. Billy Nacewicz says that in the late-1970s and early '80s, "Richie made almost as much money as he could have driving a Cup car. Those Cup guys didn't have the endorsement deals they do today, so a driver's pay was basically whatever his percentage of the purse was. I think Jerry Cook felt the same way."

Cook sure did. "When I won some of those [modified] championships," Jerry says, "I'd sit back and look at it. I'd look at what I made, and I'd look at the deal I had with Pete Hollebrand as my car owner and Hollebrand Trucking as my sponsor; then I'd look through the money-won list and see what the [Cup] guys were making."

Every winter, Cookie came to the same conclusion: "We weren't doing too bad."

Evans had several seasons in which his cars took in well over $100,000; as the owner and driver, he didn't have to divvy up that haul. Yes, he had plenty of overhead, but he was also very skilled at figuring out little ways to keep those costs down. "What you've got to remember," O'Brien says, "is that Richie had a lot of deals. All the stuff that would cost the typical car owner a bunch of money—gas, tires, shocks, motors—he either got for nothing, or somebody else was paying for."

No, Richie Evans never made anything close to Jeff Gordon-level dough—or even Joe Nemechek-level dough—but his take-home pay sure wasn't bad. He had a nice home; he had plenty of toys; anything he really wanted, he could afford. Plus, he had the ability to race on his own terms. John McMullin says, "I think he liked the idea that next weekend, he could run up and down the highway from Stafford to Oswego to Thompson if he wanted to."

And when you add a comfortable income to personal freedom, you get what O'Brien calls "a hard situation to give up."

"I'm content," Evans once told a *Speedway Scene* columnist. "A lot of my friends carry lunch pails and work in factories, and I'm pleased that I don't have to do that. I like what I do. What else do you need in life to be happy?"

Which goes a long way toward explaining why, as soon as he'd climbed from his car after finishing second to Rusty Wallace in that 1980 Grand American 300 at Talladega, Evans was heading for the exit gate. He had no interest in hanging around to schmooze with all the Cup team owners and drivers who were there to run the next day's Winston 500. Wallace no doubt did a bit of that; he was already aiming his career toward the big time, and had developed close ties to folks like Bobby Allison and Don Miller, the latter of whom is now his partner in Penske Racing South. It's a pretty safe bet that as soon as he finished his

A pair of kings, Richard Petty and Evans, when the seven-time Cup champion visited Shangri-La in 1985. *(Lynn Evans collection)*

post-race interviews, Rusty took a winner's stroll through the Cup garage.

Evans headed instead to a small nearby airport, where he climbed into a rented, single-engine Beechcraft Bonanza piloted by Ron Hutter. Billy Nacewicz and Thalia Hutter, Ron's wife, were also on board. They flew northeast, toward Winston-Salem, where a NASCAR national championship modified race was scheduled at Bowman Gray Stadium. Richie hadn't planned to run that show—if he had, he'd have sent one of his own cars there—but he figured there was time enough to maybe zoom up and talk his way into a ride.

When they landed and rolled up to the general aviation terminal, they found no rental cars available. They called a taxi, but, with time running short, Evans was worried about the wait. So the four of them walked out of the small terminal and waved down the first car they saw pulling away.

"It happened to be the [air traffic] controller who had worked us in over the radio," laughs Hutter. "I told him, 'Hey, we're running late, and we've got to get this guy to Bowman Gray Stadium.' He said, 'Come on, I'll take you.'"

They got briefly lost on the way, stopping for directions at a gas station. When they finally reached Bowman Gray, Thalia Hutter recalls, "We all walked into the pits together, and all of a sudden Richie was *gone*. Then, just that fast, he was back beside us, wearing his firesuit. Where he changed, I have no idea."

Ron Hutter says, "We actually got there when they were running the pace laps for the feature. He flagged a guy down, the car pulled into the infield, and Richie ran out there, still pulling his helmet on. Then he climbed in and ran the feature."

It ended up being a short night at the Stadium; the commandeered modified lost its brakes. Then Evans, Nacewicz and the Hutters climbed back into that Bonanza, headed up the Atlantic Coast toward Connecticut and a Sunday afternoon show at Thompson.

And while Buddy Baker was outrunning Dale Earnhardt and David Pearson on his way to capturing the Winston 500, Evans was fending off George Kent and John Rosati to win something called the Bronze 100.

Richie probably figured he'd had the better day.

PART FIVE

"'You Gotta Be 40 To Drive One of These Things'"

Mike Adaskaveg photo

Rebound

NO ONE SEEMS QUITE SURE just when Richie Evans first motioned toward his modified and quipped, as he so often did, "You gotta be 40 to drive one of these things." It's a safe bet, knowing Richie, that it came out in a cocky, post-victory moment shortly after his 40th birthday. That would have been in 1981, when he happened to be on a hell of a tear, and for the third straight season was, without doubt, the baddest modified man in the land. But 1982, the year that Greg Sacks "just rocked everybody," to steal a Billy Nacewicz phrase, had been a wakeup call for the Evans team.

"I don't think '82 affected his confidence at all," Nacewicz says. "In fact, I know it didn't. Richie never lost any confidence in his driving." But he never liked getting beat, either, and he certainly didn't like the suggestion—subtly and not so subtly floated in some quarters—that maybe 1982 was some sort of a signal, perhaps the beginning of the end, the start of the slide that seems to take all the great ones toward the ends of their careers.

But if watching Evans get punched around by Sacks and the Wilsberg car had planted any doubts about Richie's speed, he erased them all in 1983. To *this* gunfight, he brought an Uzi. Actually, a pair of them, two new orange Cavalier-bodied modifieds which carried something of a different look, flashy by previous Evans standards: over the hoods and down their sides, they carried broad stripes, a whitish yellow at the nose running to a deep red on their rear flanks.

And they were among the fastest cars ever to roll out of the shop on Calvert Street, carrying Richie Evans to one of the best years of his career. He won 38 times in all that season, and his NASCAR record included a stout 31 victories in 68 starts; just as importantly, in those 68

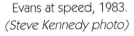

Evans at speed, 1983. *(Steve Kennedy photo)*

Left to right: Kenny Hartung, Ray Spognardi, Evans, Billy Nacewicz and Tiger Pettinelli celebrate their 1983 Dogwood 500 win at Martinsville. *(Dave Pardi photo/courtesy of Speedway Scene)*

events he tallied 57 top-five finishes. Among his happiest moments that year: a Dogwood 500 victory at Martinsville, a green-to-checker romp in Stafford's 100-lap Fall Final, a sweep of a springtime twin-30s program at Thompson, and two hard-earned 75-lap scores at Oswego, one over Reggie Ruggiero and the other over Brian Ross in a cold, damp B.R. DeWitt Port City 150. In the latter race's victory lane, winking at his sponsor, Evans told announcer Rich Goldstein, "Gene told me he was sick of giving the trophy to other people."

At season's end he picked up track championships at his Friday-night haunt, Spencer Speedway, and his Sunday stop, Thompson.

And, oh yes, in 1983 Richie Evans beat George Kent to win his sixth straight NASCAR national modified championship. Better than that, it was his seventh overall, a record and a source of quiet pride for Evans—and of loud boasting for his most avid supporters—because it gave him one more NASCAR title than Jerry Cook, with whom he had shared the previous standard.

It was one fine season for the Rapid Roman, 1983 was.

Even when he lost that year, Evans managed to do it with a flair. In that September's Bud 200 at Oswego, a late yellow flag threatened to end the event with the pack running at a caution-speed trot. That was fine with leader Gary Iulg, who had won dozens of races on the dirt tracks of New York and Canada and was also a formidable pavement shoe with good equipment under him. It was also all right with Evans, because second-place in this big show—a non-NASCAR race he hadn't been sure he'd be able to fit into his points-chasing schedule—was going to be a nice bonus. As the modifieds rolled past the Oswego flagstand in the final minutes of the race—lap 197, lap 198, lap 199—Evans casually puffed a cigarette. Then, as he followed Iulg out of the second corner, something up ahead took both men by surprise: the pace car was pulling into the infield. Evans, caught completely by surprise, said he "fired that cigarette out the window and grabbed a gear." As the lights blinked

Rebound   **253**

Reggie Ruggiero runs in tight quarters with Evans at Oswego. *(Rick Nelson photo/courtesy of Speedway Scene)*

green, Iulg hit the gas. Richie did the same. No one passed anyone during that weird half-lap sprint to the checkers, but it sure made for a few laughs later on.

Evans had some stiff competition that year. Sacks and Wilsberg were back, Ruggiero was the hot New England driver, DeWitt "teammate" Doug Hewitt was fast at Spencer and Shangri-La, and George Kent was a constant factor, shadowing Evans up and down the NASCAR trail.

And Ross, an Albany-Saratoga graduate who'd first raced with Evans all the way back in the coupe days—"prior to when he was put out of NASCAR," is how Brian says it—had worked the kinks out of a homemade orange modified of his own. He and his friend Dick Daddario had built the car in 1982, and by '83 it was running up front at Stafford, Riverside Park, Oswego, everywhere Ross hauled it. On a lot of nights that season, he was the toughest rival Evans had.

"Those were fun races," Ross says. "I mean, if you just start on the pole and you run away from everybody, there's no challenge in that. But when you're racing with guys like Richie, who are just such fierce competitors, *nothing* compares to that."

After that year, a diehard short-track fan from Ohio named Bill Davis came up with an interesting tidbit. Since 1976, he claimed, he had religiously scoured as many weekly racing papers as he could get his hands on, compiling a list of the most successful drivers in every branch of the sport. Davis reported that in that eight-season stretch between 1976-83, Richie Evans had won more feature races than any driver in America, topping Dick Trickle 293-284. If the Davis numbers are correct —and no one ever emerged to dispute them—Evans managed a remarkable 36.625 victories *per season* in that span.

So maybe the folks who thought 1982 was a bad year for the orange #61 were right. When you're supposed to win more than 36 races a year, sure, less than 30 really *is* a slump! All jokes aside, Evans was back in

Brian Ross and Richie Evans, side by side. *(Dave Pardi photo/courtesy of* Speedway Scene*)*

form in 1983. Some folks have suggested, looking back, that never in his career did he drive any better than he did that year.

Brian Ross, who certainly qualifies as a Richie Evans expert, isn't sure about that. "Richie studied racing so hard, all the time," Ross declares. "It was his life, and he was just so intense about it. And I've got to say, he just got better and better."

But Ross admits that he's happy to have figured into so many of the great Evans races from that period. He says, "Up until that time, there wasn't anything I had done that compared with the feeling of being able to put that much pressure on Richie Evans. Because, let's face it, Richie was one of the greatest drivers there ever was, maybe the greatest in our area.

"I think a lot of people figured that if Richie was there, they were going to run as hard as they could and have a good time, but they were going to finish second. Well, I couldn't bring myself to think that way. I had to feel like I could beat him, and when I finally did that once in a while, it was such a rewarding accomplishment.

"So I don't know if those were his best times, but I know they were *my* best times."

If there was a downside to the 1983 Evans campaign, it was a small thing that has paled over time. He once again contended for Winston's overall NASCAR national short track title, but it went instead to Nashville Speedway late model champ Mike Alexander, who later had a brief stint at the Winston Cup level. It annoyed Richie that, under the traditional Southern qualifying system, Alexander was able to time-trial into the weekly features and thus always started near the front while he, Evans, routinely lined up seven or eight or nine rows back for his own 30- and 35-lappers. But Evans kept his anger to himself until, as the title chase narrowed to the two of them, Alexander—urged along, some suggested, by Winston PR troops trying to drum up interest in the fight —

After years of on-track competition, Evans and Jerry Cook got on rather well once Jerry took a NASCAR job. "We've been working together," Cook told a writer. (Jim Squalliano photo/courtesy of Speedway Scene)

lettered the words "Richie Who?" on the lip of his Camaro's front spoiler.

His wife, Lynn, says, "I know that bothered Richie." *Bothered?* When publicly questioned about the matter, Evans was usually silent but tight-jawed; privately, he raged. He saw the gesture as a disrespectful put-down.

Again, the whole flap passed soon enough, and in retrospect maybe it was a good thing. It kept Evans charged up in a time when he had lost a couple of career-long motivators.

Jerry Cook was by now well into officialdom, and he and Evans actually seemed almost *cozy*. Cook explained to writer Ron Hedger, "I think he understands what my job is … In the past year and a half we've been working together to make [modified racing] better." Evans told Hedger he thought Cook was doing "a good job."

And Maynard Troyer, another 15-year Evans rival, had quietly hung up his helmet at the end of 1982, having admittedly grown more interested in building and selling cars than in driving them.

Kent was still a terrific foe for Evans, and so was Ross, but, hell, they were friends of his. Sacks, just beginning to focus on a Winston Cup effort, drove the Wilsberg 5 less frequently and finally left the ride altogether. And Richie's next great spat of consequence, with a Pennsylvania charger named Jimmy Spencer, lay down the road a bit.

Maybe all that "Richie Who?" nonsense from Alexander fired him up a bit. Because when Hedger asked him who he thought might be "the next Richie Evans," the very topic seemed almost to rankle him.

"Whoever takes my place," he told Hedger, "they're going to have to put in a lot of hours. They're not going to do it by just being a driver.

"If they're going to be me, they'll have to at least build their own car."

The Competitive Fire

BY EVERY REPUTABLE ACCOUNT, Richie Evans was not a bad loser. Billy Nacewicz says, "He'd come in after finishing second or third, and maybe on certain nights *I'd* be upset, but Rich would say, 'What the hell's wrong with that? Look who beat us.' And I'd sit back and think, He's right. We got beat by Bugsy, or maybe we got beat by Ray Hendrick. Sometimes, second or third is just fine."

Tony Siscone, who had been a part of several one-two New Egypt finishes with Evans, winning *and* losing his share, says, "If you beat Richie, he wasn't the kind of guy who came over to shake your hand and said, 'Hey, way to go!' But he'd always give you a wink or a nod from a distance, or maybe a little wave."

There is plenty of lore about Richie the Good Sport, Richie the Gracious Runner-up, even Richie the Benevolent, the guy who was always willing to give a competitor a leg-up. Richie with the Helping Hand.

This was Brian Ross on the Oswego Speedway public address system in 1983, after losing to Evans in an incredible 75-lapper: "So many times when the chips were down, this guy helped me out an awful lot. He's loaned me stuff and he's given me good advice. I can't thank him enough. The guy is really a super racer. He's the guy who makes racing what it is today, he's the guy you've got to beat. Damn, I'll tell you, he's one tough competitor, and a good friend of mine."

And this was Greg Sacks a few years ago, reminiscing about his own struggling days on Long Island in the 1970s: "One of the first things about Richie that left an impression on me happened at Islip, when he came to one of the big shows. I dropped out early with a carburetor linkage problem, and after the race he came right over: 'What happened?' Now, we were friends. We got along. But the reason he came over, I believe, was to see what put me out in case it was something that could ever put *him* out. I showed him what the problem was, and he showed me something he'd done so the same thing couldn't happen to him. Then he showed me a couple other things I could do to my car, things I hadn't learned yet, that might save me from having different problems. So, yes, he was helping himself by looking into my problems, but he turned around and helped me in return."

But make no mistake: Evans was not a guy who settled happily for anything less than victory. His years in the sport, particularly his lean days early on, had taught Richie Evans to accept defeat—"You can't win 'em all, right?" he might shrug—and even to smile through it. But he was a racer to whom defeat, on the wrong day or under the wrong circumstance, could be a bitter pill.

Once, after finishing second to Maynard Troyer, Evans called him "that SOB." In truth, the two were surprisingly tight. *(Val LeSieur photo/courtesy of Speedway Scene)*

Just because he couldn't win 'em all didn't mean he had to like every loss. And if those losses came too often at the hands of the same opponent, well, that was the worst.

Jay Hedgecock, a fine North Carolina driver and car builder, uttered one of the great lines about the competitive fire within Richie Evans. This was in 1982 at New Smyrna, in the middle of a week in which Sacks —who had sure come a long way from those broken-linkage times at Islip—was kicking Evans's ass, and everyone else's, on a nightly basis. "Man," drawled Hedgecock as he watched an unsmiling Evans load up, "I'll bet Richie is goin' back to the motel every night and just chewin' that headboard right off the bed."

It had nothing to do with how Evans felt about Sacks, and everything to do with how he felt about finishing second *again*. Veteran New York race announcer Gary Montgomery once made a similar observation after watching Richie run second to Maynard Troyer—who had been on a hot streak—in an extra-distance race at Spencer Speedway. "Evans was asked to stand in victory lane for the runner-up interview," Montgomery wrote in *Gater Racing News*. "Evans said privately to the master of ceremonies, 'I'm not standing here with that SOB.' He immediately returned to his race car and stormed off to the pit area. Later, after the crowd had headed home, Evans and Troyer had several beers together and talked of the race and their plans to play with snowmobiles as soon as there was snow. He didn't think Troyer was an SOB, he just didn't like anyone or anything that beat him."

And like all big winners, Evans would go to incredible lengths to avoid getting beat. He'd run the outside. He'd run the inside. He'd tell Jerry Cook he was going to one track, and then show up at another. He'd bolt a wing on his roof if it was legal, and plumb his carburetor to inhale nitrous oxide when it wasn't against the rules. He'd connive.

Oh, yes, the man could connive with the best of them. Pull a fast one to keep his edge on the next guy? In a heartbeat. Hell, Mario Fiore tells a great story about Evans pulling a fast one on the closest thing he had to a real teammate, fellow B.R. DeWitt flag-bearer Doug Hewitt. It happened in 1978, when Fiore and Reggie Ruggiero—basically bullring racers at the time, winning frequently at Riverside Park and Monadnock —were anxious to strut their stuff in the big-track special events at season's end.

"We really wanted to run the Thompson 300, but we didn't have a motor that was up to snuff," Fiore says. "Richie called me and said, 'Do you need a motor for Thompson?' I said yes. He said, 'OK, I'll make you a deal. I've got a motor sitting up at B&M in Rochester, and if you go up there and pick it up for me, you guys can use it at Thompson. It's sitting there right under the bench.' It was a motor Smokey Yunick had originally built, and all I had to do was go out there and pick it up. I thought that was pretty good. Then Richie says, 'One other thing. There's a brand-new motor up there, too, and I also need you to bring that one

Tony Siscone learned first-hand how helpful and/or competitive Richie Evans could be. (Marc Rohrbacher photo/courtesy of Speedway Scene)

back.' I said, 'Sure.' Why not? We'd be going right through Rome on the way home, anyway.

"Well, it turned out that B&M was building that new motor for Doug Hewitt. It was their latest and greatest piece, and Richie coveted that motor. He knew they'd give it to us if we said we were picking it up for Richie [because it was, after all, Gene DeWitt's engine]. But he didn't want to be the one who went up there and got Dougie's motor. So he was looking for a fall guy, somebody to go up there and get that motor."

Grinning at the memory, Fiore says, "He just *had* to try that motor before Dougie Hewitt got it. When we dropped it off at his shop, he was like a kid in a candy store, with his brand-new piece. I found out later on that Dougie wasn't happy about it."

It was a mind-game victory, sure, but it was a victory. You have to look at it from Richie Evans's perspective, because the big winners look at *everything* from their own perspective: If he had let that engine slip past his hands and it turned out to be some fire-breathing monster, and Doug Hewitt had beaten him with it, well, that would have been the kind of headboard-chewin' loss Jay Hedgecock saw at New Smyrna a few years later.

Richie the Good Sport? Richie the Benevolent? Sometimes.

Just not all the time.

"I've got a great story about that," Tony Siscone says. "When I first starting running at New Egypt, Richie would come in for the 100-lappers and the 150-lappers, the national championship shows, and there were nights when he would just about lap the field. I was driving for Dick Barney, and Dick said, 'We've got to do our homework, and get better. We've got to work harder.' And he was right; we had to step it up to the next level to run with Richie, and we did. Pretty soon we could run in the same lap with him, and after a while we could maybe finish second or third behind him. Well, eventually we caught up; in fact, in the last couple seasons that we all ran there together, the dominant guys were me, John Blewett [Jr.] and Richie.

"I'll never forget this one particular race there, a 150-lapper. I won

The Competitive Fire **259**

the show and Richie finished second, and I lapped the entire field except for Richie. At the end of the race, he was going into [turn] three as I was coming off [turn] two. Dick Barney came on the radio and said, 'Do *not* lap him,' and I didn't *want* to lap him, because that would have been like insulting Richie.

"Anyway, right after this, there was a big show at Stafford. I'd only been there a few times, and of course Richie had been a regular there, so I went over to ask him about tires. I think we had three different right-rears to choose from, and I wanted his opinion. Now, anytime I went to Richie—at Martinsville, Riverhead, it didn't matter—he'd always help me out. That's how he was. But this time he turned to me, put his hand on my shoulder, and with that sly smile he said, 'You've been drawing off me for a long time. After that New Egypt race, class is out.'

"I said, 'What are you talking about?' Richie said, 'Man, you smoked the field, me included. I'm done helping you.' I said, 'You're *really* not going to tell me which tire to run?' He said, 'Nope.'

"I walked back to our pit, and Dick Barney was waiting for me. He said, 'Well, what did Richie say?' I told Dick what had happened, and he just laughed. He said, 'There is the *greatest* compliment you'll ever get.' And, you know, Dick was right, because what Richie was saying was, 'OK, you're a threat now. You're on your own.'"

Same story, different characters, this time Fiore and Ruggiero. "When we started running the bigger tracks regularly [in 1981], our first race was in the Spring Sizzler," Fiore says. "We finished third, and Richie ran second to Bob Polverari. He was really happy that day; he hadn't done many customer cars up to that point, so he was really proud of the fact that we ran that good. But a few races later, there was something we needed—some part, I can't remember what it was—and we asked Richie if we could borrow one. He said, 'Well, you guys are running good. You should have your *own* stuff.'

"It's like it took him a while to accept that you could run with him. But I'm sure it was the same with everybody. When Geoff Bodine first started beating him, they were at odds; same thing with Sacks [in 1982], same thing with us. In '84, we really started to put everything together and hit on a great combination, and we were really fast …"

Fiore laughs. "And it didn't go over good with Richie."

Losing was something he tolerated. Losing too often was something he could not stomach. And looking bad? Well, Richie Evans had long since passed the point where he was going to put up with looking bad.

Siscone remembers Evans showing up at Wall Stadium for a 70-lap mid-summer event called the Budweiser Classic. "He flat-out hated Wall," Siscone says, "but they were paying big money, like $4500 to win and $50 for every lap you led." The top 10 qualified through time trials, and the rest of the pack had to run heats.

"Gil Hearne and I are on the front row," Siscone says. "I think Richie qualified 11th or 12th. I took a walk through the pits, and there's Richie, standing by his truck, smiling. I said, 'I guess you're on the pole in your heat.' He says, 'Nah. I'm not in the mood for this.' I said, 'Whaddaya mean?' He says again, 'I'm not in the mood.' Then he turns to his guys and says, 'Let's go to the casinos.' And he loaded up and went to Atlantic City."

Sounds completely implausible, unless you really knew how competitive he was.

"That was his way of getting out of things gracefully," Siscone says. "It was like saying, 'Look, I can't stand this freaking place, and we're not hooked up.' It wasn't a [NASCAR] points deal; he was only there because the race paid so good. And if he wasn't running good enough to win, he wasn't going to go out there and just ... *ride around*."

 # Headliner

EVANS GOT HIS FIRST NATIONAL INK not long after he'd clinched his initial NASCAR modified championship in 1973. It ran in the April '74 issue of *Stock Car Racing* magazine, and in those days SCR was the only glossy publication paying any attention to the modified division. Pete Zanardi, who at that point was covering sports for the *Hartford Times*, drew the assignment. Zanardi had long been a familiar face at New England's weekly tracks and all the major modified events, but he says he hardly knew Evans at the time. For the story, Pete traveled to Rome and spent, he recalls, four days with Richie and his friends, pinballing between the Calvert Street garage, Coalyard Charlies, the Rusty Nail and other sites of local interest.

"I went up there with Phil Smith, and I think Phil knew Richie a little better than I did," Zanardi says. "Anyway, we'd spend all day at the shop, and then at night we'd go to one gin mill or the other."

All that bouncing around, Zanardi sees now, was Evans's way of feeling out this stranger from Connecticut. "I think he wanted to test you, to find out, 'Just what kind of guy am I dealing with?' Richie had to find out if I could stand riding in his car while he drove down the main drag, hitting [marker] barrels and trying to get them to fly up over the hood. He had to find out if I was able to hang out in the bar and drink with him and his friends. I think that was Richie's way of sizing you up, to find out who you were."

Apparently satisfied, Evans granted his visitor a lengthy, candid interview in his bachelor digs upstairs from the Coalyard. "I distinctly remember sitting at a table in the apartment above the bar," Zanardi says, "and talking to Richie about him growing up on the farm and things like that. I remember him having serious answers to serious questions."

Tolerating the media: Evans confers with crewman Kenny Hartung while pesky columnist Bones Bourcier lurks. *(Val LeSieur photo/courtesy of* Speedway Scene*)*

Wilbur Jones, alongside Evans from the start, remembers that in his earliest racing days, "Richie didn't like doing interviews at all." But at some point he came to the realization that, as Billy Nacewicz puts it, "the press was important to racing." And thus began what amounted to a pretty long honeymoon between the modified racing media and the division's most celebrated driver.

"As a rule, the media treated him pretty well," says Nacewicz. "I think they liked Richie because you could always get an opinion out of him. It didn't matter if it was something to do with racing—a tire rule, and engine rule, whatever—or some fun thing that was going on, he always had something to say."

If Evans didn't always *enjoy* the media—and, really, no one in his right mind enjoys being pestered in the workplace, which was what happened every time some columnist cornered him at the track or phoned his race shop—he certainly tolerated it politely enough. Sometimes, he could even spin it to his own advantage.

Dick O'Brien, who in addition to his Oswego Speedway duties covered motorsports for the *Syracuse Herald*, says, "Richie wasn't afraid to stir the pot [in the press] a little bit, if he thought he had to. And he was smart enough to know when he could use an interview to get his point across, whether it was to NASCAR or whoever. He knew how to come around through the back door that way."

And Evans had a grasp on the media-participant dynamic, the subtle interaction between the two sides.

"Richie understood that whole thing very well," says Pete Zanardi. "See, Richie always knew what he was about. Even when I made that first trip to Rome, he was already a folk hero up there; when we went into a bar or a restaurant, people came around to talk to him. They wanted to talk to *Richie Evans*. He was something special to them, and he was not naïve about that. It was the same with the media. He truly understood what that relationship was all about, and what he meant to the sport.

"I have yet to meet anyone who told me that Richie was anything but professional with the newspaper guys. He was always going to give you an answer."

Andy Fusco, one of the first to cover Evans on a regular basis, uses an oxymoron—"both guarded and open"—to describe the champion's approach to the press. His explanation sounds a bit like Zanardi's theory about Evans wanting "to test you."

Fusco: "What I mean is, Richie was quite guarded and aloof until a writer earned his confidence. Then, once he trusted you, he became a wellspring of information. At first, I had a difficult time overcoming the *guarded* part, because he knew I was close to Jerry Cook and especially the Pete Hollebrand family, and Richie generally disliked Cook's associates. But once it became obvious that my interviews were for purely journalistic purposes and not to rat him out to Cookie, Richie became a terrific source. And a pal."

Yes, a pal. Because while Evans recognized as well as any short-track racer the professional lines between the media and those it covered—which can sometimes be real "us against them" boundaries—he also allowed those lines to blur when the work was done. When Nacewicz suggests that Evans "had a lot of friends in the media," it is something of an understatement.

Stop and think about the number of times Evans interacted with, say, Fusco and Mike Monnat and Dick Macco at the New York tracks, or Phil Smith and Toodi Gelinas and Charlie Mitchell in New England, or, going way back, Gary London and Lou Modestino at the old All Star League events. He came to know many of the daily sportswriters who showed up only occasionally, and certainly all the modified columnists from *Gater Racing News*, *Speedway Scene*, *Area Auto Racing News* and *National Speed Sport News*. And then there were the photographers: guys like Bob Hunter and John Grady had snapped Evans from the beginning, and then there were Fred Smith at Shangri-La, Mike Adaskaveg and Clint Lawton in Connecticut, Ace Lane Jr. down in New Jersey, David Allio on those Southern trips …

"The people who covered modified racing, we'd see a lot of them two or three nights a week, every week," says Billy Nacewicz. "They got to be almost like family. It got to the point where some of 'em were part of our gang."

Val LeSieur recalls his friendship with Evans building right along with Richie's career, as the driver and the publisher—whose *New England Speedway Scene* morphed into simply *Speedway Scene* in the late 1970s—began to see more of each other. "Because Richie was winning all the time, he became one of our key guys," LeSieur says. "Before him, Bugsy Stevens had been more or less the key, the guy that got the most coverage. But then Bugsy had a few quiet years, and that's when Richie was winning all over the place—Stafford, Thompson, Riverside Park, and of course in New York—and so he got a lot of coverage."

Print and broadcast journalist Dick Berggren tapes a radio interview with Richie. *(Dick Berggren collection)*

That got sticky because LeSieur, the kind of outsized character Evans always got a kick out of, was one of those Nacewicz cites as being "part of our gang." The *Speedway Scene* office received the occasional complaint from readers who figured that Evans appeared so often on page one—which some drivers back then likened to a musician being on the cover of *Rolling Stone*—because of their friendship.

"I heard the same thing when we used to put Bugsy's picture there a lot," says LeSieur. "But when a guy is winning all those races, and he's popular, too, are you supposed to *not* put him on the front page?"

LeSieur and Evans ignored the hubbub, and their friendship rollicked on. It went the same way with Evans and Dick O'Brien, who in the course of covering races and/or representing Oswego often fell in with the Evans caravan as it rolled up and down the highway.

"One year at Oswego, we did a little promotional deal on a Wednesday," O'Brien says. "And we had this idea that Richie could take some of the local media people for rides around the track in his race car. This was a strong area for the pavement modifieds back then, and, let's face it, Richie was the king of the hill. Anyway, I got [speed shop owner] Howard Conkey to give us a seat and some belts, and we got some helmets, and Richie moved some tin around inside one of his cars and put in that second seat.

"We had a handful of people lined up: the three TV stations from Syracuse, that kind of thing. It was perfect for Richie, because he didn't have to do any kind of formal interviews, just explain the car, maybe talk about how fast they'd be going, and then scare the cameraman a little bit as they were running around the place.

"So the day comes, and as I'm in the middle of introducing him to the guy from Channel 3 or wherever, Richie turns to me and says, 'Hey, you write for the Syracuse paper. *You're media.* Get in.' Well, I'm a pretty big guy, but I finally wiggled into that thing and buckled up, and I'm pulling on one of the helmets we had brought. I've got the helmet about three-quarters on, and I'm fighting to fasten that double-ring thing on the strap—I mean, I haven't put on many helmets in my life—and, *vrooooom*, off we go. Richie took right off out of the pits, before I was even all hooked up.

"Naturally, he takes the car right up to the wall out of the corner, and he's on the gas hard. I'm hanging on to the roll cage with one hand and trying to keep that helmet on my head with the other hand. I looked across at him, and he was laughing and looking right back at me. I said, 'Don't look at *me!* Look at the *race track!*' We did about five laps—five *fast* laps—and, I'll tell you, it was a huge thrill. Even when I look back on it now, I'll think, 'I got five fast laps around Oswego Speedway with Richie Evans.' I'll never forget that."

O'Brien pauses. "In the last four or five years of his life, especially, I felt like I got to know him really well. He became a good friend. I loved to shoot the shit with him, just because I enjoyed his company."

Evans and *Speedway Scene* publisher Val LeSieur shoot the breeze on a damp day at Stafford. (J&J photo/courtesy of *Speedway Scene*)

So the lines had blurred a bit. So what? Richie didn't think that was any big deal. In fact, he seemed to get a kick out of the idea that blurring things in that manner might aggravate others who were, well, more rigid about such things. One night he spotted Andy Fusco in the Albany-Saratoga pit area. Evans grabbed an orange T-shirt bearing his name and his familiar #61, and tossed it to Fusco.

"Hey, Andy," Evans laughed, "could you do me a favor and wear this next time you go to Hollebrand's house for dinner?"

Lucky Man

TRUE STORY: Richie Evans is standing near the handicapper's board at the Riverside Park Speedway. It's an early-'80s Saturday night, and Evans is grinning like the proverbial cat who has just eaten the proverbial canary. Riverside is hosting an extra-distance modified race tonight—100 laps, 200, it doesn't matter—and, for a change, qualifying is being done by time trials rather than heat races. The plan is to line up the feature by inverting the top 10.

Evans, having time-trialed early on, has strolled over to watch the last group of guys go against the clock. He says he would have preferred to see the fastest 10 guys redraw, because in his opinion the inversion process encourages guys to soft-pedal their way around the track, hoping to end up, say, eighth or ninth quick. Just to prove his point, he proclaims, he has done just that: he ran his time-trial lap at 95 percent rather than the usual flat-out 100, hoping to buck the system and start the feature up front.

So far, it's looking great. As the qualifying line grows smaller, Evans is seventh … then eighth … then ninth … and, finally, that magical 10th.

"How'd I do?" he asks, beaming, gloating. There are only a few cars left to run, none of them very good ones, and the big Riverside Park feature is going to begin with Richie Evans on the pole.

Now, let's get one thing straight: Evans was as smart a driver—and as smart an observer of his division—as any who ever turned a wheel. Smart enough to qualify early and guess correctly how slow he'd need to be to sandbag his way into the first couple of rows? Sure. But smart enough to get it *perfect*, to have the whole thing figured out exactly right, to place himself 10th, and therefore first? Nobody, not even Richie Evans, is *that* smart.

Evans knows this, of course, but he's not about to let on. "How'd I do?" he asks again, laughing now.

Suddenly, his face grows taut, the laughter disappears. Just as the qualifying session is about to end, Evans has spotted a red ramp truck rolling into the pit area. It belongs to Joe Brady, a Boston-area modified owner who has been a winner over the years with drivers like Leo Cleary, Bobby Santos, Bugs Stevens and Ken Bouchard. Some sort of trouble—a crash the previous night, or mechanical problems on the way to Riverside, who remembers?—has delayed Brady's arrival. Even his driver on this evening, local Agawam hero Marty Radewick, had all but given up on Brady showing. But here is that red ramp truck pulling to a halt, and here is the familiar Brady Bunch #00 being hastily unloaded, and here are the track officials confirming to Brady and Radewick that, yes, they will be allowed to take their time-trial laps.

And here is Richie Evans, suddenly not looking so smart, because if Radewick goes out there and gets it right—a solid bet—he'll likely be good for a top-10 run, and Evans will be bounced from a pole-position start to the sixth row.

Well, everything works out for Evans tonight, ... but barely. Marty Radewick, hustling like hell, can only manage 11th. Evans will see the green flag up front, and he will still be there when the checkers fall.

"As good as he was," George Kent says with a chuckle, "Richie was also lucky."

Sure enough. In fact, Evans was a big believer in luck, good and bad. He had the usual racer's superstitions—"I remember being told that we couldn't eat peanuts in the stands," daughter Jodi says, "and we couldn't wear green on a race night"—and a couple more of his own. He once recounted to writer Toodi Gelinas something that took place in the middle of a mid-'70s hot streak: "Someone gave us some champagne to keep in our truck to open at our next win. Several races went by, and I had nothing but bad luck until we broke the bottle. That same night, we won the race." Gelinas also wrote of what had become a nightly Evans ritual: "Moments before Richie takes to the speedway for the feature event, his main men from the B.R. DeWitt crew reach in and clasp his hand, wishing him good luck and a safe ride. For [Evans], it's become a tradition he wouldn't race without."

At the turn of the '80s, Evans got on a bit of a hot streak in New England, winning with regularity at Stafford, Riverside Park and Thompson. It dawned on him that whenever he received a pre-race handshake from wrecker driver Booker Jones—who in years past had blazed a trail as the area's first African-American modified racer—the night seemed to end with the #61 parked in victory lane. It became a necessity for Evans, but nobody, apparently, informed Jones about this. One Saturday night at Riverside, as the field got ready to rumble off the grid to start the main event, Billy Nacewicz's radio headset crackled: "Where's Booker?" asked Evans, with some urgency. Nacewicz spotted the Booker's Garage tow truck in the pit area and directed it toward the frontstretch, where Jones reached into the orange Pinto and clasped his friend's right hand. Evans won another feature that evening.

A pre-race visit from Booker Jones, Richie believed, was a sign of good things to come. (Clint Lawton photo/courtesy of Speedway Scene)

Supermodified star Joe Gosek was a first-hand witness to Richie's respect for fate. Evans had taken his division's half of a July 1985 mod/supermod twinbill at Oswego; Gosek was running off with the supermod main, looking for his first-ever win, when a driveshaft broke in the closing laps. The two had met just that year through some mutual friends, and Evans invited the youngster to a big bash he was hosting the following day at his Freeman Hotel in Osceola. At the party, remembers Gosek, "Richie said, 'Goddam, you had their asses kicked last night.' I said, 'Yeah, I've had a *lot* of races won, but I haven't finished one off yet.' He said, 'Well, I'll give you some good luck.' He went into the rig and got me his trophy from the previous night. He said, 'Take this. You can give it back when you win one.' I got my first win that August, but I never did hook up with Richie to give him back his trophy before he died. I've still got it, right beside my [Oswego, Star and Sandusky] Classic trophies."

There are those who define "luck" as that mysterious place where preparation meets opportunity. Well, if that's true, Richie Evans must have been in a constant state of preparedness, because opportunity came knocking on his door fairly regularly.

There was the September Sunday at Islip in 1980 when he and Charlie Jarzombek had staged their brilliant game of cat and mouse in the All Star 300. When Jarzombek's engine exploded with Evans on his tail, both cars spun wildly in the oil. Jarzombek, absolutely out of control, bounced off the wall; Evans, absolutely out of control, bounced off ... Jarzombek. One white Vega, badly busted up, was hauled by wreckers to the infield, while one orange Pinto, bent by the relatively soft car-on-car impact rather than broken by a hard car-on-wall smash, limped around under caution, in the lead, until the laps ran out.

This photo may have been blurred by alcohol! Evans "lends" Joe Gosek an Oswego trophy in a party at Richie's Freeman Hotel. (Linda Holdeman collection)

Now, it's one thing to be fortunate enough to win one major race that way, caroming off the leader's car as you both slide helplessly through the slop of a greased-down track. But Evans did it *twice*. George Kent says, "We were at Martinsville one time, me leading him, and we were coming up to lap some cars. Then I saw that green [coolant] fog; one of the lapped cars had broken either a hose or a radiator. I said, 'Oh, shit, here we go.' I went sliding in, and Richie came sliding in, too. But him and his damn luck! His car slid right into mine, which drove me into the wall, and he pulled away. In fact, he went on to win the race."

Kent smiles. "Yes, Richie was very good, but he was very lucky, too. Oh, that used to drive me crazy."

It drove Tony Siscone a little bit crazy, too.

"At New Egypt, after time trials the top eight or 10 guys would draw for starting positions in the big shows," Siscone says. "Richie was phenomenal with that draw. He'd always pull a number in the top three, usually the pole, and some people used to swear it was fixed. Well, this one night, we're all out on the front straightaway for the draw, and Richie pokes me with his elbow. He says, 'Listen, why don't we swap tonight? I'll tell the announcer I'm drawing for you, and you're drawing for me. They all swear it's fixed, and this'll shut 'em up. Just draw for me, and I'll draw for you.'

"I said to him, 'You're on.' But as we were standing there, I kept thinking about how terrible I'd always been at drawing. I said to myself, 'Watch, tonight I'll probably draw the front row, and I'll have to give it to him.' So I chickened out. I said, 'No deal.'

"Well, that freaking Richie. I pulled sixth. He pulled second. Man, he razzed the shit out of me."

From Outlaw to Company Man

THE FACT THAT RICHIE EVANS gave up his outlaw ways in the early 1970s didn't mean he decided to live his racing life completely within the lines. He still got a pretty fair kick out of beating anything that *looked* like a system, whether it was put in place by a sanctioning body or a track operator. The guy, as we have already seen, had a wide anti-authoritarian streak, and it never really went away.

"Even after he came back to NASCAR, Richie would do things to tweak you," Dick Waterman remembers. "For instance, we used to pay a bonus to any of our regulars who ran the [Permatex 300] at Daytona and painted 'Utica-Rome Speedway' on their cars. Bill Wimble painted it on there in letters a foot tall, and so did Lou Lazzaro. Well, Richie put it on his car, too, but it was so small you couldn't have seen it with a magnifying glass. Of course, by our rules he had it on there, so we had to pay him.

"Richie had that outlaw streak in him, and he wanted to do things his own way. He didn't bow down to NASCAR, or to *anybody*. Any rules you wanted to mention, he didn't want to follow. That's just the way the man was built."

But as his career flowed along and he got more entrenched—as he became a brighter part of the fabric of modified racing—Evans became less radical about such matters. He still enjoyed playing the occasional practical joke on a promoter, or maybe shooting him a barb during an interview, but in time Evans began to view the relationship between himself and the sport's decision-makers as more of a cooperative thing. Anything that helped modified racing also helped him, he realized. And in the last several years of his life and career, he may have been the division's ultimate company man.

Oh, he remained his famously independent self, always ready and willing to take a principled stand. When Stafford Speedway owner Jack Arute instituted a one-brand tire rule in 1982, Evans avoided the place except for its special events. But when things went smoothly between Richie Evans and the dozen or more track bosses he might interact with in a given season, they went *very* smoothly. The late Bob O'Rourke, the old All Star League's chief steward and pit boss for years at Islip Speedway—and a man to whom Evans often turned for advice—once said, "Richie was a promoter's dream."

"I think Richie enjoyed knowing that he contributed to racing," says Lynn Evans. "Now, I never heard him say it this way, but I think he looked at racing as a pie, and you needed all the slices to make a whole pie. That meant the racers, the press, and of course the promoters."

Billy Nacewicz says, "If a promoter needed something, Richie would usually try to accommodate him. He did a lot of telephone interviews from the shop, radio shows and things like that, to help them promote their upcoming races. Sometimes he'd go out to New England or up to Oswego or out to Rochester for press things the promoters had lined up."

Oswego's Dick O'Brien recalls Evans doing "a lot of promotional work for us, TV interviews or anything we wanted. And if he made a commitment—'Yeah, I'll be there'—he kept it."

That was especially important to places like Oswego, independent tracks whose events Evans ran when he wasn't busy chasing those national titles. In a real way, a lot of NASCAR promoters got lucky with Richie Evans. They knew they'd have him at least a few times each year for the extra-points races, and once they received his entry blank they were free to advertise that the—pick one: three-time, four-time, five-time—NASCAR national modified champion was coming in for the big 150-lapper. He'd be there, whether he wanted to or not.

With folks he respected, Evans could be "a promoter's dream." That's Oswego's Dick O'Brien on the right. *(J&H photo/courtesy of Speedway Scene)*

Non-NASCAR track operators have always had to hustle harder to attract the top stars, enticing champions like Evans and Jerry Cook (or before them Bugsy Stevens and Fred DeSarro) with convenient dates and fat purses. And, yes, sometimes with those quietly arranged appearance fees that have always been part of the short-track fiscal picture. Deal money.

In the case of Oswego, its rich payoffs and its proximity to Rome—and the fact that Evans just plain liked the joint—were generally enough to bring him up Route 69 and out Route 104, to the great old track not far from the shores of Lake Ontario. But if he could get a little extra something on the side, he wasn't about to turn that down.

"You know, Richie never really asked for a lot of money," O'Brien says. "But sometimes he'd ask for *tickets*. If we had the Bud 200 coming up and we needed him to do something, he'd say, 'Gimme 20 tickets on the backstretch. My friends like to sit back there.' Isn't that funny? Most guys, if they want tickets, would say, 'I want seats at the start-finish line.' But Richie wanted 'em out back, way down by turn three.

"Well, that was a great deal for everybody. For us, it meant a few more people in the seats, and for Richie, he could pass out those tickets to his buddies from Rome. That was more important to him than some big up-front deal."

New England promoter Russ Conway, another non-NASCAR guy, occasionally dealt Evans for special events he and partner Ken Smith staged at Thompson, and for the Yankee All-Star League small-block series he and Smith co-promoted with Thompson's Don Hoenig, Waterford's Harvey Tattersall and Monadnock's Bill Brown in the late 1970s. In the '80s, when Conway brought Winston Cup stars Richard Petty, Dale Earnhardt, Buddy Baker, Tim Richmond and Ron Bouchard to New England for a touring pro stock mini-series, he also contracted Bugs Stevens, Bentley Warren and Evans "because we wanted the local flavor." And he jumped at any opportunity to lure Evans to midweek modified events at the Star Speedway, home base for the Conway-Smith organization.

Without revealing figures, Conway calls his financial arrangements with Evans "a standard thing. We'd say, 'Look, Richie, if you don't do well, we'll make sure we take care of you a little bit.' In other words, even if he got into a jingle, we'd make sure he left with at least 'X' number of dollars."

Conway, whose races were usually well off the beaten path for Evans—particularly Star, tucked up there in Epping, New Hampshire, some 330 highway miles from Rome—came to enjoy the simplicity of their negotiations. He says, "What I appreciated about Richie was the fact that he wouldn't lead you on. Some guys tell you, 'Yeah, I'm pretty sure I'm coming,' and then leave you hanging. With Richie, either he could come or he couldn't come, and that was that.

"Once, we were running the modifieds at Star on a Wednesday

night. He wasn't sure he could come, but he said, 'If I can, I'll let you know in time for you to pump it up.' If you were a promoter, he was always aware of your side of things, and he didn't want to mess you up. He understood his value to a track, yes, but he also understood that if he just showed up out of the blue and you couldn't *promote* him, it did not do either of us any good. We wanted him for one reason—to attract the people who followed Richie Evans—and he knew how that worked."

Even when his answer to a promoter was a flat no—and Linda Holdeman remembers Evans stubbornly refusing to run an Oswego ASA show because he wouldn't be receiving any deal money, as he suspected the visiting Winston Cup stars were—you got it on time. That night, he went someplace else and raced his modified instead. Holdeman was upset about the matter, certainly, but she admits she couldn't fault Richie's honesty.

"He was," she says, "one of the most straightforward, tell-it-like-it-is people I've had the pleasure of dealing with."

Billy Nacewicz says, "For the most part, Richie had a lot of respect for the promoters and the track owners. He had been around long enough that I think he understood what they went through just to put a show on."

There was ample evidence of that. In a radio appearance with Arnold Dean, Evans responded to a caller's ire over ticket prices at one Connecticut track by defending the promoter—or at least giving him the benefit of the doubt—even though he never raced at the facility. "I would say that operating expenses of the speedways have gone up," Richie pointed out. "And we are *constantly* on the promoters for more purse [money], because our parts [costs] have gone up ... Basically, between the purses, probably the insurance, the help, *everything* ... inflation is into every category of every business."

Sometimes he couldn't help thinking like a promoter even when he was competing. Dick O'Brien recalls one such night, when Evans crashed in the closing stages of an Oswego Budweiser 200. "We've got five laps to go, eight laps to go, something like that," O'Brien says. "At Oswego we always used corner men, officials right down beside the track, and Ed Lynch was our guy down in turn two. Richie's car is bent up pretty good—front, back, everything's wrecked, and it's got maybe one wheel on it—and Eddie's out there with the safety crew. They try to haul it off by the front end, and there's all this crashing and banging and cracking in the car. Eddie said the rear end sounded like a bag of marbles. They need another wrecker on the back, that's all there is to it. It's a cradle job. But the problem is, that takes time, and in the Bud 200 the caution laps count. It's clear that if we call over that other wrecker and cradle Richie's car back to the pits, the race is going to end under yellow.

"So Richie says to Eddie Lynch, 'Just drag that sonofabitch off and lay it in the grass over there.' He did *not* want to see that race end under caution. They pulled that car off the track with the frame dragging, and we got the thing finished under green. He knew that made it a better show for the fans."

Linda Holdeman says, "He had an immense dedication to modified racing. His thoughts were, 'How can we make this better? How should we do things different?' He was always calling to say, 'Why are you doing this?' or 'I don't think that will work.' His mind was always thinking about that side of things, and he was on that phone *constantly*. He was always promoting modified racing."

O'Brien says, "Richie was smart. He knew what was good for business. If the tracks made money, they'd pay better, and some of that extra money would end up in his pocket. He understood that progression. I think he realized that if he was going to stay in that division—and he'd made up his mind that he was a modified guy—it was in his best interest to see that the division was healthy."

In fact, O'Brien believes it was this same paternal instinct Evans had developed for the division that led him to sometimes stick young drivers into his backup cars for one or two appearances. In particular, O'Brien cites Mike Stefanik and Tony Jankowiak, neither of whom had made any deep impression on the modified scene before Evans took an interest in them.

Stefanik's turn came in 1980, when he was a modified rookie. He was a fast kid who had won plenty of late model events at Stafford, but even with solid equipment—a current Troyer car fielded by Mert Bell—he'd had a tough first year in the modifieds.

"We managed to win a race at Riverside, but the season didn't go as well as we'd hoped," Stefanik says.

Then, in the days before the season-ending World Series at Thompson Speedway, he got a phone call from Evans. The two had raced together quite a bit that year, particularly at Riverside Park, and something about the kid—just 22 years old then—had caught the old champion's eye. Evans got straight to the point: "Would you be interested in running one of my cars this weekend?"

Stefanik says, "You just can't explain what that meant. I mean, this was *Richie*. He said later that he wanted to pick up my morale, and he did; I was so excited I couldn't sleep. I ended up doing laundry in the middle of the night, just to do *something*."

His Thompson ride, carrying the number 61X, was the straight-axle Pinto designed by Kevin Reap, and it was fast.

"You know, I almost won that race," Stefanik recalls. "I was running second to Ron Bouchard and then Richie passed me, but he got a flat. Now it was back to me and Ronnie, and my car was wicked fast. Then, with eight laps to go, the motor started skipping. I thought I had broken a valve spring, so I shut it off. What really happened was, Richie used to run these small motorcycle batteries, and the electric fan had killed the battery.

Mike Stefanik (right) drove an Evans car at Thompson as a modified rookie in 1980. "You just can't explain what that meant," says Mike. (Steve Kennedy photo/Stefanik collection)

The late Tony Jankowiak was "a kid Rich took a real shine to," says Billy Nacewicz. *(Don Fast photo/courtesy of Speedway Scene)*

"If I had only shut off that fan, I might have won the race, because Ronnie had a flat tire later on. Greg Sacks ended up winning without passing any of us."

In the years since, Stefanik has won six NASCAR modified championships and two Busch North series titles—doubling up, incredibly, in both 1997 and '98—and yet he still counts that Thompson race as "one of the neatest things that ever happened to me."

Stefanik says, "Driving for Richie gave me instant credibility. I still remember standing in the pit sign-in line and having people ask me what I was driving. And I was like, 'Um, the 61.' Just to say those words blew my mind."

Tony Jankowiak knew the feeling. A Buffalo-area kid who had made some noise at Lancaster and Spencer, Jankowiak first showed up on a lot of modified radar screens when he tagged along with Richie's gang on road trips to New England in 1984.

"Tony was a kid Rich just took a real shine to," says Billy Nacewicz. "I'll never forget this one particular race at Stafford. We popped in there with two cars, and we had Tony practicing with one of them. Not a lot of people out that way knew him yet, so everybody was wondering who the heck was in our other car. Well, Tony had one of Richie's suits on, so we were telling people he was Richie's son.

"At one point Tony was in the car, waiting in line to go out and practice. Bugsy Stevens walked up, thinking it was Rich, and sat down on the nerf bar to talk. Tony said he was thinking to himself, 'Man, here comes Bugsy. He's the big kingpin here. What's he want with *me*?'"

Just being associated with Evans helped the careers of both Stefanik and Jankowiak, got more people—fans, sponsors, car owners—looking in their directions. Dick O'Brien says, "You know, Richie did things like that for a reason. Yeah, he liked those guys, but he also did it for the overall good of the division. I'm convinced of that."

And remarkably, given that some of his biggest career headaches involved NASCAR, there seems to be near-unanimous agreement that Evans's approach to the sanctioning body took on that same all-for-one, one-for-all feel as the 1970s turned into the 1980s. Whenever he felt the bosses in Daytona Beach had the division's best interests at heart, he was, in Dick O'Brien's words, "a big, big NASCAR supporter."

And when something didn't feel right to Evans, says Brian Ross, "he'd dial the phone to Florida, and they would take the call."

"Richie was one of the few guys to speak up to NASCAR," says Val LeSieur. "Most of 'em didn't dare to say 'boo.' But he'd always tell 'em what he thought should be done, and they listened to him."

Billy Nacewicz remembers, "He had almost weekly conversations with the people who were important in NASCAR at that time, whether it was [president] Bill France Jr. or [vice presidents] Jim France or Jim Hunter. He had a good rapport with all those guys. They knew he was their champion, year after year after year, and I'm sure they also knew he was a nine-time Most Popular Driver winner, which meant he carried a lot of weight with the fans. And I'm sure they respected what he had done against some of their biggest names at Daytona.

"So there was a very good working relationship there. Like I said, they had regular conversations about whatever was on their minds, or on his mind. Say they had an idea about a rules change; they would call Rich to see what he thought, because they knew he would give them a straight answer. They might not *like* the answer, but they knew it was his honest opinion.

"Rich had his ups and downs with NASCAR, that's for sure. But, you know, any sports star who is around for 20 years is going to have some ups and downs with the governing body. I think Rich knew he needed NASCAR to further his career, and I think NASCAR knew that with him, they had an outstanding personality who was also a champion."

Hunter, who previous to joining NASCAR's executive team had been a sportswriter, a public relations rep for Firestone and Chrysler, and part of the promotional squad at Talladega, was like Evans in one regard: he looked at things from many angles. He was a frequent visitor to the Northeast's tracks in the early '80s, often in Jim France's company, and spent considerable time discussing the state of the modified union with Evans. What impressed him most, Hunter once admitted, was the NASCAR modified champion's passion for the breed.

"Richie was candid, to say the least," Hunter recalled. "But we knew how much he loved modified racing, and that he always had the best interests of the division at heart. He was thinking about the division more than about how some rule would be helping or hurting Richie Evans."

From outlaw man to company man—"a promoters dream"—Evans had come quite a distance. But let's not blow the guy's anti-Establishment reputation altogether.

Richie gets another round of goodies as NASCAR champion. That's STP's Steve Tucker handing Evans a check. Down the line are Winston's T. Wayne Robertson and, at far left, NASCAR's Jim France. (courtesy of Speedway Scene)

Like Dick Waterman said, Richie never lost the thrill of giving those in charge a good tweaking now and again. He held onto the winner's check from his first Daytona victory for so long that the International Speedway Corporation's bookkeepers started pestering him; why, they wondered, hadn't that $18,500 transaction ever taken place? Well, at first it had been just a pride thing with Evans, a big check to show off to friends, but later he loved the idea that it was getting some noses out of joint in Daytona Beach.

One of the great Evans tweaks, back in 1983, involved Jim Hunter, who understood Evans well enough to artfully tweak him right back.

"I saw him at Martinsville," Hunter said, "and for some crazy reason we got talking about Christmas trees. I told him my wife, Ann, had always been after me to get a real, live tree, because we usually didn't have one. Richie told me, 'I'll get you one. Up where we live, there's a million Christmas trees.' I told him, 'Forget it, Richie. I don't want to owe you *anything*.'"

The two men laughed, and that was that. Or so Hunter thought.

"One day toward Christmas, I get home from work and there's this *giant* Christmas tree lying in my garage. My wife said some guy had driven up, asked if this was where Jim Hunter lived, and dropped off the tree.

"There was a little note attached to the trunk of this beautiful Christmas tree. It said, 'Dear Ann Hunter ... Do not be anywhere near this tree when the lights are plugged in. I have soaked it in inflammable liquids, and when Jim plugs it in, he's history.' And it was signed, 'Richie Evans.'

"I sent him a note back saying, 'Sorry to disappoint you. The tree looks beautiful with all the lights on.'"

From Outlaw to Company Man

Smelling the Roses

BY 1984, EVANS HAD BEEN LEADING a racing life—hell, he had led the mother of all racing lives—for better than 20 years, struggling at first to find money and then later to find time, dreaming of the road and then essentially making it his home, longing to be a professional racer and then discovering, probably to no great surprise, that it isn't always heaven when you get what you wish for.

And, always, he seemed to have it handled. Smack in the middle of that span, in 1973, he told Pete Zanardi, "If I couldn't have fun racing, I wouldn't race. Some people let it get to them, and then it becomes a hassle for them. It is no longer a pleasure thing. I don't think racing would be worth it if it became a hassle."

It never did seem to become a genuine hassle for Evans, but toward the end there were signs that he was beginning to pay more attention to a life outside racing, even a life *after* racing. Racing was still that "pleasure thing," to be sure, but he seemed to go to greater lengths than ever to seek out life's other little pleasures, the ones that couldn't be found looking out over an orange hood.

He was well into his 40s, and roses were no longer just colorful decorations in a victory wreath after a big 200-lapper. Roses were something he seemed to want to stop and smell a bit more often.

For one thing, he spent increasing amounts of time with those in his world who didn't happen to hold wrenches.

"In my opinion, Rich started to become a family man late in his life," says Rita Marcello. "He really started getting involved with his youngest two kids. In his first marriage, he didn't have the time to spend with the girls, because his career was taking off. He was go, go, go, and travel, travel, travel.

"But now he would do things like take his son fishing, and he would be really excited about that. And he'd bring Little Rich to the shop, and even to some of the races. Rich was a macho guy, and I think he liked having his son with him. It was different to some extent with Tara, because she was just a little girl, but he paid a lot of attention to her, too. He not only spent time with those two kids, he *made* time for them."

Maybe that was some sort of belated reaction to his own father's passing, just before Christmas in 1978. Ernest Evans had been stricken while riding a snowmobile with friends; it was a hobby his son had gotten him into, and Ernest, reluctant at first, was soon spending hours on the trails around Westernville. ("Rich was the one who got us through my father's funeral," Sandy Jones remembers. "The three of us were sitting there—Rich, my mother and I—and whenever one of us got a little emotional, Rich would whisper, 'Stare at a flower.'")

Man's best friend: Evans relaxes in 1985 with Suzy, a terrier belonging to supermodified owners Skip and Lois Matczak. *(Bones Bourcier collection)*

Richie and Richie Jr. at a high school graduation party for daughter Jodi. *(Jodi Meola collection)*

And Sandy, who by the 1980s had relocated to Pennsylvania, recalls Richie being all smiles every September when much of the clan—some of his own kids, mom Satie, Sandy and her boys, Bob, Ed and Joe— would turn up at Pocono for the Race of Champions. "We were never one of those hugging families," she says, "but it was almost like a grand reunion."

Smelling the roses ...

Late in the 1982 season, interviewer Roger Bear asked Evans if he ever got "weary of the drudgery." Without the slightest hesitation, Richie replied, "Yeah, I'm ready for the snow to come. Then I know this car can't race anymore." It wasn't something you could imagine him admitting in, say, 1968 or 1975.

There remains some debate among those who knew him as to exactly how weary Evans was getting. Wilbur Jones says with absolute certainty, "He was thinking about retirement. I *know* that." On the other hand, Billy Osmun maintains, "He never said anything about quitting around me."

Either way, the fact that he was a lot closer to the end of his career than the beginning had obviously entered Richie's mind. As Dick O'Brien points out, "He knew he might be coming toward the end of the driving deal. Let's face it, he was at the age when you're thinking about things like that."

Yes, the age thing. Evans couldn't have helped but sense it looming in 1982, '83, '84. Jerry Cook and Maynard Troyer, two of the modified heroes whose careers had helped shape his own, had retired. The pair bracketed Evans in age—Troyer less than three years older, Cook less than three years younger—and had simply decided that the desire to

Left to right: a 1980s reunion of coupe-era teammates Joe LaMonica, Wilbur Jones, Richie Evans, Ted Puchyr and Ron LaMandia. *(Ted Puchyr collection)*

compete no longer outweighed the sacrifices they had to make in order to do it.

And it wasn't just desire that faded as a man got older. There hasn't ever been a driver fast enough to outrun Father Time; even the greatest racers, if they keep at it long enough, cross that invisible threshold beyond which they just don't win like they used to. Troyer and Cook were still competitive when they hung up their helmets, but nothing like they'd been in the 1970s. Ed Flemke had captured the Stafford 200 and the Thompson 300 in 1977, when he was 46, but even then it had been a few years since Steady Eddie was a steady winner. It was also in '77 that Bugsy Stevens had his last truly great season, when he was Stafford's dominant driver and Seekonk's track champion at age 43. Of course a fan of any of those guys could rattle off reasons why their favorite was struggling, and in some cases the arguments would be valid. The bottom line, though, was that those men *did* struggle, just like all drivers seemed to, as they rolled past the big four-oh. And Richie Evans —a keen observer, remember, of all that happened in his division—was no doubt well aware of that.

Sure, that threshold was different for every driver, and, sure, Evans had won 38 times in 1983 at age 42, and, sure, every now and then he'd still proclaim, "You gotta be 40 ..."

But he understood that his time at the top was limited. He understood that because he was human.

Richie still carried himself well: active, animated, plenty tough. But he also had all the usual aches and pains of middle age, and then some. Wilbur Jones says, "Sometimes he'd be bent over from the hard work he'd done. His back bothered him a lot, and he'd go to the chiropractor. In fact, I remember that he always used to go to the chiropractor right before he left for Daytona, because then he could lay down for about 24 hours on the ride down there."

Lynn Evans says, "One thing that really bothered Rich was the idea of getting old. No, he never *acted* old, but it was like he was really, really angry about getting older. He wanted to live life, and I think in some respect he thought getting older meant that life was getting away from him. He had finally reached a plateau where it was getting easier for him to do the things he'd wanted to for so long, and yet at the same time he didn't want to get old."

She pauses. "He was going through some changes. I don't think he was any less *driven*, but maybe he was looking at things differently. Toward the end of his life, I remember him saying, 'Lynn, sometimes I wish I could just get away from all this. I'd live in a tent out in the middle of nowhere, with no phones, no nothing.' I couldn't understand that at the time, but now I can. I mean, he had reached that [point] where the phone is ringing 24 hours a day, and everybody wants a piece of you, and you just don't like that part of your life anymore."

Billy Nacewicz says, "He talked about wanting to slow down, to take more time for himself."

Again, it wasn't something you could imagine Richie Evans admitting in, say, 1968 or 1975.

By 1984 or so, Nacewicz recalls, "Rich did get to a point where he was taking things a little easier. He started spending less time at the shop; he'd basically come in when he felt like he *had* to be there. He was still there every day, don't get me wrong, but you were never sure exactly when he'd show up. But most days he'd still be there until pretty late at night."

Cutting down on his shop hours, Evans told Ron Hedger, was a therapeutic move: "I still like racing, but I feel like I have to pick a part of it to get away from a bit."

There it was, a public version of the same things he had been saying privately, to Lynn and to Nacewicz and to others. And if you stared at his words long enough—the bit about picking "a part of it to get away from"—they seemed to hint that Evans saw this as a warm-up for the day when he would "get away" even further. By, say, climbing out of the cockpit, maybe a little at a time.

That was something he and Nacewicz talked about occasionally, on late-night hauls back to Rome or in the after-dinner hours at the shop. There was no doubt, Nacewicz says, that Evans wanted to hang around the sport as a team owner once his driving days were done. But just how that transition was going to take place was something they never quite resolved.

"We did kick around a few ideas," Billy says. "The way I think we'd have gone is, we'd have probably brought on another driver and entered him in whatever races Rich wanted him to run. That would have been a good way to break him into our team. Or maybe we'd have given him a car to run at, say, Spencer Speedway every Friday night, while we went off and did our usual deal. In other words, Rich would have said, 'You go and do *this*, and I'll go someplace else and do *that*.' Don't forget, he

What might have been: Evans and George Kent talked about teaming up as owner and driver. *(Val LeSieur photo/courtesy of Speedway Scene)*

had done that with Eddie Flemke [in the outlaw days], running two cars at two different places. Then I think Richie would have eventually backed off on chasing the championship and started hitting just the big-money shows, and worked the *other* guy into doing more and more races.

"He talked about a few different drivers. We talked about Tony Jankowiak, of course. And we talked about George Kent quite a bit, because we both thought he'd have been a good fit with our team."

Indeed, Evans often admitted to being a fan of Kent's. He told Hedger, "Of anybody I've raced against, if I were not driving but running a car myself, I'd specifically go after George as my driver. And that's no bull."

No bull at all, according to George Kent himself. "A lot of people don't know it, but we had sort of already made that deal," Kent says. "Richie told me he wanted to cut back on his driving, and he asked me if I'd be interested in driving for him. I was 10 years younger than him, and I think we both figured we'd make a great team."

They never did get around to discussing timetables or scenarios: when it would all happen, who would race where, that sort of thing. "Richie had his superstitions," Kent says. "It's like he didn't want to talk about it *too* much. He just asked me if I'd drive, and I told him I would, and we let it go at that.

"I guess we both figured we'd talk about it later."

Later. That's when Richie Evans was going to decide, once and for all, what he would do with his racing, and with everything else, too.

This much was certain: he planned on keeping the old shop humming for quite some time. He'd continue racing, even if only as an owner. Maybe he'd expand the chassis-building side of things, although he had no aspirations of keeping pace with his busy pal Troyer. "I'd overlook the operation," Richie told Ron Hedger, "but I'd leave Billy pretty much in charge. I've dedicated enough years to race cars and race tracks that I don't want to be totally involved like Maynard."

And maybe he'd dive deeper into the world of used street cars, an activity which began to occupy his spare time as the 1980s passed. Dick O'Brien used to attend the Wednesday-night auto auctions in Cicero, just north of Syracuse, and he recalls occasionally running into Evans there. "Richie would come up and buy a few old rats for Bondo and the boys to patch up and crank out for beer money," O'Brien chuckles.

By that point, Bill "Bondo" Clark was a Calvert Street full-timer. He says, "I had been doing so much of Richie's stuff that one day he said, 'You'd be better off just coming to work here. We'll set you up right in that corner over there, and you can keep all my stuff painted.' I'd go to the races, drive the spare truck, whatever he needed. And, yeah, we did the used cars.

"We'd go and buy six or eight cars at the auction. I was real clever with the bodywork and making 'em look good, and of course he was a genius mechanic. That man could actually diagnose an internal engine problem by placing a piece of broom handle or a socket extension up against the motor, then putting his ear to it and listening to the thing run. I watched him do it. You'd think the problem was terminal, and he'd discover it was just some small thing he could fix. Anyway, we'd get those cars ready through the course of the winter. Then, come spring, he'd let it be known that they were for sale, and they'd all be gone that same week. A lot of those cars were bought by people he'd done work for back in his gas station days, people who just trusted him."

Evans told Hedger, "I'm not going to work too hard when I quit [racing]. I'm going to say that I need 'X' dollars this week, and I'm going to earn what it takes. I've actually done pretty well, though a lot of people probably think I squander a little money now and then."

His friend Donny Marcello confirms that. "Rich watched his money," Marcello says. "He saw to it that things were taken care of. He had things figured out."

Smelling the roses …

Kent, or somebody, would drive the race cars. Nacewicz would crank out modifieds for customers. Clark would take care of the previously-owned vehicle department. And Richie Evans would oversee the whole shebang.

OK, fine; that's a pretty busy schedule. But, remember, Evans was a work-hard, play-hard guy. If all that activity on Calvert Street was going to satisfy the first half of that equation, what was going to fulfill the second? What in the world would Richie Evans do for fun if he couldn't hang out in the Islip Speedway parking lot or the Thompson Clubhouse or Josie's Outpost Lounge, drinking beer with the folks he'd just beaten in the feature?

Richie's orange '34 Ford Victoria. (Don Bok photo/Lynn Evans collection)

"We were a lot alike," says Maynard Troyer, here at the Freeman Hotel. (Linda Holdeman collection)

Well, at least two things his friends can think of: he'd play with his hot rods, and the Freeman Hotel up in Osceola.

It was Maynard Troyer who helped hook Evans on street rods. Richie got his hands on an orange '34 Ford; Troyer had a red one. "Richie and Maynard had always been close, but I think they were getting closer," Wilbur Jones muses. "They both had their hot rods and their toys, and they were starting to enjoy other things in life besides race cars. Branching out, I guess you'd say."

Troyer says, "We were a lot alike. I mean, I didn't party like Richie did, but I partied *some*. And we were alike in other ways: I had a street rod, he had a street rod. I had a snowmobile, he had a snowmobile. And neither one of us had anything *stock*; it was all tricked-out. Hell, if I couldn't beat him on the race track, I'd want to whip his ass on a snowmobile, and vice-versa. We just had at it, no matter what we were driving or riding, and that never changed."

And the Freeman, "a good half-hour drive from the shop," Nacewicz says, was proving to be both a perfect getaway and a great source of quiet labor for Evans. Maybe it represented that "tent out in the middle of nowhere, with no phones, no nothing," that he had spoken to Lynn about. He and Billy Osmun and a handful of cohorts—Max Baker and Fred Ulrich among them—whipped into shape its 13 guestrooms, its bar, and its bathrooms.

"Billy Nacewicz's father helped us clean up a bunch of the rooms and get them ready," Osmun says. "Before long, we got it to the point where we could at least stay in the place ourselves. It was still pretty crude, but through the years we just kept chipping away at it."

Almost immediately, it was suitable for partying, and some of the goings-on during the Evans-Osmun tenure at the Freeman Hotel live on in the chronicles of racing-related debauchery.

"This one time, we were going to have a pig roast," Nacewicz remembers. "Well, Richie said, 'We've got to do something to perk this party up. Let's attach some money to the end of a long pole, and then we'll sink one end of the pole into the ground, and we'll grease it. And whoever climbs the pole to the top first gets to keep the money.'

"So, in the middle of the week, up to the hotel we went. We planted this pole into the ground—it had to be about 30 feet high—and wired it so it wouldn't break. Richie ended up talking Maynard into matching him dollar for dollar; I think they each stuck $200 onto that thing. And when everybody showed up for the pig roast, we had a ball watching people try to climb that thing."

They tried it solo. They tried it in tandem, getting piggyback boosts. They tried it in teams, forming pyramids. They tried using all kinds of inventive strategies. Nacewicz laughs, "Some pretty well-known females from the modified circuit figured they could get a better grip on that pole by taking off some of their clothes, and that was OK with us. And, you know, nobody ever did get that money, but they sure did come down greasy."

It was some party, all right. "People were riding four-wheelers," says Joe Gosek. "Guys were rolling 'em over, crashing, going to the hospital. Oh, they had all kinds of shit going on."

Bob Polverari remembers another Freeman Hotel bash getting a little out of hand. "We were blowing off quite a few salutes," Polverari grins. "You know, fireworks. We had M-80s, we had everything. Anyway, a police cruiser showed up. The policeman said he'd appreciate it if we'd stop doing that, and of course Richie was giving him a hard time, but in a fun way. In fact, he blew off a couple of salutes right in front of the cop, just kinda daring him. Well, the cop came over to talk to me, seeing if maybe I could calm Richie down and get things quiet. Meanwhile, Richie jumps in the cruiser and starts rolling down the road.

"The cop pulls out his gun, and he's got it pointed straight at Richie. He says, 'You've got to *stop*, or I'm gonna shoot you.' The cop wasn't serious, of course. He obviously knew Richie—or at least knew *about* him —and there was no way he was going to actually shoot him. But this was one time when Richie carried things a little further than I would have, for sure."

Lifelong pals Max Baker and Richie Evans in 1985. *(Sandy Jones collection)*

(bottom left) Here's trouble brewing. The famously persuasive Evans is clearly goading shirtless columnist Dick Macco into doing something zany as supermodified shoe Joe Gosek listens in. *(Linda Holdeman collection)*

(bottom right) Lookout below! Lynn Evans makes an unsuccessful run at the $400 "pole climb" at a Freeman Hotel pig roast. *(Linda Holdeman collection)*

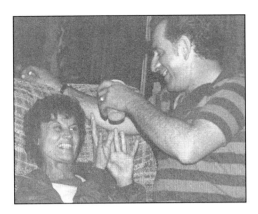

(left) Linda Holdeman gets threatened with a beer shampoo. *(Linda Holdeman collection)*

(right) The Freeman at party time. *(Linda Holdeman collection)*

Partner and friend Billy Osmun at the wheel of the Evans ambulance. *(Val LeSieur photo/ courtesy of* Speedway Scene*)*

Billy Nacewicz says, "That hotel was really a great outlet for Rich. Yeah, we partied up there quite a bit, but I think it also helped him relax. He could go up there and hang out, do some snowmobiling if it was winter, or just get away from the telephone.

"I've said that racing was Gene DeWitt's golf game. Well, that hotel was Rich's golf game."

And Osmun, Evans's partner in the whole affair, says, "I think we both liked it a lot. We had some good years there, some good times together. Just not *enough* time."

There were a few other things Richie was thinking about doing in those final years, things that seemed like fun. He would mention them every now and again, bouncing one idea off this friend and another off that one, just sort of thinking out loud.

Joe Jones: "He wanted to get into the [street car] tire business. He and I had talked, and we were getting older. I told him, 'Rich, you're making some pretty damn good money. You'd better not be spending it all. You'd better be putting a little aside.' Well, he got talking about this tire thing. He knew a guy [through] the racing circuit who was selling tires wholesale, big time, like hundreds of tires every day. Richie was wanting to maybe lean into that, and we discussed it."

Tiger Pettinelli: "Richie told me a few times that when he retired, he had ideas about doing something again with a farm. He said, 'You know, I'd like to have a little farm, maybe have a few beef cows.' I think he'd had enough of milk cows from growing up on the dairy farm, but he did talk about having a few beefers."

Bill Hatch: "He mentioned to me a couple times that he had this dream of building one more coupe. You know, an old coupe-style body, but with all the new stuff that the modifieds were running then. He wanted to take that coupe and outrun all the modern cars. Wouldn't that have been something?"

But the lodge, the Freeman Hotel, that was going to be the big thing. That was going to be the sweet spot, the reward for all those hours and all those laps and all that work. He'd run up there with his hot rod, and just hang out, and smell those roses.

Wilbur Jones says, "Rich always told me, 'Man, I can't wait. Someday we're gonna sit on that front porch in rocking chairs, and laugh about everything we've done.'"

1984: Some Excitement with Jimmy

IT'S HARD TO SAY EXACTLY WHEN the relationship between Richie Evans and Jimmy Spencer began to deteriorate. When Jimmy, the son of Pennsylvania dirt-track tough guy Ed Spencer, started popping up at NASCAR modified events in the early '80s, he and Evans initially appeared friendly enough. Richie sold him a car at one point, and grinned as he spoke of this fast young kid who was finding his feet at Shangri-La.

But, make no mistake, the relationship *did* deteriorate. By mid-1983 or so, Evans seemed to have run out of nice things to say about Spencer. And by the summer of '84, when it was clear that the chase for that year's NASCAR modified championship had come down to Richie and Jimmy, neither of them was acting especially cordial toward the other.

Why all the animus? Well, the answer kind of depended on whom you asked.

Spencer himself told writer Herb Dodge, "Richie doesn't want the stiff competition I'm giving him." But that hardly seemed like a complete examination of the situation. Did Jimmy really think he was any tougher in 1984 than Dutch Hoag and Maynard Troyer had been when Evans first ran up against them at Fulton? Did Spencer really believe he was putting up a stiffer fight than Charlie Jarzombek and Freddy Harbach had given Evans at Islip in the 1970s? Did Jimmy really see his challenge as being harder than the ones Evans faced from Bugs Stevens and Ron Bouchard in Stafford's heyday? After all, nobody could recall Evans having any kind of lasting disagreement—never mind any ill will—toward those guys.

Did Spencer see himself as being a stiffer points chaser than George Kent had been in 1982-83? Or—wait just a minute here—than *Jerry Cook* had been for all those years?

Was that correct? Had Richie Evans—having faced Eddie Flemke, Ray Hendrick, Gil Hearne, Jim Hendrickson, Paul Radford, Fred DeSarro, Merv and Roger Treichler, giants from *everywhere*—suddenly grown testy at the idea of a little competition?

With all due respect to Jimmy Spencer, there are a couple of other plausible explanations.

In 1982, Evans borrowed Jimmy Spencer's car for a Thompson Speedway match race. By mid-'84, things were less cordial. *(Steve Kennedy photo/ courtesy of* Speedway Scene*)*

The first was Spencer's driving style. From the time he began showing up at most of the bigger NASCAR events, he had always been more than a little bit ... well, *enthusiastic*. For all his obvious natural speed, he was frequently bumping into things: other cars, fences, you name it. More than one modified veteran suggested back then that once Spencer lost some of that youthful aggression, he was really going to be something. But that process was taking some time.

"Jimmy always went for the win, and sometimes it got him in trouble," George Kent remembers. "He just didn't understand that sometimes you're only going to finish third or fourth."

Early on, all that was something to grin about. Stafford announcer Ben Dodge dubbed Spencer "Mr. Excitement" after one particularly hairy Spring Sizzler performance, and the nickname stuck. But within the next few seasons, there were those who felt that Spencer's act needed updating, that he was too rough and too crude; after four or five years at the modified level, they pointed out, he should have developed better manners.

"Some of the stuff he did was a little over the line," Kent says. "It wasn't *my* idea of racing, OK?"

And then there was this: too often, confrontations with Spencer on the track resulted in confrontations with Spencer—and sometimes lots of Spencers—*off* the track. Jimmy's modified career was dotted with stories of, shall we say, loud discussions between his family-based team and whatever team he'd happened to clash with.

Richie Evans didn't look favorably upon rough driving, and he certainly seemed to have no tolerance at all for pit-area brawls. Think about this: For all his feuding with Cook, and for all the fierce battles he'd fought with Geoff Bodine, there is no recorded evidence of Evans having ever lifted a hand toward either man, nor they toward him. One of Richie's professors, the diminutive Eddie Flemke, used to say that he'd

All of 1984's drama centered around these two men, Evans and Jimmy Spencer. *(courtesy of Speedway Scene)*

fight any man alive as long as they both had steering wheels in their hands; in other words, all disputes were settled on the race track. Evans left behind no lasting philosophies on the matter, but he seemed to adhere to that same code.

Was Evans worried about Spencer and his stiff competition? Maybe. Or was he just tired of Spencer's rough-and-tumble shtick? Again, maybe. Either way, here they were in the heat of 1984, Richie trying to hold onto a crown that he had grown rather fond of wearing, and Jimmy trying to take it away.

That '84 points chase was the last run under the system that had forged champions like Stevens, DeSarro, Cook and, yes, Evans, with every NASCAR-sanctioned race counting—to varying degrees—toward the title fight. Oh, a couple of things had been fancied up as NASCAR looked to update its oldest division; just as in '83, the races which paid the most points, the old "national championship" or "NC" shows, were now termed "Circle of Champions" events. But the idea was the same: hit all those big races, certainly, but then fill the holes in your calendar with every NASCAR-sanctioned modified show you could get to.

Early in the season Kent made some noise, and so did Reggie Ruggiero, and so did Connecticut nice guy Corky Cookman. But at the top of the heap stood Spencer—who came out of the box with two Circle of Champions wins in 24 hours, the Riverside Park opener and the Spring Sizzler—and Evans, who was in it for the long haul.

It was, for much of the season, a good old-fashioned points chase, the two protagonists shadowing each other to all the usual modified citadels: Martinsville, Thompson, Spencer Speedway, Islip and Riverhead, New Egypt, Shangri-La …

Then came a couple of conflicts centered around the Oswego Speedway, still an "outlaw" track, still a good payday for modified racers four or five times a season. Evans loved Oswego because it was home, as we have already seen, but he also loved the idea that it almost always paid better than whatever alternatives existed on those same race dates, regardless of sanctioning body. If his NASCAR schedule was blank on a date when Oswego was hosting modifieds, the decision to head to Harry Caruso's track was a no-brainer. Even when there *was* a conflict, he often tried to negotiate his way around it.

To Evans, running Oswego was a matter of dollars and sense.

"For a long time, Richie missed more of our races than he made, simply because of the points thing," says Dick O'Brien, who counts 14 Oswego events Evans was forced to pass up. "And when I'd see him later, I'd always kid him and say, 'Hey, too bad you missed our show. It was easy pickings for somebody else.' See, we always paid the mods good money, same as the supers; if we had a doubleheader that paid the supermodified winner $2000 or $5000, whatever it was, that's what we paid the mod winner, too."

As O'Brien recalls it, those payoffs often proved too tempting for Evans to resist, even if that meant missing the occasional NASCAR race. "He started calling our purses 'instant point money.' He knew he had to run all year long to see that NASCAR money, but if he went to Oswego he got the money that night. So he'd say, 'Well, I can run for two grand at Oswego or a grand at this NASCAR show; that's $1000 in instant point money!' And as time went on, he was a real cornerstone-type guy for us. He not only ran our races, he'd go out of his way to get the other [points-chasing] guys to skip a [NASCAR] race so they could come up and run for some good money."

Evans's theory was that in a typical two-man slog toward the championship, neither contender suffered if both skipped a NASCAR event and chased the Oswego dollars instead. There were exceptions to that rule, of course; if a fellow was trailing by some huge number of points and he desperately wanted that title, it was in his best interest to run every NASCAR event he could get to, regardless of what Oswego was doing. But if the fight was a close one, why not call a temporary cease-fire and run Oswego?

That was how Evans played it with John Blewett, with George Kent, and even, amazingly enough, with Jerry Cook. Yes, the two Romans eventually got over their 1970s shell games—guess which car, at which track, is the real one, and which is the backup?—and often appeared together at Oswego's modified events. Cook may have loved piling up those NASCAR points, but he was also as smart with a buck as any racer who ever strapped into a short-track car. Again: dollars and sense.

But in 1984, Spencer wasn't having any of that. He pointed out that the tracks whose events normally went up against Oswego's—Islip, Riverhead, New Egypt, Riverside Park—were bullrings where he excelled, and where he had sometimes gotten the better of Evans in 1983 and '84. Perhaps, Spencer hinted, Richie's sermons about dodging the small tracks and their small purses were masking something deeper:

"Knowing he didn't want to go there," Spencer told writer Herb Dodge, "gave me a psychological edge."

That sort of talk does not sit well with Billy Nacewicz, who declares, "Richie was an excellent bullring driver. I mean, we won six All Star 300s *in a row* at Islip! I think that might have been the most incredible feat of Richie's career, even bigger than winning nine championships or winning Daytona twice. I mean, [all those] laps around Islip Speedway without him running into somebody or somebody running into him.

"Richie wasn't afraid to go wherever we needed to go to run for the points. In fact, that always worked in our favor. See, everybody wants to go out and chase the championship, but when they get out there, they find that it's a lot harder than they thought. You're running up and down the road, coming home just long enough to get prepared, and then you're gone again. We'd get home Monday morning, and by Wednesday or Thursday we had to be back on the road. But, you know, we were used to that. So our attitude was, 'Hey, if somebody wants to chase us, we'll drag 'em around the country with us.'

"But there were also times when that didn't make sense. If there was a big-money show at Oswego and the only thing running against it was a regular show at Islip or Riverside Park, Rich would say, 'Hey, let's use our heads here. Do we really need to pass up that race to go and run a 30-lapper somewhere?'"

On Memorial Day weekend in 1984, Evans and Spencer did just that, skipping the Port City 150 in favor of a NASCAR event at New Egypt. Adding insult to Richie's injury was the fact that the Oswego race happened to be sponsored by B.R. DeWitt. "I told Gene I'd go to his race," Evans told writer Ken Tesoriere. "I said, 'Just say the word, Gene, and I'll be there.' But he said it was up to me, knowing the points are critical …"

That July, another Oswego modified race came and went without Evans and Spencer, who instead spent their evening finishing fifth and ninth, respectively, at Riverside Park.

Had they been chummier, Richie might have pulled Jimmy aside and told him the classic Bugs Stevens story he always loved. As Evans recalled it, he and Stevens were walking away from an early-'70s pit meeting at Albany-Saratoga, about to share the front row for the start of a long-distance modified show. Bugsy was a three-time NASCAR champion by then, and a celebrated veteran; Richie had only recently begun to peak. Curious about what sort of pace Stevens planned to run, Evans came right out and asked him.

"Bugsy didn't say anything for a minute," Evans remembered. "Finally he said, 'Kid, it's like the story about the two bulls on the hill.' I asked him what he meant. Bugsy said, 'There's these two bulls standing at the top of a hill, looking down on a field full of cows. It's one old bull, and one young bull. The young bull says, 'Hey, I think I'm gonna run down this hill and fuck one of those cows.' And the old bull just sort of nods his head and says, 'You go right ahead. I'll *walk* down this hill and fuck 'em all.'"

The old bull, Bugs Stevens was preaching, sees the big picture.

Sure, Spencer and Evans could have had that kind of talk. Jimmy was 16 years younger than Richie, but then Richie had been nine years younger than Bugs Stevens. A young bull can learn a lot from an old bull if he's willing to listen. But across that season, Evans just stood there and watched, frustrated, as Jimmy Spencer, 1984's young bull, insisted on running down his own personal hill.

"I got annoyed at the way things went," Evans admitted to Herb Dodge. "[Jimmy] ran me around. We missed some good-paying shows."

The funny thing was, as all this happened Evans only extended his NASCAR points lead. And while Spencer did indeed capture Circle of Champions events at Riverhead, New Egypt and Holland, Evans was hardly slumping on those bullrings he was supposed to be so worried about; he won a Circle show at New Egypt himself, and was runner-up in all three of those Spencer victories.

Dick O'Brien says, "You've got to give Spencer credit. It was a real knock-down, drag-out deal. Not too many guys lasted too far into the season against Richie in those years, and yet Jimmy was right there with him."

But, as the NASCAR record book later noted, "Evans pulled away in the last third of the year." He did it, you might say, by walking down that hill.

The pot was at full boil by the first of September, just in time for two classic modified races that became two classic tales in the Evans-Spencer saga.

The first was the Labor Day weekend running of the Budweiser 200 at Oswego. Both Evans and Spencer had indicated they'd be there—outlaw status or not, it was one of the richest modified shows anywhere—and both figured prominently in the track's advertising. But ...

"The closer we got to that weekend," O'Brien remembers, "the more we started to hear that Spencer was going elsewhere—Islip, I guess—and if he went there, Richie would have to go, too. Naturally, we wanted them both at Oswego. I was getting a little worried, so I asked Richie about it. He said, point-blank, 'I'll be there if Jimmy's there.'"

In the days leading up to the race, O'Brien hustled to dot every "i" and cross every "t." He arranged a three-way conference call between himself and the two drivers. Evans, O'Brien recalled, went quickly into his usual pro-Oswego rap: "Richie kept saying that it made more sense for them to be at the Bud 200 than to be at some little obscure race that just happened to pay NASCAR points." But Spencer wasn't quick to bite, and O'Brien remembers the conversation taking on a combative tone: "Oh, yeah, they went at it a little bit. I guess both of them had to air out some laundry."

In the end, Spencer and Evans reached an accord. Each swore that come the Saturday of Labor Day weekend, he'd be at Oswego. Still, some doubt lingered.

"Toward the end of the call," O'Brien says, "Richie said to Jimmy, 'I'll meet you for breakfast at 10 o'clock that morning, right across the street from the track. That way, we'll each know the other guy is there.' Jimmy said he couldn't be there that early, but that he'd show up at Oswego for sure. 'I'll be there,' he said."

The night before the Bud 200, both men struggled in a Spencer Speedway 100-lapper. Evans finished 10th, Spencer fell out.

"On Saturday morning," O'Brien grins, "Richie is in the pits bright and early. He's looking around. No Spencer. Time goes by, and still … no Spencer. Every time that pit gate swung open, Richie had his eye on it. Finally, in comes Jimmy, with two cars, and everybody breathes this sigh of relief. Now we can race."

Billy Nacewicz, also grinning, says, "That was nerve-wracking all the way to the last minute. I don't think we knew for sure that Jimmy was going to show up until we saw his truck pull into the infield."

Looking back, Spencer probably should have gone to Islip. He finished 17th in the Budweiser 200. It was won by a chap named Evans, who hauled something over $17,000 back to Rome later that night. You have to wonder what this whole experience did to Jimmy's spirit of détente.

One week later, the two men showed up at Thompson for the 1984 Winston 300. It stands as the one event which best defines their rivalry.

Evans, who had earned the 300 pole by winning a qualifying race held earlier in the season, was a Thompson no-show on Saturday; his schedule that day called instead for a leisurely drive from Rome to Shangri-La, which had a 200-lap Circle of Champions show scheduled for Saturday night. Spencer timed 16th at Thompson and then caught a private plane to Shangri-La, some 230 miles to the west. Evans won the Shangri-La race, while Spencer—who later groused to Herb Dodge, "I passed Richie three times"—got wrapped up in a couple of tangles and finished 12th.

At Thompson on Sunday, Jimmy Spencer had on his war paint. His NASCAR championship bid was all but over. He had finished behind Evans in the four most recent Circle of Champions events. The Winston 300 wasn't part of the Circle program, but it had a fine purse and a great history; in nine previous runnings, its winners had been Geoff Bodine, Eddie Flemke, Ron Bouchard, Ray Miller, Greg Sacks and Evans. It was a nice opportunity for Spencer to rescue a drowning season.

The first half of the Winston 300 showcased Evans (who led laps 1-44), Reggie Ruggiero (45-82), Brett Bodine (83-93), Mike McLaughlin (94-132) and then Evans again. Lurking just outside the lead, meanwhile, were Kent, Jarzombek and Spencer. But in the tire-mad 1980s, when one guy might be sprinting on gumball rubber and the next fellow biding his time on a harder compound, the Thompson 300 was a hard race to read. You had to sort of sit back, and watch things unfold.

And unfold they did. Kent crashed. Brett Bodine had an oiling problem. Jarzombek crashed. Ken Bouchard, always fast at Thompson, got lapped early after suffering three flat tires, then made up his lap and actually took the lead at the two-thirds mark, only to blow another tire almost immediately. McLaughlin, quick all day, slipped and slid toward the end, out of rubber. Evans, leading, pitted under caution at lap 219 for a new right-rear tire. Several teams had experienced problems with left-rears during the day—chiefly Kenny Bouchard's—so Evans and Billy Nacewicz played it safe with the one they had. They measured the car's rear stagger on the stop, adjusted the air in the hot left-rear, and hustled the orange Cavalier back into the fray.

Up front, Spencer and Ruggiero—both of whom had pitted earlier and were set for the duration—waged a spectacular duel. (It was, really, a forecast of the great fights they had in the post-Evans era.) Meanwhile, Evans charged up to 10th … seventh … fifth … fourth at lap 260 … past a loose McLaughlin for third on lap 270.

On lap 282, Ruggiero coasted to the pits, his car's rear-end gears chewed up. That left Evans second, but still a good ways back. His only shot at the win was a caution, which he got when Mike Stefanik spun on lap 284. That put the season's two best drivers, and every little drama that had carried them to that point in the year, in a straight fight for the checkers. What followed was some of the most riveting modified action ever seen at Thompson, or anyplace else. Herb Dodge wrote that Evans "tried to go under Jimmy, and Spencer cut him off. Richie went to the outside, and Jimmy came up high. The two cars hit in turn three, and a great puff of white tire smoke ensued." He quoted Spencer as saying, "[Evans] hit me so hard going into three, I knew he wasn't going to be a gentleman today."

All this, mind you, was on the very first lap after the restart. From there, it got *really* interesting. Every assault by Evans, and there were many, was rebuked by a Spencer slide, a Spencer chop. And Evans was no choirboy himself; few in attendance could remember him ever using his front bumper so freely. Richie explained away his aggression by telling Dodge, "[Spencer] sure can wind you up."

It wasn't pretty, but it was thrilling.

"Let's just say that I thought we were getting blocked more than our share," Billy Nacewicz says. "It actually got to the point where I mentioned to Rich on the radio that maybe he ought to do something about it. Richie said, 'Well, we can take second place and $7000, or I'll end up on my roof and we'll take a wrecked car home.' He could see that there was no way he was going to get by.

"Of course, he could have just *dumped* him. We had fresher tires, so we were faster. But that wasn't Richie; he wasn't going to just knock him out of the way. Even though he was getting driven all over the track, he wanted to pass clean."

Champions all: Nacewicz, Hartung, Evans and Spognardi, 1984. *(Marc Rohrbacher photo/courtesy of Speedway Scene)*

It didn't happen. Spencer's blue #24 crossed the line ahead of the orange #61.

As Jimmy and his family whooped it up in victory lane, Evans seemed more disappointed than angry. It was hard to tell if he was disheartened by the loss, or by the tone the race had taken on. He told Herb Dodge that Spencer "was all over the race track," and added, "If I raced like him, neither of us would have finished today."

Spencer's response? "Richie is a sore loser. He's been on top so long, he doesn't know how to take second." He defended his blocking by pointing out that he'd been on older rubber, and that he had altered his rhythm to maintain control.

"I won on worn-out tires," Jimmy crowed to Dodge. "I don't know of anybody else who could have won this race driving my race car."

Well, not even Evans ever suggested that Spencer lacked talent, only that he sometimes lacked good judgement. Speaking to Dodge, Richie conceded that Jimmy was "a good driver when he's not in his cuckoo head."

By year's end, Evans and Spencer had each won five of the 30 Circle of Champions events. But it was in the weekly events, the grinding heart of the schedule, that Richie locked up the 1984 NASCAR modified championship. In 66 NASCAR starts that season, he won 14 times, with

49 total top fives and 58 top-10 finishes. Jimmy, meanwhile, took a very respectable 11 victories, but scored 10 fewer top fives than his rival, and five fewer top-10 results.

That 1984 crown was Richie's eighth, a NASCAR record. At that point, only Richard Petty, with seven Grand National/Winston Cup titles, was close. Pressed on that statistic by the NASCAR public relations department, Evans was humble. "I like records," he said, "but it's hard to compare Richard's record with mine. They are totally different types of racing." But he got a kick out of the idea that Petty's earliest championships had come while running hectic schedules of 60 races and more, many on short tracks where Evans himself had won: Martinsville, Hickory and Bowman Gray in the South, plus Albany-Saratoga, Thompson, Islip and Oxford. "That's something I like," he said.

But didn't he take any special pride in being the only man in NASCAR history to win more than seven championships?

"I'm pleased with it," he admitted to the *Rome Daily Sentinel*. "Nobody else has done it. Nobody else is foolish enough to work that hard, I guess."

 # "Milk and Cookie Racers"

IN THE 1984 Bud 200 at Oswego, Evans won only by turning back a relentless challenge from Jeff Fuller. Fuller had been winning races in New England for several years, and in his first couple modified seasons he had picked up a reputation for being a little bit wild. By the early '80s, though, he had been transformed. He got better rides, and his driving smoothed out, and ran regularly near the front of the pack. Fuller's maturation, really, was not unlike the change Richie Evans had gone through between 1969-71.

In that Bud 200 in '84, Fuller—27 years old by then—was terrific. Evans's car had never turned a lap prior to that night, and though fast, it was not as consistent as he'd have liked. Fuller's car, meanwhile, seemed to get better as the night rolled along. He tracked down Evans, the leader, and by lap 185 they were nose to tail, with Fuller, visibly faster, ready to pounce.

Across the next 15 laps, they threw a show as fair and as good as anything seen that year. Fuller made serious stabs high and low, and on a couple of occasions, with both cars pointed straight, he tagged Evans's rear bumper. Had Fuller been able to nose ahead, he'd have finished in the next county; he was that fast. But Evans never missed a beat, and Fuller got nothing more than a sniff of the lead. Jeff Fuller went home to Massachusetts thinking about what might have been, and Richie Evans went back to Rome with another Oswego Speedway trophy.

On a day that wore out all the "milk and cookie racers," Evans bagged the hot, humid 1985 Thompson 300. *(Rich Oakley photo/courtesy of* Speedway Scene*)*

"Rich loved it whenever something like that happened," Lynn Evans says. "He loved the idea that he could not only still compete with those young guys, but *beat* them."

Age, as we have already examined, was sometimes a prickly issue with Evans. A *Speedway Scene* columnist once wrote about the "old man," Evans, still showing the way to all the hot kids. It was a favorable piece, and Evans had no quarrel with the column itself. He did, however, complain pointedly about the word "old."

And he did seem, uh, less than overjoyed with a playful barb thrown his way by Bugs Stevens in a podium interview after the '85 Fall Final at Stafford. Brian Ross won the 100-lapper, and Evans had charged past Stevens late in the show to grab second, and now the three of them were being interviewed by announcer Ben Dodge. Stevens told Dodge, "The right-rear tire must have let go, and I was just hanging on."

Ever the needler, Bugsy glanced toward Evans and continued, "And then I watched ol' Grandpa Richie come by …."

Evans looked happy with his run. He also looked like he wished his longtime buddy and frequent party mate had chosen his words a little bit differently.

On the other hand, there were times when Richie would turn things completely around and play the age card in his favor. When he pipped Ross in a tight Oswego 75-lapper in 1983 and Brian complained on the public address system that his neck had given out, Evans, 42, leaned in and playfully kidded Ross, 33, about getting old.

And in 1985, after a Thompson 300 run in hot and devilishly humid conditions, winner Evans was first astonished and then amused to see the next three finishers—runner-up Doug Hewitt, third-place John Rosati and fourth-place Mike Stefanik—lolling around in various stages of distress, being attended by medical personnel.

"Those guys were laying up against their cars, tongues hanging out, firesuits unzipped, getting oxygen," Billy Nacewicz says. "And Rich, even at his age, looked like he could have run another 300 laps."

Ron Hutter grins, "Richie got out of the car that day and he was just bouncing around, happy, but they had to *drag* all those younger guys out of their cars."

As he was being driven by golf cart to the press tent for interviews following the victory lane ceremonies, Evans glanced over at the gasping trio and declared with a mean chuckle: "Look at 'em. Milk and cookie racers."

"I remember that," Nacewicz says. "And when he came back from his interviews, he said, 'Gimme a beer.' We partied half the night. The rest of 'em probably went straight home, took a cold bath, and went to bed.

"We laughed about that all week. 'Milk and cookie racers.'"

PART SIX
Just Passin' Through...

David Allio photo

Nine-Time Champion

IN HIS POINTS-CHASING DAYS, Richie Evans had met and turned back serious challenges from Jimmy Spencer, John Blewett Jr., George Kent, Bugsy Stevens, and, of course, Jerry Cook. Stevens and Cook were already hardcore road warriors before Evans took them on; it is probably safe to say that Evans made Kent, Blewett and Spencer into the road warriors they became. Following that man around could teach a fellow a thing or two about chasing points. Even when the points systems changed—from the everything-counts era to the national/regional twin championships, then to the "touring" concept designed largely by Cook and introduced in 1985—Evans was the guy giving the lessons.

In '85, it was Mike McLaughlin's turn to learn. McLaughlin was driving for the great Len Boehler, who had won three NASCAR modified titles with Stevens—and who would later win three more, with Wayne Anderson in 1994 and Tony Hirschman in '95-96—and it was partly thanks to Evans that he had that ride in the first place. After McLaughlin's previous car owner, Norm Foster, got out of the sport in April of '84, Boehler hired him on the strong recommendations of Evans, Ron Bouchard, and veteran modified wrench Clyde McLeod. McLaughlin and Boehler had won their first race together, in May of '84 at Thompson; in '85 they were winless on the NASCAR tour, though they did win elsewhere, most notably in the lucrative Budweiser 200 at Oswego. Tour-wise, McLaughlin had 16 top-five finishes and 22 top-10 scores in 29 starts, and was rock-steady race in and race out.

"Richie was consistent and fast," McLaughlin says. "We were just consistent. We were always just kinda *there*, you know? We had just enough speed and just enough consistency to let Richie know we were there."

Of course, chasing Evans was somewhat easier in '85 than it had been, say, for Cook in '78. No longer was points-hunting a matter of juggling double-pointers and national championship events, and then filling out your schedule with regular weekly shows. In theory, the inaugural tour schedule of 29 races, all extra-distance events, was akin to lumping all of the old NC events together, and if a driver wanted to run anything else, that was up to him. (And Evans did, by the way, which was no surprise; as tough as ever in the weekly 30-lappers, he won the Spencer Speedway and Thompson track titles.)

The 1985 modified championship was Richie's ninth, and his eighth in a row. And while those numbers are impressive, you can add this: Those nine titles came in just 10 years of all-out trying. Evans won the championship in 1973, lost it in a straight fight to Cook in '74, never really gave the points a full effort in '75, and then stayed out of the battle altogether in 1976-77.

Spring Sizzler, 1985: Richie Evans, winner. *(Dave Mavlouganes photo/courtesy of Speedway Scene)*

The Rapid Roman cops a 1985 Spencer Speedway feature. *(Bev Ver Straete photo)*

History will remember him mostly as a winner, but he also happened to be the best points racer in the history of NASCAR. He always seemed slightly uncomfortable with that "points racer" label, probably because it smacked of the "stroker" tag everybody hung on Cook in the 1970s.

In fact, when he was interviewed by Winston's Roger Bear in 1982 and Bear suggested to Evans that he was "a traditional points-chaser," Richie's body language—he shifted on his feet and furrowed his brow—led Bear to quickly add, "Not in the worst sense … but in the best sense. You run hard, you run to win. But you're a guy who knows how to go out and win championships."

He told Bear, "We like to do a lot of racing. That's how we end up in the points thing at the end [of every season]."

But it was hardly as simple as that, because winning even just one championship, let alone nine, is a complicated thing. In 1985, even with fewer races than ever counting toward the national title, it was as complicated as ever, because there was obviously less mathematical room for error. But that was OK; aboard his orange #61—this particular year carrying a blue accent stripe instead of the red—Evans made very few errors.

"You *never* have points-racing down to a science," Billy Nacewicz says. "You know what you need to do, but you've still got to go out and do it. You've got to work hard and prepare the cars right, and we did that, because we had very few mechanical failures. But you've also got to have a driver who understands how important it is to be consistent. That was Jerry Cook's biggest asset over the years: He really knew how to be consistent.

"Everybody says that if you run up front, the points will come, and that's true. I mean, if you finish first, second, third, fourth, all season long, you're going to be tough to beat." And in 1985, that was just what Evans did.

Evans won a 1985 NASCAR Modified Tour stop at Riverhead, where he battled Don Howe's 34, an Evans customer car. *(Rich Oakley photo/courtesy of* Speedway Scene*)*

He won 12 of his 28 NASCAR tour starts. The victories came, in order, at Thompson's Icebreaker and Stafford's Spring Sizzler in April; New Egypt in May; Claremont (New Hampshire), Stafford, Thompson and New Egypt in July; Holland, Riverhead and Thompson in August; the Thompson 300 and Oxford Plains in September. (The Claremont-to-Holland string came consecutively, a reminder of the five straight national championship events Evans had captured back in '78.) And when he wasn't winning, he was usually coming close: five other top fives, and then four more top-10 finishes.

"For Richie, a bad day was a top five," McLaughlin says. "When you can have a bad day and still do that *good*, it adds up."

Outside the Tour, in his weekly-show stops at places like Spencer, Thompson, Shangri-La, Riverside Park, Stafford, Riverhead—hell, depending on the weather, Evans might turn up anywhere—he won 18 more times, giving him 30 total victories in 1985. It was, by any standard, a wonderful season.

Which brings to mind another thought ...

For all the talk of the various "Golden Age" periods in the history of pavement modified racing—the coupe '60s, the freewheeling middle '70s—it is too easy to overlook the fact that in 1985 the division had an incredible depth of quality, particularly at the major NASCAR events. George Kent and Jimmy Spencer, of course, were constant players; Brian Ross was still at the top of his game in his homebuilt #73; Reggie Ruggiero was a rocket on tracks of all sizes in the Fiore #44; Brett Bodine and the Sherri-Cup #12 team, in their fourth full season together, were always in the mix; Charlie Jarzombek had finally found his footing on the half-miles, dominating Stafford with the Wilsberg #5 and also shining at Thompson, Oswego and Martinsville; Jeff Fuller and George Brunnhoelzl were blindingly fast, if both a little unlucky; supermod phenom Doug Heveron was campaigning his own modified, and looking more comfortable by the week; Jamie Tomaino, John Rosati and Corky Cookman had a knack for qualifying near the front and staying there; Greg Sacks, a NASCAR Cup semi-regular by then, was popping in and out to drive Art Barry's car; Mike McLaughlin and Mike Stefanik were the coming kids, and Bugs Stevens was the steady veteran.

Adding to that mix were guys who, in their own neighborhoods, were as tough as nails: Tony Siscone, Jerry Cranmer and John Blewett in New Jersey; Stan Greger, Marty Radewick and Ray Miller at Riverside Park; Doug Hewitt, Jan Leaty and Billy Griffin at Shangri-La and Spencer.

Asphalt modified racing in 1985 was absolutely stacked with talented racers. And yet, one more time, Evans came out on top. He was the king of them all.

George Kent insists that in '85, Richie Evans was every bit as good as he ever was. "He still had that drive," Kent says. "Richie had one place to go, and that was to the front."

Five times that season, Evans wandered up to Oswego for that track's modified specials, which, while unsanctioned, were every bit as competitive as any NASCAR tour race. He dropped out of one, the Bud 200 on Labor Day weekend. In the other four outings, he won the B.R. DeWitt Port City 100 and a 75-lapper in June, ran second in an August 75-lapper, and won a 35-lap sprint in October. That October show, part of a then-traditional mod/supermod program held annually on the night before the Super DIRT Week biggie at Syracuse, marked the 13th Oswego victory for Evans.

And, oh, yes, it also happened to be the last race he ever won. There was no way to know that at the time, of course. But, looking back, you'd have to say that Evans walked away from his adopted home track in style.

Dick O'Brien recalls, "It was a cold night, windy, like it always seemed to be for that October race. Well, Richie was still going to party, and he was still going to be the last guy out of that race track. One by one, everybody was shuffling out of the infield because it was just so cold, but he and his gang weren't ready to leave. So they pulled everything into the little tunnel area at Oswego, where you go under the grandstands to cross the front straightaway, and they shut the gates on either end of it just to get out of the wind. And there they stayed, drinking beer and carrying on.

"The last two Oswego employees to leave the track that night were me and [track owner] Harry Caruso. Harry pulls up to that crowd in his Suburban, opens up the door, and says, 'Hey, guys, you've got to leave. I've got to lock up.' Richie walks over to Harry—they'd always had a good relationship—and he starts trying to con Harry into giving them some more time. And eventually, Harry hands Richie the keys, and he says, 'OK, here you go. Lock the gates and turn out the lights when you're done.'

"Now, if you knew Harry Caruso, you understood that Oswego was his speedway, his baby. Nobody—*nobody!*—could have just walked off with, literally, the key to the joint. I'd been there since 1964, and I'd never seen anything like that happen. But Harry basically said to Richie, 'I'm trusting you to do this,' and, believe me, that was a tribute to how he felt about Richie Evans.

"Richie said, 'Don't worry, Harry. I've got it covered.' Sure enough, when the party finally fizzled out, he locked the door and he left."

Evans and company went home to Rome. The next Friday, the week's maintenance behind him, he was doing his last little bit of preparation for the NASCAR's tour's penultimate event, the World Series at Thompson. He was going there with a solid lead in the points race.

It was supposed to be a family thing, Lynn Evans says, she and her husband and their two kids. But she had just come home late on Thursday from an extended trip to San Diego and, after a day full of laundry and packing, a long weekend at Thompson was not looking all that inviting.

"I had [another] four-day trip the next week," she recalls, "and I was going to have to leave at six o'clock Monday morning after getting home from Thompson at God knows when. So by the time I got all this stuff done on Friday, I was just broken-down tired. I said, 'Rich, I can't go. I'm exhausted. You go alone. We'll stay home.' And he said, 'Well, I'll take Richie.'

"That was the first time that the two of them went away together, and I was so happy about that. Little Richie was so excited. But then I remember the two of them pulling out of the driveway, and I was standing there bawling my eyes out. I mean, it's my boy's first road trip."

The thrill of victory, even after several hundred of 'em. Evans and Billy Nacewicz at Claremont, NH, 1985. *(Burt Gould photo/courtesy of Speedway Scene)*

Her son was growing up. First had come the Cub Scouts—Lynn was his troop's den mother—and now he was going to be gone for the weekend, Little Rich hanging out with Dad.

"Later on, I called the garage, knowing that they hadn't left yet for Thompson," Lynn says. "I was still crying, and the guys were laughing in the background because Rich was telling them all this. In fact, I remember Bondo saying, 'Mamas, don't let your babies grow up to be cowboys.'"

It was a sweet-and-sour weekend for Richie Evans. He finished an off-the-pace sixth in the World Series feature won by George Kent over McLaughlin, and Richie seemed, at least outwardly, not at all happy about that. How do you get excited about a *sixth*? But soon it sunk in that, in the big picture, this one result meant very little. Evans had clinched the NASCAR modified title. Again.

That thought seemed to reinvigorate him, slowly, and by the time the car was loaded up and the party moved across the vast Thompson Speedway parking lot and into the clubhouse, Evans seemed ... *content*. He grabbed a bite to eat, then put his son to bed in the comfortable sleeper compartment of the hauler truck, and returned for a celebratory round of drinks with his crew and several friends, among them his championship rival, Mike McLaughlin. It wasn't a wild night, but a fun one, lots of laughter and some loud music on the clubhouse jukebox.

"Like we always said, Richie raced hard and he played hard," McLaughlin smiles. "And I'm glad I was able to play with him that night."

"We're All Just Passin' Through ..."

"A RACE DRIVER," Reggie Ruggiero declares, "doesn't foresee anything bad happening to *him*. We go to the track, and we race, and in the back of our minds we know it *can* happen. You know you can get hurt. You know you can get killed. But you block that out of your mind, and you go and race, week after week."

Somehow, some way, Richie Evans had never been seriously hurt in a race car. He had sailed his coupe out of Cayuga in 1970, rolled down the frontstretch at Weedsport in '71, battered the Martinsville wall with Geoff Bodine in '81, and run headlong into dozens of guardrails, and he had done all this without ever having spent a night in a hospital.

Billy Nacewicz says, "He got burned at Pocono [in 1978] when our Mustang went up in flames going through the tunnel turn. He had some burns on his back, second-degree, I think, but nothing to the point where he had to be hospitalized."

Pocono, 1978: Evans suffered burns on his back and shoulders after blowing up an engine in his super-speedway Mustang, but did no hospital time. *(Ray Masser photo)*

Incidents come to mind, and images of Evans in pain: one Saturday at Riverside Park, he limped around the pits all evening thanks to a hard crash with Bob Park at New Egypt the previous night. Then Evans went out and ran a sporty third in the Riverside feature, and afterwards the limp had disappeared. "Guess I worked the kinks out," Richie had laughed. And there was the time in the '70s when he had a cast on one leg—maybe he cracked it in a racing accident, or maybe, as his daughter Janelle insists her dad told her, he stepped on a beer can and tore something—but cut it off because he was afraid a track official might prevent him from racing in plaster.

And, yes, there was the night in 1976 when his Pinto jumped a wheel at Spencer Speedway and he went for a violent flip, badly wrenching his neck. Lynn Evans, then still in the girlfriend stage, remembers what her future husband told her later that night: "This is the first time in my life I was really scared racing.'"

But considering all those years and all that hard competition, all those nights when he followed a snarling pack into a fast corner and somebody slipped, Richie Evans had been lucky enough—blessed enough—to have gotten away with a lot.

And when you get away with a lot, and in the process you pile up hundreds of victories and track championships and more national championships than anyone in your brand of racing, you begin to look almost indestructible, to your fans and even to those closest to you. They never stop caring about you, but they sure stop wringing their hands in fear, because you're seemingly above anything going wrong.

Lynn Evans says, "So many times, people would ask me, 'So, what does your husband do?' I'd tell them, 'He drives race cars.' They'd say, 'Don't you worry about him?' Well, I never, ever worried. This was Rich. Nothing was going to happen to him that he couldn't handle."

In 20-plus years of racing, Evans had never been seriously hurt. *(Jodi Meola collection)*

In fact, the most beaten-up Evans ever looked at a race track didn't have anything at all to do with racing. It was in that hot, muggy stretch of the summer of 1981, when the effects of a virus normally found in children—a silly *kid's* disease!—laid him low for a couple of weeks.

"Chicken pox," Lynn Evans says, smiling at the memory. "Little Richie brought it home, and then two weeks later Tara got a case. I'd had the chicken pox as a kid, and we talked with Rich's mother and she though he'd had chicken pox when he was a boy. So we thought the two of us were safe, because you can only get this thing one time.

"Well, Rich went racing in New England for the weekend. It must have been a Monday morning when he got home. He was going to take a quick shower and then catch up with the guys back at the shop. The water's running, and all of a sudden I hear, *'Lynn!'* I don't know if it was the hot shower that brought it out, or what, but I have never seen a worse case of chicken pox."

Within a couple of days, she recalls, "he was running a fever of about 103, and that's bad. But, of course, he wouldn't go to a doctor. He'd always see his chiropractor for his back, but he had no time for doctors. Those chicken pox were killing him; he couldn't sleep, and it made him so mad. He was *livid*. So do you know what he'd do? In the middle of the night, he'd get up and go for a drive. He told me that as long as he had a cigarette in one hand and the steering wheel in the other, he wouldn't be able to scratch."

Missing a day at the shop was out of the question. Skipping a race? Come on.

Nacewicz remembers, "He had this big ol' beard, because he couldn't shave. He couldn't scratch, and you knew it was killing him, and he was all sweaty and hot. He looked like hell. He'd still win races, but that's probably the worst shape I ever saw him in."

"When Rich started racing," says Billy Nacewicz, "nobody even had a firesuit." (Lynn Evans collection)

Imagine that? Nacewicz went through hundreds of features with Richie Evans, maybe a thousand, and never saw a race car rough him up harder than the chicken pox did.

Did Evans ever believe that his sport might really hurt him? Him? Forget it. He was just like Ruggiero and all the good ones: *You block that out of your mind, and you go and race, week after week.*

Dick O'Brien says, "Richie always told me, 'You know, I'm amazed that I didn't get killed before I got into racing.' He'd say, 'Here, I've got a helmet and a harness and a well-built car. In those days, we were crazy. We'd race in the streets, race in the fields.'"

"Rich realized the dangers," Billy Nacewicz says quietly. "I *know* he realized the dangers. It's not something we sat down and discussed, but he'd been around long enough to understand what was involved. I used to wish he'd wear [fireproof] gloves—and he sometimes did toward the end of his career, because he got used to 'em after we'd go to New Jersey, where they *made* you wear gloves—but he always thought he had a better feel for the steering wheel with his bare hands. He would never run a full-faced helmet, either, because he thought they blocked his peripheral vision. Sure, a closed helmet is safer, but he preferred the open-faced helmet. I wasn't in a position to force him to do anything, and he was certainly capable of knowing what he wanted."

Nacewicz shrugs. "Don't forget, Rich started racing when the drivers wore T-shirts. Nobody even had a firesuit. Ask Bugsy Stevens or Jerry Cook or a lot of those guys what they used to wear. And I'm sure they thought they were as safe as they could be."

New Jersey driver Tony Siscone knew, as well as anybody, both the value of being safety-conscious and the consequences of being cavalier about the subject. In a 1982 Martinsville modified feature, he had taken off his sweat-soaked gloves to dry during a caution period, but then found himself unable to get them back on before the green flag reappeared. He tucked them away, figuring he'd slip them on during the next yellow. The next yellow, though, was for him; Siscone, his view blocked by swerving traffic, plowed into the rear of Ray Evernham's stalled car. The high-speed wreck split Evernham's fuel cell, the contents of which flew back into Siscone's cockpit. His hands were terribly burned in the inferno, leading Siscone down a miserable, months-long road of hospitalization and therapy.

After his return to racing, Siscone would occasionally try to nudge Evans toward looking deeper into the latest safety gear—hoping to make a big impression by showing Richie his hands, and their awful scarring—but was usually met with the expected resistance.

"When I told him that wearing gloves was real important," Siscone told Dick Berggren, "he just looked at me and said, 'Look, we're all just passin' through.'"

Martinsville: Home Away From Home

ONE OF THE GREATEST LINES EVER WRITTEN about Evans came from Ron Hedger, who once described Richie strolling into the pits at Martinsville "just before high noon, with the appearance of a man who had thoroughly enjoyed himself the previous evening."

That was a pretty good bet.

Evans liked going to Martinsville, and for much of his career—certainly all of his point-chasing seasons—he went there three or four times a year, hauling out of New York on I-81 and then, at Roanoke, meandering down twisty Route 220 toward Collinsville, with its popular Dutch Inn and Holiday Inn hotels, and Martinsville, where the track itself sat.

For a long time, Martinsville hosted the modifieds as a Saturday undercard to its April and September Grand National/Winston Cup events; those shows, typically, were 150 laps in length. But Evans thrived, competitively and socially, on Martinsville's traditional March and October doubleheaders, the Dogwood 500 and the Cardinal 500.

By the time Martinsville rolled around in March each year, Evans might have already run a dozen races, at New Smyrna and Daytona and Hickory and Lord knows where else. And he managed to sneak in his share of November shows over the years, too, at places from Chemung to Wall Stadium. But Martinsville still *felt* like it opened and closed every season; all the big names were there, and carloads of Northern fans showed up to say either hello to a new racing year or goodbye to another one gone.

Two more things about Martinsville: It always had a big-event feel,

(left) Old friends: Evans with Martinsville Speedway founder H. Clay Earles. *(Lynn Evans photo)*

(right) Evans loved Martinsville's doubleheaders. Here, he shares a 1978 victory lane with late model sportsman winner Sonny Hutchins. *(courtesy of Speedway Scene)*

and it had the coolest winner's trophies in the world, full-sized and very functional grandfather clocks.

"Martinsville was sort of like the Daytona 500 of modified racing," says Billy Nacewicz. "Of course, you had the Race of Champions, and that was huge, too. But everybody wanted to win Martinsville. They wanted one of those clocks, man. And Richie had won, what, 10 of them?

"So he had fallen in love with that place. He liked the track, he liked the atmosphere, and he got along really well with the promoter, Clay Earles, and Dick Thompson, the PR man. It was always a fun time."

Lynn Evans says, "Richie loved Martinsville. *Loved* it."

And from the first trips down in the coupe days—when Evans discovered proper Southern moonshine—through the championship celebrations and the "greatest finish of any race, anywhere" with Bodine in '81, imagine the memories he had of the place.

Hell, imagine the Martinsville memories he created for others … at the track, at the Good Times Lounge (owned by Southern modified ace Perk Brown) just over the North Carolina line in Eden, at whatever hotel would have him and his rowdy friends.

In 1975, not long after it took the kindness and bail money of Clay Earles for Evans to make it to the starting grid one Sunday, writer Rich Benyo described Richie as "a tough New York modified driver who knows every little nook and cranny in the town of Martinsville, and is on a first-name basis with everyone from the innkeeper to the chief of police, from repeated run-ins with both."

Which summed things up nicely.

"We used to stay at the Dutch Inn until they threw us out of there," recalls a grinning Nacewicz. "The final straw, I think, had something to do with some shrubbery getting removed and carried into a room, or something like that. Lenny Boehler might have been involved in that one. It's hard to remember, because there had been a few incidents.

"But kicking us out wasn't totally fair. I've seen some awful, awful behavior there, and it wasn't *always* us. I saw Jarzombek's gang hanging off the old windmill out front, and I saw [journeyman Massachusetts driver] Jerry Capozzoli ride his mini-bike into the swimming pool. He'd already ridden it up and down the halls and into the bar; now we're all standing around by the pool, and he's dragging that damn mini-bike up onto the diving board. We figured he was just going to sit there. Next thing you know, he fires up that mini-bike and rides it straight into the pool!

"Don't get me wrong, we got away with some stuff there, too. We weren't completely guilt-free. Fortunately, one of our biggest fans and good friends, Cathy Carter, worked at the Dutch, and she turned her head a couple times. But we also got blamed for a lot of stuff we didn't really do by ourselves. I know we had a lot of co-conspirators who were still living at the Dutch Inn after we were asked to leave."

Actually, Nacewicz's terminology—"asked to leave"—is on the mild side.

"It got to the point that we actually weren't allowed on the property," Billy says. "In fact, they told us they had a court order that said we couldn't even turn our truck around in their parking lot! Rich said, 'Boy, I guess they really didn't want us around.'"

Here, Nacewicz laughs. "We told 'em that was a big mistake, and it was, because when we moved over the hill to the Holiday Inn, we moved the whole social scene with us. And it thrived there for several years."

Nightly, one of Martinsville's best parties ran in the Holiday Inn bar until it closed at midnight, and then shifted to the parking lot outside the corner room where Evans most often bunked. "All our friends would stop by," Billy Nacewicz says.

Bobby Hutchens remembers being "probably 12 or 13 years old, just a naïve kid" when he and his father took a room at the Holiday Inn. He says, "One evening after practice, we went out to eat. We got back to the hotel and got ready to go to bed, and there was a bunch of guys next door just raising hell. This started at about seven o'clock, and I swear they were still going at four o'clock the next morning. Dad wouldn't let us go outside at my age, but I found out later on that it was Richie and his guys having a good ol' time. They kept me up all night."

And how did Evans do that weekend? "The best I remember," Hutchens says, "he set it on the pole in qualifying and pretty much checked out in the race."

If there wasn't enough fun to be had right there at the Holiday, Evans might go looking for some. On one Martinsville night, recalls George Kent, "He and I went out with his hot rod. I drove, and of course he was constantly reaching for the emergency brake. The sun was coming up before we got back. It wasn't pretty. I was just happy we had stayed out of jail." On another, smiles Ron Hutter, "Richie rented a van and hauled everybody up to some cowboy bar in Roanoke so they could ride the mechanical bull. He said he couldn't ride it himself, because his back was bad, but he talked the rest of us into doing it."

Then there was the night when, with the bar closed and all readily available beer gone, Evans pronounced the party over by climbing into someone's compact rental car, wedging it into the breezeway beside his room, and then slithering out the window and heading off to bed. Tom Baldwin recalled, "He just left the car right there! Oh, the next morning everybody went crazy."

Normally, this was a man who couldn't wait to get to Martinsville to dig into all the fun it held. But things were different in October of '85; a lot was changing for Richie Evans. He had another championship behind him. He had the used-car thing rolling along, and the hotel, too. And time was marching on. On the day before he left for the Cardinal 500, his daughter Janelle dragged her mother down to the Calvert Street shop to inform her father that she had just gotten engaged.

"Richie and I were getting along pretty well by then," Barbara Evans says, "and Janelle said, 'Mom, come with me so I can tell Dad!' So we went, and he thought that was great. He said, 'Oh, good, we can have a party up at the hotel!' I said, joking around, 'The heck we will! There's no way we're having a party up there with all *your* friends.' He sent Janelle and I down to the drugstore to get him a new leather watchband and a carton of Winstons. And that was that."

When the familiar orange Ford cube van and its open trailer bearing the B.R. DeWitt #61 left for Martinsville, Richie Evans was not on board. He opted to fly down instead. That was rare, but, again, things were different, changing. Lynn Evans was away working, so the youngest two Evans children, Richie Jr. and Tara, were at a neighbor's house; Lynn recalls the neighbor telling her, days later, that Richie had stopped over that night to kiss the kids goodbye, which was unusual. Daughter Jodi, hearing the same story, remembers the neighbor saying her dad "seemed real hesitant, seemed kinda funny. He left, and then he came back" to see the kids again.

Mark Lyon, a crewman on the Evans-built #44 owned by Mario Fiore, recalls his surprise at bumping into Richie at the airport in Pittsburgh, where they caught the same connecting flight to Greensboro. Evans told Lyon that by flying rather than riding down in the truck, he had been able to sneak in some extra work time up at the Freeman Hotel.

He rented a Lincoln in Greensboro, legged it up to Collinsville, checked into the Holiday Inn and then did the usual night-time thing. At some point he ran into Charlie Roberts, a New Jersey radio producer with whom he had been friendly for years. Roberts congratulated Evans on championship number nine, and asked him about the future.

Richie Evans grinned. "You can't quit on an odd number."

On Thursday morning, he headed the few miles down Route 220, bound for Martinsville Speedway.

The Day the Music Died

HOW DO YOU TELL THE STORY of what might be the most important crash—and thus the blackest day—in the history of a racing division? How do you recount how a marvelous Virginia Thursday went so bad so quickly? How do you capture the way modified racing changed, and changed forever, just because one race car hit the Martinsville Speedway wall at a little before 11 o'clock on October 24, 1985? How do you sum up what happened in the first warm-up session for the final NASCAR event of that season? How can you put down on paper how unbelievable—as in *truly beyond belief*—it all seemed?

"You just never, ever in a million years thought we'd lose Richie Evans in a racing accident," says Brett Bodine. "Number one, he never wrecked. I mean, the guy was the best at avoiding accidents. He'd be in a pile of smoke, with cars spinning everywhere, and he'd drive right out of it and win the feature. I'd be side-by-side with him when there was a crash right ahead of us, and I'd end up on the wrecker with a wheel torn off and he'd wind up in victory lane."

So how do you tell that story?

Well, you just tell it the way people remember it.

"I was talking to Richie that morning, before practice," George Kent says. "He was *real* happy that he'd won the championship, because they had changed the points system and he'd still managed to win it. He was pretty excited about that. We were talking in his hauler, just shooting the bull."

As practice time approached, the champion and his peers changed into their firesuits. Engines were being warmed up, so things were getting noisy along the backstretch pit at Martinsville, where most of the modified teams were clustered. On the back of the orange Evans truck, there was one last little bit of socializing, two short-track legends passing time the way they had a hundred times before.

"I was with Richie, what, two minutes before he got killed?" Bugsy Stevens says. "We were sitting there, shooting the shit. He told me he had been trying to find me the night before, looking to raise a little hell, but he never could. We joked that it was probably just as well, because we were a handful when you got us together.

"And he said, 'Come on, Bugs. Let's go out and practice.'"

The late Fred Ulrich remembered, "I know we were parked near Art Barry, and Rich was going to build a new chassis for Art. Anyway, Rich jumped in the car for warm-ups, and Art and I were standing there. Rich

One last light moment: Evans with Bugsy Stevens, October 24, 1985. *(courtesy of Speedway Scene)*

motioned for me to back him out—you know, to make sure he was clear of traffic—so I did that. Then he gave me that little look he had, almost like a wink. And away he went."

Away he went, for all time. Evans brought the car up to speed—checking things, warming fluids, just getting set—and then he got on the gas. He had won 10 times at Martinsville. Nobody knew the track better. He was now a nine-time national modified champion. Nobody was more on top of his game. Richie Evans hot-lapping at this place was worth paying attention to.

"Martinsville was a funny track," says Mario Fiore, whose long, successful collaboration with Reggie Ruggiero had just ended and who now had Doug Heveron in the seat of his Evans-built car. "In the first couple warm-ups it would be slow, and our team was somewhat limited on the tires we had, so I didn't want to send Dougie out until the track was good. So I was watching Richie, knowing that if the track was good, he'd run fast. He turned a good lap, and I said, 'OK, the track is coming in. Let's go.'"

Then Fiore stole one last glance at Evans, speeding by and heading toward turn three. "I saw him go into that corner," Fiore says, "and I saw him hit the wall."

It seemed almost unreal to Fiore, and to his ex-driver Ruggiero, now driving for Connecticut team owner Mike Greci. Ruggiero, who was standing on the pit wall, also timing Evans, remembers, "I watched him go down the backstretch, and he never turned the corner. It was so … *unusual*. He just didn't turn. He went straight into the fence."

Brett Bodine says, "There are points in time that you will never forget, and for me this was one of them. I was sitting in my car, the Sherri-Cup car, and we were making a spring change on the backstretch pit road when I saw Richie's car go straight into the third-turn wall. I just looked up and saw him go in. That moment, that snapshot, was, like, branded into my brain. I got on the radio and said, 'Richie just wrecked,' never even *imagining* how bad it was."

At that point, maybe the only guy in the place who appreciated how bad a crash it had been was Tony Siscone, who, as fate had it, was both the closest witness and the first man on the scene. Nearly 20 years on, when he says quietly, "I remember it like it was yesterday," you do not doubt him.

Siscone: "I had run about seven consecutive laps, hammer down; there were only about four or five cars out there, so I had a nice, clear track. We had a brand-new Jack Tant motor, and I had cut some really good laps. I slowed down on the backstretch and pulled to the inside. I looked up into my mirror, and I saw Richie coming off the second turn. I radioed my guys and said, 'I ought to jump in behind Richie and see how good we really are.' Well, he went by right at that moment, and he drove into the third turn …" Pause. "And never turned. When he hit, I was no more than, oh, 50 yards behind him."

A longer pause. "After he hit, his car was sliding backwards in the outside lane. There's steam, smoke, the whole deal. And now I'm literally driving along next to him in the inside lane. I mean, I'm down by the curb, slowing down, and he's up high, going the same speed. And I see Richie slumped over."

Number 61, the B.R. DeWitt Cavalier, orange and blue, scraped to a halt beside the fourth-turn pedestrian crossover gate, its right-front corner gone, its frame twisted grotesquely. Siscone stopped his car nearby. Because of his own horrific 1982 accident at Martinsville, he had just one thought: *Fire!*

"The fuel pump was sheared off Richie's car, of course, and there's fluid running everywhere," Siscone says. "I'm thinking about fire the whole time. I bailed out of my car without taking off anything; I'm still wearing the helmet, gloves, the whole deal. I ran over and literally ripped his window net down. And then I saw Richie."

Violent crashes have violent results. In automobile racing's television era, maybe folks have grown immune to that; even the worst wrecks are contained in a box across the living room, behind a glass screen, with the director careful not to allow anything too disturbing to slip onto the airwaves. Drivers might die, but they die out of view; if one camera shot is too horrific, you simply run another, or cut to a commercial. Tony Siscone did not have the benefit of such filters when he reached his friend's car, and saw what he saw. This was awful. This was bad.

"I started yelling for help, waving for an ambulance," Siscone says. "The thought of fire became secondary, because I was certain that Richie was dead or dying. I felt so helpless; I wanted to help him, and I *couldn't*.

"It seemed like an eternity, but probably only seconds later—it's so hard to judge time—Bugsy Stevens got there. I remember grabbing him, saying, 'Bugsy, we've got to help Richie!'"

Like Siscone, Stevens had been on the track, had seen the impact, had stopped to help. In his autobiography, Stevens wrote: "I leaned in to get Richie's helmet unbuckled, and right away I knew he was gone."

For Stevens, the whole thing was grimly reminiscent of another October day—Sunday, October 8, 1978—when his friend and fellow champion Fred DeSarro had crashed at Thompson. In that case, too, Stevens was on the scene immediately, joining Kenny and Ronnie Bouchard in an effort to free DeSarro. "I was struggling to get Freddy's helmet unbuckled with one hand, trying to hold his head still with my other hand," Stevens wrote, "and his blood is pouring out onto my uniform." DeSarro never regained consciousness, and died three weeks later.

Now it was another friend's helmet, another friend's blood. Stevens sized up the situation. This was not just DeSarro all over again; this scene was worse. Bugs Stevens stepped away.

Siscone: "I was going crazy, and Bugsy was as calm as could be. He knew. *He knew.* He said, 'Richie's gone.' I said, 'No, no, no …'

"He said again, 'Richie's gone.' And he told me, 'Tony, I went through this with Freddy.'"

And Bugs Stevens was right. Richie Evans, who had earned nine NASCAR modified championships and nine Most Popular Driver awards, who won on the biggest tracks and the smallest, who went from ducking bill collectors to sitting in suits at banquet-hall head tables, who lived without a time clock, who loved nothing better than racing and its highway life, who had such a interesting past and yet had only just begun to truly look ahead … was gone.

Siscone sagged. Stevens walked back toward his own parked modified, threw his helmet at its door, and said out loud, "These fucking race cars are killing all my friends."

Back in the modified pit area, few people had any idea of the severity of the crash. Again: they were on the backstretch, and the emergency workers surrounding the Evans car were over in turn four. In between, there were their own hauler trucks, some infield buildings, and the Busch Series transporters. Besides, they had their own cars to worry about. Guys crash in practice all the time; that's no reason to stop airing up tires, warming engines, checking bolts.

And then there was this: NASCAR modified racing was then in the midst of a relatively safe era. Sure, DeSarro had died after that Thompson wreck in '78, but his car had flown over a sand-bank barrier and landed hard, far down an embankment; it was easy enough to mark that tragedy down as a freak thing and just roll onward. It was the same when Jim Shampine was killed in the 1982 Bud 200 at Oswego; Jimmy was driving a fine, safe modified, Billy Taylor's, but after a simple spin he was unlucky enough to be drilled in the side by another fellow with no place to go, and Shampine suffered massive internal injuries. Again, tragic, but close enough to freakish to be written off as an anomaly. Even when Dave Furioni, a young driver from Agawam, Massachusetts, lost his life at his hometown Riverside Park Speedway in '82, there was the sort of twist that led folks to mark it down as a one-in-a-million thing: Furioni's car had speared savagely under an Armco barrier after his throttle apparently hung wide open.

In 1985, it seemed almost inconceivable, even to folks who had been around the block, that you could run a modified into a wall and get killed doing it. That sad truth sunk in gradually, late in the morning of October 24.

"I never put *death* with Richie's crash," Mario Fiore remembers. "In fact, the first thing I thought was, 'Oh, poor Richie. Now he's going to have to figure out a way to get his backup car down here.' See, I had talked to Richie earlier, and he told me he had only brought one car because he had already clinched the title. But then Mark [Lyon] ran over there to see if Richie was all right, and when he came back, he had tears in his eyes. That's when I knew it was serious. Until then, I had no idea it was that severe."

Nor did Evans's own team. Fred Ulrich said, "We were thinking, Well, he's crashed. He'll be getting out of the car, and he'll be mad. But he *didn't* get out. We started heading over there, and Bugsy grabbed hold of me. I looked at him, and he just shook his head."

Bill Hatch was beside Ulrich. "I remember Bugsy," Hatch says quietly. "That's what stopped us: Bugsy shook his head, and then he walked back to the pits."

Richie Evans was transported to Memorial Hospital of Martinsville and Henry County, where everything was made official. He was pronounced dead on arrival at 11:20 a.m., the first fatality in Martinsville Speedway's 38-year history. The cause of death was multiple trauma. The autopsy contained the words "basilur skull fracture," a term which was then foreign to NASCAR fans but which in more recent times, owing to the deaths of Dale Earnhardt, Kenny Irwin, Adam Petty and others, has become a brutal part of the sport's lexicon.

Bill Hatch: "We went to the hospital, but ..."

His voice trails off.

Lynn Evans was at home in Rome, rushing through a busy day. She had a dental appointment at noon, a Cub Scout meeting to host later in the day, and her mother was in town, visiting from Wisconsin.

"The phone started ringing," she remembers. "I wasn't going to answer it, because I didn't want to be late for the dentist." She let it ring, thinking her mother might pick up. "But then my neighbor knocked on the door, and my mother started talking with the neighbor, so I said, 'Oh, I'll just answer it.' And I picked up the phone."

It was Billy Nacewicz.

"I thought it a prank call at first, because I couldn't really hear the voice, it was so low," she says. "I noticed that whoever it was, was saying, 'Lynn ... Lynn ... Lynn.' I was ready to hang up the phone, because it was scaring me a little bit. Then all of a sudden the voice said, 'Lynn, this is Billy.'

"I was like, What the hell is *he* calling me for?"

A million things ran through her mind, and yet a racing crash was not among the first. That was not as strange as it might seem; it was easy, if you happened to skip an October event at Martinsville, to forget that practice for the modifieds opened on Thursday morning. No, this had to be something else ...

"My biggest fear for a long time was that the guys would be in an accident on the highway, because of all the traveling they did," she says. "I always thought it would be something with the hauler, because they did have a couple of close calls."

A million things ...

"And then Billy told me," Lynn Evans whispers, "that Rich ... was no longer with us."

There was shock, she says, and immediate denial. She remembers blurting this strange news to her mother, and asking, "Why would Billy say something like that?" But then her mother took the phone and spoke directly, quietly, with Nacewicz. "And as they talked," Lynn says, "it hit me."

She knew she had to get to Martinsville as soon as possible, and she knew there were people she needed to call. First on her list was Gene DeWitt; as it turned out, he had already heard. Fortunately, DeWitt had a company plane, which would take care of the immediate travel problems.

Then she called Barbara Evans, Richie's first wife and the mother of his four eldest daughters; you stop to think of all the drama they'd had in their lives—the divided households, the shuttling of the kids, the two of them putting up with this human handful called Richie Evans—and now it had come to this.

"I'll never forget Lynn calling me," says Barbara. "I was having what I guess you'd call a blue day. I remember watching a soap opera and it brought tears to my eyes, and I'm not usually like that. Later my phone rang, and it was Lynn. She said, 'I have some news to tell you' ..."

It was left to Barbara Evans to break that news to her four girls. Jodi, the oldest at 20, was living in Florida, but Janelle (barely 19), Jill (16) and Jacki (15) remained in their hometown. Jodi got the news by telephone. Janelle, having graduated high school, was at home; she describes herself as "the tough one" among the first set of Evans kids, and her first response backs that up: "I knew that in racing, something *could* happen. But with him, it was so routine; he went to the track, he raced, and then he'd come home. It was his *job*, and you just don't think of somebody getting hurt or killed doing his job."

Jill and Jacki were attending school at Rome Free Academy when they were called from their classrooms and told to report to the principal's office. Jacki was puzzled, Jill terrified, but for the wrong reason. "I had skipped a class the day before that," Jill says, laughing. "So when they called me down to the office, I thought I was in trouble for that. I actually told my friend, 'Well, I guess I got caught.' I remember walking into the office, and I saw my mother there. My first thought was, Oh my God, they're calling my *mother* just because I skipped a class?

"But then I got this nervous feeling in my stomach, and I knew something was wrong."

Barbara Evans took the girls outside, and told them their father was gone.

Richie Evans Jr., nine at the time, too young to get those nervous feelings Jill had, was in his grade-school cafeteria when the principal walked over and told him he was going home. "I didn't ask no questions," he told writer Bruce Bennett years later. "I just looked at all the other kids and said, 'Ha-ha. You've got to stay in school …'" He was at a neighbor's when they told him about his dad. "I threw the usual kid temper tantrum," he told Bennett.

Lynn Evans and Gene DeWitt flew to Virginia that afternoon. DeWitt, who nine championships and 13 seasons earlier had made his handshake deal with this floppy-haired racer with the twinkle in his eye, was drained. He later told Dick Berggren that he'd felt "just like you'd feel when you lost your best friend."

Lynn remembers being met in Martinsville by, among others, Gladys and Eileen Jarzombek—respectively, the matriarch of the famous Long Island clan and the wife of Ricky Jarzombek, always his brother's head wrench and right-hand man—and Sue Cook. For all the feuding their two husbands had done over the years, "Sue and I were always cordial," Lynn says.

Down in Hollywood, Florida, Jodi, the eldest daughter, packed a bag and headed to the airport to catch a flight home to New York. "I left that day," she says. "I remember being on that airplane, just sitting there like a zombie."

And back in Martinsville, *everybody* was like a zombie. A *Rome Sentinel* reporter who interviewed Kenny Hartung described the veteran crewman talking "as if in a trance." Dick Thompson, longtime PR director at the Virginia track and a man who counted Evans as a friend, later claimed he hadn't seen such an overwhelming air of despair over a racing death since the mid-1960s losses of Grand National stars Joe Weatherly, Curtis Turner and Fireball Roberts. "I heard veteran newsmen breaking up on the telephone after calling about the incident," Thompson wrote in a tribute. "I watched NASCAR's Jerry Cook and Andy Hall trying to do their duties while wiping away tears. I watched Clay Earles [and] Clay Campbell going about their tasks in complete shock."

Cook told the Rome newspaper, "This is probably the worst day of my life."

John Tallini, who throughout the 1960s and '70s had waved a lot of checkered flags over both Cook and Evans, could read that despair on Cook's face. Tallini had driven to Martinsville, and—as was common in those pre-cellular days—the trip passed without any info from the track. It was only when he reached the speedway that Tallini got the bad news, and he got it straight from Cook.

"Jerry was very, very distraught," Tallini remembers. "He just looked at me and shook his head."

Everything seemed somehow unbalanced. Dick Berggren later quoted the Motor Racing Network's anchor, Mike Joy, as saying, "It was like John Wayne being shot by the Indians. It wasn't supposed to happen."

Doug Hewitt, Evans's quasi-teammate under the B.R. DeWitt colors, loaded his equipment and headed home for New York. He never raced again.

There was a quick bit of talk about the race being postponed, but that faded quickly. "Richie would not have wanted that," Cook told *Gater Racing News*. "Richie was not a quitter, he was a racer. He would not have wanted the show to stop."

Jerry was probably correct. Hadn't Evans himself, on another tragic day, climbed aboard a supermodified whose chief mechanic had just been killed? Hadn't he then driven that car to victory in the 1975 World Series at Thompson? *Richie was not a quitter ...*

"You had no choice but to sit there and think about what Richie would do himself," Tom Baldwin said. "I was saying, 'What would Richie do if it had been me? What would he have done if it had been one of his best friends, say a guy like Sonney Seamon?' And the answer I kept coming up with was, 'Richie would continue on. He'd go racing.'"

And so—minus Hewitt—the NASCAR modified field carried on with the program, even if it felt more like going through the motions.

"I can't tell you a thing about the rest of the weekend," says Brett Bodine. "Everything else just happened."

George Kent echoes that: "It was a strange, strange weekend, there's no doubt about that. I tried to put it out of my mind, but, you know, you can't. It was like Superman died. That's what it was like."

A couple hours after the Evans crash, Charlie Jarzombek won the Martinsville pole position. Siscone, having just seen a hero "dead or dying," snapped down his visor and gutted out a time-trial run good enough for the outside front-row slot. In the post-qualifying press conference, Jarzombek threw a reporter's own question back at him: "What does Richie Evans mean to modified racing? What does Richard Petty mean to Grand National racing? What does A.J. Foyt mean to Indy car racing? *That's* what Richie meant. Richie was the best."

Right up until they waved the green flag, says Mario Fiore, "everybody was kind of in shock. We had always raced with Richie there. ..."

Virginian Johnny Bryant won the Martinsville modified main—a 200-lapper for the first time, down from the previous 250—over a despondent Bugs Stevens. "I would have loved to win that thing for Richie," Stevens told anyone who would listen, and he may well have done just that under the old format. By gambling on a nonstop run over the new race distance, Bryant had gotten the lead when his faster rivals pitted, and he never gave it up. Every car in the race carried a "61" sticker on the right-front corner of its roof.

The winner, not surprisingly, was asked about Evans in the post-race interviews. He admitted that on a late-race restart with 10 laps remaining, a vision of an orange car kept creeping into his brain. "I said to myself, 'Richie, just help me this one time,'" Bryant relayed.

Mike McLaughlin, runner-up to Evans in the NASCAR points chase, led the race briefly, then spun twice, and finally fell out with a failed ignition. He remembers leaving Martinsville thankful that the title fight had been decided a week earlier, at Thompson. "I've always been glad that Richie had it clinched before Martinsville," McLaughlin says. "Because I know I wouldn't have won it under those circumstances. I don't know what I'd have done, but I wouldn't have won it. I'd have given it up, absolutely. I really believe that. But I didn't have to worry about that, because it ended up the way it should have, with him as the champion."

Mario Fiore recalls "thinking about the [funeral] arrangements as soon as the race ended. Because, you know, Richie had been good to us." He was talking specifically about his team, but Fiore was thinking like hundreds—*thousands*—more.

And Where Were You?

DICK O'BRIEN ASKS, "You know how everybody says, 'Where were you when JFK got killed?' Well, it's the same, identical thing when you talk with people about Richie. Sure, it's a different perspective, but if you live a life in racing and you tend to look at things from a racing perspective, the impact is the same. If you knew him at all, you'll always remember the circumstances of how you heard about it."

O'Brien himself, this guy who knew Evans on so many levels—track manager, *Syracuse Herald* writer, friend—had still another level to him. Though his Oswego Speedway role gave him a high profile on the Northeast racing scene, that was actually a part-time gig; during the week, O'Brien drove a semi for UPS, bouncing along the Interstates for years. So where was Dick O'Brien on Thursday, October 24? "Running I-81 down to Tamaqua, Pennsylvania, just south of where you cross I-80. We'd run trucks down from Syracuse, and the guys from Baltimore and

For most of his friends, Richie's death provoked a common reaction: Not him! *(Rene Dugas photo/courtesy of Speedway Scene)*

D.C. would come up, and that was halfway for both of us; we'd exchange trailers and head home. Well, the guys at the *Herald* found out about Richie, because it was on the wire services. They called UPS looking for me, but I was on the road. Don't forget, this is all long before cell phones. Whoever took the call at UPS said, 'Can I take a message?'

"I got back to Syracuse at five o'clock. The dispatcher said, 'Hey, your paper called.' I asked him what they wanted, and he read the message, just like this: 'Richie Evans killed at Martinsville.' I was totally stunned. It was so out-of-the-blue, so unexpected."

Joe Jones, Richie's one-time filling-station boss and short-term partner in stock car ownership, does not need to think about it: "I was having lunch at the Anchor Inn in Utica. We went down there for a sandwich and a beer, me and a couple friends of mine. We went into the bar and I looked up at the TV and they said, 'Richie Evans was killed today.' I couldn't believe it. Couldn't believe it. Not *this* guy."

It happened like that across Motorsports America: phones ringing, radios bleating out the news, messages being passed along, jaws dropping. It happened with former rivals ("I owned a tire shop then, and somebody called," says Dutch Hoag) and old associates ("I was at my upholstery business, and the phone rang," recalls Dick Waterman, the ex-Utica-Rome boss) and young friends ("I was working as a mechanic on heavy equipment, and my mom called me," remembers Tony Pettinelli Jr.).

Wilbur Jones, Donny Marcello and Max Baker—old hands on a race team nobody ever *really* left—were all on various jobs at Revere Copper in Rome. "I was just going to work, and I saw Max," Marcello recalls. "He looked at me and said, 'Richie just got killed.' And I just said, 'Oh my God.'"

"My lunch break ran from 11:30 until noon," Jones says, "and I was walking into one of the buildings down at Revere. My boss came over and told me. I guess he had heard it on the radio."

Ol' Wilbur pauses. "Now, this might sound strange, but I didn't believe it at first, because I had heard that sort of thing before."

See, when popular dirt modified driver Jackie Evans was killed at Pennsylvania's Reading Fairgrounds in August of 1970, there occurred a textbook case of how fact, when spread too quickly, can turn to fiction. That night, some 215 miles to the north of Reading, Wilbur Jones was at Albany-Saratoga with Eddie Flemke, who was wheeling the backup Evans coupe. Richie, banned from NASCAR at the time, was racing—and winning—that night at Fulton. But just before feature time at Albany-Saratoga, word spread like wildfire through the pits that *Richie* Evans, not Jackie, had lost his life. Jones says, "I remember that Eddie wasn't going to race that night, because he thought Richie had been killed." Now, on October 24, 1985, his deepest hope was that this was another false alarm. "I just tried to put it out of my mind," Wilbur Jones says. "But then I ran into Bill Davis [husband of Richie's cousin Beverly], and when I looked at him, he was crying. I said, 'Oh, no, this can't *be*.'"

Buster Maurer, who had crewed Evans to his first national championship in 1973, was having lunch with his friend Bill Payne, the Cook loyalist with whom he had argued so bitterly prior to that initial all-Rome title fight. They were sitting beneath a shade tree outside Bartel's Machinery when, Maurer says, "somebody hollered out that I had a phone call. I went in and got on the phone, and my wife said, 'Richie's been killed at Martinsville.'" Just recounting that conversation brings Maurer to tears.

In Massachusetts, Ted Puchyr was thumbing through some paperwork. Having married young, started a family and stepped toward security and thus away from racing, Puchyr had gone from working all night on coupes to working as an executive for the Rite Aid chain. "I was sitting in my office and the phone rang. And I said, 'You've got to be kidding me.' You know, I can't even remember who called me. I should, but it's one of those things. I went *numb*."

In New Jersey, John McClellan, the T-shirt man, was on his non-racing job, installing an elevator. "I always carried a beeper with me, and it went off," he says. "It was my wife. I called her back, and she told me, 'Richie's dead.' And all I could think was, Somebody has made a mistake. This can't be right. But I could tell from her voice that he was really gone. And then I just stood there and cried."

It didn't matter how long you had been involved with Richie Evans, or even if you had been directly involved at all. Steve Hmiel had worked on modifieds for Jerry Cook and others; Robin Pemberton had worked on modifieds for Ron Narducci and others; Bobby Hutchens worked on modifieds for his father and himself and others. All three knew Evans, essentially, as competitors. None of that lessened the impact of the word they got on October 24.

"Not only do I remember exactly what I was doing, I remember exactly where I was *standing*," says Hmiel. "I was working for Billy Hagan, and Terry Labonte was our driver. I was packing wheel bearings, and one of the guys came in and said, 'It just came on the radio: Richie Evans got killed at Martinsville.'

"I'll tell you, his death made a man out of me. It was a sign to me: Things are going to change, man. Nothing is forever. And I'm not trying to make this sound too deep, because, hell, I was only 20-something years old. But I could tell somehow that everything was ... *different*. I knew that anything could happen to anybody at any time."

Pemberton, working then as a crew chief at the now-defunct DiGard team, recalls somebody calling the shop with the news. "I remember just thinking, Goddam, that can't be right. I mean, when Richie died, it *crushed* me. It was like a whole part of my life—something I had grown up with—was gone. I know there's been other drivers who left us, because of accidents or whatever, but Richie was a guy I had seen as a young kid, a pre-teen kid. He was supposed to just always be there."

Listen to Hutchens, and note that he was working with Richard Childress Racing when Dale Earnhardt was killed at Daytona in 2001: "It was like the whole world had crashed in when Richie died. It was definitely one of the two worst days of my life, let's put it that way. I look at losing Richie the same way I look at losing Dale: I still really don't believe it happened."

Bill Wimble, who had first put Evans together with Gene DeWitt, can relate to Hutchens's surprise. A veteran of the risky 1950s, Wimble says, "Unfortunately, I had seen enough of this business to know that it was a dangerous thing. I can remember losing six or seven guys I raced with in one year, and I know I'm extremely lucky to still be around. So by that point in my life, I shouldn't have been shocked by *anybody's* death, but Richie's death was still a very big thing."

Across the United States, *National Parts Peddler* publisher Corky Stockham was strolling the aisles of the Speed Equipment Manufacturers Association show in Las Vegas when he learned of his friend's crash. Moved by the emotions he saw from some industry heavyweights at the SEMA event, and by his own long relationship with Evans, Stockham penned a tribute that ran in the next week's *Gater Racing News*. It said in part that when "the news hit of Richie's death, it was like a shock wave across the show ... Earlier that Thursday I had noticed how many of the speed equipment exhibitors [had] arranged Richie's photos of endorsement for their products. I thought about how times had changed. Only a few years ago when I had attended the trade show with Richie, the people hardly knew us."

By 1985, everybody knew Richie Evans, and everybody felt his loss. His old coupe-days foe Dave Lape, a bonafide superstar for years on the DIRT circuit, remembers running the Eastern States 200 that weekend at the Orange Country Fair Speedway.

"Everybody there was just stunned," says Lape. "We had kind of lost touch, Richie and I, but we were still friendly. If we did see each other, we'd always talk. But once we went our separate ways, me on dirt and him on asphalt, we didn't see each other much. Still, losing him was such a shock.

"A guy like Richie, you think he's ... I dunno, invincible."

Goodbye, Champion

WHEN THEY HAULED Richie Evans's modified back to Rome for the last time, it was met by the same kind of crowd—indeed, by many of the same people—that used to greet its driver in victory lanes and pit areas and race-town taverns. This time, though, they had shown up out of heartbreak. They had shown up because ... well, because none of them knew just what else to do. So they gathered on Calvert Street, which at almost every turn in their lives had been, aside from a few rough patches, a happy place.

It was past dark when the hauler arrived on the block.

"I remember everybody standing out in front of that garage," Dick O'Brien says. "In fact, Tony Jankowiak was standing there; he had driven down all the way from Buffalo. I'll never forget that. Well, around the corner, here comes that orange truck. It starts down the street toward the shop, and then it stops. I'm sure whoever was inside had seen all these people, and now they were mapping their strategy. Well, the truck pulled up, and Billy rolled up the garage door. In went the truck, down went the door, and that was that. And people, *grown* people, just stood there bawling like babies.

"Every family, every person, goes through things like this: a sudden, unexpected death that you're not ready for. But this was just *huge*, because the 'family' was so big."

Wilbur Jones remembers, "I went down to the garage and, holy cow, everybody was there. I just wanted to see if there was anything I could do. I went over to the Elks and made arrangements over there, thinking that people might eventually need someplace to go and sit down or have a drink or whatever. I kept the bar open all night, and people kept coming in. Jesus Christ, it was a long night."

O'Brien says, "Just to show you how tough a night it was, every time anybody ordered a round of drinks, Billy would order one 'for the boss.' Then the bartender would take the old drink away, untouched, and replace it with a new one. That is still stuck in my mind."

The memorial services, it was clear, were going to be a logistical nightmare. People called acquaintances in the area to inquire about lodging in Rome, Utica, Vernon. Anyone even remotely connected with the Big Orange #61 was besieged by requests for information about visiting hours, driving directions, you name it. Obviously, Richie's family had enough on their minds, so much of the planning fell to friends.

Fred Ulrich, having quietly attended to a hundred small details in Evans's busted-out early years, now attended to one more. Looking for advice, he spoke to a friend who ran a funeral home; how in the world, Ulrich later remembered asking the fellow, could any of the local mortuaries handle anything on this scale? "He told me they'd had some big funerals at his place and never had a problem," Ulrich recalled, "I said, 'You don't understand. This is going to be the biggest funeral you've ever *seen*.'"

Linda Holdeman and Dick O'Brien, married then, were checking into things, too. "If it wasn't for Linda and Dick," Lynn Evans says, "I wouldn't have known what to do. I pretty much let them take the reins." They agreed that none of the local funeral homes could handle the crowd, and investigated other venues. At some point somebody suggested the auditorium at the Capital Civic Center, which had opened in

1928 as a movie theatre. It had a huge capacity, and they could put the casket up on the stage. That was a possibility...

The old moving-picture house had never before hosted a funeral. But "we went in there and looked it over, and you could see how it would work," Dick O'Brien says. "[The mourners] would walk down one aisle, cross the stage to pay their respects, and then go out into the theatre and take a seat."

And that was how it went: two evenings of viewing on Sunday and Monday, and then a final session prior to the burial on Tuesday. An amazing cast of racing names passed through the Capitol theatre over those three days: NASCAR president Bill France Jr., Martinsville Speedway owner H. Clay Earles, New Smyrna track boss Clyde Hart, Merv Treichler, Greg Sacks, Mike McLaughlin, Billy Osmun, Kenny Brightbill, Ron and Ken Bouchard, Jerry Cook. The *Rome Sentinel* estimated that more than 100 drivers paid their respects.

Wherever you turned, different racing faces from different racing places. The common denominator was sadness.

"I was down at the theatre, at the funeral, and Maynard Troyer came in," Wilbur Jones says. "He had some people with him, and those folks walked right on in. But Maynard didn't. He just didn't want to go into the building. I had to talk him into it; I had to go in with him. Maynard really had an awful time with the whole thing."

Lynn Evans says, "The funeral was overpowering. I sometimes think I could have been stronger—I *should* have been stronger—when the different drivers came up to me. But when I talked to those guys, I'd really lose it. I knew how much they meant to Rich, and how hard it was for them to be there."

There were, by a local reporter's count, more than 175 floral displays, including several with checkered or orange motifs.

At every memorial service, the priest or minister or rabbi will remind one and all that the point of the assembly is not to mourn, but to celebrate the life of the deceased. Well, the funeral of Richard Ernest Evans came as close to that as any imaginable. Oh, there was mourning, and sorrow, and lots of tears. But the diverse turnout and the unusual venue made everything just surreal enough to seem, yes, celebratory. Here was this often insecure man who somehow loved being the center of attention up there on a stage, his helmet and uniform set up beside him, starring one last time in his own final drama.

"It was almost like being at some big movie," Dick Waterman says. "After people went up and walked past the casket, they sat down in the theatre seats and visited."

The auditorium was well-lit, at the request of Lynn Evans. "Rich was so full of life," she says, "so I needed it to be bright." And for the two evening services it was also loud, in a wonderful way, with a tape loop playing an eclectic mix of music: Sinatra's "My Way" because it fit the moment so well; the ZZ Top rocker "Legs" because, thanks to the hot-rod theme of its video, it was an Evans favorite; the theme from the movie "Shaft" because its weekly play on the Stafford Speedway public-address system had made it something of a Northeast modified anthem; the familiar 1973 radio tune "Stuck in the Middle with You" by the one-hit wonder band Stealers Wheel because, according to Lynn, "Rich loved that song. He couldn't sing, but he'd always sing that one." Once the initial shock of hearing pop songs at a wake wore off, people grinned, nodded, tapped their feet.

"I heard some comments later on about the music," Lynn says, "but that had a lot to do with a talk I'd had with Rich. He had befriended a fellow through Billy Osmun, and this man was a mortician. Somehow they'd talked about a funeral where they played all these songs that related to the person who had died, and Rich told me, 'You know, that's pretty cool. Instead of that church-type music, they should play music that makes you think of good things. Why should people have to just sit there feeling so bad?' So in my mind, I thought that's what Rich would have wanted."

The Tuesday morning service—attended by about 1,000 people, said the *Sentinel*—was more subdued, with an organist playing hymns. The Reverend Eric Harer of St. Paul's Catholic Church called Evans "the best at what he did" ... "awesome both on the track and off" ... "a legend in his own time." He added that Richie Evans "did not come to greatness by stepping on others, by putting others down, or by holding them in contempt."

The funeral cortege, dozens of cars long, had a sheriff's department escort. That was another Fred Ulrich touch: "I had gone to the chief of police and told him he'd better be ready for a lot of traffic." Up front was Evans's orange '34 Ford, followed closely by Maynard Troyer's bright red rod. The procession snaked out of downtown Rome, through the same streets where his victories and championships had been marked a few years earlier on Richie Evans Day.

Janelle and Jodi Evans beside dad's hot rod, smiling through their grief in the hours after his burial. *(Jodi Meola collection)*

Sorrow and laughter at one last Richie Evans party. At left, Dick O'Brien consoles Lynn Evans; at right, Val LeSieur tends bar. (courtesy of Speedway Scene)

In 1896, the English poet A.E. Housman wrote down some lines that fit the scene, in a piece about the funeral of a celebrated local sportsman as seen through the eyes of his friend, a pallbearer. Housman's famous "To An Athlete Dying Young" contains the following stanzas:

The time you won your town the race
We chaired you through the market-place;
Man and boy stood cheering by,
And home we brought you shoulder-high.

Today, the road all runners come,
Shoulder-high we bring you home,
And set you at your threshold down,
Townsman of a stiller town.

The burial service was held in the cemetery behind a pretty little white church in the center of Westernville, Richie's hometown. After the graveside prayers were said and folks began to drift slowly back to their cars, there came another strange musical moment. A young woman, seemingly unknown to those who remained, stepped forward with a small boombox-type tape player. She pushed a button, and out of the speaker flowed a simple homespun tune, with stark and heartfelt lyrics about her favorite driver. "When the tape finished," wrote Ken Tesoriere, "she took up the recorder, went to her car, and left." It was a chilling end to a wrenching morning.

When it had all ended, several dozen of the Evans inner circle changed into casual clothes and headed north toward Osceola and the Freeman. There, at what was supposed to be his retirement getaway—where he was going to sit on the porch with the rest of the gang in their rocking chairs—they saluted his memory with a long, all-out bash. They laughed, they cried, they ate, they drank, they told hundreds of stories, and they laughed and cried some more.

"I remember Val LeSieur tending bar, with his shirt off but still wearing a tie," Dick O'Brien grins. "I mean, you could just picture Richie cracking up over that."

In another culture, it would have been called an old-fashioned Irish wake. On this cool October afternoon, evening and night, it was one last Richie Evans party.

Mystery

FIGURING OUT WHY A RACE CAR has crashed is, even in the best cases, an inexact science. Today there are cameras everywhere at the biggest events, and yet even the clearest videotaped replay, shown from multiple angles, cannot always pinpoint the root cause of a wreck, the exact reason the wreck unfolded.

For instance: If a driver loses control and spins to the infield, *why* did he lose control? Was he simply driving too hard, or did he perhaps happen upon some unseen fluid on the track? If a tire blows, *why* did it blow? Did the driver run something over? Did the tire blister and explode?

Sometimes, there is never going to be a single explanation that satisfies everybody. Such was the case when Richie Evans hit that third-turn wall. There remains considerable debate, even after all this time, and not just about *why* this or that happened; folks who were there and saw the whole mess with their own eyes cannot seem to agree on what happened in the first place.

It shouldn't matter, really. Still, because there is that unknown—and probably because this was Richie Evans, the division's biggest name and grandest champion—it somehow *does* matter to many people, and likely will for a long time to come.

There was plenty of instant speculation about a stuck throttle, because modified racing had been through a handful of serious crashes (including the 1982 Dave Furioni fatality at Riverside Park) in which throttles were blamed. But a subsequent inspection deemed that the car's throttle and linkage were still functional. And Reggie Ruggiero, who saw the crash from the pit wall, maintains, "It wasn't a throttle, because if the throttle had stuck, you'd have seen the front tires lock up. Richie never put the brakes on. Your first reaction in a race car is, the throttle sticks, you put the brakes on, and the front tires lock up."

Standing only yards away from Ruggiero, Mario Fiore watched the same crash but saw something different: "He had the brakes locked right before he hit; I saw the puffs of smoke come off the tires."

Maybe Evans was on the brakes, maybe he wasn't. George Kent, trying to rerun that "strange, strange weekend," cannot say for sure. "I don't remember [seeing] any skid marks, or anything like that," is the best that Kent can come up with.

And if not the throttle, did something else fail? Crewman Kenny Hartung—speaking in that "trance" to the newspaperman from Rome—had little doubt: "Something in the right-front broke," Hartung declared.

Brett Bodine says, "I think there was a mechanical problem. That's not laying anything off on anybody; it's just that *mechanical things happen*. And at Martinsville in a modified, you drive so deep into the turn that if a mechanical failure happens, the time you have to react is so little. It's not like a Cup car, where you're letting off the gas way back on the straightaway. You drive a modified way down into the corner, and *then* you let off. There *is* no time to react."

Ironically, the guy you might figure to be the most reliable witness saw nothing in the way of any evidence. Tony Siscone says, "After Richie went by me down that back straightaway, I could only see the back of the car. Honestly, to say what happened ... I don't know. To me, it just seemed like the wheels never turned, because he went straight in. But I can tell you this: He went in full-bore."

Certainly, no one has put as much thought—or sheer physical effort—into figuring out that crash as Billy Nacewicz has. He says, "I don't know what happened. I wish I could tell you something definite. I wish I could tell *everybody* something definite, but I can't.

"NASCAR looked at the car. They brought in Maynard Troyer and Jerry Cook—Maynard because of all his building experience—and they couldn't find anything they could pinpoint [as having caused the crash]. Yeah, there was a lot of busted stuff on it, but nothing you could say for sure broke before the impact."

Cook, quoted by *Gater Racing News* in the wreck's aftermath, said, "We took the car into [a trackside] garage and we looked it over. The car was intact, the accelerator worked ... the pedals worked ... the seat belts worked ... the roll bars were intact. Except for the damage sustained when the car hit the wall, there was nothing wrong with the car that we could find."

Nacewicz says, "There are still a couple big questions in my mind. One [involves] the right-front wheel assembly, which was taken away at the scene and never returned. So we don't know if there was a failure of some kind on the right-front.

"I had the car in my possession for a year [in Rome], and every now and then I'd go back and look at it, just hoping that by looking at it with a clear head I might find something. Finally, it got to be too overwhelming. We cut it up and got it out of there."

In the absence of any definitive mechanical culprit, there arose speculation that perhaps something had happened to Evans himself, some medical crisis that left him incapable of slowing his car down and rounding that corner. Billy Nacewicz again: "There are theories out there about that, too, but we don't know. As far as a physical problem, different drivers in the vicinity have said different things: that he was slumped over before he went in, or whatever."

A heart attack, perhaps? A stroke? An aneurysm? Richie Evans smoked. Richie Evans drank. Richie Evans often skated by on too little sleep.

"Let's face it," his friend Dick O'Brien says, "Richie was never the guy who looked at the calendar and said, 'Well, it's time for my yearly check-up.'"

Dutch Hoag proclaims, "Right from the day it happened, I said, 'Something happened to Rich, something physical.' I've heard them say it was a stuck throttle, or whatever, but he was such a fast thinker, such a *responsive* kind of driver, that he'd have been able to do something. Get the brakes on, get the car sideways, *something*. That's what I believe to this day."

George Kent concurs: "Something happened to him. That's my opinion. I don't think it was the car, or anything else. I think something happened to him. I mean, Richie was awful good at trying to keep a car from wrecking bad, and that car wrecked too hard. If he'd had *any* control over it, it wouldn't have wrecked that bad."

Who knows?

"I've gone back and looked at the autopsy [report]," says Jodi Meola, the eldest daughter, "and there's no indicators that anything was wrong with him."

And yet ...

"He was starting to get headaches toward the end," Lynn Evans says. "But, again, he wouldn't go to the doctor. I used to say, 'Rich, go and get a physical. All these headaches are not normal.' Of course, he was a smoker, and he wasn't what I'd call a healthy eater; with the traveling, he ate at all hours of the night. Rich was a meat-and-potatoes guy, and everything had to be fried. And he loved his ice cream."

Ah, the ice cream. In the 1960s, Ted Puchyr remembers, "Richie would say, 'Come on, let's go up to the house.' Then he'd say, 'You want some ice cream?' He'd give you a bowl and a couple of scoops, then he'd sit there and eat the whole half-gallon." Daughter Janelle remembers her dad's freezer jammed with "all these half-gallons of maple walnut and chocolate chip."

Who knows? Headaches, a broken part, that atrocious diet, a hung throttle, the cigarettes. Who knows?

"I think we'll always have that mystery," says Dick O'Brien. "What happened?"

Jodi Meola says, "It still ... I don't know if 'haunts' is the right word, but it still eats at me today."

Lynn Evans has this thing in her head, this idea, her own way of having the mystery of October 24, 1985 make sense. She says, "I like to think that in that one instant in that car, he had a talk with the man

Richie Evans at work, 1985. *(Mary Hodge photo/courtesy of Speedway Scene)*

above. And the man above said, 'Richie Evans, I can take you out as a star, a champion, and nobody will ever be able to say they beat you. But there's a sacrifice: I'm going to have to take you right now.'

"And you know something? I really believe that Rich would have been OK with that. I really believe that's how he would have wanted to go."

Missing Man

IN THE WINTER OF 1985-86, the modified awards-dinner circuit was understandably low-key. At many of the same banquet venues Richie Evans had once turned into parties, his widow and his team and his sponsor instead posed stoically, accepting whatever awards he'd had coming.

That year, the Spencer Speedway dinner and the first-ever banquet for the NASCAR Modified Tour were scheduled as a combined affair. Evans had won the Tour championship, of course, and had also wrapped up the Spencer track title. It should have been, *would* have been, one hell of a night. Instead, it was a sad occasion—the Thompson Speedway banquet, which also honored an Evans track championship, was another—to pay silent tribute to a hero who wasn't there.

When the snow cleared, NASCAR modified racing prepared for the first season in more than a dozen years in which Evans wouldn't play some sort of a lead role. Even when he stayed close to home in his mid-1970s NEARA phase, he had remained a factor in the biggest NASCAR races, winning a Martinsville here, a Spring Sizzler there.

For all the speculation in his final years about how Evans might eventually ease out of the driver's seat, one thing became clear in 1986: modified racing wasn't ready for so abrupt a departure. Nobody in the division ever figured on one day waking up and not having him around.

"I'm sure we would have gone for the title again," Billy Nacewicz says. "Rich had accomplished pretty much everything he could in modified racing; we had won every big race at least once, and most of them we'd won twice or more. But I *know* he wasn't ready to retire yet."

That '86 NASCAR schedule opened, as usual, at Martinsville, where the race had a strange twist: the winning car, Art Barry's brand-new maroon #21 with Brett Bodine in the seat, was the last customer project Evans had taken on before he died. The media made a lot of that, with one headline even blaring something about the "ghost rider" in the car; corny in retrospect, sure, but such was the emotion of the day.

Springtime in the Northeast brought a slew of memorial races, many

of them 61 laps long, some at speedways where Evans hadn't raced in years, others at tracks where he had *never* raced. "A lot of tracks asked me about doing that," Lynn Evans recalls, "and how could I say no? Rich's fans meant so much to him. *People* meant so much to him. I went to most of those races, at least in the beginning, and at times it was very hard. I mean, to have grown men walk up to you and cry, that's a tough thing."

Jodi Evans remembers her and her sisters always being "honored to be there," but adds, "it was also very, very emotional."

At Oswego's traditional May date—in 1986 a 125-lap NASCAR Modified Tour show named in his honor—came perhaps the most moving tribute. Just prior to the feature, the loudspeakers called everyone's attention to the old electronic scoreboard in the first turn, where Evans's number was posted in lights. Then the bulbs blinked off, and track announcer Roy Sova, who had called so many of Richie's wondrous moments there, said, "That is the last time you'll see the 61 on the scoreboard here at the Oswego Speedway."

As Richie's superspeedway Camaro made a slow lap around his old home track, with Billy Nacewicz driving and Kenny Hartung beside him, the PA system loudspeakers blared a song Lynn Evans had handpicked for the occasion. It was George Harrison's "Faster," a tune the ex-Beatle said was inspired by Formula One champions Jackie Stewart and Niki Lauda and written especially in memory of his late friend, the star-crossed Swedish F1 driver Ronnie Peterson. On this day, in the bright sun of another spring on Evans's home turf, it sounded like his life story set to music:

(left) NASCAR founder Bill France Sr. presents Richie's 1985 championship honors to Lynn, Richie Jr. and Tara. *(Lynn Evans collection)*

(right) Lynn Evans wipes away a tear, Riverhead Raceway owner Barbara Cromarty offers a consoling hand, and daughter Tara hangs tough at one of 1986's many memorial races. *(Kevin Kane photo/courtesy of Speedway Scene)*

The Evans Camaro, Billy Nacewicz and Kenny Hartung aboard, at Oswego in 1986. *(Howie Hodge photo/courtesy of Speedway Scene)*

Chose a life in circuses
Jumped into the deepest end
Pushing himself to all extremes
Made it – people became his friend

Now they stood and noticed him
Wanted to be a part of it
Pulled out some poor machinery
So he worked till the pieces fit ...

Faster than a bullet from a gun
He is faster than everyone...

As the Camaro rolled slowly out of turn four and down the front straightaway, it passed a starting grid full of Richie's peers, many of whom had spent their entire careers either looking up to, trying to catch, or racing alongside the man in the #61. Those were a hard few seconds, whether you were thinking about Evans or about the men preparing to race for the trophy bearing his name.

Jamie Tomaino, who had raced against Evans for 10 years, topped the modified field. Joe Gosek, Richie's young friend, took the accompanying supermodified feature.

In time the stream of memorial events slowed as teams got into the Friday/Saturday/Sunday rhythm of the season, but that didn't mean things were back to normal. For many folks, modified life felt ... different. Some ultimately decided it was too different.

"A lot of people just stopped going to the races," says Millie Hatch, counting herself and her husband Bill among them. "We just started following the Cup races instead."

Another Rome-area couple, Donny and Rita Marcello, went the same route. When they go to a race these days, it's more likely to be at a place like Charlotte than, say, Oswego or Stafford. "I still love racing, believe me," Donny says. "But without Richie there, it's like my heart isn't in it anymore."

Dick O'Brien, looking at the situation from his multiple perspectives of fan, friend, and longtime official, says, "I had been through this before, when we lost Jimmy Shampine. See, Jimmy was the absolute king of the supermodifieds, especially at Oswego, so that was a huge impact. But with Jimmy, the impact was on a smaller group of people, because the supermodified community was a smaller thing. With Richie, it was more widely felt. I wish I had a $10 bill for every time this happens: I'll run into people at the mall who I haven't seen for years, old-time fans. I'll say, 'Hey, how are you? Where the hell have you been?' They'll say, 'I haven't been to the races since Richie died.' And they're not lying.

"Don't forget, things had been changing in asphalt modified racing. You also had a lot of guys leaving: Maynard had retired, Sacks had moved on, Ronnie Bouchard had moved on, Cookie had retired, and a lot of guys like Merv Treichler were now doing other things. Richie was, literally, the last real link to the old guard, the last guy you *knew* was going to be at all the big races. So when he went away, they just gave it up."

Those who stuck around saw, over the course of the next decade, a very different sort of modified racing emerge. Several tracks dropped the modifieds as a weekly headliner; one was Stafford, which had enjoyed a couple of stints as the premier modified track in the Northeast but axed the class in favor of the more restricted SK division after the 1986 season. And the touring concept continued to evolve, moving toward the one-event-per-week formula now followed by NASCAR's Whelen Modified Series. Lost forever were the days when Evans, Cook, Bugs Stevens, Ernie Gahan and Fred DeSarro had run gypsy-like up and down the highway, running 60, 70, 80 events in the course of winning their national modified titles.

"It makes me kind of sad," muses Billy Nacewicz. "They're down to about 20 races, and it seems like half of 'em are at Thompson and Stafford. Nothing against the guys who are there now, because it's not their fault, but what kind of championship is that?"

And along with the changing schedule came changing procedures. First, the length of the races rose dramatically; fans raised on a regular-season diet of 30-, 35- and 50-lap features—with the odd 100 thrown in —watched modified race distances soar to the point where the *average* race on the 2004 NASCAR Featherlite slate was 156 laps. (One wonders what impact that had on annual classics like the Bud 200 at Oswego and the Race of Champions, which once stood out as great endurance tests but became just a couple of slightly-longer-than-average modified shows. In the 1990's, Oswego axed the Bud 200 from its schedule, and a series of financial scandals led longtime ROC boss Joe Gerber to sell his event's once-proud name to Empire State promoter Andy Harpell. These days, the Race of Champions is a New York show with a few invaders tossed in.)

Second, cost-cutting rules regarding tire brands, compounds and total number of tires allotted did away with the widely-varying strategies once seen in long-distance modified events. In a typical 150-lapper allowing teams to change three tires, the bulk of the front-runners will pit during any caution period close to halfway, effectively dividing the race into two halves. In an old-school 150, a gambler like Richie Evans might dive onto pit road at lap 110, take on a couple of soft Firestones or Goodyears, and then carve his way back through the pack. You'll not see that again.

Third, time trials gradually replaced heat races as the standard method of qualifying for major modified events, to the point where even the last-chance consolation race became a thing of the past. If a driver doesn't make the cut through time trials, he'd better be high enough in the NASCAR points standings to earn a provisional starting spot. Failing that, he's going home.

You can argue all day whether these changes have helped or hurt the division, and certainly there are plenty of diehards on either side of that fence. What cannot be debated is that things look a whole lot different than they did when Evans was around. And it is reasonable to wonder just what the Rapid Roman might have made of it all.

Dick O'Brien says, "Jerry Cook was always a modified car owner, and when he set up that [NASCAR] tour, he set it up for a modified car owner. Time trials, no heats; there's not even a consi! Hell, when you went to the Bud 200 or the Spring Sizzler in the '70s, some of the best racing of the weekend happened in those heats! I mean, you could have had a ho-hum [race], but if somebody asked you how the show was, you'd say, 'Geez, they were dog-eat-dog just trying to make the feature! So-and-so started 13th in his heat and just barely made it in!'

"They've forgotten that they have to *entertain* people."

While Evans himself was also a car owner, he was on the record as favoring heat races over time trials, telling radio interviewer Arnold Dean that heats were "generally more interesting, as far as the fan goes" and that they "make the show move along quite a bit faster."

Maybe an against-the-grain opinion like that wouldn't register loudly today. Maybe NASCAR was so determined to push its modified division in this direction that even a nine-time champion would have had little choice but to follow along for the ride. We'll never know. But this much is clear: Richie Evans was probably the last modified racer powerful enough to (A) rally the rank-and-file to support a cause, and (B) get

NASCAR and/or the track promoters to at least *examine* that cause. Today, to compete in the NASCAR Modified Series is essentially to acquiesce to whatever schedule, whatever rules, whatever procedures come out of Daytona Beach.

Again, that might be good or it might be bad, but it sure is a change from the days when a guy like Evans could—and would—take his case straight to Bill France Jr. or Jim Hunter.

"When Richie died, the modified people lost more than just a star," says Evans crewman Ray Spognardi, who in 2004 could still be found in the pits, spinning wrenches for Art Barry. "They lost their voice. They don't have a guy like that anymore, somebody who'll stand up for them, somebody who'll lead them. Instead, they've got people telling them what to do and how to do it, and they just go along."

To listen to Ed Flemke Jr., a modified lifer with 30 years behind the wheel, is to understand that the balance of power between the division's decision-makers and its racers has tilted in the absence of a strong presence like Evans. "We go to these meetings, and we know we're getting snowballed and railroaded and lied to," Flemke says. "And I'll think, *This* is when you need a guy like Richie."

"He had the clout," says Mario Fiore. "He had [the attention of] the big boys from NASCAR, for sure."

No matter how you view it, the modified picture is not the same with Richie Evans missing.

But Bobby Hutchens—like countless others—believes one thing has not changed.

"For anybody running modifieds today," says Hutchens, "Richie still ought to be their benchmark. Because that was The Man, right there."

Scattered

THE FATES AND FORTUNES of those whose lives Evans touched have gone in a thousand different directions.

Billy Nacewicz, who had built so many winning cars in the old shop on Calvert Street, tried to keep the place rolling by hanging out his chassis-building shingle. He named the business RE Fabrications in memory of his driver, boss and friend. It seemed for a while like a good move, because Nacewicz was held in high regard in the modified community and the early interest was high. The only problem was, he could hardly bear to be at a race track anymore. The wound was too fresh, his nerves still too frayed.

Nacewicz: "I remember a race at Oswego [in 1986] when Tony Jankowiak was driving one of my cars. He went into the first turn and got into a three-car tangle. I was standing in the infield and my view

Seventeen months after Evans died, the great Charlie Jarzombek lost his life at the same track. *(Val LeSieur photo/courtesy of Speedway Scene)*

was blocked by the hot dog stand, but I heard this terrific crash into the wall. And as I turned to watch the cars coming out of turn two, the only car I didn't see come out was Tony's. My knees started shaking so bad. I thought to myself, 'This is not for me.' Then I heard them say Tony was out of the car, that he was all right. It was the greatest thing I'd ever heard."

Then, early in 1987, came the blow which sent Nacewicz reeling.

Charlie Jarzombek and Ernie Wilsberg were the first truly high-profile customers Nacewicz had. They unveiled their new RE Fabrications car that March, shaking the bugs out in the NASCAR opener at the Orange County Speedway in Rougemont, North Carolina. Then came Martinsville. Jarzombek had high hopes for the car, and so did everyone around him. The day before the race, his father, Charlie Sr.—known in every modified pit area as Super—motioned a friend to look into the cockpit. There, in lieu of the rooftop Evans memorials many cars still sported, Charlie Jarzombek had requested that a number 61 be lettered.

"He wanted Richie in there ridin' with him," Super Jarzombek said.

When the modified portion of the Dogwood 500 went green, Billy Nacewicz was sitting with some friends atop a van inside turn one. Which happened to be right across from where Jarzombek, his engine screaming from an apparent stuck throttle, slammed into the concrete wall with deadly force. Seventeen months after Billy's life had careened off its tracks on the other end of this same speedway, he was forced to absorb the loss of another friend.

What followed was a period cruel not just to Nacewicz, but to all of asphalt modified racing. Within three years and one month of Jarzombek's death, the division was rocked by four more fatal crashes, those of Corky Cookman (at Thompson in 1987), Tommy Druar (Lancaster, 1989) Don Pratt (Pocono, 1989) and Tony Jankowiak (Stafford, 1990). The loss of Jankowiak was especially hard on Nacewicz; young Tony had hung out with the Evans crowd almost from the time he had started racing at tracks across New York. In the middle of all that, Nacewicz had to bury his father.

RE Fabrications struggled because its owner's *life* had become a struggle. "There was just a series of deaths," he says. "It took a lot out of me. I kind of lost my spirit, and the business started going downhill." In the middle of that rocky road, Nacewicz and his wife divorced. In time, he sold the chassis business and moved to North Carolina, eventually finding work with Busch Series teams and companionship beside another former resident of Rome: Lynn Evans.

It's one of those strange stories that spin out of tragedy, surprising even those involved.

Shell-shocked in the wake of her husband's death—"For the next year," says her friend Rita Marcello, "we would sit together for hours, all night long"—Lynn slowly began the process of tying up all the loose ends relating to Richie's racing and his sideline businesses. No one person had a handle on *everything* Evans had going on, but Billy Nacewicz came as close as anybody did. These days, Lynn refers to him as "William" partially as a way of distancing him from the "Billy" her husband was always talking about.

"I leaned on William a lot after Rich died," she says. "He became my strength, and that was so unselfish of him because when Rich died, William lost a lot more than people realize. He loved Rich, too."

She laughs, thinking back 30 years to when Nacewicz first joined the Evans team. "When William came into the picture," Lynn says, "I didn't really care for his personality. Because, see, until you really got to know him, he wasn't always very friendly. I remember saying, 'Rich, if you and I are going to be together, I'm sorry, but you've got to get rid of this guy.' And he told me, 'Well, OK. But if I do that, I'm gonna have to park those race cars, because I *need* him. He's the guy I need.'

"Well, that was pretty smart of Rich. By that point, I knew him well enough to know that racing was his life. So I said, 'Well, all right.' I remember Rich saying, 'Just give him a chance. You'll really like him.'"

Out of tragedy ...

"Neither one of us ever imagined it would become anything on an intimate level," Lynn says, still sounding amazed by the whole thing. They were a couple before most of their friends knew it, and they have stayed together. Again: if it sounds strange, maybe you haven't been through the kind of sorrow those two walked through together.

Richie's children—the four from marriage number one, the two from his second—have grown up and established their own lives. Jodi, her husband William Meola and their kids, Ryan and Gianna, live in Rome, as do Janelle and Doug Walda and their children, Kara and Trevor. Jill and her daughter, Megan, also remain in town. Jacki and Mark Williams live in Horseheads, New York, with their daughter Jenna. Richie Jr. has bounced around a bit, having lived in New York, New Jersey, and, presently, North Carolina. His sister Tara, the baby of the

Daughter Jodi with a couple of Richie's grandchildren at a Rome parade. In the car is Jim Ball, whose displays carried on the Evans story for years after the champ's death. *(Jodi Meola collection)*

bunch, attended Appalachian State University in Boone, North Carolina, and resides now in New Jersey.

"The kids are the ones who really lost out," says Lynn, "because they didn't get to know their dad like they could have." She points out that at the time of their father's death, the older girls "were at an age when most kids aren't really *into* their parents. And Richie and Tara were very little, so they don't have many memories."

Daughter Jill says, "I had started to admire him more and more as I grew up, especially the year he died. I was at the age where you're learning more about life, and I was starting to realize the way everybody liked him."

And if his children missed out, so did the next generation. First wife Barbara, who never remarried, says, "I look around today at his beautiful grandchildren, and I think, Dear God, what Richie is missing! I can see him today really *enjoying* these grandchildren."

In the winter of 2003-04, Jodi's son Ryan and Janelle's boy Trevor, then 16 and 13, respectively, were building what Janelle called "this mini-bike *thing*, out of a snowblower." Both moms, shaking their heads over the gearheads they had raised, interrupted the construction to announce this: "Boys, your grandfather would be proud of you two."

Jodi says, "I get sad, because I think back to the way he was with us, even with the limited time he had, and I know he would have been an *excellent* grandfather. He'd have more spare time on his hands, and I'm sure he would have enjoyed being with the kids. That's the only time I get angry about him being gone; I'll think, Why did you have to go so early?"

No one would blame Richie Jr. for asking his father that same rhetorical question. He wanted to be a racer from the time he could remember, and as a toddler was a frequent visitor to the Calvert Street garage, where his dad seemed to delight in his daredevil antics. On a 1979 radio show for WTIC in Hartford, host Arnold Dean asked Evans what he might do if his only son, then three years old, someday wanted to race.

DEAN: "Would you encourage him?"

EVANS: "I will help him if he shows that he has the ambition. But if he doesn't want to hold up his end, I will not have anything to do with it."

DEAN: "You would not *dis*courage him from it, though."

EVANS: "I will not go either way. He's going to have to show that he wants it, and then I'd go right along with it. But he's going to have to work at it."

The son tried that, but without Dad around it was tough. He dabbled with karts as a youngster whenever he got the chance. After a stab at college in North Carolina, he hot-lapped a few borrowed street stocks and did short stints driving late models in Virginia and local modifieds at New Jersey's Wall Stadium. His Wall ride was owned by the Blewett family, a noteworthy footnote given his father's 1981 NASCAR title fight with John Blewett Jr. At any rate, neither situation lasted, and by 2004, the guy so many folks still call Little Rich, no longer little at age 28, was back in North Carolina, working as a fabricator. His bloodlines, he told writer Bruce Bennett, hadn't opened many doors: "Being the son of Richie Evans actually makes it a little harder ..."

Lynn Evans says of her son, "My heart bleeds for Richie. I knew it wasn't going to be easy for him, because even Dale Earnhardt Jr. had to work for what he got. But Little Richie never was able to get the help Rich could have given him. And I really think that being the same age as so many of these kids who come in—some with their dad's money, or their dad's connections—has to be painful for him. I look at that as a mother, and it makes me sad."

The elder Evans did pass on a little bit of competitive advice to his youngest child, daughter Tara, when at five years of age she joined a soccer league that pitted her against the boys. Her memory of his pep talk is priceless: "I remember my father saying, 'Tara, don't let those boys push you around. When the refs aren't looking, stick your foot out and trip 'em.'"

Ernest Evans, Richie's father, died late in 1978, a little more than a month after his son had clinched his second NASCAR championship. Satie Evans, the quiet little mother who would stand there beaming whenever her Richie had won, died in 1996. She is buried beside her husband, in a plot next to their son's.

Sandy Jones, the sister, today lives outside Baltimore, in the suburb of Lutherville.

Like the Evans family, the old race team has scattered around a bit, too. Billy Nacewicz says, "I talk to Kenny Hartung a couple times a year, and Ray Spognardi a few times a year. We don't keep in touch as much

The late Satie Evans with her granddaughter Tara. *(Jodi Meola collection)*

Richie, Jr. prepares for battle at Wall Stadium. *(Michael Pares photo)*

as we should, and a lot of that is my fault as much as theirs. You get busy living your own life."

He shrugs and adds quietly, "Absence and distance. There's a lot of people I'd like to have kept up with, but I haven't done it, for whatever reason."

Fred Ulrich died in 2003, but Wilbur Jones is still in Rome, as is Bill "Bondo" Clark, and Buster Maurer is just up the road a piece in Lee Center. John McClellan, a New Yorker now, is in nearby West Leyden. But the gang gets together only rarely, and that takes prompting, like the time in 2002 when McClellan threw a small party. "Little by little," John says, "a lot of the old stories came back out."

The old shop at 608 Calvert has changed hands a few times since 1985, but belongs now to Tony Pettinelli Jr., which seems rather fitting. He came of age stooging on the #61 before becoming a valued team member, and, after all, his dad had sold the building to Evans in the first place. There, Tiger builds racing machines of another kind: all-terrain vehicles and snowmobiles, both popular forms of competition in the region.

Gene DeWitt remained in racing after Richie's death, sponsoring DIRT star Jack Johnson and, with some initial reluctance, returning to the NASCAR modified scene by backing George Kent. "Gene was obviously pretty depressed over what had happened to Richie, and I think his kids talked him into calling me as a way for him to get back in," Kent says. "Anyway, he made me an awful good deal, so we went racing together." The pair won numerous races. Sadly, DeWitt himself passed away in 1988. As the new millennium arrived, his heirs sold B.R. DeWitt, Inc. and several other family companies to Hanson PLC, described in the business pages as an "international building materials company."

Kent, for his part, remains one of the toughest regulars on the New York pavement modified circuit. Other ex-Evans foes still going strong: Jamie Tomaino, Tony Hirschman and Mike Stefanik, now part of the old guard on the NASCAR Whelen Modified series, where Reggie Ruggiero, Jan Leaty and Ken Bouchard make occasional starts; Jimmy Spencer, Mike McLaughlin and Jeff Fuller, all hanging on in the dog-eat-dog Nextel Cup and Busch Series world; and Doug Heveron, now tooling around Florida's asphalt tracks in a winged sprinter.

And, of course, Geoff Bodine, still climbing through Cup, Busch and Craftsman Truck Series windows. One of his more ironic rides came a few years back as a Rockingham fill-in for the injured Tim Fedewa at BACE Motorsports, where Billy Nacewicz was among the lead mechanics. "That led to a little bit of ribbing around the shop," Nacewicz says. "Those guys busted me about teaming up with Geoffrey. But that was OK with me. I knew what he could do. Geoff did a great job, and he was good to work with."

Strange as it might seem, never across that weekend did those controversial Evans/Bodine modified finishes come up. Nacewicz laughs, "It was better to leave that alone. We still had to work together. But, honestly, whenever I see Geoff, obviously there's some mutual respect there from our past accomplishments. We'll always say hello. But it's a very casual thing; we don't go out and have a beer together, and we've never had a chance to sit down for 20 minutes and talk about the old days."

Most of Richie's surviving rivals, however, have hung up their helmets. Jerry Cook has been through a series of promotions within NASCAR and is now a Daytona-based administrator with the organization. Bugs Stevens, admittedly rattled by the deaths of Evans, Jarzombek and Cookman, climbed out of modifieds in 1987, raced pro stock late models for a while as a hobby, and finally quit in 1991. Ron Bouchard walked away from NASCAR's Cup circuit in 1988, and now owns several successful automobile dealerships in Massachusetts. Brian Ross steers trucks rather than race cars. Mike Loescher operates a driving school in Florida. Merv Treichler helps run his family's large floral business. Roger Treichler, sadly, has been confined to a wheelchair since a 1999 roofing accident. Dick Fowler moved to Florida, as did Bill Wimble, Leo Cleary, Gene Bergin and God knows how many more as the 1960s modified crowd edged into their golden years.

Doug Hewitt parlayed his modified experience and his technical know-how into several NASCAR crew-chiefing positions. In 2004, he was spearheading the Busch, Cup and ARCA efforts of young Joe Gibbs Racing shoe J.J. Yeley.

Lee Osborne retired from sprint car racing in 1984, and in time became a highly-respected builder of street rods; among his customers were A.J. Foyt and Jeff Gordon. Divorced from his first wife in 1988, Osborne and his old flame, the former Donna Hoag, reunited thanks to some old modified friends, Jerry and Sue Cook. Donna, widowed, was visiting Daytona, and got together with the Cooks. Ozzie remembers, "I was living in Brownsburg, Indiana, when Sue called and said, 'Somebody here wants to talk to you.' I hadn't talked to Donna in 26 years, but I recognized her voice right away." He moved back to New York, and he and Donna—married now—live high on a Penn Yan hilltop with a postcard view of Keuka Lake. Out back in a tidy barn/shop, he builds about one rod per year, "traditional stuff" like 1932-34 Fords. His cars are always steel-bodied because Osborne insists that putting a fiberglass body on a hot rod "is like getting a boob job. Yeah, it'll look good, but you know it's not the real thing."

Osborne's father-in-law and ex-teammate, the great Dutch Hoag, still looks tough enough to climb into a modified and win himself another Race of Champions. Hoag still owns a trucking outfit in Bath, New York, the town his Langhorne wins put on America's racing map. His grandson Alex races dirt modifieds at the Black Rock Speedway in nearby Dundee. "I'm there every Friday night," says the Dutchman, "but I don't travel much." He did show up at Oswego in October of 2003

(left) Two Evans cronies: Billy Osmun, left, still runs the Freeman Hotel; Sonney Seamon passed away in 1994.

(right) Old friends and rivals, both now gone: Richie Evans and Lenny Boehler. *(Val LeSieur photos/courtesy of Speedway Scene)*

to serve as grand marshal for the Race of Champions, after years of turning down personal invitations from ROC rep Marilyn Toal and other old friends. Why the change of heart? "Marilyn caught me in a weak moment," Hoag smiles.

Maynard Troyer, having sold his race car business to former modified shoe Billy Colton, divides his time nowadays between New York and Florida. Ten years after Evans's death, Troyer talked about missing the fun times they'd had off the track: "He had the hotel, of course, and we went up there quite a few times and played."

Here, Maynard paused. "Osmun's still got the place, and he's invited me up a number of times, and I'm sure we'd have a good time. But it's just ... I don't know, *different*. If Richie had been around, I'd have been there."

Other familiar faces are gone now, too. Ray Hendrick died in 1990, Sonney Seamon in 1994, Lou Lazzaro in 2000, Lenny Boehler in 2002, Tom Baldwin in 2004, and the sad list goes on.

All that family, all those friends, all those foes, scattered in the winds of time.

Legacy

IN 1998, as part of NASCAR's 50th anniversary celebration, Bill France Jr. commissioned a panel to come up with the 50 greatest drivers in the sanctioning body's history. It was announced to a Speedweeks gathering of international motorsports media and invited guests in a theater inside the Daytona USA attraction. The list, as expected, was chock full of superstars from the Grand National/Winston Cup/Nextel Cup league. But four short-track giants also made the cut: the late Ralph Earnhardt, ageless Alabama Gang leader Red Farmer, and a couple of modified champions named Jerry Cook and Richie Evans.

Around that same time, an ESPN poll ranked the century's 100 greatest North American race drivers. A.J. Foyt topped the survey; Richie Evans slotted in at number 32, ahead of such motorsports luminaries as Don Prudhomme, Ned Jarrett, and Jacques Villeneuve. The only other short-track star on the list was World of Outlaws sprint car icon Steve Kinser, right behind Evans in 33rd.

In 2000, Jersey-based *Area Auto Racing News* polled 23 motorsports journalists—including, admirably, several not connected with AARN—to come up with a listing of the top 25 asphalt modified drivers of all time. Every voter who responded had Evans on his or her list. Out of a possible 575 voting points, he registered a 573. Twenty of the 23 picked Evans as being number one.

In 2003, NASCAR compiled its own selection of all-time modified greats. Theirs was a tricky task: not only was consideration limited to men who excelled in NASCAR events—handicapping open-competition luminaries like Dutch Hoag and Ed Flemke—but there was also the complexity of comparing today's series to the more footloose pre-touring era. The NASCAR list left plenty of room for garage debate, but there was never really any doubt about the man in the lead slot. From 10th to first, the list included Reggie Ruggiero, Jimmy Spencer, Fred DeSarro, Bugs Stevens, Tony Hirschman, Geoff Bodine, Ray Hendrick, Jerry Cook, Mike Stefanik ... and Richie Evans.

Evans has also been named to several halls of fame. He was a shoo-in, of course, for the New York State Stock Car Association and New England Auto Racing halls. It was a bit more surprising when in 1986 he became a first-ballot inductee to the National Motorsports Press Association hall; never before had the Southern-heavy NMPA voting bloc ushered in a driver who hadn't competed at the Grand National/Winston Cup/Nextel Cup level.

The capper came in 1996, when, in a black-tie ceremony at Talladega, the International Motorsports Hall of Fame inducted Evans. His "classmates" included three-time Indianapolis 500 winner Johnny Rutherford (who, serving as an NBC-TV analyst, once interviewed Evans after a Martinsville victory); 1970 NASCAR Grand National Champion Bobby Isaac; John Surtees, a World Motorcycle Champion who later won Formula One auto races as a driver and car builder; Donald Healy, world speed record holder and father of the fabled Austin-Healy; and Dr. Ferdinand Porsche, who designed and built a line of road and race cars you might be familiar with.

Richie's family and a small band of friends attended, and daughter Jodi Meola called the event "a huge, huge thing for me. It helped me realize my father's place in things, and how he fit into all that." Donny Marcello, a long way from the Rusty Nail and Utica-Rome Speedway on this Talladega night, remembers, "Richard Petty was there, and he stopped to talk with us. Richard put his arm around me, and he said, 'I'm glad I didn't have to run against that guy.' That was a hell of a compliment to Richie."

In 1978, three-time Indy 500 winner Johnny Rutherford interviewed Evans at Martinsville; in 1996, both were inducted into the International Motorsports Hall of Fame at Talladega. *(Balser and Son photo/courtesy of Speedway Scene)*

And the compliments have kept on coming, from all kinds of places. The International Race of Champions for years featured a car bearing a color its mechanics, many of them New Jersey natives and modified fans, called "Evans orange." Jeff Gordon's Nextel Cup Chevrolet rolls off the starting grid every Sunday with a small #61 on its front bumper, a tribute from Steve Bergh, a Hendrick Motorsports fabricator originally from Howell, New Jersey. "I just thought it belonged on there," Bergh says. And in October of 2003, Dale Earnhardt Jr.'s Busch Series team ran the Charlotte 300-miler with a car painted up to resemble the same scheme—orange, of course, with red and yellowish accent striping—carried by the B.R. DeWitt Cavalier in 1983, one of Richie's best seasons.

"Richie Evans is a pioneer of the sport and he was a big inspiration to many in NASCAR," said Dale Jr. "Myself included."

Martin Truex Jr., whose father and uncle Barney had both raced Evans-built modifieds at Wall Stadium and elsewhere, drove that orange Earnhardt car at Charlotte. In a Speed-TV "Wind Tunnel" interview, he declared the experience "real cool for me. Richie Evans, everybody knows, was the greatest modified driver of all time. It was a huge honor for us to put his paint scheme on our car. It was big. It was *real* big.

"I've heard so many stories about him," Truex grinned. "They pretty much said he could win a race with a car on three wheels, and all kinds of amazing stories like that."

Those who co-starred in those stories won't ever forget them. George Kent says, "I know some people think about other things when it comes to Richie—the partying or whatever—but I think mostly about all those good races." And if you ask Jerry Cook what first comes to mind when somebody mentions his fellow Roman and perennial championship rival, Jerry does not hesitate: "The tough competition."

Bobby Hutchens says, "One of the greatest thrills of my life came at

Martinsville, not long before Richie was killed. I had a pretty competitive car and a really good motor, and I actually got to race some with him. After he died, that's something I told my daddy; I said, 'Even if I never do another thing in racing, I got to run wheel-to-wheel with Richie Evans.' That will always be very special to me."

And those who have only *heard* the stories can't help wanting to hear more. "Even today," says Ray Spognardi, "people come up—people I haven't seen in years, and people I've never met, but they know I used to work with Richie—and sooner or later, that's what they want to talk about. That is a real tribute to the man. Some of these younger guys, the kids just getting into the game, they know about him, but they don't know much. And yet the thing I like is that they ask a lot of questions about him: how we did this, how we did that, how Richie looked at things."

The Evans legacy, clearly, is more than just a compilation of statistics and a listing of the institutions where he is enshrined. A big chunk of his legacy is the curiosity that still swirls around the man, the fact that he's still … *cool*. "Think about it," says Dick O'Brien. "Whenever you see a driver do anything really special, who's the first guy you compare him to? It's Richie."

A lot of that is due to what pop psychologists call "the James Dean factor." O'Brien says, "It's that whole 'he died with his boots on' thing. Richie died with his helmet on, running balls-to-the-wall. He died as a champion, and we all want to remember him that way."

Billy Nacewicz agrees: "Unfortunately, we lose some performers at the peak of their careers. To their fans it's hard, but to the performers themselves I think it's how they'd *rather* go out.

"I look at a guy like Arnold Palmer. He's still out there, and he'll still play a tournament every now and then. He's a great man, and he's still very popular with golf fans, but it bothers me to see a champion struggling to shoot an 80 while some kid is out there shooting 65. And that happens in racing, too; there are drivers who overstay their careers. You almost wish everybody would get out while their star is still shining, and not go through those five or 10 extra years of not winning.

"So, yeah, the fact that we remember Richie as being a champion right until the end has kept his luster going," Nacewicz says. "We never saw him running 12th with all these new kids going by him. You still think about him being wide open, on the track and off the track."

"You never saw him deteriorate," declares Buster Maurer. "Nobody can say, 'Well, gee, Richie had started to slow down,' because, no, he didn't. He was always good."

Steve Hmiel says, "Obviously, it was an absolute tragedy, losing him like that. On the other hand, I have a hard time picturing Richie Evans, 70 years old and miserable because he couldn't race anymore."

That's an Evans we'll never know.

"Nobody ever beat him," Nacewicz says. "He went out on top."

Evans in 1985. "You still think about him being wide open, on and off the track," says Billy Nacewicz. *(Burt Gould photo/courtesy of Speedway Scene)*

"Like He's Still Here"

TONY PETTINELLI JR. is sitting in his office at the former Evans shop on Calvert Street. He basically works out of one half of the building, the part where all those #61 modifieds and customer frames were built. An auto-repair shop fills what used to be the main garage.

"A lot of the stuff here is left from back when Richie had it," he says. "Over on that post, you can still see the mount where we had the tube-notching tool. And the lifts Richie put in are still there on the other side of the shop. They get used every day.

"There aren't too many days that go by here when I don't have a conversation involving Richie or something he did. Even if I'm not thinking about him, somebody else will bring his name up."

Without question, the old shop still holds a bit of orange-tinted karma.

"People will drive by this place sometimes just to see it," Pettinelli says. "And, I mean, they're more than welcome to stop in. Sometimes they do that, and I'll show 'em around. I know what Richie meant to people—fans, acquaintances, whoever—so I know how important that is."

Wilbur Jones, knows, too. "He's been gone a long time," sighs Wilbur, "but they still remember him."

They sure do. Around Rome—indeed, all over Oneida County—you can walk into bars, sandwich shops, go-kart tracks, you name it, and glance up to find a picture of Richie Evans hanging on the walls. His daughter Jill says, "That used to bother me, because it just reminded me that he was gone. But I don't feel that way anymore. I think about the way people smile when they look at those pictures, and the way they tell all the old stories, and it makes me happy."

It never goes away, according to Jill. "I work as a travel agent, and I'd say that at least twice a week, to this day, somebody will come in and we'll end up talking about my father. They'll notice that my last name is Evans, and they'll ask me if I was related to Richie. Once they find out that I'm his daughter, they always have a story to tell.

"That amazes me, to see the way so many people liked him and followed him. It feels good that he's remembered that way. It's an awesome thing to think that he lived his life so fully that people haven't forgotten about him."

And it isn't just limited the old hometown. Jill's kid sister Jacki has lived in Oswego, in New Hampshire, and now in Horseheads, and at every stop she's heard Richie Evans stories. She says, "I can't tell you how many times I've heard, 'Oh, I knew your dad!' I had a girlfriend who went to college in Massachusetts, and her professor found out she was from Rome, New York. He said, 'Have you ever heard of Richie Evans?' That just blew my mind."

Same sort of unexpected reference, but with a racing twist: Janelle and her husband Doug were in a camping area outside the New Hampshire International Speedway for a Nextel Cup race. "This other couple was parked near us, and somehow we got talking about where we were from," Janelle says. "They were from Agawam, Massachusetts, and I knew my father used to race there [at Riverside Park] but I didn't say anything. Well, we said we were from upstate New York, and then we narrowed it down to Rome, and the first thing they wanted to know was if we'd ever heard of Richie Evans. And I was like, 'Um, well …'

"Once they found out he was my father, it was a big to-do. They came over and started telling stories. I just sat there and took it all in."

It doesn't take much, it seems, to jostle the memories. Recently, Dick O'Brien was driving down the road, with Bill Merkling riding shotgun. The two are old friends, fellow Oswego Speedway veterans—Merkling was a longtime assistant flagman there—and traveling partners who had downed a few post-race beers with the Evans crowd up and down the East Coast. Now, they were riding home from an afternoon on the golf course. "As I was passing through Oneida, I went past Ross Holmes Collision," O'Brien says. "Ross was a guy who raced modifieds; in fact, he ran with Richie quite a bit. Anyway, there's this beautiful pickup truck in front of his shop, and it's that perfect shade of orange. I said to Merk, 'Look at that!' And Merk said, 'Richie Evans orange.'"

Which would come as no great surprise to Maynard Troyer. "Richie was one of a kind," says Troyer. "You know, Richard Petty's name is going to be coming up for years after he's gone, and it's the same with Richie. There are certain people who just kind of stand out."

No surprise, either, to Lee Osborne, who grins, "Some people you forget about the next day, and some people you *never* forget about. Richie was one of those guys you never forget."

Or John McClellan. "Sometimes," he admits, "I catch myself saying 'Richie is' instead of 'Richie was.' It's like he's still here."

Or Buster Maurer, who chokes up if you get him talking too much about his friend: "It's pretty hard," he says quietly. "I miss that guy."

Well, there was—*is*—a lot about Evans to miss, no matter what your relationship with the man. Maybe you thrilled to his driving from a seat high in the grandstands at Spencer or Thompson or New Egypt. Maybe you spun wrenches on those coupes back at the gas station. Maybe you slid him some deal money or busted him for some rules infraction. Maybe you chased him around Hickory or through the Trenton dogleg. Maybe you just nodded in anticipation from the press box when he ended his 1984 Bud 200 victory interview with the words, "Thanks everybody for coming," and then, raising a cold can of the race-sponsor's product toward the Oswego crowd, added this as an invitation: "Have a party."

Yeah, there's a lot to miss.

"You know, it's funny," says Mike McLaughlin. "I'll always remember Richie saying, 'We're all just passin' through, so while you're here you've gotta make your mark.' Then he'd laugh that little chuckle he had: *Huh-huh-huh*. But, you know, he left his mark, all right."

Bill Wimble, who watched Evans come and watched him go and knew all along that he was seeing something special, sums it all up with a quiet smile.

"Anybody who accomplished what Richie did is bound to have many, many people remember him," says Wimble. "They'll be talking about him for years."

Epilogue

ON OCTOBER 8, 1956, in Game 5 of the World Series, a right-handed hurler by the name of Don Larsen walked to the mound as the starting pitcher for the New York Yankees. Larsen was a star-crossed fellow. Two years earlier, his won-lost record with the Baltimore Orioles was 3-21; nobody in Major League Baseball threw away more games that year. He had come to the Yankees as part of an 18-player trade, and finished the '56 season a respectable but hardly spectacular 11-5. Now, here he was, smack in the middle of a World Series against his team's archrivals from across the East River, the hated Brooklyn Dodgers.

Game 6 was Larsen's second start in the 1956 Series. He didn't make it past the second inning in Game 2, having been yanked off the mound after blowing a six-run lead. There was no reason to expect that his three days of rest had turned him into Cy Young, to that point arguably the greatest pitcher of all time.

And yet, for this one afternoon, Don Larsen was better than the greatest. He was perfect. With 64,519 fans filling every seat in Yankee Stadium, he threw the only perfect game—no hits, no runs, no men on base—in World Series history. Today, nearly half a century later, footage of Yankee catcher Yogi Berra jumping into Larsen's arms plays from time to time on the TV highlights shows.

Two things happened in the wake of Larsen's improbable flash of brilliance. First came one of the best-known sports headlines of all time: "Imperfect Man Pitches Perfect Game." Shortly thereafter, his estranged wife, alleging that Larsen was delinquent in support payments, filed a court action in an attempt to grab a share of his World Series earnings.

Man, doesn't that struggle sound a little bit familiar? Doesn't it ring a coupe-era bell? Wasn't Richie Evans that same sort of imperfect man, capable of perfect things?

As we have seen, Evans had a good-guy streak a mile wide, as evidenced by the helping hand he so often extended to younger drivers and friends in need. And steadfast? I think of a tale dating back to 1978, when Firestone was bailing out of short-track racing and Goodyear was on the verge of taking over the modified tire market. Every top Firestone driver but one had jumped ship. Bobby Summers, the old Firestone rep—and even today a familiar modified face with Hoosier—was telling the story not long ago. "When it was clear that Firestone had lost interest in racing and things were going downhill," said Bobby, "I had to beg Richie to get off our product for his own sake. I had to tell him, 'Richie, we're done. Forget about it. We can't do it any more.' He was a loyal, loyal person."

Good guy? Great guy. But, still, imperfect, because this was the same

Richie Evans who, according to his own testimony, was a collection man's nightmare in his gas-station days. This was the same Richie Evans who, according to the testimony of his friends, sometimes raised a little too much hell. This was the same Richie Evans who went through spells when he tried so hard to be a family man but, according to the testimony of all concerned, sacrificed that because his racing job—his racing career, his racing life—demanded sacrifice.

Imperfect? Certainly.

And then you come across an old Evans friend and rival named Bob Polverari, and you hear him saying softly, "Richie was the perfect driver, in my mind. He was such a clean driver, and yet he was also aggressive enough that he was the fastest guy out there. Just the perfect driver."

Imperfect Man Drives Perfectly.

I was asked on a radio show not long ago who I thought was the most interesting racing personality I'd ever covered. "Richie Evans," I said. "Hands down." And I meant it. If Hollywood ever decided to make a movie about what race drivers are truly like—don't worry, they won't—they could start by taking a close look at Richie. No, he wasn't perfect, but he was ... *real*. Which is why, after all this time, his name and his image and his legacy still carry so much weight.

And now, on a cold, gray Monday evening in Rome, I am checking into the Quality Inn, the same hotel that used to be a Holiday Inn, the same hotel where Evans went crazy with his Loctite one evening. I don't know how many nights I have spent here in the course of this book going from mental notes to printed words, but it's a bunch. I plan on staying here tonight and tomorrow night, wedging in a few last interviews and a couple of social calls.

The guy at the front desk is in his 30s, Italian-looking, and his nametag says Romano. It catches my eye. If you know anything at all about stock car racing in upstate New York, you know all about the Romano clan from Johnstown, over near Fonda. There was papa Joe, the patriarch, and his son Andy—who won on dirt and blacktop at Fonda, Plattsburgh, Devil's Bowl and Utica-Rome— and Andy's boys, Mike and A.J., both double-digit winners in the dirt modifieds. Johnstown and Rome are maybe 70 miles apart on the New York Thruway, so as I fill out the registration card I take a shot.

"You wouldn't happened to be from the racing Romano family, would you?"

The guy says, "You mean, like, car racing?"

"Yeah," I reply. "There's a bunch of racing Romanos around here."

"No," the desk clerk says. "Sorry."

Then he pauses. "But you know, there was a guy from right here in Rome, Richie Evans. He was a pretty big in car racing."

I mention that I'm familiar with the name. His eyebrows arch. Turns out that as a kid in the 1960s, he grew up just across Dominick Street from Evans's Shell station. He says he used to listen to the engine in that orange coupe roar whenever they test-fired it. Then he tells me that Richie used to go at it pretty good with another driver from Rome, a fellow by the name of Cook.

I have been driving for several hours, and I'm tired. There is probably nothing he can tell me that I haven't heard, oh, a million times across the years. The common-sense thing would be to just end the conversation politely, grab the key from my man Romano, and head for the room and the pillow. But instead I stand there and I nod, almost certainly with a smile, and I let it roll.

After all this, I'm still in the mood to hear a Richie Evans story.

Feature Victories

THOUGH WE DON'T CLAIM THIS to be a complete list of Richie's career triumphs, it's pretty darned close. It is based on a list started by New York statistician Mark Southcott—thanks, Mark!—and padded by several more wins uncovered in the author's research. The total: at least 477 modified wins (one track's records were incomplete, and we chose not to estimate) plus one supermodified win and a limited sportsman score.

NEW YORK
Utica-Rome Speedway, Vernon – 33 modified (1965-78)
Lancaster Speedway, Lancaster – 22 modified (1969-76)
Holland Speedway, Holland – 11 modified (1977-85)
Spencer Speedway, Williamson – 49 modified (1969-85)
Shangri-La Speedway, Owego – 66 modified (1972-85)
Oswego Speedway, Oswego – 12 modified (1972-85)
Fulton Speedway, Fulton – 42 modified (1968-77)
   (plus 1 limited sportsman win)
Chemung Speedrome, Chemung – 2 modified (1978)
Albany-Saratoga Speedway, Malta – 17 modified (1970-76)
Evans Mills Speedway, Evans Mills – 1 modified (1970)
Weedsport Speedway, Weedsport – 1 modified (1971)
Islip Speedway, Islip, Long Island – 17 modified (1970-83)
Riverhead Raceway, Riverhead, Long Island – 1 modified (1985)
Freeport Stadium, Freeport, Long Island – 2 modified (1972-76)

MASSACHUSETTS
Riverside Park, Agawam – 32 modified (1978-84)
Seekonk Speedway, Seekonk – 2 modified (1979-83)

CONNECTICUT
Stafford Speedway, Stafford Springs – 38 modified (1975-85)
Thompson Speedway, Thompson – 32 modified (1975-85)
   (plus 1 supermodified win)

NEW HAMPSHIRE
Monadnock Speedway, Winchester – 3 modified (1978-1981)
Claremont Speedway, Claremont – 1 modified (1985)
Star Speedway, Epping – 1 modified (1979)

MAINE
Oxford Plains Speedway, Oxford Plains – 2 modified (1982-1985)

NEW JERSEY
Wall Stadium, Wall Township – 1 modified (1971)

New Egypt Speedway, New Egypt – 23 modified (1978-1985)
Trenton Fairgrounds Speedway, Trenton – 2 modified (1973-78)

PENNSYLVANIA
Pocono Raceway 3/4-mile oval – 2 modified (1972-80)
Pocono Raceway 2.5-mile superspeedway - 1 modified (1979)

VIRGINIA
Martinsville Speedway, Martinsville – 10 modified (1973-1983)
Franklin County Speedway, Calloway – 1 modified (1979)

NORTH CAROLINA
Bowman-Gray Stadium, Winston-Salem – 2 modified (1979-1980)
Caraway Speedway, Asheboro – 2 modified (1973-1979)
Hickory Speedway, Hickory – 2 modified (1978-1979)
Metrolina Speedway, Charlotte – 1 modified (1974)

TENNESSEE
Kingsport Speedway, Kingsport – 1 modified (1979)

FLORIDA
New Smyrna Speedway, New Smyrna Beach – 39 modified (1976-1985)
Daytona International Speedway, Daytona Beach – 2 modified (1979-1980)

CANADA
Capital City Speedway, Stittsville, Ontario – multiple wins
  (records incomplete)
Deux Montagnes Speedway, St. Eustache, Quebec - 1 modified (1979)

# Track Championships

THE BULK OF THE following track titles earned by Evans were full-fledged, full-season points championships, although a few—such as Oswego—are based on abbreviated "mini-series" schedules. Not counted are his six World Series championships at New Smyrna.

1970 Fulton
1971 Fulton
1972 Utica-Rome
1973 Utica-Rome
1974 Fulton, Utica-Rome
1975 Shangri-La
1977 Shangri-La
1978 Utica-Rome, Chemung, Holland
1979 New Egypt, Holland
1980 Stafford, Riverside, Thompson, Holland
1981 Stafford, Thompson
1982 New Egypt, Shangri-La
1983 Spencer, Thompson, Oswego
1985 Spencer, Thompson

Index

Abbott, Dick, 11, 117, 212
A-to-Z Automotive, 22, 23
Adams, Kenny, 133
Adaskaveg, Mike, 133, 263
Airborne Park, 18, 21, 30, 54, 160, 163
Albany-Saratoga Speedway, 18, 21, 22, 32, 35, 39, 49 and throughout
Alexander, Mike, 255
All Star League, 33, 39, 53, 55, 59, 66, 121 and throughout
Allard, Lee, 171, 173
Allio, David, 263
Allison, Bobby, 144, 159, 245,249
Allison, Donnie, 33, 244
Anchor Inn, 320
Anderson, John, 146, 154
Anderson, Wayne, 205, 212, 298
Appalachian State University, 338
ARCA, 341
Ard, Sam, 73, 196
Area Auto Racing News, 82, 106, 263, 343
Armstrong, Dick, 56, 107, 109, 111, 113, 132, 133 and throughout
Arute, Jack, 144, 269
ASA, 157, 242, 271
Associated Press, 89, 90
Auto Palace, 11

B&M Speed Shop, 36, 67, 78, 132, 152, 159 and throughout
B. R. DeWitt Inc., 67, 68, 69, 70, 73, 74, 181 and throughout
BACE Motorsports, 340
Baker, Buddy, 250, 270
Baker, Max, 12, 26, 42, 55,116, 220, 282, and throughout
Baldwin, Tommy, 138, 177, 185, 188, 205, 209, 211 and throughout
Baldwin, Tommy Jr., 177
Ball, Jim, 338
Balough, Gary, 150
Baltimore Orioles, 349
Barney, Dick, 189, 259, 260
Barry, Art, 187, 301, 311, 312, 330, 335

Bartel Machinery, 220
Batchelder, Dick, 238
Bear, Jerry, 96, 101, 116, 166
Bear, Roger, 116, 217, 218, 219, 241, 277, 299 and throughout
Beavers, Sammy, 235
Beebe, Jack, 193
Bellinger, Eddie, 241
Bennett, Bruce, 317, 339
Benway, Bob, 86, 108, 112, 141
Benyo, Rich, 34, 88, 98, 146, 308
Berra, Yogi, 349
Berggren, Dick, 10, 29, 32, 53, 70, 94, 101 and throughout
Bergh, Steve, 344
Bergin, Gene, 17, 52, 58, 40, 341
Best, Dave, 166, 222
Bianco, Junior, 122
Bisci, John, 48, 58, 111
Black Rock Speedway, 341
Blackie the dog, 4
Blewett, John Jr., 98, 197, 206, 208, 212, 259, 288 and throughout
Bodine, Brett, 150, 187, 192, 291, 300, 311, 312 and throughout
Bodine, Eli, 56
Bodine, Geoff, 21, 52, 53, 56, 78, 80, 81, and throughout
Boehler, Len, 67, 74, 140, 163, 190, 223, 298 and throughout
Bonneau, Rich, 185
Bonnett, Neil, 154, 155, 156, 157, 158, 159, 180 and throughout
Boos, Chuck, 52
Boot Camp the dog, 130
Bosley, Len, 19
Bouchard, Kenny, 88, 171, 207, 230, 292, 314, 324, and throughout
Bouchard, Ron, 56, 59, 72, 78, 81, 82, 96 and throughout
Bowman Gray Stadium, 77, 99, 134, 135, 164, 169, 249 and throughout
Boyd, Lew, 44, 122
Brady, Joe, 223, 266
Brightbill, Kenny, 235, 241, 324
Brooks, Dick, 173

Brooklyn Dodgers, 349
Brouwer, John, 211, 236, 237
Brown, Bill, 270
Brown, Perk, 308
Brunneau, Bob, 134
Brunnhoelzl, George, 300
Bryant, John, 87, 319
Busch Series, 248, 273, 310, 314, 337, 340, 344 and throughout

Cagle, Will, 39, 55, 122, 141, 222, 241
Callaway Speedway, 76, 86, 161
Campbell, Clay, 317
Campi, Don, 89
Capital City Speedway, 99, 100, 110
Capital Civic Center, 323
Capozzoli, Jerry, 309
Capua, Frank, 176
Caraway Speedway, 76, 80, 85, 134, 161, 169
Carillo, Joe, 29, 31
Carpenter, Junior, 161
Carpenter, Milton, 45, 47
Carter, Cathy, 309
Carter, Jimmy, 174
Caruso, Doug, 171
Caruso, Fats, 217
Caruso, George, 171
Caruso, Harry, 171, 287, 301, 302
Caruso, Romey, 171
Catamount Stadium, 22, 55, 60, 134, 164
Cayuga Speedway, 303
Charland, Rene, 10, 17, 19, 37, 39, 103, 104
Charlotte Speedway, 10, 145, 243
Chartrand, Guy, 52, 53, 76
Chassis Dynamics, 194
Chemung Speedway, 56, 108
Chicagoland Speedway, 243
Childress, Richard, 242, 322
Chmielewski, Stan, 228
Ciprich, Chuck, 234
Claremont Speedway, 300, 302
Clarence's Steak House, 33, 34, 76, 81
Clark, Bill "Bondo", 23, 24, 116, 117, 164, 281, 303 and throughout
Clark, Dick, 13, 104
Cleary, Leo, 52, 169, 266, 341
Clement, John, 36
Cloce, Ed, 53, 214
Coalyard Charlies, 41, 63, 91, 92, 261
Cohen, Bruce, 94, 236
Cole Sand & Gravel, 181

Collinsville Holiday Inn, 201
Colton, Billy, 342
Colwell, George, 96, 101, 116, 162, 166
Coniam, Warren, 238
Conkey, Howard, 264
Conway, Russ, 239, 270
Cook, Jerry, 17, 32, 39, 46, 47, 52, 58 and throughout
Cook, Sue, 98, 101, 317, 341
Cookman, Corky, 230, 287, 300, 336, 341
Corbeil, Dick, 87
Corellis, Tommy, 141
Cornelius, Gary, 69
Coville, C.D., 141
Craftsman Truck Series, 340
Cranmer, Jerry, 301
Cromarty, Barbara, 331
Cuneo, Bob, 194

Daddario, Dick, 254
Dale Earnhardt, Inc., 242
Dallenbach, Wally, 189
D'Allessandro, Bruce, 118
Danbury Racerama, 237
Danko, Brian, 194
Darlington Speedway, 42
Davidson, Andy, 45
Davies, Joanne, 58
Davis, Bill, 254, 231, 320
Davis, John, 96
Daytona Memorial Stadium, 151
Daytona International Speedway, 16, 44, 49, 52, 56, 69, 70
Dean, Arnold, 8, 13, 29, 107, 115, 163, 173 and throughout
Dean, James, 345
Debais, John, 232
Dennis, Bill, 73
DeSarro, Fred, 39, 52, 56, 58, 59, 74, 75 and throughout
Deuel, Les, 98
Deux Montagnes Speedway, 169
Devil's Bowl Speedway, 55, 78
Dewitt, Byron R., 67, 246
DeWitt, Gene, 66, 67, 68, 69, 70, 71, 73 and throughout
Diddley, Bo, 201
Diffendorf, Don, 21
DiGard Racing, 153
Dimmig, Dick, 170
DIRT, 141, 232, 301, 322
Dixon, Dick, 136

Dodge, Ben, 286, 295
Dodge, Herb, 109, 285, 289, 290, 291, 292, 293 and throughout
Dole, Bob, 174
Donnelly, Glenn, 141, 232, 233, 234
Dover Speedway, 145, 148
Dowd, Russ, preface, 175,
Dragon, Beaver, 71
Druar, Tom, 336
Dunster's Restaurant, 19
Dutch Inn, 94, 307, 308, 309

Earles, H. Clay, 95, 200, 201, 308, 317, 324
Earnhardt, Dale, 242, 245, 250, 270, 315, 322
Earnhardt, Dale Jr., 339, 344
Earnhardt, Ralph, 342
Eastern Bandits, 37, 104, 163, 180
Eddy, Mike, 150
Edie's Bar, 223
Edwards, Terry, 234
Eilenberg, Carl, 203
Ellis, Bruce, 206
Empire State Concrete & Aggregate Producers Assoc., 181
ESPN, 342
Evans, Anthony, 26, 55, 67, 116
Evans (Peters), Barbara, 18, 25, 30, 41, 60, 61, 62 and throughout
Evans, Bob, 106
Evans, Ernest, 2, 3, 5, 25, 276, 339
Evans, Jacki, 9, 61, 127, 128, 12, 317, 337 and throughout
Evans, Jackie, 320
Evans, Janelle, 9, 61, 127, 128, 130, 310, 316 and throughout
Evans, Jill, 9, 103, 127, 128, 129, 130, 317 and throughout
Evans, Jodi, 9, 61, 127, 128, 129, 310, 316 and throughout
Evans, Lynn (Kreuser), 4, 5, 12, 66, 115, 123, 124, 126, 126 and throughout
Evans, Richie Jr., 126, 127, 277, 302, 303, 305, and throughout
Evans (Jones), Sandy, 2, 3, 4, 5, 6, 106, 276, 277, 339
Evans, Satie, 2, 3, 6, 25, 126, 339
Evans, Tara, 126, 127, 128, 305, 310, 331, 337 and throughout
Evans Mill Speedway, 112
Evernham, Ray, foreword, 307,
Farmer, Red, 73, 342

Farone, John, 224
Figari, Lou, 39
Fiore, Mario, 104, 117, 118, 119, 136, 137, 170 and throughout
Firestone, 90, 97, 135, 136, 145, 169, 274 and throughout
Flemington Speedway, 234
Flemke, Ed, 17, 18, 19, 21, 36, 37, 38 and throughout
Flemke, Ed Jr., 37, 50, 90, 121, 123, 186, 188 and throughout
Fonda Dragstrip, 8
Fonda Speedway, 19, 44, 46, 66, 87, 141, 235
FONDA!, 44, 122
Foote, Red, 37
Ford, Gerald, 174
Foster, Norm, 298
Fowler, Dick, 13, 45, 46, 51, 94, 140, 220 and throughout
Fox, Ray, 68
Foyt, A.J., 318, 341, 343
France, Bill Jr., 274, 324, 342
France, Bill Sr., 47, 331
France, Jim, 274, 275
Franklin County Speedway, 138, 169
Freeman Hotel, 230, 231, 267, 281, 282, 284, 326 and throughout
Freeport Stadium, 59, 89, 164, 205, 243
Frings, Dennis, 189
Fuller, Jeff, 294, 300, 340
Fulton Speedway, 18, 20, 21, 39, 44, 45, 46 and throughout
Funk, Lou Jr., 237
Furioni, Dave, 315, 327
Fusco, Andrea, 100
Fusco, Andy, 32, 44, 49, 88, 89, 96, 99 and throughout

Gagliardi, Cam, 66
Gahan, Ernie, 17, 75, 102, 122, 123, 217, 333 and throughout
Galullo, Danny, 136
Gant, Harry, 85, 139, 147, 155, 156, 157, 158 and throughout
Gater Racing News, 53, 167, 206, 258, 263, 318, 322 and throughout
Gaudreau, Al, 224
Gaudreau, Peg, 224
Gelinas, Toodi, 93, 104, 171, 23, 263, 266
Genessee Stone Products, 181

Geoff Bodine Fan Club, 202
Gerber, Joe, 183, 334
Gherzi, Moe, 136
Gibbs, Joe, 341
Gioia, Steve, 238
Giroux, Dennis, 72, 140
Gitchell, Fran, 108
Gold, Eli, 197, 198
Golden Isles Speedway, 89
Goldstein, Rich, 253
Good Times Lounge, 308
Goodyear, 135, 136, 137, 145, 169, 210, 334 and throughout
Gordon, Jeff, 248, 341, 343
Gosek, Joe, 267, 283, 332
Grady, John, 263
Greci, Mike, 312
Greco, Bill, 39, 136, 137
Green, Tom, 18
Green Gables, 227
Greger, Stan, 138, 301
Griffin, Billy, 301
Griffin, Pee Wee, 135, 146, 147, 152, 154, 155, 157 and throughout
Griffis Air Force Base, 16
Griffiths, Jack, 49

Hagan, Billy, 32
Hall, Andy, 317
Hamilton, Pete, 18, 19, 67, 102, 158, 245
Hanley, Junior, 150
Hanson PLC, 340
Harbach, Fred, 39, 51, 52, 138, 140, 150, 205 and throughout
Harer, Reverend Eric, 325
Harman, Billy, 17, 223
Harpell, Andy, 334
Harrison, George, 331
Hart, Clyde, 149, 324
Hartford Times, 261
Hartung, Kenny, 169, 226, 227, 228, 253, 262, 293 and throughout
Hatch, Bill, 13, 93, 106, 165, 218, 224, 284 and throughout
Hatch, Millie, 13, 93, 106, 165, 218, 332
Haynes, Jim, 144
Healy, Don, 343
Hearne, Gil, 260, 285
Hearst, Tom, 214
Hedgecook, Jay, 258
Hedger, Ron, 115, 213, 256, 279, 280, 281, 307 and throughout

Hendrick, Ray, 33, 52, 53, 54, 56, 59, 80 and throughout
Hendrick Motorsports, 344
Hendrickson, Jim, 87, 285
Hensley, Bill, 58
Herbert, Jeep, 44 (Pete Moss, Flex Hose, Bob Alou)
Heveron, Doug, 300, 312, 340
Hewitt, Doug, 150, 156, 182, 254, 258, 259, 295 and throughout
Hickory Speedway, 76, 85, 109, 133, 294, 307, 347 and throughout
Hill, Elton, 17
Hirschman, Tony, 298, 340, 343
Hmiel, Steve, 53, 54, 96, 101, 134, 139, 148 and throughout
Hoag, Alex, 341
Hoag, Dean, 120
Hoag, Donna, 341
Hoag, Dutch, 20, 21, 33, 39, 45, 47, 52 and throughout
Hoenig, Don, 202, 270
Holdeman, Linda, 215, 216, 271, 272, 284, 323 and throughout
Holland Speedway, 112, 182, 203, 212, 290, 300
Hollard Patent School, 8, 12
Hollebrand, Pete, 67, 89, 100, 248, 263, 265
Hollebrand Trucking, 248
Hollywood Restaurant, 43
Holman-Moody, 132
Holmer, Phil, 170
Holmes, Ross, 347
Hoosier Tire, 210
Houseman, Charlie, 41
Housman, A.E., 326
Howe, Don, 118, 205, 300
Hudson, Bobby, 20, 91
Hunter, Ann, 275
Hunter, Bob, 26
Hunter, Jim, 274, 275
Hutchens, Bobby, 164, 188, 242, 309, 321, 322, 335 and throughout
Hutchins, Sonny, 308
Hutter, Ron, 132, 133, 135, 157, 159, 169, 172 and throughout
Hutter, Thalia, 249

Ifft, David, 154, 158
IMSA, 144
Ingersoll, Bernie, 16, 31, 32
Ingram, Jack, 73

International Motorsports Hall of Fame, 343, 344
International Speedway Corp., 275
Irwin, Kenny, 315
Isaac, Bobby, 343
Islip Speedway, 76, 77, 86, 87, 99, 112, 134 and throughout
Iulg, Gary, 253, 254

Jankowiak, Tony, 272, 273, 280, 323, 335, 336
Jarrett, Ned, 213
Jarzombek, Charlie, 39, 52, 108, 134, 138, 149, 151 and throughout
Jarzombek, Charlie Sr., 336
Jarzombek, Eileen, 317
Jarzombek, Gladys, 317
Jarzombek, Rick, 151, 205, 206, 317
Johnson, Alan, 36
Johnson, Bob, 82, 155
Johnson, Danny, 36
Johnson, Jack, 141, 340
Johnson, Junior, 245
Johnson, Milt, 36
Jones, Bob, 106
Jones, Booker, 266, 267
Jones, Harvey, 89
Jones, Joe, 7, 8, 9, 11, 12, 29, 91 and throughout
Jones, Wilbur, 6, 12, 13, 14, 18, 23, 26 and throughout
Josie's Outpost Lounge, 224, 227, 281
Joy, Mike, 107, 197, 198, 200, 318
Judkins, Bob, 58, 139, 144, 173, 223

Kelly, Joe, 189
Kennedy, President John F., 11, 319
Kenseth, Matt, 243
Kent, George, 96, 109, 111, 112, 141, 146, 162 and throughout
Kent, Ron, 165
Kingsport Speedway, 139
Kinser, Steve, 342
Kneisel, Dave, 234
Knipe, Teddy, 72
Kosinksi, Red, 170
Koszela, Sonny, 56, 85, 132, 140, 144
Kotary, Cliff, 12, 69, 102
Kotary, Dave, 13, 17
Kotary, Robbie, 51
Kotary, Tom, 17
Krebs, Buddy, 136

L and R Speed Shop, 19
L Truck Stop, 16
Labonte, Terry, 321
LaJoie, Don, 83
Lamandia, Ron, 27, 278
LaMonica, Joe, 27, 278
Lancaster Speedway, 39, 40, 48, 50, 54, 55, 58 and throughout
Langehorne Speedway, 20, 42, 48, 52, 68, 80, 146
Lape, Dave, 19, 20, 22, 40, 235, 322
Larson, Don, 349
Lauda, Niki, 331
Lawton, Clint, 263
Lazarro, Roseanne, 126
Lazzaro, Lou, 17, 39, 46, 47, 51, 58, 59 and throughout
Leaty, Jan, 301, 340
Lebanon Valley Speedway, 44, 141
Lee Speedway, 55
LeRoy Lime & Crushed Stone, 181
LeSieur, Val, 151, 220, 225, 226, 227, 228, 263 and throughout
Lesik, Joe, 10, 16, 18
Lime Rock Park, 144
Lind, Dave, 170
"Little T", 94
Loescher, Mike, 20, 84, 149, 150, 220, 241, 341, and throughout
London, Gary, 263
LoPiccolo, Steve, 111, 113
Lund, Tiny, 72
Lux, Ron, 68
Lynch, Eddie, 237, 271
Lyon, Mark, 310, 315

M&H Tire, 135, 145
Macco, Dick, 240, 263, 283
MacTavish, Don, 18, 19, 22, 46, 47, 49, 51 and throughout
Maggiacomo, Jocko, 136
Mahoney, Chuck, 10, 11, 230, 231
Malcuit, Mark, 169, 172
Manchester Oil Heat, , 207
Mangino, Gene, 51
Marcello, Dominic "Donny", 26, 32, 38, 42, 43, 51, 63 and throughout
Marcello, Rita, 91, 93, 220, 222, 226, 276, 333 and throughout
Marshall, Harley, 238
Martin, Mark, 150
Martinsville Speedway, 32, 33, 34, 42, 76, 79, 83
Maseles, Howard, 225, 226

Mason's Garage, 81, 139
Matczak, Lois, 276
Matczak, Skip, 240, 241, 276
Mathalia, Frank Sr., 13, 17
Matthews, Banjo, 132, 146, 152, 156
Maurer, Randy "Buster", 54, 55, 58, 59, 60, 102, 116 and throughout
McArdell, John, 234
McClellan, John, 220, 223, 230, 321, 340
McCreadie, Bobby, 110
McLaughlin, Mike, 226, 291, 298, 300, 301, 303, 318, 324, and throughout
McLean, T.K., 192
McLeod, Clyde, 298
McMullin, John, 171, 195, 221, 226, 227, 228, 248
Meahl, Kenny, 66
Memorial Hospital, 315
Mendelsohn, Larry, 39, 59
Mentus, Ron, 177
Merkling, Bill, 347
Metrolina Speedway, 85
Miller, Bernie, 17, 32, 140
Miller, Bobby, 96
Miller, Don, 249
Miller, Ray, 171, 209, 291, 301
Miller, Wayne, 214
Millington, Lee, 54
Mitchell, Charlie, 263
Mitchell, Clayton, 52, 55
Modestino, Lou, 263
Mohawk Airlines, 123, 124
Monadnock Speedway, 138, 139, 169, 171, 180, 207, 258 and throughout
Mondale, Walter, 174
Monnat, Mike, 167, 263
Montgomery, Gary, 258
Moon, Don, 17
Morabito, Vinnie, 88
Morgan, Danny, 26, 55, 116, 161, 166, 220
Motor Racing Network, 197, 318
Muldowney, Shirley, 8
Murphy, Mike, 118

Nacewicz, Billy, 8, 35, 36, 42, 70, 77, 84 and throughout
Nagle, Dave, 71, 133
Namath, Joe, 98
Narducci, Ron, 39, 321
NASA Space Shuttle, 146

NASCAR, 5, 10, 11, 12, 16, 17, 19 and throughout
National Speed Sport News, 263
NEARA, 108, 109, 111, 112, 113, 131, 132 and throughout
Neff, Tom, 32, 39
Nelson, Willie, 114, 161
Nephew, Dick, 24
New Egypt Speedway, 99, 100, 110, 111, 134, 138, 141 and throughout
Newman, Art, 116
Newman, Paul, 176
New Smyrna Speedway, 109, 132, 133, 146, 147, 148, 149 and throughout
New Systems Laundry, 58
New York State Fairgrounds, 54, 87, 102, 301
New York Yankees, 98, 243
Nextel Cup, 10, 53, 54, 242, 243, 247, 248 and throughout
Nice N Easy, 11
North Florida Raceway, 89
Newman, Paul, 176
North Wilkesboro Speedway, 162
Nashville Speedway, 255
Newport News Herald, 174
New Hampshire International Speedway, 347
New York Bituminous Concrete Assoc., 181
Nu-Style Jewelry, 192
New London Waterford Speedbowl, 193
NEDOC, 210, 211
NEAR, 343
Nazareth Speedway, 234
Nemechek, Joe, 248
National Parts Peddler, 322
New York State Stock Car Assoc., 343
New York Yankees, 349

"On the Road Again", 161
Oakland A's, 98
O'Brien, Dick, 25, 26, 115, 171, 176, 216, 236 and throughout
Olsen, Budd, 39
Orange County Speedway, 141, 322, 336
O'Rourke, Bob, 66, 209, 269
Ortiz, Ed, 10
Osborne, Lee, 20, 21, 22, 38, 39, 44, 48 and throughout

Osgood, Bryan, 59
Osmun, Billy, 220, 230, 231, 232, 241, 277, 284 and throughout
Oswego Speedway, 16, 21, 24, 48, 59, 112, 113 and throughout
Ouderkirk , Ralph, 45
Outlet Tire Sales, 181
Oxford Plains Speedway, 180, 213, 294, 300
Page, Bill, 93
Page, Sally, 93
Paige, Satchel, 243
Park, Bobby, 212, 304
Parsons, Benny, 154
Pavilion State Bank, 181
Pavilion Truck Sales, 181
Payne, Bill, 78, 78, 95, 321
Pearce, Al, 174
Pearson, David, 200, 244, 250
Pemberton, Robin, 18, 19, 35, 191, 321
Pendergast, George, 223
Penske Racing South, 249
Peters, Barbara, 8, 9
Peterson, Ronnie, 331
Pettinelli, Tony, 58, 116, 117, 119, 221
Pettinelli, Tony Jr., 58, 161, 166, 186, 219, 220, 221 and throughout
Petrocci, Bob, 69
Petty, Adam, 315
Petty Enterprises, 246
Pfeiffer's Restaurant, 9
Phil's Chevrolet, 194
Picard, Buddy, 86
Pickerall, Clarence, 33
Pieniazek, Eddie, 78
Pocono Speedway, 56, 59, 77, 101, 107, 139, 145 and throughout
Podolak, John, 234
Polverari, Bob, 112, 136, 138, 171, 175, 178 and throughout
Porsche, Ferdinand, 343
Potter-DeWitt Corp, 181
Pratt, Don, 336
Puchyr, Ted, 11, 12, 13, 26, 27, 28, 29 and throughout
Punch, Jerry, 197

Race Hill Farm, 193
Radewick, Marty, 118, 135, 266, 301
Radford, Paul, 33, 52, 76, 80, 81, 86, 138 and throughout
Rafter, Billy, 10

Ray, Mike, 96
Ray, Sue, 66
RE Fabrications, 337
Reagan, Ronald, 97
Reap, Kevin, 190, 272
Rebello, Gene, 236
Reichert, Gary, 20
Reutimann, Buzzie, 39, 83
Revere Copper Products, 26, 101, 320
Rich Evans' Shell Service, 25, 26, 27, 28
Richards, C.J., 141
Richmond, Tim, 270
Rite Aid, 321
Riverhead Raceway, 88, 89, 134, 138, 141, 164, 205 and throughout
Riverside Park Speedway, 118, 123, 134, 135, 136, 141, 148 and throughout
Roberts, Charlie, 197, 310
Roberts, Fireball, 317
Roberts, John, 237, 238
Robertson, T. Wayne, 275
Rockingham Speedway, 340
Rolling Stone, 264
Rolling Wheels Raceway, 69, 122, 141
Romano, Andy, 17, 350
Romano, A.J., 350
Romano, Joe, 350
Romano, Mike, 350
Rome Cable, 101
Rome Free Academy, 12, 23, 317
Rome Sentinel, 317, 325
Rosati, John, 134, 171, 195, 207, 250, 300
Rose Garden, 91, 224
Ross, Brian, 138, 177, 181, 185, 188, 206, 253 and throughout
Ruggiero, Reggie, 118, 136, 137, 138, 179, 187, 188 and throughout
Rusty Nail Café, 41, 42, 43, 101, 123, 124, 125 and throughout
Ruth, Babe, 243
Rutherford, Johnny, 343, 344

"Shaft", 171, 325
Sacks, Greg, 149, 177, 178, 185, 204, 205, 210 and throughout
Safari Motel, 128, 133
Sampson Hauling Corp., 181
Sandusky Speedway, 239, 267
Santos, Bobby, 140, 266
Schneider, Frankie, 39

Seamon, Rita, 61
Seamon, Sonney, 13, 17, 36, 37, 38, 45, 46 and throughout
Seekonk Speedway, 56, 193, 210, 278
Seifert, Bill, 152
SEMA, 322
Senneker, Bob, 242
Serwacki, Ed, 145, 148
Shampine, Jim, 236, 238, 333, 241, 315
Shangri-La Speedway, 20, 56, 59, 77, 78, 79, 108 and throughout
Sherri-Cup, 300, 313
Shippee, Dave, 211, 236, 237
Shoemaker, Ken, 17, 21
Shullick, Dave, 240
Silva, Ollie, 59, 85
Singer, Pat, 106, 110
Siscone, Tony, 180, 211, 212, 213, 214, 257, 259 and throughout
Slater, Bill, 173, 217
Small, Jim, 67, 116
Smith, Fred, 263
Smith, Ken, 270
Smith, Phil, 86, 107, 220, 261
Solhem, Ralph, 116, 187, 191, 229
Sova, Roy, 331
Speedway Scene, 58, 157, 203, 211, 214, 220, 226 and throughout
Spencer, Ed, 285
Spencer, Jimmy, 149, 150, 256, 285, 286, 287, 288 and throughout
Spencer Speedway, 20, 39, 48, 49, 50, 54, 69
Spognardi, Ray, 149, 166, 169, 216, 243, 244, 253 and throughout
St. Paul's Church, 226, 325
Stafford Springs Speedway, 58, 76, 77, 78, 85, 99, 105 and throughout
Stahl, Jere, 133
Star Speedway, 164, 239, 267, 270
Statewide Racing Team, 235
Stefanik, Bob, 136
Stefanik, Mike, 181, 190, 272, 273, 295, 301, 340
Stevens, Bugs, 18, 21, 39, 40, 41, 42, 50 and throughout
Stewart, Jackie, 331
Stewart, Tony, prologue
Stock Car Products, 158
Stock Car Racing, 261
Stockham, Corky, 120, 322
Summers, Bobby, 90, 135, 170, 349
Surtees, John, 343

Sutton, Willie, 37
Suzy the dog, 276
Swift, Nolan, 111, 236, 237, 238, 241
Syracuse Herald, 262, 319, 320

"To an Athlete Dying Young", 326
Talerico, Mike, 111, 113
Talladega Speedway, 157, 158, 159, 248, 274
Tallini, John, 12, 80, 318
Tant, Jack, 33, 52, 55, 132, 134, 313
Tasnady, Al, 39
Tattersall, Harvey III, 236, 237, 238, 270
Taylor, Billy, 21, 170, 194, 314
Taylor, Elizabeth, 174
Taylor, Phil, 194
Tesoriere, Ken, 326
The Hutch, 41
The Nutshell, 41, 192
"They Called Me The Shoe", 22
Thomas, Dave, 173
Thomas, Mel, 182
Thomas, Wayne, 145
Thompson, Dick, 42, 201, 308, 317
Thompson Speedway, 94, 131, 142, 148, 163, 173, 175 and throughout
Thurman, Joe, 155
Toal, Marilyn, 342
Tomaino, Jamie, 155, 300, 332, 340
Tomasi, Ken, 67
Tommy Frank's Mobil, 16
Treichler, Gordy, 54
Treichler, Merv, 19, 20, 36, 53, 81, 85, 91 and throughout
Treichler, Roger, 52, 53, 83, 90, 285, 341
Trenton Speedway, , 55, 58, 72, 80, 81, 83, 84 and throughout
Trickle, Dick, 151, 156, 158, 242, 243, 254
Trinkhaus, Frank, 46, 54
Troyer Engineering, 133
Troyer, Maynard, 21, 24, 45, 47, 51, 52, 59 and throughout
Truex, Barney, 118
Truex, Martin Jr., 344
Tucker, Steve, 275
Turner, Curtis, 42, 20, 48, 68, 317
Turner, Donnie, 20, 48, 68
Turner, Ray, 20
Turner, Tommy, 132

Ulrich, Fred, 12, 25, 31, 32, 36, 37, 49 and throughout
Union Oil, 118
Unitas, Johnny, 98
UPS, 319, 320,
USAC, 157, 158
Utica-Rome Speedway, 10, 11, 12, 13, 16, 18, 20 and throughout

Van Horn, Fuzzy, 39
Vaughn, Linda, 154
Vee, Bobby, 145, 194
Vernon Speedway, 10, 11
Victoria Speedway, 42
Vollertsen, Jim, 108, 113

Wagner, George, 87
Wall Stadium, 55, 173, 209, 260, 339, 344
Wallace, Rusty, 157, 158, 159, 190, 248
Waltrip, Darrell, 73, 152, 153, 154, 244
Waterman, Dick, 16, 17, 18, 31, 32, 37, 39 and throughout
Watkins Glen, 145, 148
Wayman, Don, 54
Weedsport Speedway, 141, 232, 233, 234, 303
Wesnofske, Teddy, 91
Westernville Flying A Service, 7, 8
Williamson, Speed, 11
Wimble, Bill, 17, 24, 35, 44, 51, 69, 70 and throughout
Winston Cup, 19, 255, 256, 270, 271, 293, 342 and throughout
Wood Brothers, 33, 244, 246
World of Outlaws, 48, 342
Worley, Satch, 33, 80, 81, 107, 108, 138, 169 and throughout
Wright, Cliff, 22, 23
Wright Brothers, 146
Wyckoff, Ron, 136, 171
"Winning", 176
Westboro Speedway, 164, 193
Weather Channel, 165
Warner, John, 174
White House, 174
Wilsberg, Ernie, 210, 252, 254, 256, 300, 336
Wilsberg, Jamie, 210, 252, 254, 256, 300
World Series, 349
Wright, Bill, 238
Wallace, Ronnie, 239
Warren, Bentley, 241, 270
Weatherly, Joe, 42, 317
Wayne, John, 318
Williams, Mark, 337
Whelen Series, 340

Yankee All-Star League, 131
Yankee Stadium, 349
Yarborough, Cale, 245
Yarbrough, LeeRoy, 69
Ye Old Eagle, 226
Yeley, J.J., 341
Yerrington, Ed, 205
Young, Sy, 349
Yunick, Smokey, 132, 146, 258

Zanardi, Pete, 5, 12, 25, 32, 57, 59, 72 and throughout
Zautner, Donnie, 22, 23
Zervakis, Emanuel, 196
Zimmerman, Dennis, 37, 10, 163
ZZ Top, 324

J&H photo/courtesy of *Speedway Scene*